REMEMBERING AND THE
SOUND OF WORDS

Remembering and the Sound of Words

Mallarmé, Proust, Joyce, Beckett

ADAM PIETTE

CLARENDON PRESS · OXFORD

1996

Oxford University Press, Walton Street, Oxford OX2 6DP
Oxford New York
Athens Auckland Bangkok Bombay
Calcutta Cape Town Dar es Salaam Delhi
Florence Hong Kong Istanbul Karachi
Kuala Lumpur Madras Madrid Melbourne
Mexico City Nairobi Paris Singapore
Taipei Tokyo Toronto
and associated companies in
Berlin Ibadan

Oxford is a trade mark of Oxford University Press

Published in the United States
by Oxford University Press Inc. New York

British Library Cataloguing in Publication Data
Data available

Library of Congress Cataloging in Publication Data
Piette, Adam.
Remembering and the sound of words: Mallarmé, Proust, Joyce, Beckett/Adam Piette.
Includes bibliographical references and index.
1. French literature—19th century—History and criticism. 2. French literature—20th
century—History and criticism. 3. Mallarmé, Stéphane, 1842–1898—Language.
4. Proust, Marcel, 1871–1922—Language. 5. Beckett, Samuel, 1906–   —Language.
6. Joyce, James, 1882–1941—Language. 7. Literature, Comparative—French and
English 8. Literature, Comparative—English and French. 9. English
literature—20th century—History and criticism. 10. Memory in literature. I. Title.
PQ283.P44 1996   840. 9—dc20   95–16585
ISBN 0–19–818268–6

1 3 5 7 9 10 8 6 4 2

Typeset by Pure Tech India Ltd., Pondicherry
Printed in Great Britain
on acid-free paper by
Biddles Ltd,
Guildford and King's Lynn

For Diane

a voice murmuring a trace. A trace it wants to leave a trace,
yes, like air leaves among the leaves, among the grass,
among the sand

Texts For Nothing XIII

Acknowledgements

I would like to thank Queens' College, Cambridge, Trinity College, Cambridge, and the University of Lausanne for their support.

I am grateful for the help and advice of many friends and colleagues, particularly to: Neil Forsyth, Alex Holdcroft, Alison Harvey, Alban Harvey, Ralph Pite, David Taylor.

I am indebted to Rosemary Lloyd, Christopher Ricks, and Malcolm Bowie for their guidance and example at different stages in the writing of the book.

I would like to thank Diane Piette and my family for their tireless encouragement, forbearance, and help.

My greatest debt is to Eric Griffiths, *il miglior fabbro*, who saw me through it all.

A. P.

Contents

Introduction

Reduplication of Sweet Sounds

When Shelley heard a bird sing, he thought of himself:

A Poet is a nightingale, who sits in darkness and sings to cheer its own solitude with sweet sounds; his auditors are as men entranced by the melody of an unseen musician, who feel that they are moved and softened, yet know not whence or why. (116)

When we read poetic prose, or prose we believe to be poetic, we are in the position of those auditors: hearing sweet sounds, a certain melody, being moved and softened, yet not knowing the precise causes. Is the music within the prose simply there as a meaninglessly 'softening' adjunct to syntax and sense—or is the author merely cheering him- or herself up along the bare and bitter tracts of narrative? Shelley's sentence is sweet in this mysterious way. The s-run along 'sits'-'sings'-'solitude' resolves itself sweetly and aptly into 'sweet sounds', with the slight after-shock in 'unseen'.[1] 'Melody', similarly, finds echoes in 'men'-'musician'-'moved', reinforced by a vowel-sound chiasmus. But beyond noticing this, how far can one go? The sounds of prose, even within the most intense passages, seem condemned to remain either pretty little mimetic tricks like the 'melody'-'sweet sound' echoes, or unseen musical accompaniments threading through the half-silent words to the satisfaction of the author alone. But Shelley's poetic prose has another mimetic trick up its sleeve the mimesis of memory, memory of writing poetry.

Thinking in prose about the poet as bird, he remembers writing a poem about a bird as poet, 'To a Sky-Lark': 'Like a Poet hidden/In the light of thought,/Singing hymns unbidden,/Till the world is wrought/To sympathy with hopes and fears it

---

[1] The ɪ-repetition in this phrase climaxes on its long-vowel counterpart, the iː of 'sweet'.

heeded not'.[2] The poem is, like 'A Defence of Poetry', concerned with the unseen, quasi-divine influence of solitary poetic inspiration upon the rest of the world. Given the narrow range of Shelley's imaginative world this coincidence is perhaps not surprising. But Shelley's tact lies in feeling the analogy between that unseen moral influence and the 'unseen', half-heard sonorities of his words. The sound-repetitions in the sentence from 'A Defence of Poetry' recall the *internal rhymes* of 'To a Sky-Lark'.

The s-run can be found in the analogy between sky-lark and the high-born maiden in her tower:

> Soothing her love-laden
> Soul in secret hour,
> With music sweet as love which overflows her bower[3]

The unseen musician behind the sweet prose sounds of the 'Defence of Poetry' sentence has a name: Shelley's memory of the secret music of internal rhyme overflowing the bower of its poetic form, sending waves through the later prose. The music in the words has its source in the poet's self-therapeutic soothing of secret pain. The music that is at the heart of a poet's craft is, for Shelley, primarily made up of internal rhyming effects.[4] Sound-repetitions in prose are the technical counterpart to those effects. In Shelley's case, their main function is to remind the reader that, though writing prose, he is a poet—and the easiest way of nudging our memories is for Shelley to recall his own poetic technique within the sound-traces of his prose.

But it is important to acknowledge the fact that, despite this 'sounding-off' tone, Shelley's dedication to the sounds of his words was absolute, as absolute as his dedication to the Platonic-poetic expression of humanity's eternal 'majestic form and graceful motions.'[5] His sweet sounds, whether in internal rhymes or prose sound-repetitions, are the real accent of his neo-

---

[2] *Complete Works*, ii. 2, 303, stanza IX/S, ll. 41–5

[3] *Complete Works*, ii. 2, 303, stanza VIII/S, ll. 36–40.

[4] Donald Reiman underlines the importance of internal rhyme patterns in Shelley's poetry in the chapter on style in *Shelley's 'Triumph of Life'*, 93–98. Neville Rogers has shown how end-rhyming was in many cases decided in advance by Shelley—the main toil of his writing being the internal sound-system (*Shelley at Work*, 208).

[5] 'A Defence', *Complete Works*, v. 5, 117.

Platonism; unseen yet heard and felt, they were meant to soar that high.

In 1830, Mary Shelley recalled a conversation between Shelley and Byron discussing Shakespeare's poetry:

Shelley. . . . Is not a line, as well as your outspread heroics, or a tragedy, a whole, and only as a whole, beautiful in itself? as, for instance, 'How sweet the moonlight sleeps upon this bank.' Now, examining this line, we perceive that all the parts are formed in relation to one another, and that it is consequently a whole. 'Sleep', we see, is a reduplication of the pure and gentle sound of sweet; and as the beginning of the former symphonizes with the beginning *s* of the latter, so also the *l* in moonlight prepares one for the *l* in sleep, and glides gently into it; and in the conclusion, one may perceive that the word 'bank' is determined by the preceding words, and that the *b* which it begins with is but a deeper intonation of the two *p*'s which come before it; sleeps upon this slope, would have been effeminate; sleeps upon this rise, would have been harsh and inharmonious.

Byron. Heavens! do you imagine, my dear Shelley, that Shakspeare had any thing of the kind in his head when he struck off that pretty line? If any one had told him all this about your p's and s's, he would just have said, 'Pish!'

Shelley. Well, be that as it may, are there not the coincidences, I suppose you would call them, that I showed in the line?

Byron. There are. But the beauty of the line does not lie in sounds and syllables, and such mechanical contrivances, but in the beautiful metaphor of the moonlight sleeping.

Shelley. Indeed that is also beautiful. In every single line, the poet must organize many simultaneous operations, both the meaning of the words and their emphatic arrangement, and then the flow and melting together of their symphony; and the whole must be united with the current of the rythm.

Byron. Well, then, I'm glad I'm not a poet! It must be like making out one's expenses for a journey, I think, all this calculation!

Shelley. I don't say that a poet must necessarily be conscious of all this, no more than a lady is conscious of every graceful movement. But I do say that they all depend upon reason, in which they live and move, and have their being; and that he who brings them out into the light of distinct consciousness, beside satisfying an instinctive desire of his own nature, will be more secure and commanding. But what makes this metaphor beautiful? To represent the tranquillity of moonlight is the object of the line; and the sleep is beautiful, because it gives a more intense and living form of the same idea; and the rythm beautifully falls in with this, and just lets the cadence of the emphasis dwell upon the sound and sense of the sweet word 'sleep'; and the alliteration assimilates the rest of the line into one harmonious symmetry. This line, therefore, is not altogether a work of art?[6]

Leaving aside the prickly problem as to whether the two phonemes s̲ and l̲ are necessarily 'pure and gentle', Shelley's sensitivity to the 'simultaneous operations' of the meaning of words and their symphony in cadenced, rhythmical lines is something to be admired. The hearing of the 'sweet'-'sleep' reduplication, the registering of the s̲ and l̲ repetitions, Shelley's sensing the way in which these sound-effects prolong, stress and 'dwell upon the sound and sense of the sweet word "sleep" ' is a remarkable revelation of his workshop secrets.

It is also a powerful, symphonic defence of internal rhyming technique; thus, by implication, of sound-repetitions in poetic prose. It is noticeable that the key-rhyme Shelley sees at the centre of Shakespeare's line is the 'sweet'-'sleep' consonance, or coincidence; 'sweet' is, as we have seen in the sentence from the 'Defence of Poetry', one of the words whose phonemes Shelley himself loves to reduplicate. His symphonizing theory of sound-repetitions is basically a musical means to key-word emphasis: the key-word is prepared for and determined by the preceding words, their sounds gliding into it, supported by emphatic cadence. Assimilating alliteration lies at the centre of Shelley's search for poetic value in abstracted human speech.

Musical sound-repetitions, for Shelley, were therefore the fundamental agent in this search for an ideal symphonic harmonious-

---

[6] From 'Byron and Shelley on the Character of Hamlet,' *New Monthly Magazine and Literary Journal*, 29:2 (1830), 330–1. For evidence for the attribution to Mary Shelley, see E. Houghton (ed.) *The Wellesley Index to Victorian Periodicals*, iii. 213 (entry 1565 for *NMM*). Furthermore, the dialogue form recalls an earlier Mary Shelley contribution to the journal in 1824, where the author falls asleep in the Coliseum and hears, simultaneously, a conversation between two ancient Romans and between two modern British dandies ('Rome in the first and nineteenth century')—the 1830 article rewrites this as overhearing the two dead poets in the style of Landor's *Imaginary Conversations* (reviewed in the *NMM* the year beforehand). In my analysis of the dialogue, 'Shelley' should be understood as referring both to Mary Shelley and Shelley.

ness—the neo-Platonic idealist in him heard music as a natural, organic force of persuasion towards bodily and spiritual unity. The possibility of such a harmony lay in what he heard as the perfect quadruplet-rhyme between the beat of blood through the heart, rhythm and sound of voice and breath, artistic and natural music-making, and supernatural 'circles of life-dissolving sound'.[7] 'To Constantia Singing' shows this clearly: Constantia's voice is a 'Spirit', and the 'blood and life' in her fingers bewitch the strings. Shelley listens with his blood: 'The blood is listening in my frame', and dissolves like Lionel: 'I am dissolved in these consuming extasies.' The s and l repetitions Shelley identified in the Shakespeare line reappear in this poem: 'Thy voice slow rising like a Spirit, lingers/O'ershadowing it with soft and lulling wings'.[8]

Byron might very well have cried 'Pish!' to all this—after all, it would take some considerable act of mechanical contrivance to hear in a girl singing a parlour-song a manifestation of the Spirit in the blood, the air, the song, and the poet's own sound-repetitions. More important is Shelley's obstinate sense that sound-effects are agents of inspiration of a very hypnotic kind—'soft and lulling', dissolving, flowing and melting—that may prove fatal (Lionel and the listener's swooning deaths). Though the crossing of ecstatic experience with neo-Platonic music- and essence-theory may seem hopelessly restricted to contemporary concerns, there is something to take away from this aspect of Shelley's weirdly fanatical feeling for the sweet sounds of words and music; namely the possibility that over-rich sound-effects may be danger-signals, ethical markers of a liquid drift towards a self-languishing mystique. Shelley's approval of dream-like 'eloquent blood' did

[7] 'Rosalind and Helen', Complete Works, ii. 2, 1166. The poem contains the boldest expression of Shelley's Hellenistic aligning of poet and bird. Lionel listens to the 'sweet words' of the 'poet-bird', the nightingale, speaks to Helen, who is inspired to play the harp and cry her song; the song in turn inspires Lionel to such a pitch that he dies away—'as every strain/Grew fainter but more sweet, his mien/Sunk with the sound relaxedly' (ll. 1168–70)—the 'strain-sweet-sunk-sound' string reinforces Shelley's acoustic pun between sounds gliding, dying away into each other along the phoneme-repetitions and Lionel's relaxing into his own death on hearing the inspired sweet sounds of Helen's singing voice.

[8] Complete Works, iii., 155–6. Alastor's dream of the veiled maid accords with this: 'The beating of her heart was heard to fill/The pauses of her music, and her breath/Tumultuously accorded with those fits/Of intermitted song', 'Alastor', ll. 169–72, Complete Works, i. 181.

considerable harm to Yeats, for example. But Shelley, in the recall of his poem in his prose, found out another way of earthing the aerial tendencies of his musical ear: in memory.

Memories lived with Shelley like guilty incrustations:

> The curse of this life is, that whatever is known, can never be unknown. You inhabit a spot, which before you inhabit it, is as indifferent to you as any other spot on earth, and when, persuaded by some necessity, you think you leave it, you leave it not; it clings to you—and with memories of things, which, in your experience of them, gave no such promise, revenges your desertion.[9]

Words are rather like spots on earth to Shelley. He inhabits them, often slackly, carelessly—but he carries the memory of them (their sounds) on with him through line after line of poetic territory. Their revenge is often the creation of an emptily repetitive echo-chamber.

But at times, Shelley heard those sounds strange again on the ear, and a real, poignant beauty is born on the air of his words, on a remembered spot on earth. A nightingale sings:

> now loud,
> Climbing in circles the windless sky,
> Now dying music; suddenly
> 'Tis scattered in a thousand notes,
> And now to the hushed ear it floats
> Like field smells known in infancy,
> Then failing, soothes the air again.[10]

We are accustomed to four of these kinds of Shelleyan music: loud, spiritual bombast ('See, where the Spirits of the human mind/Wrapt in sweet sounds, as in bright veils, approach!'), dying falls ('Music when soft voices die,/Vibrates in the memory'), words scattered every which way ('No leaf will be shaken/While the dews of your melody scatter/Delight'), and a failing, quiet restraint ('The sounds that soothed his sleep').[11]

---

[9] Letter to Peacock, Milan, 20 Apr. 1818, in *Peacock's Memoirs of Shelley*, 123.
[10] 'Rosalind and Helen', *Complete Works*, ii. ll. 1105–11.
[11] *Prometheus Unbound* II. IV. v. 245, ll. 81–82; 'To—', 'music when soft voices die', IV. 94, ll. 1–2, *Poems: 1820*; 'To Jane' ('The keen stars were twinkling'), IV, 204, ll. 16–17; 'Alastor', l. 198.

But a rarer sound is there too: 'And now to the hushed ear it floats/Like field smells known in infancy.' This is no empty synaesthesia—the way the floating birdsong seems to drift through the air to the suddenly expectant attention ('hushed' very finely catches our breath) recalls quite precisely remote memory's sudden quiet shock of recognition and its steady aftermath. The rarity is in the superfine quality of the comparison (two tiny, hushed delicacies) but also in the slight awkwardness of phrasing: the clumsy f-repetition, the gulps in 'known in in-', the poverty of English when it comes to the olfactory (only 'smells' and 'odours'—both words cannot keep the farmyard out). The lines bear witness to the human side to Shelley's gift, the tangible, embarrassed memories of childhood sensation, and his own embarassment in admitting this strange, halting music as evidence. Sound-effects can give rare accents away, discovering a strange sense to Shelley's preoccupation with sweet sounds and spirits: a trembling protectiveness about remotely singing, evanescent memories of a child breathing in the fields.

The Meaning of Individual Phonemes

Shelley's fidelity to his sound-systems, though, raises many difficult questions about the very chanciness of the chances of language. These questions are primarily suspicious about the arbitrary subjectivity of any ascription of sense-values to sounds, and they can be concentrated down to four main areas of debate in the field of phonolinguistics.

First, whether it ever makes sense to ascribe meaning to units of sound divorced from their context within words (s and l as 'pure and gentle', for example).

Secondly, whether it is legitimate to believe that, in some manner either onomatopoeic or physiological, the sounds of words 'represent' the sounds of the world or the emotions attached to objects, or whether there is some mystical imitative relation between signifier and signified (whether the phonemes in 'sleep' mime, in some way, the sweetness of repose).

Thirdly, whether the sounds of words are not of purely structural significance within literary works, acting as 'musical' figures with absolutely no sense beyond the sensuousness of pleasing figures of pitch and sound-repetition (Shelley's 'harmony' and 'symphony').

And, lastly, if a sound-sense argument can be proven, whether it should not merely be described as a local, unconscious, and transient effect within a particular context that cannot be extrapolated from (all that Byron implies with his 'Pish!' and 'mechanical contrivances').

Paul Delbouille, in his 1961 study, *Poésie et sonorités*, addresses the first two questions with some vigour. Maurice Grammont's ascription of predicates to every single vowel and consonant independent of word or syntax is exploded mercilessly and at angry length. There may be some words where particular vowels have a mimetic effect as in obvious onomatopoeia but these are few in number and are an insufficient basis for generalization (27–37). He concedes that the illusion amongst language-users that there is such a link might prompt certain identifications (the vowel 'i' with littleness, for example[12]) that then enter the process of word-change over time (72–73), but the links in general can never be absolutely systematized and anyway, when they occur, they always occur with the sense of the words uppermost. As F. L. Lucas joked in unconscious support of Delbouille, 'If "forlorn" meant a kind of potato, would it still ring like "a bell"? '(249). Delbouille proves that theses like Grammont's, where each individual acoustic component of language has a definite nuance, merely rely on the arbitrary nuances in the words they choose to describe the sounds. Therefore Grammont, in arbitrarily calling a certain basketful of vowels 'grave' and another 'aigu' and then listing examples where sound-patterns in poetry mime those accents is in reality only transposing his impressions backwards from the accumulated senses of his examples onto the vowels he says he is isolating (92–110).

Grammont's own categories of sound-values, for Delbouille, make this quite clear:

Grammont établit une rapport entre les sonorités et toute une série de sentiments aux nuances subtiles. S'il y a des sons *graves* et des sons *aigus*, y a-t-il des sons *idylliques, timides, haineux, douloureux*, des sons de *l'immensité*, de *l'indignation*, de *l'inquiétude* ou du *dépit*—tous sentiments ou im-

---

[12] This is Jespersen's famous thesis: "Symbolic Value of the Vowel *i*", in *Linguistica* (Copenhagen, 1933) (1922), 283–303.

pressions qui [. . .] figurent à côté de cent autres, la table des matières du *Vers français?* (Delbouille, 50)

This is not to deny that language-users may also share many of Grammont's superstitions. Maxime Chastaing, for instance, is generally open-minded as to whether it is unconscious phonic symbolism that affects language change or rather the sonic coincidences pre-existing in the lexical stock. Either way, in an experiment with students, he found that they felt the phoneme R̲ to be 'très rugueux, fort, violent, lourd, âcre, dur, voisin, amer', whilst l̲ was felt to be 'léger, débonnaire, clair, lisse, faible, doux, distant' (502 ff.)

Such folk feelings may have some effect in word-creation; for instance, in certain kinds of doublet—'teeny-weeny', 'Lady Luck', 'rough and ready', 'spick and span', 'itsy-bitsy', 'shim-sham' etc. But it is impossible to tell whether these reduplications are exploiting coincidences already available in the lexicon, or whether they are created by folk feelings about the symbolic value of certain phonemes. For my part, I feel the existence of lexical saffinities between separate words in a language ('flip' and 'flop', for example) helps create the illusion of a superstitious ground of acoustic symbolism in the minds of language-users. The fact that snakes 'hiss' (onomatopoeia) may have determined the collocation of 'slither' and 'grass'. But to move from saying this to identifying the phoneme s̲ with a snake's hiss is wholly illegitimate. It would be like saying that because 'woof' imitates a dog's bark, all uses of the phoneme w̲ recall a dog's bark. Onomatopoeia, childrhymes, doublets, comic riddling are small-scale, local phenomena in a language. They cannot be used to justify a dark faith in phoneme demonology. The language will always disprove such endeavours. If Jespersen, Chastaing, Jakobson *et al* insist that the phoneme i̲ is identified with littleness, then how do they explain words such as 'big', 'immense', 'massive', 'limitless'?

Mimetic Phonemes and Kristeva's Babies

Delbouille has even less time for exponents of the second area of debate, whose champion he identifies as Spire with his physiological explanation for the feeling in words. Spire attempts to prove that there is a mimetic re-enactment of the sense of words in the way one articulates them. So, in saying 'murmurer', for instance, one's mouth executes 'une suite de moues analogues à ses mouvements dans l'acte de murmurer'. From similar examples he proves that the consonant 'm' always articulates a sense of things 'molles'. 'L's are liquid and lulling because the tips of the tongue in their articulation are always 'humectés de salive', and so forth (319–324).

Delbouille simply argues that Spire is also reading backwards. Delbouille concedes that feeling has an influence over articulation that makes one pronounce the 'l's in 'lullaby', for example, in a soft and childlike way, whereas in 'low labour costs' one would naturally ignore them. But the inverse, that 'l'articulation pouvait suggèrer le sentiment' is both arbitrary and fantastic (63). What possible atomistic theory of articulation could give individual values to the fricatives, labials, explosives, etc. (the 'danse laryngo-buccale' in Spire's phrase ('Delbouille, 63)) that would cover the huge difference of sense between 'frontal lobotomy' and 'a bottle in front of me'?

A new version of the Spire–Grammont wrong-headedness can be found in the work of Julia Kristeva, whose eagerness to discover signs of rhythmical sex-drives in texts has made her fall in with this most curiously French superstition. A great deal of time is spent in *La Révolution du langage poétique* demonstrating that Freud and Klein can be proved down at the phonemic level of sound-repetitions. Her analysis of the first stanza of Mallarmé's 'Prose' is typical:

La pulsion agressive phallique /tR/, /dR/, /f/, etc. et anale /gR/ de la première série s'oppose à la pulsion orale incorporante (succion) de la seconde /m/. La série de voyelles commence avec un coup de glotte devant /i/, traverse toute la gamme des fermées antérieures /i/, /e/, aux ouvertes éventuellement postérieures /wa/ ou /wo/ de 'mémoire' et 'grimoire', et, après ce relâchement, revient de nouveau en avant /e/, /i/, /y/, esquissant ainsi un mouvement de tension (sublimation): aggressi-vité-analité-tension. (242)

The argument behind Kristeva's extraordinary transformation of these phonemes into units of differing unconscious drives is circular. She says phonetic repetition is a return to the pre-linguistic state of infanthood (221); she then says that each phoneme therefore carries a meaning supplementary to the words it occurs within ('*les sons du langage sont plus que des phonèmes*' (222)), in other words, all the conflicting, mother-directed 'pulsions' that go to form the metalinguistic *chora*; the proof that all these revolutionary 'drive-sounds' exist can be found in avant-garde writing and its sound-repetitions (226).

The error can be put simply. Kristeva is making this kind of move:

Babies babble. Babies have unconscious desires. *Therefore* babies' babble is the expression of those unconscious desires. Babies' babble is essentially a series of repetitions of individual phonemes. Those phonemes *must* mean something. Each phoneme *should* be assigned to a particular unconscious desire and its drive. Avant-garde poets use a lot of sound-repetitions. *Therefore* their phonemes *must* be the expression of the *same* unconscious desires and drives. The proof that babies' babble means all these things is avant-garde poetry.

Apart from the circular argument (the proof starts at the wrong end), each one of the moves in italics is illegitimate and arbitrary. It is not clear that babble is an expression of unconscious desires— many researchers rather interpret the majority of the articulations in terms of practice play or arbitrary responses to immediate needs and events.

M. A. K. Halliday, for instance, sees in the little language of the protolinguistic infant (8 to 101/2 months old), signs which are 'functional in respect of the child's intent', the vocal expressions meaning 'yes, we're together' and 'look, that's interesting', 'I want' and 'I don't want' (about specific objects), 'do that—I insist!', 'that's nice', 'that tastes good', signs associated with attention to surroundings, 'yes, here I am', 'I'm sleepy' etc. (183–6). All the signs are immediate responses with practical, instrumental, regulatory and interactional purposes, very much more humdrum then the mystical, narcotic *chora* of Kristeva's dream world. Of course, Halliday may be reading the jargon of sociological 'interpersonal' beliefs into the child's babble. But accepting this would only serve to heighten the improbability of Kristeva's hypotheses, the ruinous rhyme between childish babble and psychobabble.

Other researchers, such as Oller, have argued that early infant sounds are a product of infant anatomy (the high proportion of velar and uvular sounds in gooing, for instance, being made

possible by the high position of the infant larynx) and are fun-
damentally exploratory and reflexive, not passive (86–87). Their
motivation is to prepare 'the skills for communication as he or she,
the child, understands those skills'(101).[13] The pre-verbal child,
many researchers believe, spends a great deal of time *listening* to
adult talk, classifying the sounds it cannot itself reproduce.[14] The
six early stages of development of speech production set out by
Stark show a more complex picture than Kristeva's monolithic
pre-linguistic phonetic-phonemic drive-sounds suggest: (1) reflexive sound making (cry, discomfort, vegetative sounds) (2) cooing
and laughter (3) exploratory vocal play (4) reduplicated babbling
(5) non-reduplicated babbling (jargon, protowords) (6) referential
words (79). Whether or not the infant, at stage one, is responding
to the adult world (it is important for Kristeva that this be untrue,
though this goes against the grain of research), it is sheer fiction
that prompts her to read anal and oral 'pulsions' into the body
contractions that accompany the early sounds on the basis that
'anterior' phonemes affect the digestive tract, and 'posterior'
sounds the sphincter (*Polylogue*, 445).

Moves such as these characterize the superstitious and mystical
search for the meaning of individual phonemes, divorced of context in ordinary speech and text. The folk feelings that will hear a
snake's hiss in an s-repetition, or 'brightness' in a string of aɪ
sounds run very deep. They are of the same order as Kristeva's
desire to discover the 'semiotic rhythm', 'indifférent au langage,
énigmatique et féminin, cet espace sous-jacent à l'ecrit [. . .] ryth-
mique, déchaîné, irréductible à sa traduction verbale intelligible'
(*Révolution*, 29). Perhaps the image of Kristeva wiring ten baby
infants up for sound and all the while checking the contractions in
their sphincter and digestive tubes might warn the world of what
terrible comedy there is in the rage to give isolated sounds the
meaning one always wanted them to have.

Alerting-Devices

It is in the second two areas of debate about the relations between
the sound and sense of words (the fugitive and the musical) that

---

[13] See also Fischer and Corrigan, 'Skill Approach', 245–274.
[14] Jakobson and Waugh, *Charpente du langage*, 79.

the phonolinguist is engaged with real difficulties. To begin with the contention that sound-effects have only a fugitive significance. Delbouille strongly prefers the argument that sound-effects in literary passages are of local significance only and even then at a level secondary to the sense. He argues that a reader must first be alerted before sounds are taken into consideration at all:

nous considérons que les sons ne peuvent souligner le sens, jouer en accord avec lui, que si le lecteur est alerté, même s'il ne prend pas nécéssairement conscience du pourquoi ni du comment, par une présence insolite [. . .] Ce que nous entendons, ce que nous lisons, ce ne sont pas des sons ou des lettres qui évoqueraient des sens. Le processus est infiniment plus rapide: nous identifions mots et rapports au plus vite; parfois même nous identifions déjà avant d'avoir tout saisi ou, si on préfère, nous comprenons à demi-mots. Le signifiant n'existe qu'à peine le temps de se faire reconnaître. Il faut bien autre chose pour que nous le remarquions, pour que nous acceptions de nous arrêter à lui ou d'y revenir. (29)

That 'autre chose' is, according to Delbouille, either an 'étrangeté sonore' or a simple 'mise en relief'. Noticing the sound-repetitions in Delbouille's prose, for instance (the run on the sounds of 'sons' in the sentence beginning 'Ce que nous entendons' perhaps), would, in other words, require the superaddition of an alerting device before one could be confident that the effect is there to be heard as anything more than accidental.

What kind of alerting device, though? Is it something to do with the sense of the words? The density of the sound-effects? The presence of some key term? On Valéry's 'Elle n'écoute ni les gouttes dans leurs chutes,/ Tinter d'un siècle vide au lointain le trésor', Delbouille writes that 'c'est le sens du vers, et particulière-ment du verbe *écoute*, qui nous met sur la voie de la suggestion' (23). Certain words by their sense ask us to go over the words again to discover how the sounds are organized. He stresses this again in his comment upon Anna de Noailles' lines, 'Bruit des sources errant dans le jardin d'Armide,/Bruit d'air, de fifre d'eau, de tambourin liquide,/Bruit argentin, luisant, circulant, blanc et blanc,/ Bruit de brise qui glisse et de poisson volant!'. Delbouille writes, 'la triple répétition de "bruit" force notre attention (par son sens), qu'elle nous oblige, pour ainsi dire, à tendre les oreilles de l'imagination' (24). But cues for the ears of the imagination might be more easily read in poetry. Are there any corresponding alerting-devices in prose? An answer to this question is essential if the fugitive argument is to be resisted. This argument is neatly summed up by Dell Hymes: 'the longer the work or passage, the less any particular selection of sounds can escape being submerged by the normal frequencies of the language' (50).

One of Swift's madmen in his digression on madness is one 'that has forgot the common *Meaning* of words, but an admirable Retainer of *Sound'*(338–9). Is it then mad to listen to the sounds of words when reading a long piece of prose? Delbouille, with his point about the indifference to sound in prose in rapid, skimming eye-reading, would tend to agree. When we come across this sentence in a 250-word paragraph five sentences long from *David Copperfield*, for instance, would we even notice the close rhyming prose?

The walls were whitewashed as white as milk, and the patchwork counterpane made my eyes quite ache with its brightness. (80)

Leaving aside the fact that Dickens's novels were often read out loud, what matters here is that the eye *will* catch that oddly childish repetition of 'white'. The other sounds (w initial alliteration; the 'milk'-'ache' half-rhyme with 'work' as intermediary, the 'quite-bright' rhymes) may seem superfluous, but they strengthen the odd childishness of the tone, the storybook simplicity of the expression; they support that basic repetitiveness. The style is like Time in the early chapters: 'as if Time had not grown up himself yet, but were a child too, and always at play.'(87). Childish prose tends to be more vocal; as Swift pointed out to Stella, when writing their 'little language': 'Do you know what? when I am writing in our language I make up my mouth just as if I was speaking it. I caught myself at it just now.' (657) There is no need to seek out some fanciful predicate to tack on to a w-repetition in this context— all one need acknowledge is the proximity of the narrative voice here to childish diction, rhythms, and sound-effects. The 'white' repetition, which would be frowned on in 'adult' prose, signals an adult voice recalling the tonalities of a child's mind at play among simple words—in effect it is asking us to make up our mouths, and vocalize the accents of childhood, to recapture the white simplicities of childish wonder and its chanting language. The 'white'-repetition is one example of an adequate alerting-device.

Rhythmical regularity, to eye and ear, is another alerting-device; as in this sentence from *David Copperfield*, describing one of Betsey Trotwood's 'pedestrian feats': 'she kept passing in and out, along this measured track, at an unchanging pace, with the regularity of a clock-pendulum.' (645). This is a sentence about rhythmical bodily regularity, and Dickens neatly achieves similar feats in his prose sentence, with a regular, measured three-beat rhythm. The comma-strung phrases *look* regular too, and ask a reader, again, to move over the words with the internal ear, and to catch the pace of the voice in the *p*-repetitions ('passing-pace-pendulum') which mark out a supportive rhythm—they time the sounds, getting them in step with the sense.

Dense prose will tend to demand the help of the listening ear, if only to help pick out the sense—a crowded sentence will slow the eye down to listening speed, and Dickens can give the unreal energy to the clutter of objects in his close, crammed world; like the description of the mad old man's shop:

at the corner of a dirty lane, ending in an enclosure full of stinging-nettles, against the palings of which some second-hand sailors' clothes, that seemed to have overflowed the shop, were fluttering among some cots, and rusty guns, and oilskin hats, and certain trays full of so many old rusty keys of so many sizes that they seemed various enough to open all the doors in the world. (239)

A jumble of phoneme-repetitions crams the words together into discrete lumps, little runs and strings: s̱—'stinging-some-second-sailors';—'clothes-overflowed'; p̱ and ʌ—'shop-flutt-among-some-cots-rusty-guns'; visual and acoustic half-rhymes—'cots-hats-trays-keys'—supporting the repetitions of generic plurals; another s̱-run—'certain-so many-rusty-so many sizes-seemed'. Rhythmical effects allied with these sound-effects condense the prose, make it *denser* to eye and ear once heard, concentrate the prose into the accent of quiddity that is so important in Dickens, not only to describe the infinite rubbish in little room of his London nooks and crannies,[15] but also the bustling, fairy-tale business of his characters—as with this string of ḇs helping describe Omer the haberdasher: 'a fat, short-winded,

---

[15] The 'bawling, splashing, link-lighted, umbrella struggling, hackney-coach-jostling, pattern-clinking, muddy, miserable world' (344).

merry-looking, little old man in black, with rusty little bunches of ribbons at the knees of his breeches, black stockings, and a broad-brimmed hat'(178).

'Black' is the key term or motif in the Omer passages ('the black things' David calls them (179)). The presence of motif-terms is often a sufficient alerting-device. Acting in much the same way as the rhetorical repetitive sentence- and paragraph-openers so common in *David Copperfield*,[16] they train the mind to attend to repetitions as such and to correlate and account for their significances. 'Earnestness' is such a motif-term in Dickens's novel:

Then Peggotty fitted her mouth close to the keyhole, and delivered these words through it with as much feeling and earnestness as a keyhole has ever been the medium of communicating, I will venture to assert: shooting in each broken little sentence in a convulsive little burst of its own. (111)

The phonemes constituting 'earnestness' ('3:nistnas) find themselves recalled in 'assert', 'sentence', and 'burst', a recall supported by a crowded run on n̲ in the last phrase. The straight repetitions of the words 'keyhole' and 'little' are auxiliary alerting-devices. The whole issue of hearing sounds in prose is apt here, with the sense of the sentence dealing with difficulty of communication, broken sentences and getting feeling sounds across. The key term has trouble getting through the little acoustic keyhole in the reader's eye-dominated attention. This is as much as to say that the topic of any sentence or paragraph may also be an alerting-device. Any prose sentence about sound or medium of communication, for example, demands the right to be heard.

The most powerful alerting-device in prose is when imagery, tone, and diction gather together to form what is traditionally called a 'purple passage'. The term 'purple passage' first entered the language, according to the *Oxford English Dictionary*, in translations of Horace's *Ars Poetica*: Horace's allusion to showy poetry (*purpureus pannus*) was rendered 'a purple pace [piece] . . . for vewe' by Queen Elizabeth in 1598, and 'One or two verses of purple patchwork, that may make a great shew' by Christopher Smart in 1756. The OED's definition, 'a brilliant or ornate passage

---

[16] e.g. the repetition of 'I picture myself' to begin four sentences (132); five paragraphs beginning with the exclamatory 'what' (173–4).

in a literary composition', fails to take into account the general suspicion felt about showy poetic passages, that they are generally tragic or royal in a falsely theatrical way,[17] clear in the 1895 quotation from Gosse: 'Emphasizing the purpler passages with lifted voice and gesticulating finger.' The suspicion may very well be based on the strong associations the colour has with 'the dress of emperors and kings' and thus with stage representations. It may also have something to do with the pseudo-poetic euphemism for blood, cunningly used by Shakespeare, for example, to signal a cruelly theatrical rhetoric: Gloucester, stabbing the king, talks of 'purple tears' falling from his weeping sword, in harsh mockery of the king's reference to the 'tragic history' of his drowned son, 'Daedalus'-like Edward (3 Henry VI V. vi. 64). This suspicion of insincerity in purple rhetoric has no doubt tranquillized much of the prose written in English since the Euphuistic excesses of the 1580s (in which so many of the antithetical clause recurrences were based on redundant rhetorical alliteration). As a result, many writers have had to find internal justification for their purple passages, a kind of implied ethical disclaimer of the possible charges inevitably faced when one lifts one's voice and gesticulates.

Dickens's justification was the particular choice of his occasions: in David Copperfield, the purple passages are almost entirely on the subject of good, tender, sentimental women or on the undeniable pathos of elegiac memory; returning in thought to the empty family home, for instance:

it pained me to think of the dear old place as altogether abandoned; of the weeds growing tall in the garden, and the fallen leaves lying thick and wet upon the paths. I imagined how the winds of winter would howl round it, how the cold rain would beat upon the window-glass, how the moon would make ghosts on the walls of the empty rooms, watching their solitude all night. I thought afresh of the grave in the churchyard, underneath the tree: and it seemed as if the house were dead too, now, and all connected with my father and mother were faded away. (306)

---

[17] Meredith's Modern Love is very much concerned with this feeling; sonnet XXXVII is set in a 'purple valley', rich and sweet; it has a fine, sentimental look and sound beneath the 'low-rosed moon, the face of Music mute'. But the external show does not conceal the blank, sterile mistrust that is stifling the modern lovers' marriage— 'Our tragedy, is it alive or dead?'(I. 16), a question conceptually echoed later in the sequence by the sentence 'Passions spin the plot:/We are betrayed by what is false within.'(XLIII, ll. 15–16).

The tragic gulp in the throat in the comma-timing of 'were dead too, now,' is prepared for by the sheer overpowering stress and rhythm of the long elegiac phrases—the tragic note is earned, as it were, by the very incontestability of the nostalgia for the 'dear old place' and the accompanying pain felt thinking of its ravaged present state. The voice lifts up along a quadruply repeated five-beat rhythm (from 'fallen leaves' to 'empty rooms'), a prose reminiscent of iambic pentameter; along formal symmetries of sound and syntax ('weeds ... tall ... garden'-'fallen leaves ... paths', 'I imagined how ... howl ... how .... how ...', repetition of the definite article decomposing 'the dear old place'); along nightmare patterns of childish superstition. But it lifts up most of all in the extraordinarily sustained w-run centred around the poetic locution 'winds of winter' (I-repetition underlines this) and all the 'would's of the mind's vision of devastation, visually supported by the howls of the 'how's. The emotional beat of those nightmarish possibilities can be heard in the returns of the sound and joins forces with the rhythmical uplift to give an image of the self-haunting mind of a morbid child.[18]

Great care is needed dealing with this kind of alerting-device—for the general understanding of what constitutes a 'purple passage' is so often limited to natural description or references to Narcissus and the Oreads (as in Wilde's insipid *Poems in Prose*). Impassioned prose, it seems to me, needs to show some kind of awareness of the heckler's jibe that may accuse it of stagy pseudo-tragic feeling. It needs to summon up rhythmical and acoustic resources that chime in with a dramatic presentation of a mind remembering or imagining.

These alerting-devices, then—word-repetition, prose-density, presence of motif-terms, self-referential subject-matter, overtly purple passages—summon up the reader's auditory attention to

[18] When David returns later to the house, he physically goes through the same motions, recalling 'every yard of the old road' as he goes along it, haunting the old spots 'as my memory had often done' (378)—this paragraph is rich in sounds too, particularly the church-bell 'like a departed voice to me', the 'tune' of his thoughts and his 'echoing footsteps'. It also turns round the grave. The first hundred words are characterized by repetition and sound-effects—'yard-old-road-old-lingered-lingered'—and by the rhyming endings 'when I was far away' and 'where both my parents lay'. Haunted mind, recall, and memory have a corresponding prose that is run on recall of sounds and 'haunted' repetitions. This double sense to sound-repetition is particularly emphatic as the passage itself recalls similar passages in the book.

the prose passage in question. As for the vexed question of the conscious or unconscious nature of these devices, it is not necessary to go as far as Shelley's rhyme of poetic line and beautiful woman to agree with his reasoning:

I don't say that a poet must necessarily be conscious of all this, no more than a lady is conscious of every graceful movement. But I do say that [the many simultaneous operations of sound and sense] all depend upon reason, in which they live and move, and have their being; and that he who brings them out into the light of distinct consciousness, beside satisfying an instinctive desire of his own nature, will be more secure and commanding.

The fact that a poet's work is paid such respect should not disguise the other side of Shelley's statement—that internal rhymes and sound-repetitions *should* depend upon reason. My contention is that modern prose fiction should be paid the same respect and suffer the same proof.

When Wilde writes 'the pool of his pleasure changed from a cup of sweet waters into a cup of salt tears', I can find no justification in the prose poem for the p-repetition or for the 'sweet-salt' 'waters-tears' resemblances except a sickly sweet and watery desire to make the prose sound 'poetic' or 'musical' in the abstract and conventional sense.[19] It fails where the Dickens passage earns our respect. The motives we discover to be actuating the language in Dickens's poetic prose are important enough to justify a faith in the 'conscious' nature of their presence. This does not so much resurrect the intentional fallacy as redefine it as confidence in the complex nature of sound-sense relations. The difficulty lies in the act of judgement that applies that confidence, for such a confidence will often find certain texts wanting. But perhaps it is not a difficulty as such; only a going against the grain of current morbidly anti-Platonic discourses by saying that some writers write badly and why.

So I would agree that sound-effects are fugitive, as Delbouille suggests, but that they can be intensified by the presence of the

---

[19] Quoted Simon, *Prose Poem*, 665. As Simon says, Wilde's prose poems (as well as the incriminating letter to Bosie which Wilde called 'a kind of prose poem' in the dock at the Old Bailey—a terrible proof of Wilde's replacement of true feeling by a false sense of 'true poetic feeling') 'walks between passion and poetry, and misses out on both'(667).

several alerting-devices outlined above. These alerting-devices fix attention upon the sound-effects, and, by so doing, transform their fugitive properties into important elements in the immediate and serial praxis of the novel—indeed their very fugitiveness may provide a key metaphor for aspects of the fictional world. As the Dickens examples demonstrate, a writer may have many uses for the sounds of the words he uses—for Dickens, they act as cues for the tonalities of a self-haunting mind, signals of childish thinking, crowded energies, changes in pace, emotionally charged words, the accents of memory. But in all cases, a reader will become sensitive to their fragile but intermittently necessary status; both fugitively conscious and consciously fugitive, they craft real bonds between the mind and its words.

Musical Remembering

The musical argument concerning sound-repetitions has been the most attractive to hard-headed critics who are either for or against giving senses to sounds. The idea that language can be made to sound 'musical' has occasioned many a loud snort of contempt. Jean Mourot cautions: 'quand on ratiocine sur la musicalité du langage littéraire, on fait semblant de découvrir ce qu'on a déjà trouvé, puisqu'on ne fait que justifier des goûts' (62). Wimsatt is even more dubious: 'The music of spoken words in itself is meagre, so meagre in comparison to the music of song or instrument as to be hardly worth discussion [. . .]. The mere return to the vowel tonic (the chord or tone cluster characteristic of a vowel) will produce not emotion but boredom' (327).

But doubts remain, despite these strong voices. There is music in these lines, for instance:

> And up into the sounding hall I past;
> But nothing in the sounding hall I saw,
> No bench nor table, painting on the wall
> Or shield of knight; *only the rounded moon*
> *Through the tall oriel on the rolling sea.*
> But always in the quiet house I heard,
> Clear as a lark, high o'er me as a lark,

A sweet voice singing in the topmost tower
To the eastward.
    ('The Holy Grail', ll. 824–32; my emphasis)

Tennyson, according to his son Hallam 'was fond of quoting these lines for the beauty of their sound.'[20] The lines he was fond of quoting (ll. 827–8) are placed in between lines that concern sound and music—the repetition of 'sounding hall'; the lark-like 'sweet voice' with the 'lark'-repetition are strong alerting-devices. The atmosphere of the silence within the 'enchanted towers' of Carbonek is quietly musical, so strange to the sound-tormented Lancelot,[21] and an unexpected prelude to the blast of light and heat of the vision of the Grail.

That enchantment becomes chant in the two lines Tennyson preferred, as this phonetic and rhythmical transcription shows:

əʊnlr ðə ˈraʊndɪd ˈmuːn
       - - - / - / *
θruː ðə ˈtɔːl ˈɔːrɪəl ɒn ðə ˈrəʊlɪŋ ˈsiː
       - - / / - * - - / - /

The rhythm has a certain symmetry to it; the double-stressed line-endings ('rounded moon' and 'rolling sea') flanking the two-stress 'tall oriel'. The effect is to create three phrases of equal length and rhythm. The flanking phrases are brought together by the r-repetition in the adjectives (linked by the r in 'oriel'), as well as by their rounded diphthongs, and all three pairs are unified by the long vowels. The first pair ('rounded moon') develops into the central pair through vowel-repetition (moon-through; tall-oriel);

---

[20] Note for l. 827–8, *Tennyson* ed. Ricks, 899–900. The lines are a reminiscence of Scott's *The Lay of the Last Minstrel* : 'The moon on the east oriel shone/Through slender shafts of shapely stone' (II. xi); the heavy sound-repetitions (moon-on-shone-stone, shone-shafts-shapely, three st clusters) show that Lancelot's moon-madness was a common symptom at an oriel window. Tennyson is also recalling his own 'The Palace of Art': the Soul sits between shining Oriels, singing her songs; Plato's and Bacon's faces gaze on her through 'the topmost Oriels' coloured flame' (ll. 159–162; *Tennyson*, ed. Ricks, 62). Both this quotation and the Scott identify visionary light through an oriel window with sweet sounds, presumably because of the cathedral overtones.
[21] Lancelot's mad guilt is acoustic. His decision to purify himself at sea comes after a climactic deafening: 'So loud a blast, my King, began to blow,/So loud a blast along the shore and sea,/Ye could not hear the waters for the blast' (ll. 792–4)—the 'blast' repetitions give us the accent of his deafened, blasted guilt. Lancelot, seeing the veiled vision of the Grail, is 'blasted' by the heat (l. 841).

the central into the last through the dark ls (tall-oriel-roll), and the strong lip-rounding of the three vowels.[22]

Tennyson's musical practice is a combination of a rough rhythmical regularity stressing a certain symmetry, sound-repetitions to effect glides from feature to feature, and a play of variations on phonemes of a similar class (in this case, long vowels, diphthongs, and rounded sounds). This last aspect of verbal 'musicality' is the most difficult area of any phonolinguistic analysis. The work of structuralist linguistics did a great deal to stress the 'universality' of certain phonemic and semanticizing oppositions in language acquisition and their crucial importance in the understanding of speech. Though much of this work remains crudely mystical,[23] it was instructive in proving, if only by sheer insistence, the real connections speakers unconsciously hear between phonemes sharing similar positions in charts crossing manner and place of articulation.

So, for instance, the nonsense rhyme 'Pat-a-cake, pat-a-cake, baker's man, bake me a pie as fast as you can' owes much of its pleasurable regularity not only to the little internal rhyme (bake-cake) and p initial stresses, but also to the fact that seven of the key consonants are plosives, and that b in 'bake' is a bilabial plosive like p (its twin, in fact). The two diphthongs eɪ and aɪ are also felt by hearers to be pleasurably kith and kin, and the rhythm set up by the ps and the alternation of eɪ and æ, resolves sweetly on 'pie' partly because of the proximity of æ and the first element of ai (both middle, unrounded, open vowels). And, finally, the bake-cake rhyme and the p in 'pie' mean, in effect, that the ear hears an inversion of the pat-a-cake sounds in 'bake me a pie'.

Such effects rely as much on variation within sound families as on strict sound-repetition. The Tennyson lines above owe a little of their musicality to the fact that the main vowels—əʊ aʊ ɔː uː—are all fully back and rounded. This supports the internal rhythmical and sonic correspondance between 'only the rounded' and 'on the rolling', since the diphthong in 'only' occupies the same acoustic space as the ɒ in 'on'. The music of his lines should not obscure the

---

[22] əʊː— 'quite noticeable lip-rounding'; ɔː—'quite strong lip-rounding', Roach, *English Phonetics*, 18–21.

[23] e.g. the analogy Jakobson and Waugh, following the Prague linguist Jacob, support between the laws governing phonemic structures and laws governing the nucleus (Jakobson and Waugh, *Charpente du langage*, 84).

particular occasion of the senses of the words, however. To adapt Byron's critique, the beauty of the lines does not only lie in sounds and syllables, but in the metaphor of the moon shining through the oriel upon the rolling sea, that presents a mystical rendering of a heraldic shield, cooperative light and sound being the motif of the Grail. The sounds of the words are not imitative of this metaphor in any mysteriously onomatopoeic sense. They are arranged so as to be musical in the complex manner outlined above, which is apt since sound and music are of the essence.

The real music, though, is in the combination of these sound-effects and the precise semantic and connotative values of the words. T. S. Eliot advocated a semantic and contextual sense to 'musical':

> The music of a word is, so to speak, at a point of intersection: it arises from its relation first to the words immediately preceding and following it, and indefinitely to the rest of the context; and from another relation, that of its immediate meaning in that context to all the other meanings it has had in other contexts, to its greater or lesser wealth of association. (110)

The contextual musical relations may, then, be syntactical and semantic, but are also, crucially, acoustic, according to the co-presence of alerting-devices. 'Musical', in this sense, may in fact mean so much that it means very little at all. I would prefer to limit 'musical' to the acoustic, rhythmic, or prosodic properties of an utterance that are to be placed in relation to the semantic circumstance and its differing contexts. Tennyson's 'rounded moon' is musical with rounded sounds—but only becomes truly musical when that phonemic and rhythmical music is understood in relation to the context of the 'sounding hall', the sweet lark-voice, the heraldic vision of the moon through the oriel.

That vision redeems the terrible meeting in 'Lancelot and Elaine' of Lancelot and the Queen, bickering over diamonds in petty jealousy and recrimination while all the while Elaine lies dead in her bier—the scene takes place 'All in an oriel on the summer side,/Vine-clad, of Arthur's palace towards the stream' (ll.1170–1, Ricks, 867). The lines in 'The Holy Grail' remember and transform the falsely romantic and pretty context of the mean dispute at Camelot, not simply through the repetition of the word 'oriel', but through the reduplication of the internal rhyme ('all-oriel'; 'tall-oriel') and the hemistich rhythm ('on the summer side'—'on the rolling sea'). The shield-like vision redeems that moment by bringing it into contact with Elaine's pure love for Lancelot, manifest in her hoarding of his 'sacred shield' (834). And the song Lancelot hears in the topmost tower is a transfiguration of Elaine's song of life and death, sung high in her chamber 'up a tower to the east'. The music of the lines of 'The Holy Grail' is Elaine's music, a music that recalls her sacrifice and redeems Lancelot's sin.

The music of words is as complex as this—made up of internal sound-effects, rhythmical symmetries and patterns of variations within sound-families that support or make manifest the local context, whilst recalling other key lines, the key moments that provide the true music of memory, Elaine's song at Carbonek.

Verbal music, then, though fugitive, works upon the reader's ear and eye by means of alerting-devices that serve to set the chance sound-repetitions in a double context. First the context of the words immediately preceding and following it, and the larger context of the passage; and secondly the relationship of those local meanings to all the other meanings the same words have had in other contexts. The first relation is not a relation of crude imitation of the Spire–Grammont type. It is a matter of perceptible symmetries and coherent acoustic patterns that summon intelligible questions and responses about the complex of senses the passage may have. The second relation is a matter of memory, textual recall of other occasions when sound-repetitions have worked in this particular way. The recall ushers in a broader rationale for the uses of sound-effects. To anticipate my argument a little, the two musics, contextual and intratextual, have a rhyming relation at once with each other and with the reader's own manner of attending to them, the reader's textual acoustic memory.

Fetishistic Moods and Key Words

One kind of acoustic memory at work in many passages of poetic prose is the conscious memory of poetry, inviting a modified version of ways of attending to words and their acoustic interconnections normally proper to criticism of poetry. Jean Mourot, in his work on Chateaubriand's poetic prose, writes that:

sous l'empire des 'mots puissants' dont elle a le secret et dans la totale liberté de son mouvement, cette prose rejoint parfois, soit souvenir conscient, soit sourde réminiscence, soit réinvention instinctive, le rhythme poétique, les régularités syllabiques, accentuelles, sonores, dont est tissée la versification. (35).

George Saintsbury in his history of English prose rhythm finds many passages in Ruskin's prose which recall verse: 'The brain of his style seems to have been full of these verse-matrices' (395). Such conscious memories, unacknowledged reminiscences, and instinctive reinventions of poetic effects are a crucial element in many writers' technique.

But it is important to acknowledge that such poetic reminiscences must be grounded within the prose circumstance. One should be able to discover reasons for the move into poetic prose. Many writers find such a ground in discovering the relations between sound-repetitions and their characters' particular tones and intonations, or other kinds of metonymical leaps. Thomas Hardy, for instance, was expert at demonstrating what might be termed sonic pathetic fallacy, a supersensitive hearing of resonance between the 'sounds' of external and internal nature. These sound-resemblances go to the heart of his sensitivity to the discrete mystery of hidden or buried feeling. Like analysis of the play of facial features, the registering of complex, miniature shifts in sound-values is of enormous importance to his craft as a novelist.

Eustacia on the barrow on Egdon heath, the 'Figure against the Sky', is closely observed by the narrative eye and ear, but the ear is distracted by the triple sounds of the wind: the bass notes of 'the general ricochet of the whole over pits and prominences'; the 'baritone buzz of a holly tree'; and, most mysterious, the husky, shrivelled treble notes of the wind seizing, entering, scouring and emerging from 'the mummified heath-bells of the past summer'. This last sound is the 'linguistic peculiarity of the heath'. Its 'accent', resembling 'the ruins of human song', originates in what Hardy terms 'the material minutiae' and goes to create the impression of 'the single person of something else speaking through each at once'.[24]

This 'shrivelled and intermittent recitative' has its own particular prose sound, as in this sentence:

[24] *The Return of the Native*, ed. James Gindin, 43. (Abbreviated as *RN* throughout.)

They were the mummified heath-bells of the past summer, originally tender and purple, now washed colourless by Michaelmas rains, and dried to dead skins by October suns. (*RN*, 43)

The para-rhymes, 'rains', 'skins', 'suns', knit together a combination of sound-repetitions (k̲, m̲, d̲, s̲) and an audible rhythm (two five-stress phrases from 'now' to 'suns'). But this is no empty 'wild rhetoric' (*RN*, 43). The prose-sounds take on another quality when allied to the narrative observer's attention to Eustacia. He speaks of 'attention', of 'an emotional listener's fetichistic mood' (*RN*, 43) which lead him to construe the fiction of the 'single person of something else'.

This fetichistic mood, though painfully detailed in its attention to the accent of the material minutiae, is dwelling long and hard on the mystery of Eustacia's surfaces:

The bluffs, and the bushes, and the heather-bells had broken silence; at last, so did the woman; and her articulation was but as another phrase of the same discourse as theirs. Thrown out on the winds it became twined in with them, and with them flew away.

What she uttered was a lengthened sighing, apparently at something in her mind which had led to her presence here. (*RN*, 43)

The b̲-run of the heather-bells is answered by the w̲-run of the woman's sigh, accent of the b̲ells, accent of the w̲oman. The organic 'material minutiae' have a discourse that rhymes with the minutiae of the woman's emotional nature. The 'same discourse', the discourse of poetic prose, of sounds meaningful to the emotional listener's fetichistic mood, hints at a strange, dark origin; the bells to 'the single person of something else'; Eustacia's sigh to 'something in her mind'.

This sonic pathetic fallacy is deeply felt, precisely because it forces upon our attention the precise ways Wordsworthian half-creating, half-receiving perception of nature changed the manner in which later generations responded to human nature. Hardy's prose seems to be remembering poetry—'Thrown out on the winds it became twined in with them, and with them flew away' : //- -/ ' - -///- - ' -/-/-/. The three three-stress rhythms, and the sound-effects giving hints of rhyme ('winds'-'twined in with'-'away'), seduce the ear into reminiscences of a metrical form:

Thrown out on the winds
It became twined in with them
And with them flew away

Eustacia's sigh is caught up by the winds and transformed into invisible power; the voice that narrates her and her sounds is similarly caught up by the impulses of his poetic memory and transformed into rhythm and rhyme.

The Eustacia–Heath rhyme is accompanied by a prose-poetry coupling that crosses wild rhetoric with high tragic tone. The narrator finds ways of expressing the emotional analogies he believes he is experiencing by allowing his own voice to be similarly changed and charged. Negotiation between these couples takes place on the common ground linking the sounds of the prose and the sounds described by the prose:

Between the dripping of the rain from her umbrella to her mantle, from her mantle to the heather, from the heather to the earth, very similar sounds could be heard coming from her lips; and the tearfulness of the outer scene was repeated upon her face. (*RN*, 275)[25]

Sound-repetitions (in this case literal repetition of words, plus the 'heather-earth-heard' string) and poetic rhythm (strong anapaests and third paeons) identify Hardy's prose-poetic register with this essentially *emotional* exchange between outer scene and human face ('similar sounds'-'repeated'). Hardy's poetic prose has brought into combination the two strains of his own 'linguistic peculiarity': his gothic nature-superstition hinting at dark forces, and his fantastic attention upon the minutiae of human surfaces that hint at dark feeling. These two 'somethings' break the silence of skim-read prose and impose other patterns, other modulations, create a listening attention, a peculiar form of reading-memory, bringing memory of the sounds of the words on the page into contact with memory of poetic rhythms.

Sound-effects as sign of linguistic peculiarity, accent, material minutiae pointing towards *something else*; sound-repetitions signalling the fetishistic mood of an emotional listener at the same

---

[25] This sentence occurs a little while before Eustacia drowns herself—sound-repetitions therefore negotiate between her and the heather throughout her life in the book. They thus generally reinforce the identification of Eustacia with the Heath that the light-dark opposition does so much (perhaps too much) to stress.

time as bringing memories of poetry into play; questions of origin and cause, suspicions about melodramatic and superstitious interpretations—all these concerns are articulated by Hardy's prose-sound technique. And they must be concerns that the reader as emotional listener must *demand* of a writer's poetic prose to test its strength, its credibility, and its worth.

The fact that prose can be musical in these ways is obviously dependent on a long and rich tradition of experiment and innovation in poetry. This is why reminiscence of poetic effects is so important to many writers, for such overt allusions to the rival trade justify daring moves in the sound-system of the prose. Shelley's allusion to his own internal rhyming effects had such a hidden purpose as part of its tone. Internal rhyming effects in poetry are vehicles of emotional stress; similar effects can be achieved in prose if an allusion to this poetic technique is sufficiently strong. By studying the real ways internal rhymes function in poetry, one can reach some understanding of the ambition of writers of sound-repetitions in prose; for internal rhyming so often provides their rationale.

Baudelaire's t-repetition in 'Courte tâche! La tombe attend, elle est avide' from 'Chant d'automne' II, for instance, elicits this fine distinction from Delbouille:

Cette répétition est en quelque sorte une autre manière de ponctuer, de mettre en relief pour attirer l'attention. Peut-être aussi pourrait-on se demander si une telle répétition ne va pas jusqu'à suggérer le style propre aux fortes émotions. De toutes manières, le son, encore une fois, accuse un effet sémantique, et cela sans que soit mise en cause, le moins du monde, sa nature physique. (211)

The stress-change that the 't'-repetition punctuates should be heard, then, as an emotional, dramatic signal. With two further examples, he suggests that internal sound-effects isolate and stress the key-word in the lines and subsequently emotionally accentuate it. On Baudelaire's 'Que ce soit dans la nuit et dans la solitude/Que ce soit dans la rue et dans la multitude/Son fantôme dans l'air danse comme un flambeau', Delbouille writes that 'la multiple répétition du mot *dans* [. . .] ne serait guère importante si elle n'annonçait le verbe *danse*. Ainsi préparé, ce dernier prend un relief extraordinaire' (211). Similarly, in Baudelaire's 'Mais la tristesse en moi monte comme la mer', 'l'allitération souligne beaucoup plus le verbe *monte* qu'elle ne suggère le bruit de la mer' (212).

Dell Hymes in his examination of the sound-structures of some English sonnets supports Delbouille's last argument about the relations between sound-repetition and key-words or phrases in the poems. Developing James Lynch's work on Keats's 'On First Looking into Chapman's Homer' (where 'silent' is discovered as the key-word because it sums up the poem's dominant sound-structure [211–44]), Hymes puts his sonnets through an exhaustive totting-up procedure. 'Charting and totalling the frequency and weighting of sounds directs attention to words and patterns that might be overlooked' (50), Hymes writes. The process throws up the true heart of the poems, the 'summative' words.

His analysis of Wordsworth's 'It is not to be thought of', for instance, finds that:

the words '(we are) sprung of earth's "first blood" ' contain the dominant five consonants of the sonnet, / d r s t l /, and the dominant nucleus of the sestet, /ë/. [. . .] The water imagery of the poem is caught up in 'blood'. This imagery starts with 'flood' (line 1), whose sound is echoed in 'blood'; indeed the association of /l/ and /d/ is strong throughout the poem (flood, world's, flowed, old, hold, held, blood, manifold). The dominant nucleus of the sonnet, /i y/, last appears in 'we' (line 13), and this, by the intentional setting off of the phrase by dashes, adds to the force of the whole. In imagery, theme, and sound, then, this phrase, especially 'first blood', is summative (43).

I will quote 'It is not to be thought of' followed by a phonetic transcription:

> It is not to be thought of that the flood
> Of British freedom, which, to the open sea
> Of the world's praise, from dark antiquity
> Hath flowed, 'with pomp of waters unwithstood',
> Roused though it be full often to a mood
> Which spurns the check of salutary bands,
> That this most famous stream in bogs and sands
> Should perish; and to evil and to good
> Be lost for ever. In our halls is hung
> Armoury of the invincible knights of old:

We must be free or die, who speak the tongue
That Shakspeare spake: the faith and morals hold
Which Milton held. In everything we are sprung
Of earth's first blood, have titles manifold.

ɪt ɪz ˈnɒt tə bɪ ˈθɔːt ɒv ðət ðə ˈflʌd
əv ˈbrɪtɪʃ ˈfriːdm/ ˈwɪtʃ / tə ðɪ ˈəʊpn ˈsiː
əv ðə ˈwɜːldz ˈpreɪz/frəm ˈdɑːk ənˈtɪkwɪtɪ
həθ ˈfləʊd/wɪð ˈpɒmp əv ˈwɔːtəz ˌʌnwɪðˈstʊd
ˈraʊzd ðəʊ ɪt ˈbiː ˈfʊl ˈɒfn tʊ ə ˈmuːd
wɪtʃ ˈspɜːnz ðə ˈtʃek əv ˈsælətərɪ ˈbændz
ðət ˈðɪs məʊst ˈfeɪməs ˈstriːm ɪn ˈbɒgz ən ˈsændz
ʃd ˈperɪʃ / ən tʊ ˈiːvɪl ən tə ˈgʊd
biː ˈlɒst fər ˈevə // ɪn aʊə ˈhɔːlz ɪz ˈhʌŋ
ˈɑːmrɪ əv ðɪnˈvɪnsɪbl ˈnarts əv ˈəʊld
wiː ˈmʌst biː ˈfriː ɔː ˈdaɪ / huː ˈspiːk ðə ˈtʌŋ
ðət ˈʃerkspɪə ˈspeɪk / ðə ˈfeɪθ ən ˈmɒrəlz ˈhəʊld
wɪtʃ ˈmɪltən ˈheld // ɪn ˈevrɪθɪŋ wɪə ˈsprʌŋ
əv ˈɜːθs ˈfɜːst ˈblʌd / həv ˈtaɪtlz ˈmænɪfeʊld

The principal difficulty with Hymes's approach is that he did not check his phoneme frequencies against the normal frequencies of sounds in speech. In Appendix 1, I have tabulated all the occurrences of the individual phonemes in the sonnet as percentages of the overall sounds. I have also listed the percentage of each phoneme when occurring in stressed words. These percentages are set against Fry's list of the frequency of speech sounds in southern English.

What this comparison proves is that Hymes has mistakenly called d̲ a dominant consonant when in fact the five percent occurrence is normal in spoken English. Similarly, t̲ seems high at seven per cent, but this phoneme in normal English is near 6.5 per cent; and, furthermore, only 60 per cent of the poem's t̲ sounds occur in stressed words. There is a similar problem with the s̲ sounds— many of them occur in unstressed words. The r̲ sounds, though consistently high in terms of stressed words, are only half a per cent up on normal frequency. Only the l̲ sounds out of Hymes's list are consistently and significantly above average occurrence. Hymes's method also fails to catch the significant number of the phonemes p̲, f̲, θ̲, and z̲. His assertion that 'first blood' contains the dominant nucleus of the sestet, ɜː, is tautological, since it is precisely the occurrence of the vowel in 'first' that pushes the phoneme into a high overall percentage. His argument concerning the last occurrence of the phoneme i̱ː is ruined if one scans the thirteenth line correctly—for the i̱ː of 'we' is reduced to ɪ̱ (the rhythm demands a 'we're').

Hymes rightly worries about the adequacy of his own method—the 'domain' of any series of sound-effects is a major difficulty: what are the criteria for isolating any particular passage of poetry or prose as an adequate basic sample? His splitting of his own analysis of the phoneme-frequencies into three domains, poem as a whole, octet, and sestet, is an example of this fundamental doubt. He also has doubts as to reader competence:

we do not in fact know that the use of a sound in one part of a poem has any effect on a reader in a subsequent part; we have no 'just noticeable differences' for the prominence of sounds by repetition in a sonnet. Rather we analyse the poem, construct an interpretation, and postulate (or instruct) the reader's response. (52)

Hymes's anxiety about the sensitivity of the ordinary reader's ear is crossed with the abiding fear that slightly higher percentages of phoneme frequency will really not be sufficient to justify a theory of summative phrases. 'The longer the work or passage, the less any particular selection of sounds can escape being submerged by the normal frequencies of the language' (52).

A further complication emerges. That is, Wordsworth's own private pronunciation. A northern note is perceptible in the rhyming of 'flood', 'unwithstood', 'mood' and 'good' which makes one wonder whether he heard clear assonance between the rhymes 'hung', 'tongue', 'sprung', and the 'blood' of Hymes's summative phrase. Knowing for certain whether the ʌ sounds are flattened to ʊ would considerably alter the sound-frequencies, pushing ʊ up to 3 per cent. All in all, analysis of phoneme repetition in terms of statistical frequencies is fraught with difficulties.

This is especially so considering the fact that, in rhymed poetry, many of the sound-effects are centred round the end-rhymes which, even though they may be made up of phonemes that are generally low in overall frequency, are visually and acoustically powerful in their own right. They create their own short-term frequencies. This is also the case with strong internal sound-effects. When Wordsworth writes 'the flood/Of British freedom', the f-repetition is registered whether or not the rest of the sonnet has a high f frequency; and this alliteration is fundamental in enriching the sense of 'we are sprung/Of earth's first blood'. The phrase 'first blood' contains 'flood' within itself and therefore recalls the association with freedom and the river imagery. Wordsworth makes sure of the recall by the long string of end-rhymes containing d and association of l and d. Hymes notices this essential l-d association; but the fact is one does not need a statistical analysis of that association in both poem and common speech to remark its presence. The poem's rhymes do the trick for us.

But, again, this music of association is negligible if it is not in some way found to be consonant with the sense of the sonnet. Hymes's analysis has very little to say about the meaning of Wordsworth's patriotic sonnet—he is content to prove his theory of summative phrases. I would agree strongly with this theory—sound-effects have as one of their primary functions the outlining and stressing of a key feature of the text. Where Hymes goes wrong is in believing the phrase 'first blood' is summative because of the statistically high presence of the phonemes of the phrase in the poem as a whole, firstly because these phonemes are not in fact the key presences he felt them to be, and secondly because acoustical attention is not directed in such a mechanical way. Nevertheless 'earth's first blood' is summative because of the double alerting-device of dense repetition (ɜː, s, and the fricative clash in the θsf of 'earth's first') and the cumulative rhyme and internal phoneme strings linking 'flood' and 'blood'. But observing this remains futile unless one asks and answers the question 'why?'.

An answer for me is the necessary rhyme Wordsworth wished to forge between the dangerous and glorious freedom conferred on Adam in the garden ('earth's first blood' sits happily under 'Milton') and the liberating ancient liberties of England directed, like the Thames, into the sea towards a Europe oppressed by Napoleon. The 'dark antiquity', for Wordsworth, goes back that far. As he put it in the *The Convention of Cintra*, the British nation are 'a people which, by the help of the surrounding ocean and its own virtues, [has] preserved to itself through ages its liberty, pure and unviolated by a foreign invader'(228).[26] Edenic freedom, inclined both 'to evil and to good', has been preserved on British soil. The dark antiquity refers back to the beginnings of the human race (this is important for Wordsworth generally in his patriotic writings because British freedom, passion, and justice had to be proved to be identifiable with universal values). The 'flood-blood' rhyme, then, creates a double image of 'blood' as pure spiritual inheritance of Edenic freedoms and as the stream that will redeem Europe. The rhyme makes the stream temporal as well as spatial and transforms it into a river of blood, of sacred, racial inheritance. The flood is both the Thames as image of British naval and military might inspired by 'the most sacred feelings of the human heart' (*Convention*, 228) and the power of feeling and freedom transmitted by the umbilical cords leading back to Eden. It is fitting that the means Wordsworth uses to forge the bond between flood and blood are acoustic, embedded in the sounds of the English language. For it is Shakespeare and Milton who, as guardians of the language, have done most to preserve this native and universal sense of liberty. The bonds are created by the liquid sonorities of the 'tongue/That Shakspeare spake', subtle strings of sound-effects, 'salutary bands'.

The search for the summative phrase (which sound-repetitions effectively point to and point out) is a valid one, then, if one takes pains not to push statistical analysis too far, and always to attempt to explain why that particular phrase has been chosen as summative. The use of lists such as Fry's sound-frequency percentages is essential in order to avoid mistaking ordinary frequencies for extraordinary sound-effects. But they cannot and should not be exploited as anything more than a double check on the ear's discoveries. Hymes's attempt to exaggerate the significance of

---

[26] The *Convention* includes other passages that echo 'It is not to be thought of': 'domestic love and sanctities [. . .], wherever they have flowed with a pure and placid stream', under the influence of a union of passion and justice, 'put forth their strength as in a flood' (295); 'it is in vain to send forth armies if [intellect, knowledge, and love] do not inspire and direct them. The stream is as pure as it is mighty, fed by ten thousand springs in the bounty of untainted nature; any augmentation from the kennels and sewers of guilt and baseness may clog, but cannot strengthen it' (248); 'A military spirit should be there, and a military action, not confined like an ordinary river in one channel, but spreading like the Nile over the whole face of the land' (234); and, on 286, Wordsworth identifies despotism with 'this rotten bog, rotten and unstable as the crude consistence of Milton's Chaos'. These echoes confirm the military nature of Wordsworth's flood of British freedom.

frequency analysis ignores the way poetic technique most obviously works; i.e. through concentrated clusters of effects, through rhyme, and through a trained acoustic memory on the part of the reader. In all the passages I study in this book, I have double-checked my intuitions against frequency lists such as Fry's. But my analysis is not ruled by them, just as it respects but does not collapse before Hymes's severe doubts both about sound-repetitions in long passages and about reader competence.

But I admit some argument must be found that will prove that prose writers do expect the reader, at crucial moments, to direct a 'poetic' attention to the sonic surface of their prose. This would assure anyone who has doubts about the propriety of exporting into prose fiction the reading techniques I reserved for Wordsworth's sonnet.

Over-Sounds and Symptomatic Rhyming

George Saintsbury's greatly influential study of English prose prosody is marred by his wrong-headed quantitative metres. But his ear for rhythm is nevertheless good. I am relying on Saintsbury since he takes a stand against the very idea of rhyme in prose, preferring and legislating for a variety of sounds and measures in the prose of the masters. On Landor's passage, 'Her beautiful throat itself changed colour; it seemed to undulate; and the roseate predominated in its pearly hue', Saintsbury shakes his head and tuts: ' "undulate", "roseate", and "predominate" are too near' (329–30). But he has ignored the immediately preceding sentence that puts Landor's rhymes in a certain perspective: 'Innocent and simple and most sweet, I remember was her voice; and when she had spoken the traces of it were remaining on her lips.' Landor with his '-ate' rhymes is rather clumsily making his prose itself sustain a trace of sound to mimic the trace of her voice in his own retrospective memory. The changing colour of her throat is also mimed in the changes wrought in the sounds of his prose. Such observations do not redeem the passage. The two sentences clash terribly, the delicate simplicity of the one transmuted into the stumbling pretentiousness of the second. But it does at least prove that Delbouille's point cannot be sustained. The effects here are quite enough not only to alert the reader but also to stand roughly in his or her way, demanding an explanation of themselves.

Similarly in his analysis of this passage from Hazlitt's essay 'Poetry in General', Saintsbury discovers rhymes and dismisses them despite the context (Hazlitt is discussing Coleridge):

> His voice rolled on the ear like the pealing organ, and its sound alone was the music of thought. [. . .] And shall I, who heard him then, listen to him now? Not I! . . . That spell is broken; but still the recollection comes rushing by with thoughts of long-past years, and rings in my ears with never-dying sound. (361)

Saintsbury shakes his head again: 'the juxtaposition of "years" and "ears" towards the end is a most unlucky oversight—or should we not say "over-sound"?' (361). Why not, indeed? But it is an over-sound that has surely not been overlooked by Hazlitt; instead it mimes the rushing back of his recollection. The rhyme 'years'-'ears' is a figure of sound, a rhyming sound that alerts us to the presence of other acoustic repetitions in the context ('spell'-'till'; 'spell'-'recollection'; 'by'-'my'-'never-dying').[27] Hazlitt is talking about the 'never-dying sound' of Coleridge's voice. That voice had 'rolled on the ear'. The rhyme-work recalls that phrase in a locution that is concerned with the recollection of sound. Both Landor, with the traces of his subject's voice remaining on her lips, and Hazlitt, with the recollection of Coleridge's voice, use rhyme to mime that re-sounding of the memory, proving that the reader's ear should and can be attuned to the recalling of the sounds of prose. The rhymes in conjunction with the sense-context are a form of double alerting-device, each confirming the other.

Saintsbury, indeed, shows himself to be half-consciously aware of this marshalling of sound-effects to establish a conceptual image on the surface of prose. He picks this passage from Pater's essay on Leonardo's Gioconda:

> Through his strange veil of sight things reach him so; in no ordinary night or day, but as in a faint light of eclipse, or in some brief interval of falling rain at daybreak, or through deep water. (423)

Saintsbury comments, 'the clause- , sentence- , and paragraph-closes are distinguished by that curious muffled arrest which we

---

[27] I am grateful to Eric Griffiths for pointing these out to me.

have noticed—momentary suspension of movement without a jar—a sort of whispered 'Hush!' [. . .] those slight idiosyncratic diversions of words [. . .] which affect rhythm so powerfully, though so quietly, by the slight shock they give to the under-standing' (425). 'Muffled arrest', 'momentary suspension of move-ment', 'slight idiosyncratic diversions of words', 'slight shock'—these are perfect descriptions of the manner in which the 'ight'-rhymes in Pater's sentence affect the stressing of the prose-rhythm. Saintsbury seems to half-acknowledge their influence with his repeated 'slight' and the half-rhyme 'quietly'-'slight'. I do not deny that the effect is also to do with the muffled dying falls of Pater's clauses, sentences and paragraphs (though this may have more to do with the tone of voice one adopts when reading Pater's dreamy thoughts). This does not take away from the fact that Saintsbury is himself remembering the rhymes Pater uses and is half-consciously analysing their effect.

  Saintsbury's verbal memory by his own witness was quite capable of retaining passages of prose in his mind for many years. He describes how he recalls one of Mansel's sermons decades later: 'the key of it still rings, inarticulately, but with perfect accomplishment, in my memory's ear' (417). And, equally, he is not deaf, despite his prejudice against it, to the manner in which rhymes in prose do alter, or at least ask one to alter, the rhythm of the prose. He notices, whilst analysing Ruskin's description of Rouen, that:

every now and then, in these formed or half-formed stanzas,there is actual rhyme, as in a description of Rouen:

> And the city lay
> Under enguarding hills
> One labyrinth of delight,
> Its grey and fretted towers
> Misty in their magnificence of height

where a very thinkable equivalent for 'their magnificence of' will bring the thing metrically off (395)

Here Saintsbury admits that the presence of the rhyme acts like an unsolicited pressure within the prose to alter its stress-patterns. Though assenting to the dictum of the eighteenth-century critic of prose prosody, Edmund Mason (which he publishes at the end of his study), that a writer must 'keep similarly-sounding words far apart', Saintsbury shows himself to be half-consciously very sensitive to the different stress- and memory-patterns that rhymes in prose prompt.

The problem with any theory of sound-repetitions in prose is the powerful prejudice that militates against poetic prose as such. No amount of tough arguing will soften the hard line of a Saintsbury or efface the memory of Hazlitt's distaste for Johnson's prose style:

The fault of Dr Johnson's style is, that it reduces all things to the same artificial and unmeaning level. It destroys all shades of difference, the association between words and things. [. . .] The structure of his sentences, which was his own invention, and which has been generally imitated since his time, is a species of rhyming in prose, where one clause answers to another in measure and quantity, like the tagging of syllables at the end of a verse; the close of the period follows as mechanically as the oscillation of a pendulum, the sense is balanced with the sound; each sentence, revolving round its centre of gravity, is contained with itself like a couplet, and each paragraph forms itself into a stanza. (On the Periodical Essayists', in *Lectures*, 102)

Hazlitt is wrong about Johnson's balanced rhyming in prose— Johnson often displays repetitive sound-sense relations as *symptomatic* of an over-fictional imagination, as in this sentence of Imlac's discourse on the dangerous prevalence of the solitary's imagination: 'The mind dances from scene to scene, unites all pleasures in all combinations, and riots in delights which nature and fortune, with all their bounty, cannot bestow.' Here Johnson's prose-rhyming ('unites'-'riots'-'delights', for example) is a signal of the dangerous dance of the imagination isolated among its fictions. The very balance of the four-times-four-stress structure (tightened and made more rhythmical by the two 'feminine endings' of 'combinations' and 'fortune'), the very balance of sound and sense (the repetitions, the 'combinations'-'nature' recall, the 'bounty'-'bestow' alliteration) are acoustic signals of an *un*balanced mind, feasting on the luscious falsehood of its dreams of rapture, over-fictionalizing the style of its visionary schemes.

Hazlitt's charge of artificiality against Johnson's style in prose mistakes Johnson's powers of self-diagnosis for mere symptoms of a reductive reason. But saying this does not remove the sting of the charge itself as aimed against rhyming in prose as such, for Johnson is himself resisting his own tendencies towards a false sense of balance, towards over-fictional recourse to a repetitive style. Is it possible to reconcile Johnson's fear of the possible consequences of a dancing rhyming in prose with Mourot's celebration of the leitmotifs created by key-word sound-repetitions in Chateaubriand's prose?

[S]ouvent l'allitération et la répétition de sons ont valeur d'insistance; elles accroissent le pouvoir suggestif des mots-clés dont elles multiplient le long de la phrase les caractéristiques consonantiques [. . .] comme les intermittences de vers, de mesure et d'isométries, elles signalent l'affleurement d'une prose poétique, l'apparition des thèmes qui émeuvent l'être intime de Chateaubriand, des mots qui composent ses paysages favoris ou qui vibrent pour lui de profonds résonances; retours d'identités, elles confèrent à la phrase une unité sonore, renforcent son organisation interne en jalonnant son déroulement. Non pas mécanique artificielle, mais signe de la présence d'une âme, elles donnent en même temps plus de consistance au corps du style. (76)

Mourot defines sound-repetitions here as features of emphasis, signals of key-words, mimers in prose of poetic stressing effects, as indicators of themes, as consequences of the author's affective relationship to words, as creators of identity, both stylistic and ethical, and as signs of passionate presence. This is not only poetic prose in apotheosis, but the exact negative of Johnson's deep suspicion.

Stress-Lines and Masson Patterns

One critic who has attempted to reconcile these opposing opinions about the value of sound-repetitions in prose is Kathleen McCluskey. In her work on the sound and structure of Woolf's novels, she resurrected David Masson's taxonomy of sound-repetitions and set them to work on the dense textures of Woolf's prose. Masson's taxonomy is the most far-reaching attempt to get to grips with the different ways a prose sentence can be organized in terms of its sound-repetitions. I will give a quick résumé of Masson's critical terms (c is consonant, v vowel):

Start-echoes (c-/c-)	Sound-repetitions in initial position (<u>c</u>ourt . . . <u>c</u>ase)
End-echoes (-c/-c)	Repeated final sounds (ca<u>t</u> . . . min<u>t</u>)
Simple echoes	Repeated sound is a single phoneme (ba<u>ck</u> . . . tal<u>k</u>)
Compound echoes	Repeated sound is two or more phonemes (<u>str</u>ict . . . <u>str</u>ange)
Outflow-echoes (cv/cv)	Initial syllable-sound the same (<u>fi</u>rst . . . . <u>fi</u>rmly)
Inflow-echoes	Terminal syllable-sound the same (st<u>and</u> . . . h<u>and</u>)
Solid-echoes (cvc/cvc)	Repetition of whole syllable (<u>pain</u> . . . <u>pane</u>)
Frame-echoes	Repeated initial and terminal c with v-modulation (<u>st</u>ai<u>d</u> . . . <u>st</u>oo<u>d</u>)
Grid-echoes	Polysyllabic frame-echoes ('they had <u>seen</u> her <u>dying</u> and <u>s</u>aw <u>n</u>o<u>thing</u> left to <u>d</u>o')
Tag-echoes	Repeated unstressed words (articles, pronouns, suffixes, prefices, etc.)
Cap-echoes	Prefix tag-echoes (<u>in</u>different <u>in</u>considerate)
Spur-echoes	Suffix tag-echoes (constri<u>ction</u> contra<u>ction</u>)
Elements	Generic term for the phonemes being repeated
Element groups	Repeated phoneme-cluster in same order ('the <u>c</u>ar sw<u>er</u>ved off the <u>r</u>oun<u>d</u>about into the <u>kerb</u> of the <u>r</u>oa<u>d</u>'—kɜːd-kɜːd)
Motif	Repeated element-group
Augmented element-groups	When other words in context contain phonemes of element-group
Sequence	Element-groups repeated throughout passage (i.e. finding <u>fai</u>lure/<u>fee</u>l/<u>f</u>lashing/<u>fu</u>ll in same passage)
Chiasmus	Switch in a pair of phonemes (wh<u>i</u>te <u>ti</u>de)
Interchange	Sequence with switches (<u>c</u>a<u>rr</u>ied a<u>cr</u>oss a dar<u>k</u> <u>r</u>oaring <u>c</u>ave)
Knot	Scattered elements tighten into one ('<u>tr</u>ied <u>t</u>o <u>str</u>ip as he <u>p</u>a<u>ss</u>ed')
Patterned assonance	Vowel modulation with chiasmic pattern ('wh<u>e</u>n w<u>i</u>nter w<u>e</u>pt <u>i</u>ts damp')

Masson's and McCluskey's work should not be easily dismissed, despite the heavy-handedness of their terms. Sound-repetitions in prose need to be classified and named in this way if only to demonstrate how self-conscious prose-writers sometimes are in arranging their sound-systems. I have some caveats, however, with Masson's list.

Firstly, it seems to me to place too much emphasis on strict order in the appearance of phonemes, so that his element-groups, for example, must repeat the phoneme-cluster in the right order, otherwise the sound-repetitions must go under other names, in Masson's case 'interchange', 'switching' and 'knotting'. It does not seem to me to be worthwhile differentiating between a perfect element-group and a sequence that has knotted, switched and interchanged elements. Masson was looking out for perfect structures, like a scientist sieving earth for crystals, but most sound-repetition *is* earthy, i.e. inextricably involved with the obliquities of language, of things being said. The creation of a motif will necessitate techniques of repetition that demonstrate, whilst ignoring the difference between, Masson's processes of augmentation, sequencing and patterning. I propose a simplified model of classification, that seems to me to be more workable than the pattern-obsessed taxonomy advocated by Masson and McCluskey. My list includes the following terms:

run or string	series of repeated vowels or consonants
key-word	word emphasized by runs and strings
stress-line	mixed processes of sequencing, augmentation, knotting.
motif	key-word plus runs and strings repeated in more than one passage
prose rhymes	generic name for key-words

Though doubtlessly not as scientifically exacting as Masson's list, my terms do not aim to overstress the fact that repeated phonemic elements in a text have an observable order of play. If the sound-repetitions do have such a strict order, it is not at all clear that the writer is to be congratulated for such ingenuity. It may even be the case that observing Masson's demand for strict phonemic order would mean ignoring many evident uses of sound-repetitions.

The Johnson sentence again: 'The mind dances from scene to scene, unites all pleasures in all combinations, and riots in delights which nature and fortune, with all their bounty, cannot bestow.' In

Masson's terminology, the sentence has solid-echoes (scene-scene, all-all-all), what McCluskey calls an end-start echo (mind dances), knotting in the way the phonemes in 'mind', 'dances', 'unites', 'all', 'riots' knot up into 'delights', start-echoes in 'bounty' and 'bestow', end-echo with vowel modulation in 'scene'-'fortune'. There are easier ways of saying these things (like straight repetition for 'solid-echoes') and some things would be better left unsaid (the end-start-echo is a non-starter). But more seriously, Masson and McCluskey would have been unable to find a real element-group at work here, and therefore no motif, no sequence even (since a sequence, according to Masson, needs two phonemes repeated with minimal switching). And yet, to the eye and the ear, the sentence is intensely patterned.

The real discovery of Masson's technique, however, is the knotting procedures, and the way they can be supplemented by more random augmentation. This technique I prefer to define in terms of the creation of *stress-lines*. The Johnson line, for me, would be better described as containing an s-string, stress-lines along aɪts ('unites'-'riots'-'delights'), eɪʃ / tʃ ('combinations'-'nature'), and bt ('bounty'-'bestow'). 'Dances' would be the alerting-device (with the close rhyme riots-delights in support), which, with its d-alliteration with 'delights', would tend to confirm 'delights' as the summative key-word, the other stress-lines being supportive (bt augmenting the t of 'delights', eɪʃ / tʃ the long vowel). If 'delights' were to occur elsewhere in Johnson's text, similarly disseminating stress-lines, then the word would move from key-word to motif.

The question whether the stress-lines fabricate key-words, or whether it is the key-words that are fabricating the stress-lines (they are emanating out from the key-word) seems to me to be an empty one, for it presupposes a cause-effect chronology that does not exist in texts (both key-word and stress-lines are simply there on the page). My analyses throughout the book will be using both ways of describing the process (stress-lines fabricating key-words, and stress-lines emanating from key-words) indiscriminately, to show that I think both occur 'simultaneously', so to speak, on the page. But it is also clear that the illusion a reader has that there is in fact a chronologically discrete cause-effect relationship between stress-lines and key-word is an illusion important enough actually to have force in any reading experience of sound-repetitions in prose. This is another reason why I will stick to this admittedly

clumsy way of describing the textual relationship between semantic units and phoneme repetition.

McCluskey at times abuses these findings by insisting, superstitiously, that Woolf uses these techniques to stress key-words that
are not to be found in the passages she quotes ('Even when the
word itself does not appear, its sounds echo'(17)). But her analysis
of the way a key-word is stressed (in my terms) is nevertheless
masterly, as in this example about a passage from *Jacob's Room*:

> Besides actually hearing 'the cot' five times, we are also bombarded by a
> set of words which repeat (with an occasional inversion) the element k t.
> Through the passage we hear: next, quietly, cot, book stood, take, take
> bottle, cot, quilt, looked, looked anxiously, Rebecca stole, cat, plotting
> conspiracy, clean bottles, looked, cot crossed, cot, looking at, cot, night
> Rebecca, conspirators, plotting conspiracy, clean bottles. This set,
> augmented by the frequent assonance in short o, results in our hearing the
> word cot repeatedly through the passage. (33–4)

She goes on to analyse the presence of secondary motifs in the
same passage. This analysis is placed within an argument about
the way the reader finds comfort in the aura of security generated
by the 'incantation of the repetitions' but then slowly wakes up to
the possible danger in these 'lulling effects': 'The reader is aware
of the insulation and isolation which result when the patterns of a
person's life begin to determine his/her personal development
and life possibilities'(35). The 'cot' motif, then, is deeply ingrained
in the book's argument about, and critique of, childishness, lulling
patterns of existence, incantatory self-insulation. Despite her tendency to fabulate (McCluskey falls again and again into the Spire–
Grammont trap, as in 'the end-start-echo of eyes-stared simulates
the continuous obsessive gazing'(43)), her work is a valuable
contribution to work on sound-repetitions. When showing how
motifs are built up and generated, I repeat many of her manœuvres, and I hope others will follow suit.

Masson's taxonomy needs clearing up and simplifying, then;
and this study will further prove how sound-repetitions, or rather
prose rhymes, need to be understood in relation to the ways
memory is represented in the prose under study. For instance,
McCluskey could have shown how the fact that 'cot' is disseminated in surrounding stress-lines in *Jacob's Room* is a conspiratorial
sign of child-like memory-patterns at play in the prose and in

Rebecca's mind. Masson's work, despite my caveats, needs to be taken seriously and his insistence on the importance of registering element-groups (repeated phonemes in the same order) I have tried to respect in my work. In the hope of simplifying his over-burdened taxonomy, I have christened occurrences of these particular kinds of complex ordered sound-effects *Masson patterns*. Stress-lines become Masson patterns when the recurring phonemes obey strict order, either straight repetition, or chiasmic order, or very slightly switched order. The a͟ts repetitions in the Johnson sentence form a Masson pattern, then, because the phonemes occur in strictly the same order in the three words in which they occur.

The essential technique for the discovery of Masson patterns is to set a passage to be analysed up in triple spaces and then to record repeated phonemes above the lines. This enables you to register recurring patterns in clusters of different phonemes as opposed to isolating particular phoneme repetitions. If one has doubts about the noticeability of a particular occurrence, then one must check the frequency of the sound within the passage (percentage of phonemes as a whole) against phoneme frequency charts for normal spoken language. This is extremely laborious but worthwhile to avoid undisciplined pattern-hunting. Saying this does not contradict my statements about Hymes above, for this kind of analysis I would reserve for Masson patterns where special care should be taken.

Which brings me, lastly, to perhaps my most questionable move within the body of this study. That is, the christening of the key-word sound-clusters in complex modern prose as 'prose rhymes'. On one level this is a matter of convenience. Terms such as 'alliteration', 'assonance', 'half-rhymes' when used of prose sounds do not seem to me to be anything more than imports from poetics clumsily applied. Prose sound-relations are most of the time looser and freer than their poetic counterparts. 'Loose' sound-effects in prose play a counterpart to the uses of internal rhyme in poetry but without the necessity of having continual recourse to definitions of and distinctions between assonance, alliteration, and rhyme.

I call sound-repetitions clustering around key-terms 'prose rhymes' not only, however, as a convenient catch-all, but also because the acoustic alerting-devices in prose are often full or half-rhymes, in the technical sense, which order the preceding and subsequent sound-effects into initial- and vowel-rhymes. Hearing a dense sound-pattern in a prose passage often relies on the presence within it of a sound-coupling approaching classical verse-rhyme. The third reason I prefer to call the compound effects 'prose rhymes' is because the abstract properties of verse-rhymes are analogous to the effects sound-repetitions have in prose. In other words, rhyme in a poem establishes comparison, settles the accent of the stresses, initiates memory, makes play with the senses of the words, joins the disparate to create a tertium aliquid. The key-word stress-lines that prose rhymes create have similar purposes—they line up as stress-markers (perhaps contrary to the sense), they as motifs 'remember' previous contexts, make out comparisons and create new matter by syntheses, alter the senses of the words with the different order of their sounds. These analogous effects are for the most part figurative in the sense that the accents and memory they imitate are often emotional and psychological rather than purely technical. Many verse-rhymes act in similar ways. Suffice it to say that the effects of prose sound-repetitions, when key-words and motifs are being fabricated and 'remembered' by stress-lines, have something of the consequences of internal rhymes and end-rhymes in poetry.

They are agents of the creation of conceptual rhymes between the 'present-tense' matter of the sentence and past feelings and memories not quite there, whilst also ordering that matter to a tune different to that of the syntax. Words such as 'poussière', 'poussa', and 'passant' could never be called 'rimes' in French poetry. But I feel they can in French prose. Charles Péguy, in 'Entretien sur Eve', felt similarly that the sense of the word 'rime' should expand when applied to broader forms of imaginative writing, in his case the texture of his litanies:

Comme dans une tapisserie, les fils passent, disparaissent, reparaissent et les fils ici ne sont pas seulement les rimes au sens que l'on a toujours donné à ce mot dans la technique du vers, mais ce sont d'innombrables rimes intérieures, assonances, rythmes et articulations de consonnes. (203–21)

These 'rimes intérieures' cover the whole variety of sound-resemblances but, I must add, within the limits and mode of development of proper alerting-devices. That is, those sound-resemblances become prose rhymes as such only when they are marshalled by the coordinating presence of strong acoustic and/or conceptual elements. The strength will vary according to how far down a leitmotif-chain those elements appear. As there are reasons for the 'rhymes' being there in prose, there must also be reasons for looking for the rhymes in the first place. The former reasons, I shall prove, will mostly confirm a subtle transformation of those 'rimes intérieures' into figurative rhymes in the internal life of voices narrated and narrative of the books and plays I study.

A novelist must, almost by definition, be acutely concerned with memory, as the act of creation is essentially a continual act of memory-creation, -accretion, and -synthesis, the imagination at constant service to the characters' memories. Katherine Anne Porter, reflecting on her craft, demonstrates in this passage how much the occupation of writing has made her highly preoccupied with the act of remembering:

> One of the most disturbing habits of the human mind is its wilful and destructive forgetting of whatever in its past does not flatter or confirm its present points of view. I must often refer far back in time to seek the meaning or explanation of today's smallest event, and I have long since lost the power to be astonished at what I find there. This constant exercise of memory seems to be the chief occupation of my mind, and all my experience seems to be simply memory, with continuity, marginal notes, constant revision and comparison of one thing with another. (449)

Memory work is an essential part of the work of the writer, and it is in his or her contact with language, from both a semantic and an acoustic point of view, that the work is done. Though writing has been primarily described as an act of the imagination, prose fiction is above all an act of imaginative remembering, and there is no writer who does not reflect on this strange human power, be it faculty, treasure house, or computer store.

This book will attempt to show how these reflections are integral to the heart of modern writing, and that at that heart lies a mysterious acknowledgement of the rhyming nature of memory, the remembering work of prose rhymes. If prose rhymes are miniature acts of memory, memories touch the mind and its language in the same way as sound-repetitions ripple through our words. This small-scale mystery has large-scale implications, not the least of which is a kind of literary practice, a mimesis that hears as well as sees the murmurs of the mind, a difficult music of remembered connotations and selves fugitively united.

1

Mallarmé and Poetic Prose:
Le Démon et les rimes dissimulés

Poetic prose can tend to direct its reader to meditate on the ways the imagination suffuses the people and words under its contemplation with the overflow of poetic desire, the rhythms and rhymes of the language of egotistical love. One of the direct ancestors of this tradition is Nabokov's *Lolita*. By 1955, deep suspicions about poetic prose are part of the writer's arsenal. Critique of the egotism involved in the projection of desire has become a common accompaniment to an understanding of poeticality in prose, to such an extent that the very presence of the acknowledged features of a 'fancy prose style' are sufficient witness to the rank wish-fulfilment of the narrative voice:

LOLITA, light of my life, fire of my loins. My sin, my soul. Lo-lee-ta: the tip of the tongue taking a trip of three steps down the palate to tap, at three, on the teeth. Lo. Lee. Ta. [. . .]
   Did she have a precursor? She did, indeed she did. In point of fact, there might have been no Lolita at all had I not loved, one summer, a certain initial girl-child. In a princedom by the sea. Oh when? About as many years before Lolita was born as my age was that summer. You can always count on a murderer for a fancy prose style.[1]

The fancy phonological play on dark and light *l*s, the parodies of Poe-inspired sound-repetitious poetasting ('My sin, my soul'; 'In a princedom by the sea'), childish nonsense-verse crossed with mock scientificity ('the tip of the tongue taking a trip of three steps down the palate to tap, upon three, on the teeth') make for more than a fancy prose style. They substantiate a diction and eloquence undone to death by a savagely parodic self-consciousness, a creature of dead voices. The equation of a fancy

---

[1] Nabokov, *Lolita* (Abbreviated to *L* throughout), 9.

prose style and murderousness is itself a fancy move by a pointless, put-on voice (shades of the advertising slogan blunted by a chic cultural knowingness). The voice defends the florid, antiquated nature of its desires but cripples that defence through embarrassment at not having it all in high inverted commas.

Something *is* murdered, though: any possible fine uses for imaginative movement in prose diction. The sound-repetitions are there as pure, self-murdering play, as signs of a crippled literary consciousness over-aware of the direct 'Freudian' links between his control over this adopted mother-tongue and the sexual fantasy-fulfilment at the root of his paedophilia. The memory parody and influence of the relationship with Annabel alluded to above (the 'initial girl-child') are retold with the same gamy, urbane parody of, and wised-up intimacy with, eloquence and its dubious sources:

Through the darkness and the tender trees we could see the arabesques of lighted windows which, touched up by the coloured inks of sensitive memory, appear to me now like playing cards—presumably because a bridge game was keeping the enemy busy. She trembled and twitched as I kissed the corner of her parted lips and the hot lobe of her ear. A cluster of stars palely glowed above us, between the silhouette of long thin leaves; that vibrant sky seemed as naked as she was under her light frock. I saw her face in the sky, strangely distinct, as if it emitted a faint radiance of its own. (*L*, 14)

Sensitive memory touches the prose up into arch parody of *risqué* pulp-fiction, coloured by clusters of repeated sound (the ɪ-run 'twitched', 'kissed', 'lips'), arabesques of phonemes running through crudely sentimental cliché (the eɪ and s stress-line in 'face', 'strangely', 'faint', 'radiance'). The flat comic reference to the bridge game openly keeps the ironic tone alive through all this, underscoring the self-consciousness controlling the virtuoso mimicry of the 'roman rose'.

Nabokov is stressing here how very close Humbert Humbert remains within the confines of the conventions he mocks, as though the only way he has of living both with his 'inherent singularity' and his intelligence is to play over-ripe games with the language of titillation. 'O, my Lolita, I have only words to play with!' (*L*, 32). Parody is his way out, parody above all of Proust,

grand precursor for Humbert Humbert in the analysis of obsession, perversion, and memory:

There are two kinds of visual memory; one when you skilfully recreate
an image in the laboratory of your mind, with your eyes open (and then
I see Annabel in such general terms as: 'honey-coloured skin', 'thin
arms', 'brown-bobbed hair', 'long lashes', 'big bright mouth'); and
the other when you instantly evoke, with shut eyes, on the dark innerside of your eyelids, the objective, absolutely optical replica of a
beloved face, a little ghost in natural colours (and this is how I see Lolita).
(L, 11–12)

When I try to analyse my own cravings, motives, actions and so forth, I
surrender to a sort of retrospective imagination which feeds the analytic
faculty with boundless alternatives and which causes each visualized
route to fork and re-fork without end in the maddeningly complex prospect of my past. (L, 13–14).

The seriousness of Proust's project rubs off on Humbert Humbert,
gives him room for credentials, just as his historico-literary history
of paedophilia (L, 19) borrows its seriousness from Oscar Wilde's
defence at the Old Bailey.

Similarly, a high-flown theory of memory and the imagination
attempts some kind of rationale for the poetic nature of the prose
when it describes the nymphets: memory artifice touches up the
past into fine artifice (windows into playing-cards, prose into
playful sound-effects) yet dares to represent that past as an objective replica on the innerside of the prose's surface; retrospective
imagination will cause the past to bifurcate into artificial alternatives (just as the prose multiplies its own sounds) yet is represented as natural and true to the complexity of Humbert
Humbert's past. The shifts and ambiguities in his self-analysis are
disguised behind a faultlessly serious and intellectual tone, but the
translated sound of parody reveals the desperation behind the
manœuvre.

What comes out of Lolita, finally, is the portrait of an intelligence
whose only joy is to treat language as a kind of incarnate girl-child
with whom he can play. Unfortunately, it is the same language he
has to use to justify himself. The sound-repetitions betray at once
a supercritical, ludic self-consciousness which must hedge its feelings around with jokes, and a mind whose only resource is the

momentary illusions of sensuous desire that the language of titillation affords it. The dream of an incarnate poetic prose has played itself out; what remains is a rankly and unconvincingly supercilious, discarnate display of symptoms.

Nabokov's findings are irresistibly depressing in ways some post-modern thinking finds agreeable. The Humbert Humbert style of criticism, to purify itself of infantile mimetic delusions, feels bound to subscribe to a different kind of absolutism, the absolutism of a sophistical relativism that is streetwise about power-systems, the staginess of all emotional displays, and the sexually and culturally determined nature of any textual strategy whatsoever. Literary manœuvres are to be put down to base and self-deluding motives, stylistic features labelled as mechanically playful signs of a language breeding pseudo-selves, Freudian screens, and empty artifice. In the area of phonolinguistics, patterns of phonemes should be considered the props of a mechanical theatrical, while any interpretation of them tumbles into the dark pit of enlightenment mimetic ideology.

It was Derrida who first set the tone by laying down a formidable array of philosophical and comic arguments against traditional neo-Platonic imitative theory. His finest expression of these arguments is to be found in the Mallarmé section of 'La Double Séance' in *La Dissémination*[2]. Mallarmé's rich rhyming and internal sound-effects are brought under Derrida's judgement, itself characterized by an extraordinarily rich acoustic surface. Derrida saw a direct link between Plato's theory of mimesis and interpretation of sound-repetitions in language. That link operates not only as a historical fact (Platonic mimetic theory feeds into Renaissance 'musical' readings of poetry), but also simply because Platonic theory is a theory of repetition as such. Derrida wants to argue that such a theory is not only enabled by, but *created* by, arbitrary phonemic coincidences in language. The study of Mallarmé, then, complements the deconstructing of the contradictions in Platonic mimetic propositions. Repetition as the ground of Platonic anamnesis is reduced to its basic 'poetic' agency, the dubious resemblances, correspondences and homonymic transformations that happen at the phonemic level of a self-fertilizing discourse.

[2] Jaques Derrida *La Dissémination*.

Derrida's Disseminating Rhymes

Derrida tackles the issue of sound-effects in prose head on when he looks at some 'unintentional' rhymes in a Mallarmé letter to Cazalis, and goes on to define the fundamental ambiguity in any echoic style:

Les effets de grotte sont le plus souvent des effets de glotte, traces laissées d'un écho, empreintes d'un signifiant phonique sur un autre, production de sens selon les retentissements d'une double paroi. Deux sans un. Un toujours en plus, soit en moins. Ambiguïté décisive et indécidable du syntagme 'plus de' (supplément et vacance). (Dissémination, 306–7)

Derrida's own prose plays the same ambiguous game: 'grotte' shifts to 'glotte', temporarily miniaturizing the echo-chamber down to the cave of the mouth, with any textual echoes off the face of the world reduced to the chance repetitions in voice-production. 'Sens' finds its killing opposite in 'sans'. The s̲-run in the last sentence very cleverly brings to the fore the fact that you need to *hear* the final s̲ in 'plus' to decide whether it means 'supplément' or 'vacance'. Sound-effects on the printed page are, for Derrida, undecidably ambiguous: 'meant for the whispered, not even whispered, merely mental performance of the closet, the study', as Hopkins put it,[3] they pull both ways. The possibility of not hearing them, like not hearing the s̲ at the end of 'plus', crosses any supplementary meaning they produce (if heard) with its negation.[4]

Similarly, the repetition of an acoustic signifier in a subsequent word will tend to create *something else* ('production de sens selon les retentissements d'un double paroi')—1+1=2 (you need to take one away to discover the original). But equally it will reduce the

---

[3] Letter to Everard Hopkins, 5/8 Nov. 1885, in *Selected Letters*, ed. Catherine Phillips, 218.

[4] In this, Derrida is in keeping with his subject, Mallarmé. Discussing the new innovation of rhyming the s̲ of plurals with the s̲ of the second person singular as an example of how poetry works for the eye, Mallarmé goes on: 'S, dis-je, est la lettre analytique; dissolvante et disséminante, par excellence.' For Mallarmé, though, the silent s̲ sound is a kind of proof of 'une secrète direction confusément indiquée par l'orthographe et qui concourt mystérieusement au signe pur général qui doit marquer le vers'. For Derrida, almost self-evidently, such 'rhyming' ambiguities prove the precise opposite, a self-cancelling doubling that reveals an impure, particular case of phonemic accidence. Mallarmé, 'Notes: 1895', in *Œuvres complètes* (abbreviated to *OC* throughout), 855.

sense of the two words brought together to the mere repetition of the phoneme—1+1= 1,1 (the echoic extra sound is a 'minus' sound that negates its own original). The 'double paroi' in Derrida's sentence is an elaboration of the 'grotte-glotte' metaphor—the walls of the textual cave, or the interior of the glottal chamber, resound with the traces of the echo, but where is the original cry? The 'grotte-glotte' sounds like or resounds like Plato's cave. One finds echoes, traces, imprints of an original uttered sound in the sound-repetitions on the printed page, the 'something else' created by rhyme; but the absence of that something reduces the words to mere carriers of untraceable acoustic trace-elements.

There is a serious difficulty here, once one unpacks the comic energy of Derrida's prose. Put simply, it is the problem of the undecidability of sound-repetitions in this strict sense: it is difficult to decide whether sound effects *concentrate* our acoustic attention on certain senses in the words by their density and voiced accent, or whether they *disperse* attention by emptying the words of semantic importance. The ambiguity is a common finding in neuropsychological research into memory. Rote repetition will tend to embed words and their senses into the memory, whereas other repetitive experiments prove the opposite. The phenomenon of *semantic satiation* following repetition of a single word, for example: as Ian Hunter puts it: 'The word forms a kind of closed loop with itself [. . .] the word leads only to its recurrence.' And *massed repetition*, an experiment in which the subject listens to another person saying a short sentence on a looped tape—Hunter again: 'if we listen to this repeated utterance, it seems to change. We hear other words, we hear nonsense sounds.' This phenomenon is called *verbal transformation effect*.[5] Figuratively speaking, it might be argued that any analysis of massed sound-repetitions risks these two possibilities; either the dissolving away of the semantic and syntactical power of the words as the ear reaches saturation point; or the illusory belief in 'something else' summoned up by the sound-patterns: 'other words' and 'nonsense sounds'. Semantic satiation could be said to occur when analysis reads prose or poetry in terms of purely musical and formal sound effects. Verbal transformation effects might be said to occur when criticism reads arbitrary themes and key-words into a passage,

[5] Hunter *Memory*, 109.

seduced by the patterns of sound into a state of hallucinatory intertextuality.

Derrida's line is that sound-repetitions in texts create a surplus ('supplément') that tempts the reader into indulging in verbal transformation, whilst at the same time effectively emptying those sounds of any semantic significance at all through sheer satiation. On Mallarmé's lines from 'Sa fosse est fermée', where the seagull 'Jette un écho joyeux, une plume d'aile,/Elle donna partout un doux souvenir d'elle!/De tout que reste-t-il? Que nous peut-on montrer?/Un nom!. . .', Derrida swoops down on the acoustic pun between the l-repetitions and the complex word 'aile':

toujours un supplément d'l. L'l en moins (toutes les chutes) ou l'l en trop forme le pli, 'une écriture spacieuse . . . reploie le trop d'aile' (p. 859) assure le vol de 'l'écriture ailée' (p. 173), de 'l'aile qui lui dicte ses vers' (p. 155). L'aile, qui peut être 'saignante' (sens blanc) et 'déplumée' (p. 40), se tient aussi, parfois, comme une plume ('Garder mon aile dans ta main', p. 58), 'au cas de l'écrit menacé et somme la Suprématie littéraire d'ériger en tant qu'aile, avec quarante courages groupés en un héros, votre hérissement d'epées frêles' (p. 420). Et conjuguer, plus bas, l'i avec l'l. Dès lors, il aura lui, rassemblé ses pouvoirs. L : i—. (*Dissémination*, n., 308–9; Derrida's page references are to the Pléiade 1945 *Œuvres complètes*).

The first thing Derrida wants us to say when we read such an example of his prose is just how arbitrary the wit is. If we label as arbitrary the critical move that spots l-repetitions in lines that contain the key-word 'aile' and then proceeds to pile up all the different uses of 'aile' in Mallarmé (as though they all referred to l-repetitiousness), Derrida would entirely agree. Derrida is artfully aligning the hopeless contradictions in any complex word (meaning so many things in different syntactical positions, the word may, through excessive contradictions, potentially end up signifying nothing) with the more openly arbitrary interpretation of sound-effects. The middle term is the fact that repetition both adds and subtracts, in fact leaves a 'pli' behind itself, an undecidable space at once replete with, and empty of, meaning. A complex word in different contexts can have just as many different senses: adding them together, as Derrida does Mallarmé's use of 'aile', may create a dense prose (and Derrida's prose is deliberately dense) but it also denies 'aile' any real meaning outside Derrida's comic energy. The word means at once so much and too much.

Similarly, the presence of a similar sound in various different words may increase the potential sense of that sound (each different word adds signs to the signifier), but at the same time the more the sound is used the less the senses of the words being exploited for its diffusion really matter. Any possible verbal interpretation becomes more and more openly arbitrary and open to dispute. Derrida, by equating l with 'aile', is roughly saying that any argument for an 'overall' meaning to poetic uses of a word is as questionable and laughably arbitrary as giving a strong sense to a particular phoneme. Any attempt to do so, in fact, will bring the unwitting phonolinguist into dubious regions—particularly, the tell-tale world of Freudian slips of the tongue. As Derrida shows, the conjugation of two phonemes, here l and i, for the purposes of some move towards a neo-Platonic ideal meaning or theme, is a dangerous game: 'Dès lors, il aura lui, rassemblé ses pouvoirs. L : i—' where the phonemes are deliberately rhymed with 'il' and 'lui' but made to sound 'lit', the climax, so to speak, of all the unspoken Freudian images in the host of foregoing Mallarmé references (the 'plus bas', I take it, refers to the lines from the 'ouverture' to *Hérodiade*, 'le lit aux pages de vélin, / Tel, inutile et si claustral, n'est pas le lin!' (*OC*, 42) which brings bed, book, and virginity together). Derrida, in short, is having fun at the expense of proponents of what he called in '+R' 'une théorie mimétique et hypercratyléenne du langage.'[6] His own language games are out to prove 'l'outrance même pour toute sommation lexicologique, toute taxinomie de thèmes, tout déchiffrement du sens.'(*Dissémination*, 309).

But there *is* a sense to the games Derrida plays: his illegitimate use of references. In the passage quoted above, there are several deliberately and mischievously cock-eyed 'strategies'. First, basing such an important argument on 'Sa fosse est fermée', the poem of a 17-year-old stumbling under the influence of Hugo. Secondly, misquoting from Mallarmé's preface to Leopold Dauphins *Raisins bleues et gris*. It is not the 'écriture spacieuse' which folds in its wing, but Dauphin. Thirdly, quoting from 'vers de circonstance' that are little more than playful doggerel (references are to *Dissémination*, 173, 155, 58). Fourthly, quoting facetiously from 'Don du poème', turning Mallarmé's pen-wing metaphor into something farcical

---

[6] *La Vérité en peinture*, 199.

with the '(sens blanc)' aside. Fifthly, withholding contextual information: the last quotation (*Dissémination*, 420) really refers to the aid the Academy can give to the innovative writer.

The point of this game is to abuse the subject text as though the new text (*La Dissémination*) has authorial rights over it. It is also to focus deliberately on Mallarmé's juvenile and throwaway verse (with supposedly serious psychoanalytical purposes) but in the end doing nothing with the findings except create a personal language game (a game in which the most important things said occur in the footnotes). Derrida would no doubt explain that distinctions beween important and occasional work are not only bogus, but entirely miss the point. For the main thrust of his work is to prove that secondary work is the other force upon which the primary is based—the *parergon*, or ornamental, being the unreasonable, undecideable, mad 'différance' that frames, denies, and enables. But if one cannot prove this to be so without recourse to double-talking distortion of the intellectual material used as the secondary foundation of one's argument, then it gives matter for doubt whether the parergonic structure, or supplementarity revealed is not a merely devious way of describing one's own procedures. Derrida's sense of Mallarmé's 'outrance' is based on his own sly 'outrage'.

More important than Derrida's deliberate parody of critical exactness of analysis (in this particular case, Jean-Pierre Richard's voluminous footnotes) is the philosophical crux hinted at earlier, that is, the question whether sound-repetitions concentrate or disperse a reader's attention. For Derrida they do both, but only in the sense that both possibilities co-exist in a mutually corrosive manner, creating a zone of undecideability. Derrida believes linguistic ambiguities of any kind, from broad conflictual dualities to the different senses in a word, will manufacture a 'pli' or a 'hymen' of empty energy. A word like 'hymen', because it can mean (1) a loving contract, a binding together, and (2) a separation, a membrane destroyed by that very contract, is a perfect illustration of this process.[7] In terms of rhyme and sound-repetitions, the case resolves itself down to similiar pairs of self-cancelling opposites—end-rhyme 'plie l'une à l'autre une identité et une différence',

---

[7] Derrida evidently takes 'hymen' from Mallarmé; especially the lines from *L'Après-midi d'un faune* : 'Inerte, tout brûle dans l'heure fauve/Sans marquer par quel art ensemble détala/Trop d'hymen souhaité de qui cherche le *la*' (*OC*, 51).

creating a 'hymen entre la chance et la règle' (*OC*, 309–10); sound-repetitions at once repeat the sounds of key-terms and reduce those key-terms to nonsense (and giveaway) doggerel: 'disloqué, démembré, le "mot" se transforme et s'associe indéfiniment. Le dé lit l'idée, le dais, ciel de lit, plafond et tombeau, dé à coudre tous les tissus, voiles, gazes, draps et linceuils de tous les lits de Mallarmé' (n., 317).

A complex word, in order to validate its identity, needs to be repeated in different contexts, with different senses. But the very act of repetition hollows out real self-identity—the supplement successively empties the word of its core senses. Phonemes, to arrive at any real power for the ear and eye, must repeat themselves along different words, but that very act of repetition robs the sounds of any central sense. This argument is of crucial importance to Derrida. It underpins not only the comic work of his style (the changes rung in his rhymy prose are his demonstration of this phenomenon) but also his entire anti-Platonic argument (repetition as anamnesis co-exists corrosively with repetition as dispersal into 'mimèmes, icônes, phantasmes, simulacres etc.' (*Dissémination*, 195)). Mimetic theory starts down at the phonemic level: 'la question conjointe du rythme, de la rime et du mime' (312).

But Derrida makes two important errors in his theory of supplementarity. The first mistake is to have decided that repetitions are necessarily co-present in a single textual moment. A different context may imply a different act of mind, an act of mind capable of differentiating, keeping separate, two contradictory forms, just as opinions may vary according to point of view and circumstance. As Hardy put it: 'Differing natures find their tongue in the presence of differing spectacles.'[8] A complex word may occur in two opposing senses on the same page. This does not imply that the reading or critical mind need nail them together—they can very well co-exist in their separate spaces, different textual times.

Similarly, a rhyme of 'd'aile' and 'd'elle' need not be read as a mere supplement of l. The words are in different lines, different spaces, different textual times. There is no rule or mechanism that governs the way rhymes or sound-repetitions consolidate

---

[8] General Preface to the Wessex Edition of 1912, in *The Selected Poems of Thomas Hardy*, ed. David Wright (London, 1978), 425.

differences or identities. The range of possibilities is more complex, and is predominantly context-based. In the young Mallarmé line, the rhyme of 'aile' and 'elle' brings our acoustic memory into contact with the metaphor's 'memory' of the dead girl. But this possibility is fragile and is definitely not a philosophical equation —if it is not merely the simple statement that rhymes and sound-repetitions are agents of identity and difference in the messy, human way remembering operates.

The second error Derrida makes is to believe that the double bind process, whereby addition is at once an accrual and a dispersal, necessarily leads to a hymenoid zone of undecideability. Literature is full of undecided minds. Remembering is full of undecided conflicts, anxieties, and contradictory emotive states. That does not mean that literature and memory are therefore of necessity a pair of artificial echo-chambers, grottoes or glottal stops. Logical consistency means something different in books and minds. In a book and in the mind, the self-contradictions accrue somewhat in the manner of a palimpsest—not only . . . but also . . . . They do not operate according to laws that say that if x co-exists in the same proposition as –x, then we have (x-x).

One of Derrida's favourite examples of a hymenoid construction is the word 'entre'. It can at once mean 'within the space separating people and things' and 'expressing a relationship between people or things'; it is at once the grounds of the possibility of a series and the word that blocks attempts at serialization. Derrida believes that all words operate in some measure like 'entre', their contradictions eventually deconstructing down to a between state of menace, empty energy, and potential auto-destruct. But why cannot 'entre' mean *both* things at the same time, and mean both those things in difficult community, or simply in obvious contextual distinction?

When the mind is 'between the devil and the deep blue sea', the Hobson's choice is not about what 'between' means—the context of the phrase governs that—but about the fatality of having *no* real choice. There again, part of the force of part V of *The Hollow Men*, comes precisely from a timed ambiguity in the meaning of 'between': 'Between the idea/And the reality/Between the motion/And the act/Falls the Shadow.' Four typographical pauses and two grammatical pauses stretch out the textual time before the resolution of the ambiguity—the 'Shadow' cuts in and transforms the doubt into miserable doubtlessness. It also *constitutes* the doubt, in the sense that our memory of the ambiguity is carried over into the fourth line. And, though the ambiguity is resolved ('between' definitely means 'separating'), the feeling of that ambiguity becomes part of our sense of the i̲rresolution implied by the shadow. The allusions to *Julius Caesar* confirm this—both sources are about irresolution: 'Betweene the acting of a dreadfull thing,/And the first motion, all the *Interim* is/Like a *Phantasma*, or a hideous Dreame' (II. i); 'hollow men, like Horses hot at hand,/Make gallant shew, and promise of their Mettle:/But when they should endure the bloody Spurre,/They fall their Crests' (IV. ii).[9] This complex sense and history to the word 'between' in Eliot's poem demonstrates how ambiguity in denotation can be used to substantiate a dreadfully irresolute mind. The between-state in Shakespeare and Eliot is no illustration of the hymenoid nature of all language as such; it is rather the nightmare of irresolute, cowardly minds caught in the trammels of the evil they are about to do. 'Between' as such cannot be labelled the Shadow of undecideability, for the word swerves from deliberate ambiguity to fixed denotation. But the ambiguity in 'between' is controlled, transformed, and siphoned into the meaning of the Phantasma or Shadow of evil within undecided minds.

Derrida's sense of the relations between ambiguity and supplementarity is, therefore, based on an overdetermined model of how paired opposites come into contact. The fact that repetition of sounds or words can create ambiguities, whenever paired opposites (like identity-difference, chance-rule) glide into double focus, does not necessarily imply that the spectral possibilities offered up are to be held together in vice-like corrosive relation. In his anxiety to avoid giving any room to 'mimétologisme', initiating any move from syntax to 'substantialité sémantique ou "symbolique" ', Derrida feels obliged to indulge in 'une sorte d'excès d'interprétation, un supplément de lecture'.[10] His interpretations and readings are, as a result, overladen with philosophical and referential permutation games and heavy punning and rhyming effects. But the excess cannot disguise the machinery running the readings, the machinery that is governed by the proposition that the more

---

[9] First Folio Nonesuch Edition (4 vols.; London, 1953), iii. 432, 465.
[10] *Vérité*, 306.

near-doubles a text, word, or phoneme has the more undecideable it becomes. And this machinery is factitious because it makes the illegitimate move from the given fact of surplus sounds, repetitions, readings to a crippling simultaneity of the possible contradictions.

The mind both remembers and forgets; a complex word can have a variety of senses; any paired opposite can generate a bewildering range of spectral possibilities; sound-repetitions can equally disperse and concentrate attention. But an act of memory has in its control a modest power over different times, different contexts; the mind when remembering moves over the emotive range implied in a 'not only . . . but also . . .' complex accretion, and endlessly demonstrates its capacity to hold a variety of circumstances in differing zones, hierarchies and spheres, within and across which the act of comparison, brought about by the double act of assent and dissent, creates and does not destroy.

Derrida is right to suppose that sound-repetitions are a crucial testing-ground for making one's mind up about relations between writing and the mimetic tradition, but he comes to this conclusion through fallacious reasoning. For Derrida, sound-repetitions trouble traditional philosophical relations between signifiers and signified—they in fact deconstruct any proposal of language as a supplement of a real phenomenal world by their more radical supplementarity. But the value of sound-repetitions for writers lies not in the *mise-en-abîme/mise-en-scène* problematic of language's hold on the world, but in their mimetic relation to varieties of mental language events, in particular, as I shall argue, the many varieties of remembering acts (both public and private) that take place in the same language. It would be absurd to call memories supplements to the events, imaginations, and readings that create them. Nor are they repetitions of those initiating past moments (only philosophers ever thought that). Neither do they mime them, whatever Plato thought. But literary language can and does mime memory's operations, transformations, condensations and translations—and it can do so because part of memory's work occurs in the same medium, language and its myriad combinations. Sound-repetitions are a neglected agent of this strange act of mimesis. The mimesis is not Plato's, neither is it Hegel's. It is foolishly unphilosophical to dare compare remembering in writing and remembering in the mind. But such a comparison lies at the heart of fiction, for reader and writer alike.

Baudelaire and the Prose Poem

Derrida's deconstruction of logocentrism and phonocentrism, then, bribes its readers into misrepresentation of what constitutes a literary text and analysis of it. 'La double séance' attempts to wrest Mallarmé's work out of Jean-Pierre Richard's grip, but at the cost of both double-dealing Mallarmé and misunderstanding Richard. Derrida's all-out attack on Richard bases itself on the assumption that Richard's *L'Univers imaginaire de Mallarmé* is typical neo-Platonic, ontological, classical mimetic theory in thematic mode, reducing the Mallarmé text down to its signified themes, which are somehow anterior to the text and yet mysteriously present in it, like a transcendent Idea. The core of Derrida's argument turns on the fact that Richard overvalues individual complex words and their 'polysémie', and blindly ignores the disseminating effects of Mallarmé's syntax, the machine that creates the 'white' supplementary material: 'Le "blanc" supplémentaire [. . .] libère des effets de série [. . .] Si le thématisme ne peut en rendre compte, c'est qu'il surévalue le *mot* et confine le *latéral*.' (*Dissémination*, 285).

It is clear that Derrida chose to overlook passages such as the following from *L'Univers imaginaire*:

L'ambiguïté mallarméenne nous semble exceptionelle en raison de son caractère paradoxal, et presque impraticable. Elle veut en effet maintenir à l'état de séparation et de discontinuité interne les divers sens possible qui doivent coexister virtuellement dans le mot ambigu. Les significations s'y trouveront à la fois réunies et distinctes, coexistantes et libres [. . .] Au début, souvenons-nous en, le *centre* mallarméen est absolument inerte et vide. Le mot se rêve ici comme un cristal prismatique, composé d'un certain nombre de facettes, et mis en rapport de réflexion lointaine avec autres mot-prismes. Chaque facette contient un sens possible: mais ce sens ne s'allume que s'il éveille, loin de lui, son homologue. De terme à terme circule donc un rapport pur, mais ce rapport ne dure que le temps d'un éclair d'évidence. Le remplace aussitôt un autre rapport, tout aussi fulgurant et fragile, établi avec un autre mot. Avec nous le sens semblera donc jouer à cache-cache; il sera à la fois ici et là, partout et nulle part: 'le papillon blanc, celui-ci à la fois partout, nulle part, il s'évanouit'. [. . .] l'esprit s'introduira *dans* le poème pour en faire jouer les ressorts, en mouvoir diversement les parties, essayer en lui des rapprochements, des variations, des hypothèses. Le poème mallarméen ressemblerait alors à l'un de ces *mobiles* si poétiquement agencés par l'art moderne pour faire exister, créer quoi? Non plus certes l'objet, ni même la vérité du signifié ou du signifiant, mais bien la signification qui, s'égalant à chacun des termes à partir desquels elle se manifeste, les accomplit tous deux en les abolissant.[11]

Derrida may have been right to latch on to the mysticism of Richard's feeling for a complex word (evidenced here by the crystal metaphor), but he was wrong to deny Richard's awareness of the effects of Mallarmé's syntax on those many-sided words. Richard's view of the reader–text bond is more flexible and mobile than Derrida's equation of thematic criticism with imitative text–sense dialectic allows. Despite Richard's fulsome metaphorical prose, his view of the matter is a complex one.

The Mallarmé sentence for Richard is typically one in which brief flashes of particular senses occur as words link up and relinquish their relations to each other, partly due to the reader's quizzing, partly due to the estrangement caused by the syntax. Such complex movements of the reading mind are the results of a lateral and syntactical reading-attention. This attention not only intervenes in the text by proferring short-lived hypotheses, comparisons, and variations within the limits allowed by the free play of the various ambiguities, but is also shaped and governed by the simultaneous manifestation and abolition of the text's syntactical and acoustic sound–sense relations. The ideal meanings of the words are neither anterior to, nor somewhere mystically beneath, the signifiers on the page, for Richard. The varieties and ambiguities occur '*dans* le poème', and are not the creation of an easy signifer–signified dialectic.

In other words, the disseminating supplementarity of Mallarmé's syntax is simply one of the stages the reading mind goes through in its relationship with the text. The end result may not be the New Critical crystal signification that Richard presupposes. But neither is it the fiction of a rich, empty, indescribable, hymenoid space. It is rather the complex movement of the mind through syntax, sound, and senses, through irresolution and ambiguities, conflicting and harmonizing obliquities, memories and

[11] Richard, *L'Univers imaginaire* 552–4.

inventions, not towards an end result but towards the end of the paragraph.

One of Richard's examples to prove the variety of Mallarmé's procedures is the prose poem 'Le Démon de l'analogie'. For him, it is a proof that Mallarmé's obscurity is at times a manner of engagement with the possible non-sense of phonemes:

Il peut arriver aussi que cette difficulté naisse involontairement dans le poème: sans que Mallarmé possède la clef qui la résoudrait en clarté. Toute sensation poétiquement vécue devient alors un signe, mais un signe dont celui qui l'obtient ne connaît pas la signification: nous nous trouvions alors devant une série de signifiants apparement privés de signifiés. C'est le cas, par exemple, des quelques expériences narrées par Mallarmé dans *Le Démon de l'analogie*. [. . .] D'étonnantes rencontres analogiques tissent entre le monde mental et le monde objectif un réseau de coïncidences dont nous manque la preuve, le foyer. Et c'est ce *manque* même qui désormais s'érige en signification . . . Incompréhensible, la sensation semble nous venir d'*ailleurs*. (*L'Univers imaginaire*, 418)

'Le Démon de l'analogie' was written some time in 1864, when Mallarmé was living under and through the influence of Baudelaire's *Petits poèmes en prose*. Baudelaire had set himself the task of modernizing Aloysius Bertrand's *Gaspard de la nuit* by situating the scenes of each prose poem within the context of modern Paris.[12] The prose poem, for Baudelaire, was a means of forging a correspondance between the resources of poetic prose and the complexity of the modern city:

Quel est celui de nous qui n'a pas, dans ses jours d'ambition, rêvé le miracle d'une prose poétique, musicale sans rythme et sans rime, assez souple et assez heurtée pour s'adapter aux mouvements lyriques de l'âme, aux ondulations de la rêverie, aux soubresauts de la conscience?

C'est surtout de la fréquentation des ville énormes, c'est du croisement de leurs innombrables rapports que naît cet idéal obsédant.[13]

Disguised within Baudelaire's two sentences is the contradiction that poetic prose seems at once to be a liberation, a language miraculously adapted to the lyrical movements of the mind, and a

[12] Particularly rewriting the section in Bertrand's collection of prose poems entitled 'Le Vieux Paris'.

[13] Prefatory letter to Arsène Houssaye, *Petits poèmes en prose: Le Spleen de Paris*, in *Œuvres complètes*, 161. Abbreviated to *OC* throughout.

mere symptom of modern times, a pressure imposed by the urban environment. The contradiction arises because Baudelaire, along with many of his contemporaries, metaphorically identified prose with the banal details and workaday narratives of the modern city. The muse of Baudelaire's prose poems is 'la muse familière, la citadine, la vivante' ('Les Bons chiens', in *OC*, 210). Poetry, on the other hand, was identified with the ideal, lyrical imagination of the poet.

Such a quasi-mystical distinction was most importantly promulgated by Sainte-Beuve in his collection of poems and prose thoughts *Vie, poésies et pensées de Joseph Delorme*, a book that was influential in shaping Baudelaire's practice in *Petits poèmes*:

Il y a dans la poésie deux formes: 1° l'une qui lui est commune avec la prose, savoir: la forme grammaticale, analogique, littéraire; 2° l'autre qui lui est propre et plus intime que la précédente, savoir: la forme rhythmique, métrique, musicale. La forme suprême de la poésie consiste à concilier ces deux formes partielles, et à faire qu'elles subsistent l'une dans l'autre. Mais cette alliance n'est pas toujours facile, et le poète, lorsqu'il se croit dans la nécessité de sacrifier l'une à l'autre, incline naturellement à préférer la forme poétique, proprement dit.[14]

Baudelaire himself went further and identified the prosaic with a complex, mixed tone. In this he followed Poe, whose tales he revered and whose prose practice he clearly imitates in *Petits poèmes*. In 'Notes nouvelles sur Edgar Poe', Baudelaire analyses the virtues of the short tale: 'l'auteur d'une nouvelle a à sa disposition une multitude de tons, de nuances de langage, le ton raisonneur, le sarcastique, l'humoristique, que répudie la poésie, et qui sont comme des dissonances, des outrages à l'idée de beauté pure.'[15] The poetic was defined by Baudelaire as the domain of the supernatural: 'C'est à la fois par la poésie et *à travers* la poésie, par et *à travers* la musique que l'âme entrevoit les splendeurs situées derrière le tombeau' (*OC*, 598).

The prose poem, then, was fixed and defined by Baudelaire as a genre subject to opposing pressures—the lyrical impulse (with its concatenation of all the 'poetic' technical marks excepting metre

---

[14] Sainte-Beuve, *Joseph Delorme*, 148.   [15] *OC*, 596.

and rhyme; that is, rhythm, alliteration, assonance, and repetition) moving towards the supernatural; and a prosaic, urbane rationality (ranging from a city context to a style of mixed and 'dissonant' tones). The city tones demand the sacrifice of the lyrical impulse in favour of 'cette sainte prostitution de l'âme qui se donne tout entière, poésie et charité, à l'imprévu qui se montre' ('Les Foules', in OC, 170); the pure lyrical impulse creates the inspired poet: 'celui-là seul est poète, qui est maître de sa mémoire, le souverain des mots, le registre de ses propres sentiments' ('Notes nouvelles', in OC, 597). Prose gave Baudelaire the freedom of his irony. Poetic prose presented that irony as a cruel, farcical frame to the supernatural longings and correspondances of the poetic imagination, and divested the poet of some of his power over words and his own lyrical memory.

As Baudelaire put it in *Fusées*:

Deux qualités littéraires fondamentales: surnaturalisme et ironie.

Coup d'œil individuel, aspect dans lequel se tiennent les choses devant l'écrivain, puis tournure d'esprit satanique. Le surnaturel comprend la couleur générale et l'accent, c'est-à-dire l'intensité, sonorité, limpidité, vibrativité, profondeur et retentissement dans l'espace et dans le temps. (OC, 394)

Petits poèmes, however, is more mixed than these simple dualities might suggest. David Scott has well described the variety of Baudelaire's achievement, beginning with the awkwardly poetic prose of 'Un Hémisphère dans une chevelure' (an uninteresting rewrite of the poem 'La Chevelure'), and involving many sub-genres, the essay, the short story, the 'poème-boitade', the epigram. But throughout the collection, as Scott says, Baudelaire sought 'a language capable of both lyricism and analysis, one that was able at the same time to record an instinctive, spontaneous response to phenomena and to *situate* that response in a broader rational and social perspective.'[16]

This mixed project, for Baudelaire, was an essentially modern phenomenon. Poetry itself was being seduced away from its classical purity: 'si l'on jette un coup d'oeil général sur la poésie contemporaine et sur ses meilleurs représentants, il est facile de voir qu'elle est arrivée à un état mixte, d'une nature très complexe;

---

[16] Wright and Scott, 'La Fanfarlo', 81.

le génie plastique, le sens philosophique, l'enthousiasme lyrique, l'esprit humoristique, s'y combinent et s'y mêlent suivant des dosages infiniment variés' ('Théodore de Banville', in *OC*, 52). For Baudelaire, this mixed state was not merely a symptom of the urban context but also revelatory of 'le Lucifer qui est installé dans tout cœur humain'; and Lucifer was thriving in the modern environment. The poets had found him out and bore witness to his power by playing his music: 'les dissonances, les discordances des musiques du sabbat [. . .] les glapissements de l'ironie, cette vengeance du vaincu'; 'l'art moderne a une tendance essentiellement démoniaque' (*OC*, 532).

Mallarmé's Prose-Rhyme Penultimate

It is this curious sense of the demoniacal that lies behind Mallarmé's 'Le Démon de l'analogie'. The prose poem is mixed and complex in several Baudelairian senses: it shifts its tones across a wide range; its diction rises and falls from the trivial to the sublime; it recounts the reverie of a poet within an urban context; it follows the poet's meandering 'lyrical' train of thought, yet could just as easily be read as a portrait of a mind deranged by the pressures of the mundane; it portrays a poet-figure losing control over his words and no longer quite master of his memory. It is Baudelairian in more difficult ways, too. 'Le Démon' meditates on the status of the poetic, lyrical voice, of a pure, musical language and does so at the risk (or rather by courting the risk) of ridicule, of being read as incoherent 'bouffonnerie'. It takes off from a series of trivial, pretentious details and coincidences (the discords and dissonances are bold) and rises to some kind of incomprehensible, supernatural apotheosis.

  Mallarmé is flirting with parody and pastiche, turning the prose poem as defined by Baudelaire into something very nearly sterile, threatened by the hollow laugh (in ways that look forward to Nabokov). The prose poem of Baudelaire's that it most resembles is 'Le Mauvais Vitrier', published in 1862. Baudelaire's prose poem also deals with strangely driven 'actes gratuits', incomprehensible to the contemplative natures concerned ('lui-même il ne sait pas pourquoi'), that issue out of some supernatural energy created by 'l'ennui' and 'la rêverie'. And in the Baudelaire also, the energy is demoniacal: 'J'ai été plus d'une fois victime de ces crises et de ces élans, qui nous autorisent à croire que des Démons malicieux se glissent en nous et nous font accomplir, à notre insu, leurs plus absurdes volontés' ('Le Mauvais Vitrier', in *OC*, 167). What is parodic about the Mallarmé is the lack of any violence at all, the reduction of Baudelaire's diabolic energy to what is really nothing more than a poet talking to himself in front of a shop window. But the parody is no pastiche—for what Mallarmé has done is to translate Baudelaire's demon into a phenomenon of language, created by and initiating the poet's madly wandering voice, a trick within the sound effects of French that transforms an analogy into a performative.

'Le Démon de l'analogie' begins with the question: what to do with poetic material in prose? This question is disguised within a question of shared experience: 'Des paroles inconnues chantèrent-elles sur vos lèvres, lambeaux maudits d'une phrase absurde?'(*OC*, 272).[17] A pseudo-poetic description of inspiration follows, that again quietly stresses the same mystery, the mystery as to how to deal with the musical and metaphorical in prose. The poet figure goes out into the street with a 'sensation [. . .] traînante et légère' which he 'poetically' compares to 'une aile glissant sur les cordes d'un instrument'. This feeling, defined in terms of quasi-conventional inspirational imagery, is replaced by a voice musically intoning ('sur un ton descendant') a broken alexandrine couplet, one end-rhyme and a 'rejet':

> *La Pénultième*
> *Est morte*

The nonsense of the phrase is made extreme by its poetic nature, for a variety of reasons.

First, technically: the line-ending blank and the empty space after the *rejet* place the words 'est morte' 'plus inutilement en le vide de signification'. In other words, the missing noun, the two missing half-lines, the lack of meaning itself are stressed by the heavy-handed emphasis of the enjambment. Secondly, the fact that the broken line is poetic summons up a kind of investigative enquiry, an intonational search for the right touch, the right key to counteract 'le vide de signification'. Poetry demands a peculiar

---

[17] The poem as a whole: *OC*, 272–3.

kind of attention, and, in Mallarmé's case, an attention at some extraordinary remove from analysis of city street prose. And lastly, precisely because this is a 'poème en prose', this flagrant intruder, a real piece of poetry to eye and ear, leads to blank surmising about the nature of prose poetics.

These three reasons influence the narrator too, who proceeds to indulge in elementary literary analysis. He at first seeks out the intonational *heart* of the mysterious phrase, helped by his own bodily rhythm: 'Je fis des pas dans la rue et reconnus en le son *nul* la corde tendue de l'instrument de musique et que le glorieux Souvenir certainement venait de visiter de son aile ou d'une palme.' This essential note recalls his musical, inspirational metaphor (string/wing) and leads him to consider some hidden patch of the past that lies behind the nonsense verses. This troubles him so much that he begins a more searching exploration of the nonsense sounds. He reads them out aloud, experiments with pauses after the line-ending, and long, drawn-out emphases on the syllable 'nul' taken to breaking-point. All the while, his mind is at work, again in typical literary-analytical manner: he defines the word 'pénultième' ('l'avant-dernière syllabe des vocables'), searches for the reasons why that particular word rose in his poetic consciousness ('le reste d'un labeur de linguistique par lequel quotidiennement sanglote de s'interrompre ma noble faculté poétique'), investigates the psychological causes behind the phrase's sonority and the 'lying' tone of his own analysis.

In the end, he cedes to the phrase itself, allowing its elegiac cadence to control his reading, hoping that this effort will calm his anxiety. His repetition of the sounds has behind it the desire to bury the phrase by its very 'amplification', a cross between semantic satiation and massed repetition. But at this very moment, the repetitions rise into the real voice, the perfect reading, which to the feverish mind of the narrator is as much as to say that he is possessed by the demon of the phrase, 'le glorieux Souvenir' behind the dead penultimate. At the same time, his body performs a gesture ('une caresse qui descend sur quelque chose'). The last paragraph unfolds the final twist to the mystery: the strange coincidence that at the moment he spoke and made the gesture, he is reflected in a shop-window: 'la boutique d'un luthier vendeur de vieux instruments pendus au mur, et, à terre, des palmes jaunes et les ailes enfouies en l'ombre, d'oiseaux anciens.' His reflection had played the lute or lyre; the wings that had played the strings lie scattered below: his casual metaphor has taken on supernatural life in the shop-window. He runs away, condemned to wear mourning for 'l'inexplicable Pénultième'.

The riddle of 'Le Démon' has exercised critical minds since its publication. Barbara Johnson divides them up into those who seek the meaning in the referent, signifier, and signified, and those who explicate the prose poem as a text about nonsense.[18] She herself argues for the prose poem as a text about rhyme. She reads the broken alexandrine phrase as inviting a rhyme on 'ème', which she provides from the text itself ('Je sentis que j'avais la voix même'). This encourages her to interrogate the text as a reflection on the relationship between rhyme and reason (*Défigurations*, 207–9). Rhyme, for Mallarmé, was a means of controlling the peremptory power of any single line ('la loi mystérieuse de la Rime, qui se révèle avec la fonction de gardienne, et d'empêcher qu'entre tous, un usurpe, ou ne demeure péremptoirement' (*OC*, 333)). Johnson argues that criticism, itself a 'rhyme' in relation to a literary text, can never fully explain its text. This is due to rhyme's fundamental ambivalence—it is at once the vehicle of analogy and a mode of division.

To prove this, she quotes Mallarmé: 'l'acte poétique consiste à voir soudain qu'une idée se fractionne en un nombre de motifs égaux par valeur et à les grouper; ils riment: pour sceau extérieur, leur commune mesure qu'apparente le coup final' (*OC*, 365). Criticism can only offer itself up as a broken line to the text's momentary equilibrium, at once finding analogies and fractioning them, and never discovering the 'coup final' to the 'pénultième' mystery of the text (*Défigurations*, 209). Johnson's reading is persuasive. I agree with her that 'Le Démon' is a prose poem about rhyme and reason. But it does not follow from this that the text dramatizes then subverts the difference between poetry and prose, poetry and criticism (*Défigurations*, 211). For that difference does not depend on rhyme's guardian status, its control of univocal afirmations. 'Le Démon de l'analogie' is more concerned with the relations between rhyme and remembering and their status in prose.

---

[18] Johnson, 'Le Démon de l'explication', in *Défigurations* 198–9. The critics to whom she refers in particular are G. Kahn, N. Paxton, P. O. Walter, A. R. Chisolm, J. L. Steinmetz, and Derrida.

Johnson misapplies Mallarmé on rhyme in poetry to justify her pessimistic findings about the broken couplet. First, because, in the passage about rhyming motifs quoted above, it is not *rhyme* that divides the idea into fractions. For Mallarmé, the idea splits naturally into different motifs. Rhyme is purely the agent of common measure, of grouping together, of 'parenté'. As for her use of the quotation seeing rhyme as moral guardian, this too is a half-truth. Though a political reading of rhyme is possible, it cannot be taken to prove that 'la rime empêche tout énoncé, toute pensée, toute "vérité" provisoire, de *s'imposer* une fois pour toutes' (*Défigurations*, 210). For what Mallarmé actually wrote was 'un équilibre momentané et double à la façon du vol, identité de deux fragments constitutifs remémorée extérieurement par une parité dans la consonance' (*OC*, 333). The guardian status, though it does control the rhetorical power of a single line, does so not to deny the imposition of any thought, statement, or truth, but to double them up, so to speak, to create a momentary equilibrium *between* truths, thoughts, and statements. This is an entirely different matter. And it does so by an act of acoustic memory ('identité . . . remémorée . . . par une parité dans le consonance'). In other words, rhyme is not the agent of negation that Johnson would have it be. It creates balance and signals provisional identity by way of acoustic memory.

Furthermore, Johnson fails to develop one of the most interesting remarks Mallarmé makes about literary prose. She quotes the relevant passage:

Style, versification, s'il y a cadence et c'est pourquoi toute prose d'écrivain fastueux, soustraite à ce laisser-aller en usage, ornementale, vaut en tant qu'un vers rompu, jouant avec ses timbres et encore les rimes dissimulés: selon un thyrse complexe. (*OC*, 644)

Though she applies this to 'Le Démon' with its 'vers rompu' as a clue that a full rhyme is to be found in the text ('rimes dissimulés'), it is only to lead her to the falsely depressing conclusion that, since no such rhyme can be said to occur in prose, the narrator's union with ' "la voix même" de l'Autre, c'est justement sa rencontre avec sa propre disparition, son propre silence. La prose, en tant que "vers rompu", n'est rien d'autre que ce genre de silence et de mort' (*Défigurations*, 206–7). This is falsely depressing because it fails to take into account the full value of

Mallarmé's phrase, 'jouant avec ses timbres et encore les rimes dissimulés'.

For Mallarmé felt that high literary prose is not characterized by a simple lack of full rhyme. The 'vers rompu' that is prose does not resemble the 'vers rompu' going through the narrator's mind in 'Le Démon de l'analogie'. Though prose lacks the double-wing resources of the heroic alexandrine, it has other skills: play with its own sounds and a more discrete sense to 'rime'; i.e. assonance and alliteration. Mallarmé, in the passage quoted above, is talking about poetic prose's relationship to poetry; and it is a relationship based primarily on *memory* of poetic techniques, and not their blank suppression, their 'silence' and their 'mort'. Discussing the experiments in loose metre and rhythm in modern *vers libre*, Mallarmé writes: 'la réminiscence du vers strict hante ces jeux à côté et leur confère un profit' (*OC*, 362). A similar kind of reminiscence haunts the acoustic play of 'toute prose d'écrivain fastueux'.

The movement the narrator in 'Le Démon' undergoes is similar to the mysterious process of naming described in 'Crise de vers', partly memory-invocation, partly accidental shift from statement to performative: 'Je dis: une fleur! et, hors de l'oubli où ma voix relègue aucun contour, en tant que quelque chose d'autre que les calices sus, musicalement se lève, idée même et suave, l'absente de tous bouquets' (*OC*, 368).

The process of reminiscence in 'Le Démon' turns around a particular feature of the sound-system of the prose first noticed by John Simon, in his book on the prose poem:

When [Mallarmé] wants to convey the musical obsession focused on the melodious syllable *nul* at the heart of P̲énultième, the ambiance of n̲ul is made to ring out with u̲ sounds: 'Je fis des pas dans la ru̲e et reconn̲us en le son n̲ul la corde tend̲ue de l'instr̲ument de m̲usique. . .'[19]

He could have added that the u̲-repetition is reinforced by the three-word string, 'inutilement-reconnus-*nul*'. But hear how the Mallarmé goes on:

qui était o̲ublié et que le glorieux S̲ouvenir certainement v̲enait de v̲isiter de son *aile* o̲u d'u̲ne palme et, le doigt s̲ur l'artifice d̲u my̲stère, je s̲ouris et implorai de v̲oeux *intellectuels* u̲ne s̲péc̲ulation différente. La phrase rev̲int, *v̲irt̲uelle*, dégagée d'u̲ne ch̲ute antérieure de pl̲ume o̲u de rameau,

---

[19] Simon, *Prose Poem*, 390. The book was originally a 1959 Harvard thesis.

dorénavant à travers la voix entendue, jusqu'à ce qu'enfin *elle* s'articula seule, vivant de sa personnalité.

The most important acoustic feature here is the presence of the phonemes of 'Souvenir' in stress-lines running throughout the two sentences, in particular the v-run. At the same time, the y-repetitions continue, with an 'elle' variation on 'nul'.[20] The phonemes are repeating 'le son *nul*' and the sounds of 'Souvenir'—the stress-lines along the runs make them key-words in sound as well as sense.

But the sound-repetitions are also rhyming 'souvenir' and 'nul' through the middle term 'son aile'—the agency of memory accords with the 'la corde tendue'. Here is a perfect example of a 'chute' of ls—but neither the sense nor the sounds escape into mysterious undecidable space. They are rather negotiating a common ground of sound between two key terms, and revealing the hallucinatory sound-analogies the narrator is subject to. These analogies push the narrator into an act of sonic personification, transforming 'la phrase' into a self-articulating creature, an incarnate (though absent) personality, a bird-like being, or woman, made out of remembering ('glorieux Souvenir') and forgetfulness ('le son *nul* [. . .] qui était oublié'). The phrase, within the investigative and obsessive musical quest of the narrator, is undergoing a process that resembles what happens to a dead person in the remembering/forgetting transformations of the mind.

The stress-lines reinforce and reconstitute the fleeting memory of the sounds of words; this Mallarmé rhymes with memory's powers of transcendence and resurrection. The repetitions also transform the key-words into empty sounds, with sense buried: this Mallarmé rhymes with the process of forgetting, and he demonstrates how that very process, in etherializing the woman in memory, makes the woman more apt for transcendence (murmuring the phrase over and over again is driven by 'le secret espoir de l'ensevelir en amplification de la psalmodie' but this process of semantic satiation, or deliberate forgetting, actually conjures up 'la voix même').

[20] Developed into a motif linking 'aile' and 'elle' by way of vowel-variations on n-u-l: 'son aile'-'d'une palme'-'intellectuels une spéculation'-'virtuelle'-'elle'-'seule'-'personnalité'.

The full rhyme to 'pénultième' sought after by Johnson may not exist—but prose sound-repetitions do: immediately after the m̲-string 'même'-'mensonge assumé'-'affirmation'-'tourment':

Harcelé, je résolus de laisser les m̲ots de triste nature e̲rrer eux-m̲êmes sur m̲a bouche, et j'allais m̲urmurant avec l'intonation susce̲ptible de condo-léance : 'La Pénultiè̲m̲e e̲st m̲orte, e̲lle e̲st m̲orte, la dése̲spérée Pénul-tiè̲m̲e', croyant par là satisfa̲ire l'inquiétude, et non sans le secre̲t e̲spoir de l'ensevelir en amplification de la psalm̲odie quand, e̲ffroi!—d'une m̲agie aisé̲m̲ent déductible e̲t ne̲rveuse—je sentis que j'ava̲is, m̲a m̲ain réfléchie par un vitrage de boutique y faisant le ge̲ste d'une care̲sse qui descend sur que̲lque chose, la voix m̲ême (la premiè̲re, qui indubitablem̲ent ava̲it été l'unique).[21]

These are not full rhymes—but they *are* sound-repetitions, runs forming stress-lines out of the phonemes of '-ème', obsessively recalling the key tonalities of the mysterious phrase. With a rage to forget through nonsense rhyming, the narrator paradoxically re-members, fully and distinctly, the first and unique mysterious source, and the demoniacal analogy is forged between his vocal expression and the conjured dead spirit of the words he speaks.

One of the sources for this strange narrative must be Baudelaire's 1861 eulogy of Victor Hugo, whom Baudelaire describes as being practically unique in having assembled 'un si magnifique réper-toire d'analogies humaines et divines'. His style, Baudelaire tells us, is a product of his mysticism: 'de là ces répétitions fréquentes de mots, tous destinés à exprimer des ténébres captivantes ou l'énigmatique physionomie du mystère'.[22] This repetitive style is the vehicle of analogy defined as the expression of some mysteri-ous, shadowy figure: exactly as the narrator's 'Pénultième' pos-sesses him at the very moment his expression begins to multiply its phonemic repetitions, creating the gestural coincidence. The

[21] The narrator's addition 'désespérée' itself occasions a local s̲-run: 'satisfaire-sans-secret-espoir-ensevelir-amplification-psalmodie-sentis-caresse-descend sur'. Taking the passage as a whole, m at 19 is up to 5.12% of all the phonemes, compared to 3.56% in normal frequency (cf. Hug distribution table, Appendix 2). The vowel ɛ is also up over 1%, 24 occurrences making 6.45%, compared to 5.26% normal frequency. The repetition of 'pénultième' as alerting device makes us sensitive to the e̲m stress-line particularly in the phrases 'murmurant avec', 'Pénul-tième est morte, elle est morte', 'psalmodie . . . effroi', 'magie aisément', 'j'avais ma main', 'même (la première', and 'indubitablement avait'.
[22] 'Victor Hugo', in *OC*, 510–1.

poet's voice resembles Baudelaire's Hugo too: 'J'ignore dans quel monde Victor Hugo a mangé préalablement le dictionnaire de sa langue qu'il était appelé à parler; mais je vois que le lexique français, en sortant de sa bouche, est devenu un monde, un univers coloré, mélodieux et mouvant' (*OC*, 510). The Mallarmé figure had not eaten a French dictionary, though. His fare, the 'labeur de linguistique' that risks wasting his poetic spirit, was rather a book about English words in which the mystery of sound symbolism reveals itself in its full absurdity.

T. E. F. L. and Alliteration

In November 1863, Mallarmé was forced to work for a living, teaching English at the lycée de Tournon in the Ardèche. 'Le Démon de l'analogie' was written after a year's work at this unforgiving task. Mallarmé's English was very bad (and continued to be so, as Scherer proves.)[23] Nevertheless, between 1863 and 1875, Mallarmé was involved in thinking about and codifying the linguistic peculiarities of English words, their resonance, history and sounds. Jacques Michon has shown in some detail the authorities Mallarmé drew upon for his linguistic labour[24] but these do not concern us, since *Les Mots anglais* was effectively written in the summer of 1875, and the accompanying background reading must have been done at the same time. What we can say is that *Mots anglais* gives us some indication of the work Mallarmé was doing at his schools, and tells us something about the particular philosophy of language and sound-symbolism that preoccupied him during the composition of 'Le Démon de l'analogie'.

This is all the more probable since the word 'pénultième' does occur in Mallarmé's treatise:

il surgit des cas véritablement bizarres, où signification et orthographe se mêlent, pour composer des produits nouveau. *Embûche*, terme français;

---

[23] Scherer, 'Le côté de l'anglais; in *Grammaire de Mallarmé*, 35–52. Scherer treats us to the embarrassing story of Malarmé's ill-luck at the hands of the school inspectors, who during the whole time as teacher of English, dogged him with accusations of incompetence. 'Malgré ses trente ans de professorat, qui furent pour lui un lourd fardeau, Mallarmé reste un angliciste amateur' (48). And, judging from the appalling mistakes in the lists of English words in *Les Mots anglais*, this is an understatement.

[24] Michon, *Mallarmé et Les Mots anglais*.

BUSH, veut dire buisson en anglais : d'où AMBUSH, qui signifie EMBUS-CADE, au coin d'un *bois* ou quelque part. L'idée de BUISSON naît là d'une ressemblance, favorisée par le sens, entre notre finale et un mot anglais: et, avec l'accord de tous, s'est imposée. Ainsi: d'*apprécier* qui, étant donné le renforcement habituel à la pénultième des verbes raccourcis de leur Terminaison, fit APPRAISE, car PRAISE, signifie *éloge*, et par suite, APPRECI-ATION. ('Les Mots anglais', in *OC*, 997)

The suggestion arises as to whether the narrator does not stress the penultimate syllable of 'Pénultième' precisely because the linguistic labour involved in the study of historical analogies between French and English was forcing him to discover the strange laws of stress in English, particularly the law favouring the penultimate syllable as bearer of stress. The narrator is trying to pronounce 'pénultième' with an English accent.[25]

Mallarmé, in his teaching, was forcing his own mind and the mind of his students to appreciate the complex ways French words alter in English. *Les Mots anglais* has several sections on 'terminaisons' and the laws of transplantation and historical change affecting the language's 'désinences casuelles': 'Que pouvait-il, cet état du langage existant de part et d'autre, résulter du mélange des deux parlers: sinon que certaines terminaisons d'ici glissassent peu à peu dans leurs analogues de là; ou bien persistassent, tantôt intactes, tantôt détériorées?' (*OC*, 986–7). The way the narrator rolls the 'nul' syllable out, altering the phrase, re-stressing it, transforming it, resembles the way French endings have slipped and slid into new forms, or have persisted, like an event in memory, 'tantôt intactes, tantôt détériorées'. The 'chute antérieure de plume ou de rameau' in the prose poem may very well be a transformation of the habitual ways of thinking of the crazed philologist, exhausted by tedious work tracing the way French words become abbreviated in English ('l'accident le plus élémentaire de toute transposition d'une langue à l'autre, l'abréviation des finales' [*OC*, 989]).

[25] A point also made by Jean-Michel Rabaté in *La Penultième est morte* (15). Rabaté relates this fact to Mallarmé's reminiscences of Verlaine teaching English: Verlaine, apparently would adopt a deliberately bad English accent when speaking French ('[l]a prononciation défectueuse ordinaire aux compatriotes du Dr Johnson' (*OC*, 874)), or, as Rabaté puts it, indulge in 'ce jeu de fausses traductions et de littéralismes' (103).

The search for the sense of the phrase in 'Le Démon' is more than a mere trick of English stress-patterns and suffix-alterations across languages, however. The real search in 'Le Démon' is phonolinguistic—what do these phonemes, in isolation, *mean*? *Les Mots anglais* is a work obsessed by the significances concealed within the sounds of words; and in particular alliterative connections:

Au poëte ou même au prosateur savant, il appartiendra, par un instinct supérieur et libre, de rapprocher des termes unis avec d'autant plus de bonheur pour concourir au charme et à la musique du langage, qu'ils arriveront comme de lointains plus fortuits: c'est là ce procédé, inhérent au génie septentrional et dont tant de vers célèbres nous montrent tant d'exemples, l'ALLITERATION. Pareil effort magistrale de l'Imagination désireuse, non seulement de se satisfaire par le symbole éclatant dans les spectacles du monde, mais d'établir un lien entre ceux-ci et la parole chargé de les exprimer, touche à l'un des mystères sacrés ou périlleux du Langage. (*OC*, 921)

Mallarmé warns against a scientific use of the writer's imaginative resources—for fortuitous consonance may go against the grain of sound and sense if used as the exclusive basis of etymologies ('Loin de rechercher les liaisons très lointaines, je les évite: et ne donne point *lingua* à la suite de TO LICK et de TONGUE, quoiqu'il les unisse dans une certaine mesure' [*OC*, 922]).

Nevertheless, in many sections of *Les Mots anglais*, Mallarmé gives free rein to such far-fetched liaisons, driven by the alliterative temptations of his 'Imagination désireuse'. It is clear that the demon of analogy is in many ways a superstitious name for this 'Imagination désireuse'. But it is an imagination at one remove from the language it wishes to control—the troubling phrase 'La Pénultième/Est morte' comes to the narrator as though from a foreign language (the prose context has effectively estranged it). He needs to read it out loud, listen to the rhythm and movement of the words, just as though he were trying to fathom a line of foreign poetry: 'L'étude d'un langage étranger [. . .] repose sur la lecture à haute voix des bons auteurs. [. . .] Un courant d'intelligence, comme un souffle, l'esprit, met en mouvement ces mots, pour qu'à plusieurs d'entre eux ils expriment un sens avec des nuances' (*OC*, 902–3). The foreignness of the phrase as it hits him makes him treat it with all the habits of an English teacher and amateur philologist, and furthermore, with all the superstition of his sound-symbolism.

This superstition saw in alliteration the root and law of sense-production. As Michon puts it:

Le simple choc des mots rapprochés par homonymie ou par analogie phonique, devient l'occasion d'une prolifération sémantique souvent créatrice d'une paraphrase ou d'une image poétique: par exemple, TO BREAK (briser) et BROOK (ruisseau) créent le 'ruisseau aux mille brisures' (p. 928); TO WINK (cligner) et WING (aile) assimilent la paupière à 'une aile, aux battements vifs' (p. 231). (*Mallarmé et Les Mots anglais*, 154).

These phono-semantic correspondances create miniature stories, myths and folk etymologies. And, at the level of the individual phoneme and grapheme, Mallarmé's superstitious philology makes the same illicit step, dancing to the desiring imagination's tune. The letter l, for example:

Cette lettre semblerait parfois impuissante à exprimer par elle-même autre chose qu'une appétition point suivie de résultat, la lenteur, la stagnation de ce qui traîne ou gît ou même dure; elle retrouve, cependant, de la spontanéité dans des sens comme sauter et tout son pouvoir d'aspiration avec ceux d'écouter et d'aimer, satisfait par le groupe de *loaf* à *lord*: noter aussi liaison et analogie. (*OC*, 958)

Throughout *Les Mots anglais*, Mallarmé sets down similar lists of meanings for all the 'vocables'. These individual phonemic significations contribute towards the sense of the words they are the initial consonant of; and those words, in isolation, are defined by Mallarmé as 'mots purs, voire nuls, abstrait, immobiles' (as distinguished from the same words 'mises en usage par le discours' (*OC*, 965)). The 'mot nul' in 'Le Démon' is 'Pénultième', which is wittily predicated by its own penultimate syllable[26]—abstract, pure and immobile, it hangs before the narrator's imaginary reading-eye, inviting phono-semantic play, inciting the desiring imagination superstitiously to give it a demoniacal body made up of its memory of philological analyses of a foreign language. It engenders an acoustic hallucination that Mallarmé was later to attribute to Wagner's music: 'alors y aboutissent, dans quelque éclair suprême, d'où s'éveille la Figure que Nul n'est, chaque attitude mimique

---

[26] Cf. Rabaté, *La Penultième*, 15.

prise par elle à un rythme inclus dans la symphonie, et le déliv-rant!' (OC, 545). The current of intelligence creates a rhythm along the sound-repetitions, the alliterations and assonantal strings that suddenly crystallize into a palpable, simultaneously present and absent, 'pénultième' fiction; a word out of context ('mot nul') resembles a mourned-for muse in the memory ('la Figure que Nul n'est'). And, Mallarmé acknowledges, both are products of chance, the fortuitousness of coincidental correspondences.

As Mallarmé put it in 'Un Coup de dès': 'l'ultérieur démon immémorial/ayant/de contrées nulles/induit/le veillard vers cette conjonction suprême avec la probabilité' (OC, 464)—the chances of sound-effects create strange phono-semantic conjunc-tions under the pressure of the demoniacal urge to 'rhyme' in prose, to create analogies out of the basic phonemic matter of a figurative language made foreign by being exiled within a prose context. The sound-repetitions in 'Le Démon de l'analogie' are the marks and agents of the imagination's work as it establishes links between the fortuitous and the sacred, as it indulges in the penul-timate superstition of the hidden symbol within sounds. The al-literations are witness to the effort to treat the phrase with the full attention normally reserved for the investigation into the meaning of the sound-effects of English—for do not the key-words of 'Le Démon', 'aile' and 'corde', rhyme in English? Both words appear in Les Mots anglais -'WING, aile, aux battements vif' (OC, 932); 'STRING, corde' (OC, 946). The sound-repetitions show the narrator trapped in the comic miming of an act of desperate translation.

For Mallarmé was also suffering the labours of translation from English—he had recently started work on his translations of Poe (begun in London, 1863). Mallarmé's notes ('Scolies') to his trans-lations of Poe's poems show his sensitivity to these sound-effects; he remarks on the 'effets allitératifs étranges' in Poe's 'Eulalie', particularly the line 'And the yellow-haired young Eulalie'. (OC, 233). Poe's 'The Bells' caused Mallarmé great difficulty due to its 'procédés de répétition qui, contenus par le rythme originel, se défont et comme s'égrènent dans une version en prose' (OC, 240)—he felt obliged to control the repetitions with the use of parentheses, but urges the interested reader to refer to Emile Blémont's version: 'Le vers, chez lui, a pu, s'éloignant du calque strict habituel de notre version, transposer d'une langue à l'autre, tels timbres jumeaux, et témoigner d'une ingéniosité bien faite pour réjouir Poe lui-même' (OC, 240). The mystery of sound-effects in another language are furtively remembered in 'Le Démon de l'analogie'—the 'manque' felt in the absence of the 'pénultième' being in many ways a transposition of losses registered in translation.

But their traces remain in the 'rimes dissimulés' and 'timbres' of his alliterative prose. As Mallarmé says, hoping his version will recuperate some of the magic of the English original, despite the untranslateability of the 'effets purement imitatifs' in 'The Bells': 'je crois que cette impalpable richesse ne se perd pas tout entière au passage d'une langue à l'autre, bref, qu'il est un démon pour les traducteurs' (OC, 240).

The poem of Poe's that Mallarmé specifically recalls is 'Israfel', based, as Mallarmé says, on the passage from the Koran: 'Et l'Ange Israfel dont les fibres du cœur sont un luth et qui a la voix la plus suave de toutes les créatures de Dieu' ('Scolies', in OC, 245).[27] In the poem, Poe imagines the universe rapt in attention to the divine lute-player, but asks him not to scorn less impassioned poetry; in fact, he implies that context determines the quality of any song—'If I could dwell/Where Israfel/Hath dwelt, and he where I,/He might not sing so wildly well/A mortal melody,/While a bolder note than this might swell/From my lyre within the sky'. 'Le Démon', with its lute-player and its unique voice, remembers the Israfel situation and puts it to the test. The narrator does, for an instant, change places with the Israfel demon, finds a voice and a music. The 'Souvenir' driving the narrator on with his strange obsession is partly a memory of Poe rivalling the Angel of Melody.

But it is a mitigated success, precisely because the memory is coming from another tongue, from another system of sound-repetitions. The Poe poem is tightly rhymed, almost to breaking point—the sound of Israfel's name dominates the first and last stanzas. For the last stanza, Mallarmé does his best to mimic the English rhymes in his prose calque, with 'mélodie mortelle', 'celle-ci', and 'ma lyre dans le Ciel' recalling 'Israfel'. He attempts the same thing in the first stanza ('ciel'-'Israfel'-'étoiles') but with the significant half-rhyme 'Nul ne chante si étrangement bien—que l'ange

[27] In Poe's note: 'And the angel Israfel, whose heart-strings are a lute, and who has the sweetest voice of all God's creatures. —KORAN'.

Israfel' (*OC*, 214). All these effects, one might say, are the effects of pure chance: Mallarmé is translating word for word, and the sound-repetitions on el are either pure luck or inevitable ('stars' must become 'etoiles' however one desires to create sound-effects). But 'Le Démon' is precisely about strange luck and chance. Mallarmé's prose poem recalls Poe's poem and its over-rich acoustic textures, its fantastic superstitious rivalry with a foreign spirit of music—and the traces are there of that memory in the chances of prose, the 'souvenir'-'nul'-'aile' sound-repetitions. 'Nul ne chante si étrangement bien' in 'Israfel'—in 'Le Démon', the *word* 'nul' sings strangely in the context of prose. Prose as such has replaced Poe's 'where I'; the memory of Poe's poetry has replaced 'where Israfel', and a mixed voice is created of hidden rhymes and playful 'timbres'. A 'note plus forte' has been discovered, in the little miracle of the prose poem.

But why should the narrator mourn for the 'Pénultième'? Poe's 'Israfel' has no trace of any 'deuil'. A possible answer might lie in the work of Saint-Beuve's 'Joseph Delorme', source for Baudelaire's *Petits poèmes*, one of the formative 'memories' for any French writer embarking on the prose poem. In the poem 'A la Rime', Sainte-Beuve creates conceit after conceit in honour of rhyme.[28] It is 'l'unique harmonie/Du vers' (stanza I)—we recall that the narrator discovers his voice to be 'indubitablement [. . .] l'unique'. He begs Rhyme to give company to his syllables: 'Ne laisse point murmurer,/Soupirer,/La syllabe solitaire' (stanza XI), corresponding to the way the phrase 's'articula seule' in the prose poem. But the real point of contact is when Sainte-Beuve, in the last four stanzas, develops the old Renaissance conceit of rhyme as wings:[29] 'Sur ma lyre, l'autre fois,/Dans un bois,/ Ma main préludait à peine:/Une colombe descend,/En passant,/Blanche sur le luth d'ébène.'

But instead of 'accords touchants', the dove grieves, 'me demande par pitié /Sa moitié,/Sa moitié loin d'elle absente'.[30]

[28] 'A la Rime', *Joseph Delorme*, 29–31.
[29] Ronsard, for example, in LXIV of the 1552 *Les Amours*, promises his lady that he will make her name fly high in honour and fame on the 'vent de ma voix' and with 'l'aisle de ma rime'.
[30] Another Pléiade conceit—Ronsard mourns for the death of his 'moytié', for example, in CXXVIII of the 1552 *Les Amours*. It is possible that Sainte-Beuve may also have been thinking of Ovid's Sirens, metamorphosed into birds, and endlessly in search of Proserpine (V, 533-66).

> Ah! plutôt, oiseaux charmants,
>   Vrais amants,
> Mariez vos voix jumelles;
> Que ma lyre et ses concerts
>   Soient couverts
> De vos baisers, de vos ailes
>   (stanza XIV)

The 'voix jumelles' itself rhymes with Mallarmé's 'timbres jumeaux' describing a perfect translation of Poe. 'Le Démon de l'analogie' remembers the wing-strewn lyre, the mourning voice seeking its lover 'loin d'elle absente', the wing on the lute. The 'Souvenir'-wing that plays the string is partly a memory of a poem about rhyme as a figure of marriage, and, in its 'vers rompu' form, as a figure of abandoned love and dream of the absent loved one. In recalling the Sainte-Beuve poem, the narrator unconsciously develops the primary analogy (lute and song-bird for heart and rhyme) and works it into a comic meditation about analogy as such, rhymelessness as such, à l'état pur et nul.

The 'Pénultième', as that which comes before, is a figure of occluded memory in the prose poem, memory of translating Poe, memory of reading Sainte-Beuve's poem about rhyme. What is comic about the prose poem is the radical gulf Mallarmé creates between the pettiness of the occasion and the feeling that results— a sterile recall in a prose poem of two poems about the poetic lyrical voice ('Israfel') and a conceit about rhyme ('A la Rime') turns into a supernatural event, an encounter with a terrifying gift and its power to raise the memory of the fictional dead. What strangely redeems the narrator, though, is the substitution of the lost rhyme to his 'Pénultième' or 'moitié' with the 'rimes dissimulés' of a poetic prose. The prose sound-effects acknowledge their fictional status (since they derive from an inchoate theory of sound-symbolism based on chance[31]), but nevertheless forge the necessary links between the narrator's voice and the supernatural dream of a truly absent memory. The 'aile' of literary memory, touching the chords of the voice's prose sound-repetitions, raises the ghost of 'la Figure que Nul n'est' and real feeling is born. The

---

[31] I think even Mallarmé would acknowledge this, given his admittance of the fortuitous and perilous nature of alliteration in the hands of the 'Imagination désireuse' (cf. OC, 921).

sound-repetitions, with their runs and stress-lines, recuperate
prosaic language into the region of poetic chances and analogies—
like Baudelaire's Poe, Mallarmé's narrator, though exiled in the
enemy country of prose,

rentrant dans la vraie voie des poètes, obéissant sans doute à l'ineluctable
vérité qui nous hante comme un démon, [. . .] poussait les ardents soupirs
de *l'ange tombé qui se souvient des Cieux*.[32]

[32] Baudelaire, 'Notes nouvelles sur Edgar Poe', in *OC*, 592.

2

Re-establishing Contacts:
prose rhymes in A la Recherche du temps perdu

> Il y a des moments où pour peindre complètement quel-
> qu'un il faudrait que l'imitation phonétique se joignît à la
> description.
>
> (*A la recherche du temps perdu*, iii. 333).

Paul Valéry, in the 1910s, speculated on the strange power of memory:

> Ce qui me frappe le plus dans la mémoire, ce n'est pas qu'elle redit le
> passé—c'est qu'elle alimente le présent. Elle lui donne réplique ou ré-
> ponse, lui met les mots dans la bouche et ferme en quelque sorte tous les
> comptes ouverts par l'événement. (*Cahiers*, 1221)

Memory is a ventriloquist here, throwing the voices of past selves into present tense speech. This personified faculty, memory become dramatic voice within the mouth, haunts the texts of Mallarmé, Proust, Joyce, and Beckett. With Proust, voluntary and involuntary memory, though made triumphantly distinct in 'Le Temps retrouvé', often subtly inter-mingle in the ordinary courses of the human voice. I will show how Proust demonstrates this intermingling by use of a technique of key-word emphasis that mimes memory's ventriloquist interjections. The prose rhymes are marks of a past anxiety involuntarily altering the voice as it at-tempts to speak of 'other matters'.

Proust's portrait of memory is largely celebrated as centring on the 'souvenir de la patrie intérieure' (iii. 761) which the artist's lonely mission directs him towards, the bedridden mind's con-scious reliving of its complex pasts ('la décharge douloureuse d'un des mille souvenirs invisibles qui à tout moment éclataient autour de moi dans l'ombre' (iv. 61)), or the quasi-divine grace of involuntary recall (the famous 'tasse de thé').[1] I shall be concentrating on other less well-recorded memory acts. These are the unacknowledged resuscitations of past anxiety that gather around Proust's 'rimes intérieures'. They occur during his investigations into jealousy and music.

Music, for the narrator, contains an abstract of 'l'inflexion de l'être' which reproduces 'cette pointe intérieure et extrême des sensations', feelings of extreme anxiety and 'attente' (iii. 876). The leitmotif theory the narrator develops on listening to Vinteuil is related to his discovery of 'phrase-types' in literature which adumbrate a 'Passé', 'une même sensation d'anxiété' (iii. 877–8). The phrase-motifs, in both music and literature, gather up a listener's and reader's own past sensations to concentrate them into a complex of feelings 'si organique et viscérale' (iii. 764) that they resemble neuralgic symptoms rather than technical narrative signals. Swann's story demonstrates the close links between musical motifs and the manner in which jealousy fabricates sentimental or cruel selves that pretend to represent Odette. The same transformations of material take place in both kinds of feeling, aesthetic and emotional. The mystery of the loved one's memory (the time spent away from Swann), like the mystery of the passionate impact of abstract musical signs, is transformed into the jealous lover's primary imaginative material. In other words, another person's memory becomes the matter out of which the imagination fabricates its own figures of anxiety, against the grain of its own impulses, and deep within the voice.

It might seem strange for me to concentrate on these subtle memory-effects in the voice, rather than the solitary's visions and resuscitations, in a study dealing with both Proust and Beckett. What I will show is that, though Proust's presence in Beckett's Malone, Krapp, and the voices in the late prose is obvious and central, Proust's 'rimes intérieures' demonstrate an attitude to the human voice that Beckett's work parallels.[2] Proust shows how 'un

---

[1] Most Proust critics could be cited to support my summary. One in particular, however, gives an exhaustive, quasi-Cartesian account of Prousts philosophy of memory, Alain de Lattre in the second vol. of *La Doctrine de la réalité chez Proust*, 'Les Réalités individuelles et la mémoire'. Though the style is irritating with its loose Thomist format, the account of the problems of personal identity that voluntary and involuntary memory cause is particularly revealing (251–4).

[2] This is in line with Bernard Brun's reading of Beckett's *Proust*, which, according to him, privileges 'les relations interpersonnelles et les intermittences du cœur

morceaux du passé' enters the present-tense self and effects a momentary 'substitution de personne' (iii. 536) in the minutest details of the voice's inflexions and intonation. Beckett's interest in the paradox of the 'self-accompaniment of a voice that is not mine' (*The Unnamable*, 22) is an extreme development of this Proustian concern.

Madeleine Remâcle, in her fine book on the 'élément poétique' in *A la recherche du temps perdu*, writes of the difficulty of its sentence-length:

Tout lecteur, si patient, si 'agile' qu'il soit, a été surpris et comme dépaysé devant ces phrases sinueuses, démesurément étendus, compliquées [. . .] comme à la pratique d'une langue étrangère, qui ne s'est senti devenir plus habile, si habile que la complication de cette prose rebutante a paru aussi légitime que la clarté linéaire de la syntaxe traditionelle? (149)

Malcolm Bowie has argued that this 'langue étrangère' cumulatively educates us to feel its legitimacy through its almost physiognomical mimesis of the movements of the mind:

[*A la recherche du temps perdu* is] a portrait of the mind in process. Not only have the mind's indeterminacies and indecisions been given a palpable form, but its risks feel like risks: its ideas now sing, now stammer [. . .] it is writing like this which, as we read, returns epistemological enquiry to our nerves and pulses. (15)

The risks Proust takes in his style are representative, Bowie argues, of the acts of mind (passionate reminiscences and scientific analysis) of his narrator's 'recherche de la verité', from the obsessive combing of minutiae by the jealous suffering mind to the resurrections of the past in involuntary memory. The sentence-length records and captures the complex density and detail of such anxious research, rehearing the nervous impulses of the proceeding mind. Bowie is very good about the analogy Proust finds and designs between a jealous 'recherche' of the lost time of one's lover and the artist's 'recherche' of his and his generation's past. I would like to move on from his suggestions to examine Proust himself on this 'rapport intime' at the level of his minute particulars. The 'nerves and pulses' of Proust's prose that go to create his 'langue

(Odette, Albertine, grand-mère) au détriment de l'aspect visionnaire, créateur' ('Sur le Proust de Beckett', 88).

étrangère' justify themselves down at this level. For it is at the level of the 'music' of his stresses and accents that Proust's syntax mimes and releases the powerful mobilîty of the language of inner speech, the mind reacting to the burden of past connotations within the words and phrases it articulates.

The music is the difficult music of memory in which the emotional energy and desire of past moments is conserved and felt again, memory activated and articulated by words repeated, their dubious connotations stressed along his 'rimes intérieures'. 'Ces moments du passé', Proust writes, 'ne sont pas immobiles, ils gardent dans notre mémoire le mouvement qui les entraînait vers l'avenir,—vers un avenir devenu lui-même le passé,—nous y entraînant nous-même' (iv. 70). Words, like moments in the memory, are loaded with the energy of past connotations. Proust's prose-rhymes not only mime the hallucinatory movement in 'les moments du passé'; they demonstrate the importance of words as agents for those movements. They are the lines of communication along which the currents of memory and accent flow.

At the beginning of *Albertine disparue*, Proust's alternately jealous and mourning narrator is analysing the after-effects of Albertine's death within his feverishly intermittent mind:

(et même une syllabe commune à deux noms différents suffisait à ma mémoire—comme à un électricien qui se contente du moindre corps bon conducteur—pour rétablir le contact entre Albertine et mon cœur.) (iv. 118)

The minute acoustic filiation of a single syllable across two different names is analogous to the rhyming of a vowel and a 'consonne d'appui' in French prosody. This hint at the idea of the communicative power of rhyme is playfully exemplified by the sentence itself—rhyme-play's common sounds find echoing common sounds in 'syllabe', 'rétablir' and 'Albertine'; the phrase-end string 'mémoire', 'conducteur', 'cœur'; the Latin prefix-rhymes 'content', 'conducteur', 'contact'; the common ground between 'commune' and 'comme'. These rhyme-sounds are playing around two centres of sound and sense, stress-lines emanating from the common consonances of 'Albertine' and 'cœur'.

The parenthesis is hidden within this long sentence:

D'ailleurs un mot n'avait même <u>pas</u> besoin, comme Chaumont [. . .] de se <u>rap</u>porter <u>à</u> un <u>s</u>oup<u>ç</u>on pour qu'il le réveillât, <u>p</u>our être le mot de <u>passe</u>, le magique Sésame entrouvrant la porte d'un passé dont on ne tenait plus compte parce qu'ayant assez de le voir, à la lettre on ne le possédait plus; on avait été diminué de lui, on avait cru de par cette ablation sa propre personnalité changée en sa forme, comme une figure qui perdrait avec un angle un côté; certaines phrases, par exemple, où il y avait le nom d'une rue, d'une route où Albertine avait pu se trouver, suffisaient pour incarner une jalousie virtuelle, inexistante, à la recherche d'un corps, d'une demeure, de quelque fixation matérielle, de quelque réalisation particulière. (iv. 118–19)

The alignment effected between 'le mot de passe' and 'la porte d'un passé' spreads out into the sounds of the rest of the sentence, stress-lines organized into a solid Masson pattern on RapR.[3] The sound of a word becomes an involuntary portal of discovery. Proust mimes this involuntary acoustic/remembering work by flooding his text with the phonemes of his key-words, aligning, simply and efficiently, the reader's short-term acoustic memory of the text on its way with the narrator's involuntarily jealous hearing of key-words, heard by chance along his way through the world. The narrator, under the influence of his acute suffering, undergoes a series of discoveries that there is something or someone else at work within him, an undivulged self, a memory with a will of its own. That strange will, that stranger self finds its facsimile voice in the prose rhymes, stress-lines whispering the phonemes of key passwords and past words.

What consolidates this line of communication is the fact that this passage itself recalls another a few paragraphs back where the narrator is reacting to Aimé's letter detailing Albertine's relations with the 'blanchisseuse'—Aimé's letter relays the girl's memory of Albertine's words spoken in lesbian ecstasy. Proust's prose rhymes register the reverberation of those words in the narrator's own memory of reading that crucial letter:

Par instants la communication était interrompue entre mon cœur et ma mémoire. Ce qu'Albertine avait fait avec la blanchisseuse ne m'était plus signifié que par des abréviations quasi algébriques qui ne me représentaient plus rien; mais cent fois par heure le courant interrompu était

---

[3] The three phonemes Rap all have significantly higher percentages (within the phonemes of the passage as a whole) than the Hug frequencies (cf. Appendix 2). $R = 8.91\%$; $p = 4.21\%$; $a = 7.59\%$.

rétabli et mon cœur était brûlé sans pitié par un feu d'enfer, tandis que je voyais Albertine ressuscitée par ma jalousie, vraiment vivante, se raidir sous les caresses de la petite blanchisseuse à qui elle disait: 'Tu me mets aux anges.' (iv. 109)

The narrator's words are like the quasi-algebraic abbreviations of his fitful mind—they remain a transparent medium until the current flows between his memory and his heart. When the picture summoned up by Albertine's words (themselves transmitted to him—in written words—along a chain back into the past) clears again into sharp focus, the electrocution the narrator suffers is registered in the charge of Proust's stressed 'rimes intérieures'.

A full rhyme on 'cœur', as in the parenthesis that recalls this passage, alerts one to the presence of the prose rhyme stress-lines —'heure'-'cœur', a rhyme brought into closer contact by 'courant'. This rhyme-play alerts one's attention to the R-run, both lightly at the end of words (the strange repetitions of 'par' govern these) and more significantly in the string initiated by the sound-repetitions in 'courant interrompu était rétabli'. This R-run highlights the 'rétabli'-'ressuscitée' conceptual rhyme, but I believe the real effect is, dramatically, to climax on 'se raidir sous les caresses'. Rhythmically, the R-run does this by the two double accents ('feu d'enfer', 'vraiment vivante') which tend to accustom the voice (and accelerate it into) a similar stressing when articulating 'se raidir sous les caresses' in the light of the preparative R-run. This accent on 'caresses' is reinforced by the s stress-line as well as the preceding Rε rhymes.

The word itself is burning in his heart. The prose rhymes provide us with a fascimile version of the narrator's burning verbal memory. His jealousy has been set alight by a text. His reading lodged a key-word in his memory and the word pulses there with the burning power of alternating current on live tissue. Proust reproduces this textual memory with his prose rhymes, the stress-lines not only highlighting the key-word, but also miming the charge they have. A reader is asked to roll those Rs, speak the key-word with painful emphasis, weigh the charged words heavy on the tongue.

For the word 'caresses' was a key term in Aimé's letter ('lui faisait des caresses avec sa langue le long du cou et des bras' (iv. 106)). The word reverberates in the narrator's mind as he begins to live with the memory of reading that letter and the unbearable changes it has wrought on all his imagined past with Albertine. The summative word 'caresses' is one of the terrible 'mots de passé' that suffer the surge of power within his own painful memory of the new 'passé' created by that very word.

The parenthesis about rhyming details re-establishing memory-contacts between Albertine and his heart is itself, then, a signal of a key text being digested and allowed to rhyme across the currents of the narrative voice. The agonizing key-words of a read text become the syllabic fragments of a newly fabricated voice of anxiety and literary-critical obsession. This example underlines the importance of Proust's own rhyming technique in his prose, by bringing into mimetic contact the narrator's painful reading of the key-words in Aimé's letter (and subsequent resuscitating rhyme-memories in later prose passages) and a reader's own reading of his narration of these processes.

It is clear that we need to be especially careful to avoid arbitrary selectivity of phoneme repetition within Proust's long sentences, themselves embedded in the immensely long tracts of Proust's novel. One way of doing so is by observing Proust's own very carefully planned series of alerting-devices. Proust, in the two rhyming instances discussed above, uses the full panoply of devices outlined in the Introduction. There is word-repetition ('corps'-'cœur'-'corps' in the parenthetical instance, 'cœur' in the Aimé letter instance); prose-density signalled by straight rhyme and very heavy phoneme repetitions and stress-lines; motif-terms, 'mémoire' and 'cœur'; self-referential subject-matter (both instances are talking about the secret communication system created between tiny verbal details within the memory); both show traces of 'purple' writing (jealousy as ghoul, the fires of hell) which alert the reader to pay particular attention to Proust's complex comic distance from the melodramatic emphases of his narrator's verbal memory.

With all these alerting-devices in play, I believe a reader should slow down his or her reading speed, semi-articulate the words within the mind, weigh each word as the prose rhymes accumulate, and begin to hear the dramatic emphases in the narrator's printed voice. But first, before analysing in greater detail Proust's own prose rhyme mnemonic technique, I shall prove how crucial acoustic details were to Proust, and the lengths he went to in order to ground true poetic prose within his own very exacting ethical system.

Self-Appeasement, Mourning, and Poetic Prose

The narrator, meeting Albertine for the first time at Balbec, and afterwards amongst the 'jeunes filles en fleurs', henceforth associates her with the sea. The image of her profile against the sea, like some medieval tapestry, is a constant marker of how far, and how variously, the different Albertines have altered throughout the novel, yet the sea, as an image, persists in the rhythm and details of the narrator's immediate perceptions of her, his descriptions of her effect on him. In fact, in his mind she *becomes* the sea, as in this sentence where 'au bord de son lit' is comically substituted for 'au bord de la mer': 'J'allai m'asseoir au bord de son lit pour faire cette cure calmante de brise et de contemplation' (iii. 862). The 'sea-breeze—sleeping breath' metaphor—begins earlier on in 'La Prisonnière'.

Albertine is imprisoned in his apartment, deep asleep, and, hearing her breath rise and fall, he rejoices in his possession of her:

J'écoutais cette murmurante émanation mystérieuse, douce comme un zéphir marin, féerique comme ce clair de lune, qu'était son sommeil [. . .] Ce que j'éprouvais alors, c'était un amour devant quelque chose d'aussi pur, d'aussi immatériel, d'aussi mystérieux que si j'avais été devant les créatures inanimées que sont les beautés de la nature. [. . .] Son sommeil mettait à mes côtés quelque chose d'aussi calme, d'aussi sensuellement délicieux que ces nuits de pleine lune, dans la baie de Balbec devenue douce comme un lac, où les branches bougent à peine; où, étendu sur le sable, l'on écouterait sans fin se briser le reflux. (iii. 578–9)

The prose rises and falls in the first two sentences to the rhythm of the word 'mer', its syllables breaking softly amongst the words along the stress-lines.

The last sentence resolves into a repeated rhythmical figure, a six-syllable phrase, that mimes the endless 'reflux':

> quelque chose d'aussi calme [. . .]
> que ces nuits de pleine lune
> dans la baie de Balbec

devenue douce comme un lac
où les branches bougent à peine
où, étendu sur le sable [minor elision]

Proust's prose approximates as closely as it ever does in this passage to bad poetry ; 'cette murmurante émanation mystérieuse' descends to the level of pulp anthology alliteration, the similes ('zéphir marin', 'clair de lune') worthy of Emma Bovary on a sad day, the alexandrine hemistich repetitions clumsy Chateaubriand pastiche (the 'Balbec'-'lac' hiccup is finely comic). I believe Proust is thinking in terms of pastiche here, pastiche of mass cultural reproductions of high Romantic rhetoric. The passage is perfectly judged in context. Being free to impose his imagination on Albertine's captive body, the narrator is free in his composition; only we find his free composition is held strictly within the narrow and banal limits, not only of cultural cliché, but also of the expectations produced by his wishful, callow fantasizing about the slave woman within him, fantasizing summoned by the hypnotically stress-lined word 'mer'.

This is not to say that later in this section there are not passages of a quite different quality, sentences that are suddenly shocked into an intimate simplicity:

son haleine venant expirer sur ses lèvres, à intervalles intermittents et réguliers, comme un reflux, mais plus assoupi et plus doux. Et au moment où mon oreille recueillait ce bruit divin, il me semblait que c'était, condensée en lui, toute la personne, toute la vie de la charmante captive, étendue là sous mes yeux. (iii. 579)

But the simplicity sustains the tone of the pastiche, a naïve, childish wonder at having something all to oneself combined with the accent of a proprietor's proud greed. The lyricism here appropriates and binds the body to the narrow limits of the voice's desire. It has something of the morbid, self-circling luxuriance of Baudelaire's 'La Chevelure', whose startling 'analogies inspiratrices' are later described by Proust as having been discovered 'avec plus de choix et de paresse', 'volontairement' (iv. 498).[4] The combination

---

[4] Indeed, the narrator literally does enthuse over Albertine's hair with a deliberately wild and lazily aesthetic analogy: 'parfois une mèche isolée et droite donnait le même effet de perspective que ces arbres lunaires grêles et pâles qu'on aperçoit tout droits au fond des tableaux raphaëlesques d'Elstir' (iii. 579). The drawling

of laziness and willed desire both permits a loose lyricism to govern the syntax whilst narrowing lyrical possibilities down to serve the purposes of an intense rage to possess. In hearing the soft, monotonous returns of Albertine's breath in the rhythm of the prose, one can hear, as the mannerisms accumulate, the steady pant of the narrator's indolent desire to be appeased, the over-regular returns of his imaginary 'tonalité du bonheur' (iii. 229).

The narrator's delight in possessing Albertine is, in a subtle but vital sense, an appeasement of the conflict between his own memory and her mysterious memories and desires. The fictions generated by his dwelling upon her hidden histories are the main resource of his jealousy, a process consciously modelled on his own twice-told memories of the way Swann's mind had been deranged.[5] Albertine asleep frees him from those crippling fictions, gives him moments of peace from the strict application of Swann's story to his own jealous imagination. Albertine asleep 'avait rappelé à soi tout ce qu'elle était en dehors, elle s'était réfugiée, enclose, résumée, dans son corps [. . .] Sa vie m'était soumise, exhalait vers moi son léger souffle' (iii. 578). This gathering in of the self into the body ('rappelé') strips her of her concealed and dangerous memories ('se rappeler'), and the narrator is appeased ('ce même calme apaisant que la nature' (iii. 581)).

This appeasement rhymes exactly with what he seeks for in her waking life with his interrogation of her unknown memories—his strange love for her is driven by need, 'son besoin de douceur et son refuge vers un souvenir paisible, apaisant, où l'on voudrait se tenir et ne plus rien apprendre de celle qu'on aime' (iii. 584). Having Albertine before him asleep gives him the simulacrum of this 'souvenir paisible, apaisant', because he possesses her so entirely, and because sleep has withdrawn all of Albertine's uncontrollable and mysterious memories into pure body. This simulated 'souvenir paisible' gives the narrator's voice free rein to arrange its own accents into formal, lyrical patterns devoid of the emotional accents of plausible remembering. For the narrator has disengaged himself from his own memory in order to bathe himself in this artificial world of mimic 'souvenir paisible'. He has entered the

---

pretentiousness of the prose-rhyme string along 'grêles'- 'pâles'-'raphaël' gives the pseudo-Baudelairian tone away.

[5] For an example of the narrator's self-conscious uses of the Swann–Odette story, cf. iii. 228.

mystic world of the Symbolistes and cut off his language from its remembered relations. Proust judges the artifice and wilfulness of the result.

The first draft of the narrative relating to the death of the grand-mother, particularly the section that deals with how her breath is altered by morphine and oxygen, seems to have the Albertine sea-resemblance in mind. The passages quoted appear as they do in the first typed version of the draft: the corresponding passage as finally published is the paragraph beginning 'Il me semblait', pages 639–40, volume ii of the 1987 Tadié-edited Pléiade edition:

Mais la plainte heureuse s'élancait toujours légère, tourmentée, inache-vée, élancée, recommencante. Comme on dit que tel architecte gothique s'inspira de la vue de la forêt, que tel musicien essaya de reproduire le rythme de la mer ou du vent, je ne sais si Wagner a assisté à une telle mort, et a essayé de reproduire la véritable mélodie que ce bruit pourtant naturel—la mort ayant [libéré] au milieu d'une chambre une puissance naturelle, aveugle, sans signification comme la mer, ou le vent, la où était avant une personne. Mais c'étaient les élans, les chants, surtout l'éternel recommencement, comme l'incessant besoin de respirer, de la mort d'Yseult. (ii. 1208, *Esquisse XXV*, 'L'Agonie'; cf. also typescript version, ii. 1708, note for p. 640)[6]

The Wanger sentence survived into the proofs (placed after 'effusion') as:

Si Wagner a jamais assisté à une telle mort, lui qui a fait entrer dans sa musique tant de rythmes de la nature et de la vie, du reflux de la mer au martèlement du cordonnier, des coups du forgereon au chant d'oiseau, on peut croire, s'il a jamais assisté à une telle mort, qu'il en a dégagé, pour les éterniser dans la mort d'Yseult, les inexhaustibles recommencements. (ii. 1709, note to p. 640)

All that remains in the published edition is the revised first phrase of the first draft: 'Mais la plainte heureuse de la respiration jaillis-sait toujours, légère, tourmentée, inachevée, sans cesse recommen-çante.' (ii. 639) The consonance with Albertine's sleeping breath seems clear—'une puissance naturelle, aveugle, sans signification comme la mer, ou le vent'—and one can understand Proust's reasons for setting the relation up. The narrator first goes to Balbec with his grandmother; her influence on him alternates with

---

[6] The transcriptions of Proust's first drafts in the Tadié-edited Pléiade edition's 'esquisses' and notes and variants have been double-checked against the microfilm holdings at the Bibliothèque Nationale in Paris. Microfilm 619, 1st section, 35.

Albertine's on his second visit there, particularly her involuntary resurrection and his sudden mourning for her as I shall later discuss.

Other indications that survive into the final version hint at the same conceptual rhyme. When the oxygenated breath halts for a few seconds, one of the narrator's possible explanations for the change runs, 'soit par ces même changements d'octaves qu'il y a dans la respiration d'un dormeur'. Both breaths are described as pure song, as a fluid, and both are compared to wind through a reed: 'l'haleine, insensible comme celle du vent dans la flûte d'un roseau' (ii. 636), 'haleine tirée plutôt d'un roseau creusé que d'un être humain' (iii. 621). Both sections speak of the breaths simultaneously as something less than and more than human. Why then did Proust revise his draft and proofs to erase the Wagner sentence, and what in essence is the difference between the two breaths? I believe the difference will explain the revision. The difference concentrates on the limits imposed by the pathos of the scene on the narrator's own inflections.

On the train to Balbec with his grandmother, the narrator does not realize that she is very ill—this later becomes the source of real anguish on his second visit after her death when he recalls his careless indifference to her heroic attempts to conceal her pain from him. He begins to talk, though her illness makes attention impossible: his ignorance of this makes this passage a painful one to read:

Alors je lui parlais, mais cela ne semblait pas lui être agréable. Et à moi pourtant ma propre voix me donnait du plaisir, et de même les mouvements les plus insensibles, les plus intérieurs de mon corps. Aussi je tâchais de les faire durer, je laissais chacune de mes inflexions s'attarder longtemps aux mots, je sentais chacun de mes regards se trouver bien là où il s'était posé et y rester au delà du temps habituel. 'Allons, repose-toi', me dit ma grand-mère. (ii. 13)

The sensations the narrator feels on the train suggest the self-brooding pleasures in his own voice and 'regards' that he had imposed on the sleeping body of Albertine. Proust is presenting an object-lesson in the techniques of bad poetic prose as much as an example of egotistical tactlessness; he in fact suggests they are the same thing. The narrator's deliberate mimicking to excess of Bergotte's accent ('je laissais chacune de mes inflexions s'attarder longtemps aux mots' recalling 'dans sa prose il mettait ces mots aimés en lumière' (i. 543)) carelessly forgets the implications of the word 'aimés'. The run on a in the first two sentences ('parlais', 'cela', 'pas', 'agréable', 'à moi', 'ma', 'voix'), coupled with the m-string in the second ('moi', 'ma', 'même', 'mouvements', 'mon'), reveal the phonemes of 'moi' being distributed into stress-lines in the local phonolinguistic context. This not only makes 'moi' into a key-word but stresses the monotonous predominance of the self-ish voice and its connection with repeated figures of sound in the narrator's prose.[7]

It is this intrusiveness, this lazy wilfulness of the inattentive voice that the revisions of the first draft of ii. 639–40 tried to eradicate. By so doing, Proust found himself revising passages that were too self-consciously alliterative, as though recognizing the possible identity between over-rich 'rimes intérieures' and self-delight in 'les mouvements les plus intérieurs de mon corps'. For instance he revised out of his draft the phrase 'La plainte de sa respiration semblait à ce moment l'expression passionnée, déses-perée, déchirante de douceur, de ses derniers adieux'. (ii. 1708; note to p. 640) The gracelessness of such overburdened prose is ethical as well as stylistic, converting the grandmother's 'plainte' into the narrator's own echoing-box. In withdrawing the sea-reference and the Wagner allusion, Proust withdraws the narrator's inflections and thus his own too detached purposes. Noticing the similarity between the grandmother's breath and Isolde's dying song forces our attention upon Proust hearing Wagner, a tactless aside as though Charlus had just strolled into the vigil. Presenting the grandmother's and Albertine's voice too obviously as identities would accomplish the same 'faux pas', introducing upon the scene an accent that stresses 'l'allégresse du fabricateur' (iii. 667).

---

[7] There is an interesting analogy to the narrator's selfish voice and its 'ma voix' sound-repetitions in the first paragraph of Péguy's *Clio*, where the muse of History boasts of her own past power:

J'ai fait, dit-elle (comme) soucieuse, et se parlant à elle-même tout en com-mençant de m'adresser la parole; ruminante en soi-même; mâchant des paroles de ses vieilles dents historiques; marmottante; marmonnante; mâ-chonnante; soucieuse, ayant pris soudain un air sérieux, comme pour de rire, les sourcils froncés, le front froncé, j'ai fait ce travail moi-même. [. . .] Faire une recherche, faire des recherches, mots voluptueux; tout pleins, tout gonflés des promesses ultérieures [. . .] Mots voluptueux, tout pleins des mémoires, tout pleins des souvenirs, tout gonflés des anciennes promesses, des voluptés anciennes, des anciennes promesses (à développement) ulté-rieures. (Péguy, Charles, 'Clio, Dialogue de l'histoire et de l'âme paienne', in *Œuvres complètes* (15 vols., Paris, 1925), vii–viii. 9–10).

Another revison acts in much the same way, removing an identity that only stresses the narrator's 'propre voix'. The grandmother, in the first draft, was described sucking at the oxygen-cylinders, 'la bouche suspendue à cet air délicieux comme un enfant qui tèterait' (ii. 1207, *Esquisse xxv*). This too consciously recalls the narrator's description of himself kissing his grandmother's cheeks in Balbec:

je suspendis mes lèvres à sa figure comme si j'accédais ainsi à ce cœur immense qu'elle m'ouvrait. Quand j'avais ainsi ma bouche collée à ses joues, à son front, j'y puisais quelque chose de si bienfaisant, de si nourricier, que je gardais l'immobilité, le sérieux, la tranquille avidité d'un enfant qui tète. (ii. 28)

He is able to feel that in Balbec because of his grandmother's overwhelming love for him; the image returning at the death-bed twists his memory of that selflessness into an egotistical parody.

Proust's revisions, then, remove a texture of reminiscence that suggest a mind at work upon itself alone. Bergotte's accents had been grounded in remembered family inflections. The narrator by mimicking Bergotte on the train divorces his voice from such a grounding—he forgets his grandmother and concentrates on his solitary voice alone. Just as having Albertine asleep before him had given the narrator a simulacrum of a 'souvenir paisible' which is actually cut off from his and Albertine's real memories, so his voice takes the same delight in itself precisely at the time it cuts itself off from the real relations it should attend to. The 'rimes intérieures' in these instances signal the egotistical self-idolatry of a voice made pure artifice, divorced from its memory of the affections that make it human. In revising the Wagner passage from the grandmother's death, Proust removes this self-circling voice of artifical memory from the scene.

The sea as an abiding metaphor for the natural and supernatural voice within the body, in that it had become associated with Albertine and self-appeasing poetic prose , had equally to be revised out of the text relating the grandmother's dying. Later, in *Sodome et Gommorrhe*, this point is clarified at Balbec again when the narrator suffers violent 'intermittences du cœur' between his suddenly discovered sense of loss for his grandmother and his growing dependence on Albertine. Lying in the dunes to avoid Albertine, he closes his eyes and bathes himself in the rose light of his eyelids:

Puis elles se fermèrent tout à fait. Alors ma grand-mère m'apparut assise dans un fauteuil. Si faible, elle avait l'air de vivre moins qu'une autre personne. Pourtant je l'entendais respirer; parfois un signe montrait qu'elle avait compris ce que nous disions, mon père et moi. Mais j'avais beau l'embrasser, je ne pouvais pas arriver à éveiller un regard d'affection dans ses yeux, un peu de couleur sur ses joues. (iii. 175)

The language is simple, moving out of Proust's rhyming style (registered in the light way the phonemes of 'fermèrent' can be heard in stress-lines up to 'personne') into unadorned prose. Though the narrator is dreaming by the sea, its sounds are not heard. All the narrator hears is his grandmother's breath—'je l'entendais respirer'—and all he sees is the odd sign that she can understand what he and his father are saying. His father is there, we suspect, because he had shown himself coldly detached and indifferent at the grandmother's death-bed (as the ensuing dialogue in the dream shows). The dream concentrates the narrator's deep anxiety over his past carelessness in Balbec, and his terror of sudden isolation from his grandmother's powers of affection. The prose, in its lack of movement, of complex life, has contracted to the curt, cold rhythms of the dreamt father's accent: '—Que veux-tu, les morts sont les morts.' Though he hears her breathe, her breath does not move the prose.

Two paragraphs later, he has decided he can see Albertine again. In this mood, he walks along the shore and an orchestra strikes up on the promenade—the sound of the 'concert' alternates with the sound of the sea:

montant doucement, la mer, à chaque déferlement de lame recouvrait complètement de coulées de cristal la mélodie dont les phrases apparaissaient séparées les unes des autres, comme ces anges luthiers qui, au faîte de la cathédrale italienne, s'élèvent entre les crêtes de porphyre bleu et de jaspe écumant. (iii. 177)

The enamelled preciosity of this prose recalls Legrandin and Des Esseintes rather than Baudelaire. Again the melody of 'mer' runs the rhythm and rhyme, here so overtly as to reduce the prose to mumming. The m-string is suddenly replaced with as clotted a run on k, as though the musical phrases ('c' for 'concert') and the sea ('m' for 'mer') sound out their alternations. Masson patterns appear on apRe/ εs (apparaissaient-séparé-porphyre . . . jaspe . . .

écumant), lam (la mer-déferlement-lame-la mélodie), and mã. The final phrase 'les crêtes de porphyre bleu et de jaspe écumant' is a perfect prose alexandrine,[8] book-ended by 'rhyme'-words: 'crêtes' with 'faîte' and 'cathédrale'; 'ecumant' with 'comme ces anges luthiers' and the mã.-run. The clever self-consciousness of this mimetic *tour de force* wedded to the smart *della Robbia* analogy (reinforced by the 'faîte'-'crête' rhyme), betray a suspiciously aesthetic joy in anticipation of meeting Albertine, little removed from a sense of release from the sombre restrictions, and inflections, of his anxious day-dreams over his grandmother. He has returned into the 'paresse' and 'volonté' of his own voice, 'il lève la crête' (58).

The next moment he is crestfallen—with Proust's fine comic timing, the next sentence runs: 'Mais le jour où Albertine vint, le temps s'était de nouveau gâté et refraichi, et d'ailleurs je n'eus pas l'occasion d'entendre son rire: elle était de fort mauvaise humeur.' The sound of the sea and the music of the narrator's artificial joy is replaced by our sigh of relief at some poetic justice.

The two proses contrasted on the shore at Balbec, the bare, unadorned prose of the narrator's isolation from tender feeling (deaf to the sea), the unnaturally laden and perfumed prose of self-willed artifice (sea-sick), stand at the two extremes of Proust's ethical stylistics. The question still remains, what prose attends the death of the grandmother? Wagner and the sea were removed to direct the style away from the porphyritic prose associated with Albertine and the narrator's 'paresse'. And yet it is not unadorned. There is long and complex phrasing with subtle acoustic effects. To get close to the prose necessitates a slight detour to examine briefly the narrator's deep, contradictory feelings for his grandmother.

After her death, when galvanized into a sudden recognition of her eternal absence, the shock and the accompanying involuntary memory also gives him the strongest feeling of her life. His mind then alternates between gentle memories of her and the bare fact that he will never see her again. Proust's prose adopts the movingly unadorned style:

Puis les doux souvenirs me revenaient. Elle était ma grand-mère et j'étais son petit-fils. Les expressions de son visage semblaient écrites dans une

---

[8] i.e. without the poetic convention that demands that mute 'e's before consonants be sounded.

langue qui n'était que pour moi; elle était tout dans ma vie, les autres n'existaient que relativement à elle, au jugement qu'elle me donnerait sur eux; mais non, nos rapports ont été trop fugitifs pour n'avoir pas été accidentels. Elle ne me connaît plus, je ne la reverrai jamais. Nous n'avions pas été créés uniquement l'un pour autre, c'était une étrangère. (iii. 172)

It is as though the narrator has suddenly heard the fugitive, unbearable truth of those imperfects as he shifts through the perfect into the present and future. The crux of the pain he suffers in the transition is in the complex contrast beween 'une langue qui n'était que pour moi' and 'c'était une étrangère': on the one hand, a language so intimately, natively his, bonded to his mind by his grandmother's absolute selfless devotion to him, that it is the pure language of irreducible particular tenderness; at the other extreme, a stranger so foreign as to lack a language. This violent alternation between absence and presence, hinting at the extremes of written and spoken communication, is the terrible machine the narrator's mourning is powered by that pushes his prose to the parallel extremes of absolute sentimentality ('une tendresse [. . .] où tout trouvait tellement en moi son complément') and absolute bare, unadorned descriptions of pain ('une douleur physique à répétition' (iii. 155)). Unlike his relations with Albertine, however, there is no hint, ever, that the sentimental prose might be self-absorbed or that the unadorned style might merely signal withdrawal of affection. For the strange contradiction in the narrator's feelings of mourning had been played out in the narrator's relationship with his grandmother *before* her death.

He hears her voice over the telephone. Though the 'isolement de la voix' stresses his physical isolation from her, what he receives, unadulterated, purified, is their mutual tenderness:

Elle était douce, mais aussi comme elle était triste, d'abord à cause de sa douceur même, presque décantée, plus que peu de voix humaines ont jamais dû l'être, de toute dureté, de tout élément de résistance aux autres, de tout égoïsme; fragile à force de délicatesse, elle semblait à tout moment prête à se briser, à expirer en un pur flot de larmes [. . .] ce que j'avais sous cette petite cloche approchée de mon oreille, c'était, débarrassé des pressions opposées qui chaque jour lui avaient fait contrepoids, et dès lors irrésistible, me soulevant tout entier, notre mutuelle tendresse. (ii. 433–4)

Here is the perfect example of Bergotte's accent: 'douce' moving the prose around itself with the soft dy/u stress-lines, mollifying 'dureté' into a word within the soft returns of its force, 'tendresse' taking up and transforming the hissing weight of 'débarrassée des pressions opposés'. This is the soft, gentle tongue 'qui n'était que pour moi', her voice alone sounding out as pure accent, free of the weight of the body, 'pur flot de larmes'. The sea is not here, only the flow of sweet tears, pure voice, liquid and moving.

This experience is succeeded, immediately, by the sudden revelation of her as 'une étrangère'. He is present at his own absence[9] and sees her, for an instant, before his 'intelligente et pieuse tendresse' has time to alter the body to suit the softened, gentler image of the habitual eye:

moi pour qui ma grand-mère c'était encore moi-même, moi qui ne l'avais jamais vue que dans mon âme, toujours à la même place du passé, à travers la transparence des souvenirs contigus et superposés, tout d'un coup, dans notre salon qui faisait partie d'un monde nouveau, celui du Temps, celui où vivent les étrangers dont on dit 'il vieillit bien', pour la première fois et seulement pour un instant car elle disparut bien vite, j'aperçus sur le canapé, sous la lampe, rouge, lourde et vulgaire, malade, rêvassant, promenant au-dessus d'un livre des yeux un peu fous, une vieille femme accablée que je ne connaissais pas. (ii. 439–40)

The prose departs from the accent of feeling into harsh, shocked rhythms as the image flashes onto his memory and slowly develops. The delicate phrase-end half-rhymes 'moi-même'-'mon âme', 'passé'-'superposés' picking up stress-line phonemes in 'même', 'transparence' and 'place', seem to remember a lyrical past, a lyric even—the first two phrases both of alexandrine length, a prose couplet; the rhythmical identity of 'toujours à la même place du passé' and 'contigus et superposés'. This is replaced by the short-breathed, gasping rhythms of the rest of the sentence, after the cruel blow of 'tout d'un coup', ungraced by rhyme or 'soft' sound-stresses, each cruel adjective rising and accumulating the dark stresses of unaccommodated shock. The weight of her body, its age, the foreignness of her voiceless presence, has stripped the narrator of all the memory of her accent, of the intimately native and personal language he had heard over the telephone, leaving him in a foreign tongue where his prose cannot talk of her.

[9] This is Beckett's phrase. *Proust and Three Dialogues* (London, 1965), 15.

It is one of the great thoughts of the novel, the rhyme between shock at the body unaccommodated and the reality of death, between the intimacy of a living voice alone and the tender memory of a loved one dead. That thought, instanced in the narrator's experiences before and after his grandmother's death, rises into a question: how can those two experiences, those two languages, voicelessly foreign and natively voiced, ever meet, and what would the prose be like that took them up together? One would suppose it needed a miracle.

The miracle happens, *during* her death. The oxygen and morphine, in modifying the dying breath of the grandmother, alter it into pure song, music, accent, flowing, musical, tender, detached, and yet her body is there. The effect on the 'petit-fils' is overwhelming:

Quand je rentrai, je me trouvai comme devant un miracle. Accompagnée en sourdine par un murmure incessant, ma grand-mère semblait nous adresser un long chant heureux qui remplissait la chambre, rapide et musical. (ii. 635)

The narrator understands that the effect is 'purement mécanique' and that she is unconscious of it. It is drug-induced, and the result of the change of register in the breathing brought about by the oxygen. But this understanding hears her still in the miracle, the mechanical is taken up into the feeling of real transformation:

Dégagé par la double action de l'oxygène et de la morphine, le souffle de ma grand-mère ne peinait plus, ne geignait plus, mais vif, léger, glissait, patineur, vers le fluide délicieux. Peut-être à l'haleine, insensible comme celle du vent dans la flûte d'un roseau, se mêlait-il dans ce chant quelques-uns de ces soupirs plus humains qui, libérés à l'approche de la mort, font croire à des impressions de souffrance ou de bonheur chez ceux qui déjà ne sentent plus, et venaient ajouter un accent plus mélodieux, mais sans changer son rythme, à cette longue phrase qui s'élevait, montait encore, puis retombait, pour s'élancer de nouveau de la poitrine allégée, à la poursuite de l'oxygène. Puis, parvenu si haut, prolongé avec tant de force le chant, mêlé d'un murmure de supplication dans la volupté, semblait à certains moments s'arrêter tout à fait comme une source s'épuise. (ii. 636)

Description of what these two sentences are and do is startlingly close to what they make us imagine the narrator sees and hears.

From a drugged old woman attached to oxygen-cylinders rises a song: from a sentence beginning with the cold mechanical facts ('Dégagé par le double action de l'oxygène et de la morphine') and the banal rhythms of aging pathos ('le souffle de ma grand-mère ne peinait plus, ne geignait plus') rises the strange Mallarméan lyricism of 'mais vif, léger, glissait, patineur, vers le fluide délicieux'. The subtle l-run (Masson pattern running illi-illi-li), the way the phrase 'vers le fluide délicieux' picks up so many of the sounds of the first comma-strung phrases, how the adjectives, verb, and noun set up a rhythm in the first four breaths that is reproduced in one by the rest, reinforced by the phrase-end consonance in '-eur' and '-ieux', create a music that is the perfect mimesis of a breath catching itself higher and higher to finally flow, but goes beyond that. The breath becomes, through such rhythmical, acoustic effects, the fluid it seeks and breathes. The two halves of the phrase take each other's substance up in mirroring flow. The first four-beat rhythm makes the noun and verb momentarily sound like adjectives and then vice-versa, as though what the breath is, does and is like become one and the same thing. And yet those predicates are momentarily as solid as an active substance; 'patineur', so miraculously condensed to itself alone from the draft 'glissante comme quelqu'un qui patine' (ii. 1207, *Esquisse xxv*),[10] for an instant freezes the fluid to solid ice then melts as soon to a figure of speed, like the substance of its status as a noun. The lyricism of this phrase, remembering the sentences that preceded it,[11] mechanical and pathetic, is a lyricism precise about the sound it describes and the detail of the medical operation of which it is the result. It also describes with a breath-taking complexity and theological exactitude, how a soul might escape its body and the relation of a soul to the body that incarnates it. And, also, the relation of the sound of a Proustian sentence to its meaning.

The whole passage quoted organizes itself around a long assonantal stress-line that connects 'chant' with 'accent': 'insensible', 'vent', 'chant', 'souffrance', 'sentent', 'accent', 'sans charger', 's'élancer', 'tant', 'chant', 'semblait', 'moments', reinforced by high frequencies in s, z, and ʃ. The stress-line confirms 'accent' and

---

[10] Microfilm, first section, p. 33.

[11] It shares two lines of repeated sound with the words preceding it: an ɛpɛ Masson pattern (from 'grand-mère' to 'vers') and a ʒɛ/e stress-line ('dégagé' to 'léger').

'chant' as the key-words in the sentence, the key-words in the grandmother's breath. The 'accent' the novel as a whole spends such time seeking, is here at its most refined; 'accent' returns to its etymological root-source, 'cantus'. Yet it is a song that carries within itself the mundanities of suffering and the modern world, in the minutiae of its rhythms and cause. It is one of Proust's finest songs and describes how his prose, at such heights, should be attended to. The grandmother's long phrase, her human sigh merging with the rhythm of the strange atmosphere she has been given, is Proust's too, with his accent, his feeling breath adding 'un accent plus mélodieux' to the rising falling phrase of breath, musical with the possibilities of suffering and happiness within it, releasing its song as though each sentence were the last.[12] The grandmother's breath, in becoming pure flow ('déjà, comme si un affluent venait apporter son tribut au courant asséché, un nouveau chant s'embranchait à la phrase interrompue' (ii. 639-40)), in becoming pure song at the moment of death, miraculously fuses the violent extremes of experience her grandson felt and will feel into one. She is there and not there, close to death and yet intimately in the air, both pure voice and body alone, creating a prose that runs not to the sea or the lack of it, but to the simple and concentrated flow of a river within the earth.

This pure natural voice of tenderness, heard on the telephone before her death, remembered suddenly after it, is itself both recalled and transformed in the oxygenated breath of the grandmother dying. It purely re-establishes absolute contacts between memory and heart with its deep familial singing accent. And yet it rises from the body of her, at first sight divorced, as absolutely, from such accents, purely foreign body. And this voice, detached from her conscious control and yet human with her, gives itself to the people she loves:

[12] Proust's description of the grandmother's death achieves a prose-style that remembers and answers a letter his mother sent him on the death of his grandmother. Madame Proust had then quoted this passage from Pierre Loti's *Roman d'un enfant* (ch. V):

Et je voudrais, pour la première apparition de cette figure bénie dans le livre de souvenir, la saluer avec des mots à part, si c'était possible, avec des mots qui, à eux seuls, feraient couler des larmes bienfaisantes, auraient je ne sais quelle douceur de consolation. (Madame Proust à Marcel, 23 Apr. 1890 (*Correspondance*, ed, Kolb, i. 136)).

This style can be read the way Madame Proust read Marcel's letters—'je sens très bien ton pouls et ton style battre trop vite' (Madame Proust à Marcel, Sept. 1889 (*Correspondance*, ed. Kolb, i. 128-9)).

Qui sait si, sans même que ma grand-mère en eût conscience, tant d'états heureux et tendres comprimés par la souffrance ne s'échappaient pas d'elle maintenant comme ces gaz plus légers qu'on refoula longtemps? On aurait dit que tout ce qu'elle avait à nous dire s'épanchait, que c'était à nous qu'elle s'adressait avec cette prolixité, cet empressement, cette effusion. (ii. 640)

Proust's sentences are prolix for these same reasons, when they rise to the cruces the novel hoped to capture. They are rich with the song and accent of his feeling for the memories and inflections of others, the accents given to the interior lives of his people. The music along the words, in the 'rimes intérieures', minister to their stresses in his native language made foreign by their presence, and at times, as at the grandmother's death-bed, this strange medium is humanized into an accent that goes beyond such service and gives of itself. The text, with its assorted memories and motifs, becomes pure voice transformed into the accents at the heart of memory, the accent of memory's heart.

Prose Facsimiles and Musical Acts of Remembering

It was Jean Milly who, in 1975, first proposed that how Bergotte's style is described in the novel provides valuable evidence towards an understanding of the first principles of Proust's style. His 'prose cadencée' exerts a powerful influence over the young narrator whose first piece of writing is a 'poème en prose' (i. 447).[13] This prose poem and Bergotte's work are sneeringly dismissed by Norpois as 'maniérisme' and 'afféterie' (i. 464), effeminately trifling with trivial subjects, blown out of all proportion by pretentious mandarin overwriting. The style is fatally flawed by 'ce contresens d'aligner des mots bien sonores en ne souciant qu'ensuite du fond' (i. 465). The narrator's admiration for Bergotte, formerly like a 'fluide',[14] contracts, with shame, to the tight limits of Norpois's criticism.

[13] (i. 447)—'un petit poème en prose que j'avais fait autrefois à Combray en revenant d'une promenade'.
[14] (i. 466)—his mind 'contracté maintenant, tenait tout entier dans la mediocrité étroite où M. de Norpois l'avait soudain enfermé et restreint'. The narrator is locked into an ugly clatter of 't'-sounds here, neatly turning Norpois' criticism on its head.

But his admiration is won over again when he hears Bergotte speak at Swann's house, and feels he can detect traces of his special literary intonation in his pronunciation,

certain éclairage qui dans ses livres [. . .] modifie souvent dans la phrase écrite l'apparence des mots [. . .] accent indépendant de la beauté du style, que l'auteur lui-même n'a pas perçu sans doute, car il n'est pas séparable de sa personnalité la plus intime. C'est cet accent qui aux moments où dans ses livres, Bergotte était entièrement naturel, rythmait les mots souvent alors fort insignifiants qu'il écrivait. Cet accent n'est pas noté dans le texte, rien ne l'y indique et pourtant il s'ajoute de lui-même aux phrases, on ne peut pas les dire autrement, il est ce qu'il y avait de plus éphémère et pourtant de plus profond chez l'écrivain et c'est cela qui portera témoignage sur sa nature, qui dira si, malgré toutes les duretés qu'il a exprimées il était doux, malgré toutes les sensualités, sentimental. (i. 543)

This literary accent, bearing witness to feelings unacknowledged in the words, rhymes clearly with the revealing intonations of the jealous voice. As 'toutes les duretés' resolves into 'était doux', 'sensualités' into 'sentimental', so the words spoken in rational recollection by the narrator are roused by the hidden impulses of other rhythms, other feelings 'intérieurs à sa prose, décelés seulement alors par les ondulations de la surface' (i. 94).[15] These surface waves across the words do not, however, act as the mere proof of a presence. They work with the deepest concerns of the narrator, emphasizing key-words, miming their importance with the shock waves of surrounding sound-repetitions.

Bergotte is a figure that acts as an *exemplum* of this strange procedure. There are two examples of Bergotte's style that particularly strike the narrator: one of his literary accent—'l'inépuisable torrent des belles apparences' (i. 93 and i. 542) (recalled above in 'l'apparence des mots')—and one of his special pronunciation—'visage' which he pronounces adding 'un grand nombre de *v*, d'*s*, de *g*, qui semblait tous exploser da sa main ouverte' (i. 543) (recalled in the prose rhymes). The written example shows how that accent is based on assonance and alliteration—the alternation of the b̲l̲ and ā sounds making the 'apparence des mots' move with the sense. The example of Bergotte's pronunciation emphasizes

---

[15] Eric Griffiths describes 'the cadential emphasis given here to one of [Proust's] favourite words, "doux", caught up in the lovely, characteristically mollifying chime of "toutes" and "duretés" with "était doux" '. (*The Printed Voice*, 93)

how the accent is closely related to phoneme repetition as supplementary emphasis.

His prose is also a music of key terms:

dans sa prose il mettait ces mots aimés en lumière, précédés d'une sorte
de marge et composés de telle façon dans le nombre total de la phrase,
qu'on était obligé, sous peine de faire une faute de mesure, d'y faire
compter toute leur 'quantité'. (i. 543)

As Jean Milly translates it, Bergotte's 'accent' 'tend à doter certains
mots placés en relief de marques phoniques recurrentes pouvant
suggérer un rapport avec le sens de ces mots ou avec le thème
traité' (*La Phrase de Proust*, 73). Bergotte's accent, then, is essentially
made up of prose rhymes that emphasize key-words through
recurrent phonemic marks. The 'marques phoniques' correspond
to runs and strings of recurring phonemes which readers
are asked to be sensitive to, the semi-metrical counting-game
that Proust argues the style demands of readers ('compter toute
leur "quantité" '). The manner in which the phonemic marks
surround 'certains mots placés en relief' corresponds to the way
runs become stress-lines through the agency of alerting-devices,
Proust's 'précédés d'une sorte de marge et composés de telle façon
dans le nombre total de la phrase'. The power of semantic suggestion ('pouvant suggérer un rapport avec le sens de ces mots ou
avec le thème traité') corresponds to the transformation of those
words into key terms by way of the stress-lines, Proust's 'mettait
ces mots aimés en lumière'.

This peculiar emphatic accent bears the traces, the narrator
finds, of a family trait, the inflections of the Bergotte brother and
sisters—'ces inflexions en quelque sorte familiales, tour à tour cris
de violente gaieté, murmures d'une lente mélancolie' (i. 544) which
Bergotte has transformed in his prose into 'cette façon de traîner
sur des mots qui se répètent en clameurs de joie ou qui s'égouttent
en tristes soupirs' (i. 544). Bergotte's accent, then, is a trained
transformation of the memory-traces of his family's speech-
accents. It is an inherited accent transformed to survive the fugitive nature of such fleeting intonational music. The major–minor
extremes of the Bergotte music can only be fixed by some distantly
analogous technique in prose. That technique is the sound-repetitious key-word stressing technique outlined above. The only
'music' words can have is in the arrangement of their sounds.

Proust, to underline this, describes Bergotte's dying falls with a musical analogy:

Il y a dans ses livres telles terminaisons de phrases où l'accumulation des sonorités qui se prolongent, comme aux derniers accords d'une ouverture d'opéra qui ne peut pas finir et redit plusieurs fois sa suprême cadence avant que le chef d'orchestre pose son bâton, dans lesquelles je retrouvai plus tard un équivalent musical de ces cuivres phonétiques de la famille Bergotte. (i. 544).

There is something brash and over-theatrical about the repeated strains of the Bergotte music. But there is also something in its power to dwell on key-words that recalls Swann's mesmerized admiration for a certain motif in the Vinteuil sonata, particularly the way motifs in general are only very fugitively perceived through the wash of abstract feelings aroused by the present action of the music.

They need a spectator's or reader's memory to reconstruct them, give them durable life, an intelligible structure:

Et cette impression continuerait à envelopper de sa liquidité et de son 'fondu' les motifs qui par instants en émergent, à peine discernables, pour plonger aussitôt et dispâraitre, connus seulement par le plaisir particulier qu'ils donnent, impossibles à décrire, à se rappeler, à nommer, ineffables—si la mémoire, comme un ouvrier qui travaille à établir des fondations durables au milieu des flots, en fabriquant pour nous des facsimilés de ces phrases fugitives, ne nous permettait de les comparer à celles qui leur succèdent et de les différencier. (i. 206)

As if to underline the heavy rhyme he wants between musical motifs and his own prose sound-effects, Proust thumps out a heavy assonantal stress-line of p and f strings. These are the phonetic facsimiles not of the Vinteuil motifs (as in traditional onomatopoeic imitation) but of *memory's refabrication of those motifs*.

Proust's prose rhymes, then, are facsimiles of the way memory absorbs and re-establishes key sounds, key-words, key points of vision, rhythm, and feeling. And it is because prose sound-effects are, by definition, fugitive that they work best as facsimiles of 'musical' acts of remembering.

This consonance Proust learned early on. The young Proust, in *Jean Santeuil*, was capable of using sound-effects for their powers

to mime memory relationships. The narrator, listening to Françoise playing the Saint-Saens sonata, reflects on the lovers' identification of the music with the 'tristesse' of life's passing:

le chagrin d'entendre que tout passe rendait plus profond le bonheur de
sentir leur amour durer. Ils entendaient que cette phrase passait, mais ils
la sentaient passer comme une caresse. (*Jean Santeuil*, 817).

The physical 'passing' of the sounds through the air is pun-
rhymed with their sense ('tout passe') and with their felt effect
('une caresse'). Whilst a-repetitions harmonize 'phrase' and 'la',[16]
s-repetitions tune 'sentir' and 'sentaient' into the rhymes. The
p-string ('passe [. . .] plus profond') rhythmically initiates voice-
breaks after 'sentir', 'durer', 'entendait', 'passait', 'passer' with the
double-stress sound of 'tout passe' being remembered. The whole
effect is one of hearing 'tout passe' passing through the words
along the stress-lines and registering the consequences (reverberating of the connotations of 'tout passe' in the memory) in emotional emphasis and sound. The music's caress is mimed whilst
the mental processes of the listener are captured—in the same
breath.

The Vinteuil sonata creates a similar 'musical equivalent' for
Swann:

[Swann] s'était rendu compte que c'était au faible écart entre les cinq notes
qui la composaient et au rappel constant de deux d'entre elles qu'était due
cette impression de douceur rétractée et frileuse (i. 343)

Here Proust wittily mimes the 'rappel constant' with the repeated
d's—de-deux-d'entre-due-de-douceur, backed up by the 'rappel'-
'elles' rhyme alerting-device. It would be impossible, however, to
say how precisely the spaces between five notes and constant
return of two of them gives such an impression of 'douceur rétractée et frileuse'. Except that, by this stage in Swann's relationship
with Odette, the sonata has become so intimately associated with
that relationship that even the mention of notes and silent spaces
alerts us to the powerful workings of intermittence in the affair,
the figure two to the two of them, the 'douceur' and the repeated
stress on the d-sound to how the ideal Odette might make him
feel. This might seem a drastic over-reading if the reader had not

---

[16] The French a and a vowel sounds are so close, they act as more than mere
half-assonances.

been primed throughout *Du côté de chez Swann* to understand the manner in which the sonata has incarnated Odette for Swann, beginning as an experience '*sine materia*' established then by memory into 'l'étendue, les groupements symétriques, la graphie, la valeur expressive' of the primary feeling or impression, and finally transformed into a phrase felt 'comme un amour inconnu' (i. 206), the 'déesse protectrice et confidente de son amour' (i. 342).

The parallel development of Swann's love and jealousy for Odette fattens the phrase out, giving it body and spirit, so that when Swann hears it at the Verdurins, the music has by then accrued a tightly necessitated meaning:

Le beau dialogue que Swann entendit entre le piano et le violon au commencement du dernier morceau! La suppression des mots humains, loin d'y laisser régner la fantaisie, comme on aurait pu croire, l'en avait éliminée; jamais le langage parlé ne fut si inflexiblement nécessité, ne connut à ce point la pertinence des questions, l'évidence des réponses. D'abord le piano solitaire se plaignit, comme un oiseau abandonné de sa compagne; le violon l'entendit, lui répondit comme d'un arbre voisin. C'était comme au commencement du monde, comme s'il n'y avait encore eu qu'eux deux sur la terre, ou plutôt dans ce monde fermé à tout le reste, construit par la logique d'un créateur et où ils ne seraient jamais que tous les deux: cette sonate. (i. 345–6)

The dialogue within Proust's own human words approximates as closely as a facsimile can to the clearly heard and seen communication between the two voices.[17] The 'commencement' of the piece shifts through Swann's strange comprehension of the questions and responses in the music into an image of paradise at the 'commencement' of the world through the repeated figure of analogy, 'comme', a paradise in which a voice sings for its lost 'compagne'. The responses, the recalls of 'comme', tell of the manner by which the sounds become allegory, the 'as if' of a passionate, remembering mind, whilst establishing that manner as a rhyming transformation.[18]

---

[17] A good general description of how sounds in prose 'approximate' is Alain Bosquet on *Saint-John Perse*: 'Parfois la rime et l'allitération se multiplient, involontaires mais nécessaires: elles insistent sur le sens ou sur l'idée, sans leur conférer de pouvoir fallacieux' (91).

[18] Established also by the nasal vowel-run that gathers round the repeated 'entendit' and climaxes on 'sonate' (which incidentally, by rhyming listening and

The rest of the passage aligns three phrases in a similar act of transforming recall: 'encore eu qu'eux deux', 'la logique d'un créateur', 'que tous les deux', that is a local K͜œ Masson pattern. 'They still alone' rhyming deep into creative logic, the phrases within 'la phrase' are touched into a 'rappel constant' of a creative wish. The phrase 'la pertinence des questions, l'évidence des réponses' mimes the dreamt-of complicity with the perfection of the Masson pattern (εiɑ̃s εɔ̃–eiɑ̃s eɔ̃s. This sonic complicity is echoed in the following sentence with Masson patterns in ɑ̃d, ab, waz ('oiseau'-'voisin'), the plε–lep and kɔm–kɔ̃–kɔm figures knitting the two instruments and their bird-like sounds together.

Music as such, sonority in language as such are both shown in parallel accruing the matter and weight of a passionate attention and its memories. When both articulate a complex of feeling and memory, there is no such thing as a figure of repetition, of rhyme, of musical repetition *sine materia*. Proust's formulation implies that such fugitive embodiments are never to be matched in 'le langage parlé'. But the rhymes match them fleetingly, ephemerally, within the same language that tells us before and after how intimately Swann's musical ear rings to the tune of an inward memory, resurrected from deep within him, the desire to possess the ghost he has made of Odette. The repetition of the notes, heard in the rhymes, is the anthem, not of their love, but of Swann's jealousy seeking incarnations within the features of his recurrent habitual memory. Swann's mind has turned through the same obsessive pattern, his past tastes, characteristics, social habits turned again and again back onto themselves to feed the feeling. The 'petite phrase', as elusively separated from his will, represents Odette alone magnified into a supernatural *revenante* captured by Vinteuil.[19] As parsed into minor details and figures, it represents a longed-for solitary unity of the two of them, the 'qu'eux deux' of the rhymes.

The rhymes are the accent of a dream of endless responses to the complaints of need. They are there, like the minute relations

its sound into 'sonate', brings out 'son' as the culminating stress). Such effects consciously bring Swann's listening to the music and a reader's registering of the rhymes into a rhyming relation.

[19] Swann interprets the musical signs of the 'petite phrase' as representations of a fairy creature (Odette transfigured); and then immediately reflects upon the 'signes apparents et menteurs' (i. 347) of Odette's regard for him.

between the five notes of the 'phrase', in the minutiae of the texture of the written phrase. The groupings and 'graphie' of Swann's own memory system have solidified into a fascimile version of its own goddess, a creature constructed out of musical repetitions, out of repeated jealous retracings of the possible shapes within *her* concealed memory system. Proust's prose rhymes fabricate just such a parallel system, the sound-resemblances of his double-singing prose miming the memory fabrications of his own constructed creature, Swann. Like the narrator's description of the secret effect of weather over time, the experience of memory's fabrications

agit profondément sur notre organisme et tire des réserves obscures où nous les avions oubliées les mélodies inscrites que n'a pas déchiffrées notre mémoire. Un rêveur plus conscient accompagna bientôt ce musicien que j'écoutais en moi, sans même avoir reconnu tout de suite ce qu'il jouait. (ii. 441).

Valéry's ventriloquist, Proust discovered, was a musician of sound-repetitions, accompanying the voice with the inflections of forgotten feeling.

The piano–violin passage so affects the narrator that, when retelling his reactions to Albertine's death, the memory of it filters into his sentences, as he tries to resist the dawn that announces another day without her:

Ce n'était plus assez de fermer les rideaux, je tâchais de boucher les yeux et les oreilles de ma mémoire, pour ne pas revoir cette bande orangée du couchant, pour ne pas entendre ces invisibles oiseaux qui se répondaient d'un arbre à l'autre de chaque côté de moi qu'embrassait alors si tendrement celle qui maintenant était morte. (iv. 62)

The responses of piano and violin find their painful correspondence in the dawn-chorus the narrator desperately tries to shut out of his mind. Shut out of his *memory* too: not only because of the associations the dawn has in his memory with the lost intimacy with Albertine, but because his mind has become pure memory in the isolation he suffers after her death; also because the birds sing the remembered tune of a paradise of united responses of man and woman, sing of Swann and Odette. That memory has its prose rhymes within this passage that bring memory ('ma mémoire') into contact with the self ('chaque côté de moi')—with 'revoir'

picked up along the a<u>R</u> stress-line—to stress the terrible consequence ('elle maintenant était morte'). The <u>m</u>-run corresponds to
the <u>m</u>-run in the passage narrating the 'beau dialogue' heard by
Swann, and painfully stresses the difference between Swann's
dream ('ce monde fermé à tout le reste') and the hopeless bereaved
isolation the narrator suffers ('ma chambre obscure' surrounded
by 'milles souvenirs invisibles qui à tout moment éclataitent autour de moi dans l'ombre' (iv. 61)). The 'souvenirs invisibles' articulate themselves as the 'oiseaux invisibles' that recall 'l'attelage
invisible' (i. 345) of piano and violin, stressing once again the
invisible Albertine at his side, just as the Vinteuil sonata had
summoned Odette for Swann. The comparison is tragic, Albertine's death darkening the connotations of 'invisible', making
memory a widower's grief. The motifs of musical response that
had been transformed into the 'comme'-motif in Swann's mind,
comparing memory with dream, are turned into the <u>m</u>-motif of the
narrator's bereavement, rhyming 'mémoire' with 'morte'.

The prose rhyme motifs, in Bergotte's 'accent', are musical in the
sense that they recall emotional material external to the movement
of the narrative voice, acting in some way as odd *da capo* markers
within the intonations of that voice, but *da capo* markers that are
simultaneously discordant accompaniments to the main melodic
line. This music ranges from the dark powers that assault the
narrator after Albertine's death to the traces of family inflections
in Bergotte's voice. This later 'music' is behind the reasons why
Proust sets up conscious rhymes between Bergotte's intonations,
the phrasing of the sonata, and his extended remarks on the 'génie'
of the Guermantes as manifested in voice: 'le génie de la famille se
faisait intonation' (ii. 733). The narrator's feel for the weight and
historical tremors within the ancient name of Guermantes begins,
as with Swann before the 'phrase', as something 'purement
poétique' then develops into a word, almost a place, where 'nous
distinguons, sous la projection lumineuse et rétrospective d'un
nom, l'origine et la persistance de certaines caractéristiques nerveuses, de certains vices, des désordres de tels ou tels Guermantes'
(ii. 831), roughly parallel to the development from key term
through runs to stress-lines to motif. Bourgeois awe, self-con-
fessed, develops quickly into a close and detailed hearing of the
more particular deposits and stresses of an aristocratic lineage
within the voice-patterns of the family. How the duchess describes

Mme de Gallardon as 'une vieille *poison*' (ii. 792) is the locus for the family accent rather than the stained-glass mythology and colour the narrator dreams of within their name; and this trait is proof of a linguistic limitation.

For, Proust goes on, 'il est difficile, quand on est troublé par les idées de Kant et la nostalgie de Baudelaire, d'écrire le français exquis d'Henri IV, de sorte que la pureté même du langage de la duchesse était un signe de limitation' (ii. 792). This limitation creates a new duchess in his mind expressing 'les valeurs spirituelles, l'énergie et le charme d'une cruelle petite fille de l'aristocratie des environs de Combray' (ii. 793), a duchess who is a cruelly parochial and domesticated parody of the luminous creature the name had conjured up in his imagination. What he is left with, where the traces of the old charge remain, is located within the mundane particularities of accent and pronunciation, the pressing, tyrannical detail of chatter. At this level, the narrator takes what he can, and what he takes is a slow and organic chart of the evolution of the names and genealogies of the social milieu, not at the stiff proud level of the Duc de Guermantes, nor with Charlus's haughty arrogance, but as they weigh with him, as they alter and reveal 'l'origine et la persistance de certaines caractéristiques nerveuses, de certains vices, des désordres de tels ou tels Guermantes.'

Charlus's voice and accents in particular are the focus of a remorseless attention to the facets and deposits of a family history, with the additional pressures of an aetiolated literary accent, and the burden of his secret passion for Morel. Charlus, at his pitiful, tragic height in the last four books, is a great and impossible embodiment of the three main pressure-sources on the human voice in the novel, class-hereditary, aesthetic, and sexual. His continual betrayals of his 'secret' are witnesses to the impossibility of a private containment of such allied forces within the human voice. They almost make the narrator shudder with embarrassment:

J'étais presque gêné par ses yeux où j'avais peur qu'il ne me surprît à le lire à livre ouvert, par sa voix qui me paraissait le répéter sur tous les tons, avec une illassable indécence. (iii. 731)

Proust has the narrator literally repeat 'le secret' with the repeated l sounds stressing the 'le' that refers to 'le secret' (with the alerting-device of the 'lire'-'livre' rhyme bringing readerly sensitivity to the sentence's sounds into line with the narrator's 'reading' of Charlus). The readability of Charlus's vice within his voice and face is caused by the Guermantes tone and literary vocal mannerisms of the dandy enabling a liberating expressive range. His 'Pif!' at the 'valet de pied' in *La Prisonnière* expresses homosexual desire through both aristocratic ease and an artist's daring. But the three forces also mask their own revelations by such conjunctions (by the possibility that any one might be any of the others)—that is, until the petty cruelty of the Verdurins wills his disgrace, his unmasking. The origin and persistence of historical forces of feeling and fact within the self let their presence be known in the minutest articulations of that self once the perceiving attention is engaged at an imaginative pitch.

Proust's huge task was to attempt to give a comic history of the several complex stages that attention goes through in its life among names, places, books, words, social groupings, lovers, and other minds. Like the effect of the dark side of Albertine, that other world of her unknown pasts, upon the narrator, these historical forces create an energy of research in the historian's mind, an energy resembling jealousy, resembling the violent progression of desire. In Albertine he discovers not only a multitude of Albertines but a multitude of his own desires for those Albertines, Albertine defined as:

la plénitude d'un être empli jusqu'au bord par la superposition de tant d'êtres, de tant de désirs et de souvenirs voluptueux d'êtres. Et maintenant qu'elle m'avait dit un jour: 'Mlle Vinteuil', j'aurais voulu non pas arracher sa robe pour voir son corps, mais à travers son corps voir tout ce bloc-notes de ses souvenirs et de ses prochains et ardents rendez-vous. (iii. 601)

And, for the narrator, these multiple compound ghosts of memory and desire find their prose facsimiles in the myriad intonations of voices and the memory-connections of their rhyming music, 'l'harmonieuse et multisonore salutation de toutes les Voix' (iii. 609). The narrator's own text becomes a reproduction palimpsest of the 'bloc-notes' read through Albertine's body, scored over with the traces of other voices, other desires, heard in the accumulation of stress-lines within the prose.

Contresens

In his early elegant blast against the Symbolistes, 'Contre l'Obscurité', Proust had this to say about the French language:

Les symbolistes seront sans doute les premiers à nous accorder que ce que chaque mot garde, dans sa figure ou dans son harmonie, du charme de son origine ou de la grandeur de son passé, a sur notre imagination et sur notre sensibilité une puissance d'évocation au moins aussi grande que sa puissance de stricte signification. Ce sont ces affinités anciennes et mystérieuses entre notre langage maternel et notre sensibilité qui, au lieu d'un langage conventionnel comme sont les langues étrangères en font une sort de musique latente que le poète peut faire résonner en nous avec une douceur incomparable. Il rajeunit un mot en le prenant dans une vieille acception, il réveille entre deux images disjointes des harmonies oubliées, à tout moment il nous fait respirer avec délices le parfum de la terre natale. (*Contre Sainte-Beuve*, 392–3)

The latent music in the connotative harmonics of French, Proust is saying, can never be captured if creative language determinedly relinquishes, or breaks its lines of contact with, the way French has been, and is, spoken. The Symbolistes' theories of words as pure signs within an ideal internal landscape make an obscure and narcissistic mockery of the real, substantial relations a language has with a nation's landscape and its people's sensibility through history. The cult of suggestiveness for the Symbolistes was a matter of clearing French of its historical suggestions. Emile Hennequin, in his essay 'Le poétique et le prosaique', describes imaginative writing as essentially dealing with any subject 'qui reste obscur et diffus, étrange et lointain, dont la représentation toute générale et suggestive, mais cohèrente, laisse le champ libre aux émotions qui lui sont associées et à celles même qui resultent de son idéalisation'—if these criteria are obeyed one has poetry (Lehmann, *The Symbolist Aesthetic*, 140). The only historical pressures to be allowed into the garden are the primitive cries and grunts of our earliest ancestors (Gaultier's 'ancien sens',[20] Gourmont's 'langage [. . .] d'abord' (Lehmann, *The Symbolist Aesthetic*, 147). The music of the words in the poetic phrase, being detached from the sense of the words, sings within the vague emotions that they evoke. Thus Wyzéwa:

[20] Lehmann, *The Symbolist Aesthetic*, 145.

L'émotion, moins encore que les autres modes vitaux, ne peut être tra-duite directement; [. . .] elle peut seulement nous être suggérée. Et pour suggérer les émotions, mode subtil et dernier de la vie, un signe special a été inventé: le son musical. (Lehmann, *The Symbolist Aesthetic*, 58)

The musicality is both an effect and a means of the necessary split between sonority and sense that the clearance of language's histori-cal matter entails.

This definition of music as context-free Proust, very early on, found wrong-headed about the proper relations between general propositions and particular instances of them. Proust's criticism of these doctrines relocates suggestiveness within the historically accumulated connotations of words. He understood the musi-cality of creative language to reside in mnemonically charged emotion, contexts recalling other contexts, thus redefining Sym-boliste idealization of language in terms of a recollection of the stories and histories latent in key-words. His tone may be too lyrically remembering 'le français exquis d'Henri IV', as such hardly distinguishable from his duchess, or also, indeed, from Symbolistes like Charles Morice and Jules Laforgue. But, in much of its local substance, Proust's passage can be read as making some simple but important distinctions that were to prove of essential value later in life. That words in a sentence have a connotative memory; that odd couplings can awaken the past; that both these possibilities re-establish rich, historical connections between the mother tongue and the mind; that it is language in history, over time, that has the music.

Later in *Contre Sainte-Beuve* (*CSB*), these concepts are developed into a theory of resuscitation: the 'oreille fine' that the writer needs in order to hear the harmony between two impressions is the essential means by which he is nourished—he lives and dies and is resuscitated by the intermittent sequence of those resemblances, and so is the past:

Pourquoi cette coincidence entre deux impressions nous rend-elle la ré-alité? Peut-être parce qu'alors elle ressuscite avec elle ce qu'elle *omet*, tandis que si nous raisonnons, si nous cherchons à nous rappeler, nous ajoutons ou nous retirons. (*CSB*, 304–5)

An interesting difference by this stage is Proust's change of tack about the foreignness of the language created by this strange

rehearing. In 'Contre l'Obscurité', he had emphasized the native-
ness of the writer's evocations and distinguished the acoustics of
creative French prose from how one might hear 'langues
étrangères'. He may have placed such an emphasis into his argument to satirize the Symbolistes' attempts to create a new language. In *Contre Sainte-Beuve*, however, he describes the new style
created by the writer from his sequence of resuscitations as 'une
sorte de langue étrangère' (*CSB*, 304). But here 'étrangère' is clearly
being used differently: his language is foreign, he explains, because it marshals the 'contresens' each individual registers in the
process of understanding the meaning of words (*CSB*, 305). These
minute and special differences in the connotations of words for
each particular user of the language form the harmonics of language for a writer. He communicates these sequences of 'contresens', his own as well as those that others unconsciously harbour,
all foreign to the common denotations understood by an aggre-
gate of native French speakers. But they are also, as 'Contre l'Obscurité' argues, very deeply native to the manner in which the
French speak naturally, solecisms, misunderstood archaisms, verbal tics, and so forth, features of the language which preserve the
deposits of a nation's history and innumerable private histories, a
tendency explored in *A la recherche du temps perdu* most clearly in
Proust's analysis of Françoise's use of language.[21]

Proust's sentences, in their length and in their discrete but crucial patches of rhymes, are carefully designed to be heard as a
gathering of words with family ties in their acoustics and syntax,
words that hint, through the rhymes, at an accumulation of historical counter-senses. The sentence itself takes time, has a past
and future within the text as a whole, and the words are the
material within which accents of stress peculiar to the individual
imagination, that have been stored up in its past, sound out their
differences. Two rhyme-words, like the coincidence between two
impressions, resuscitate what has been omitted by the voice's
primary denotative sense. Their harmony gives articulate life to
the secret interior pressures and 'contresens' that the double working of memory and imagination have preserved and developed.

---

[21] 'Son langage, comme la langue française elle-même, et surtout sa toponymie,
était parsemé d'erreurs' (ii. 323). One of her mistakes, the use of the phrase 'faire
réponse', is, typically, a locution used by Mme de Sévigné (ii. 323)—the error, the
'contresens', opens up a 17th-century perspective.

The 'contresens' covers verbal slips such as Albertine's and Odette's (and the peculiar emphases, malapropisms, and catachreses of the majority of the characters.[22]) But more importantly the word gathers to itself, as Proust's work grew, his difficult rhyme between all the tiny betrayals of the self in 'la voix, le silence, les yeux'[23] and the revelations of the writer's individuality within the minutiae of the sounds of his sentences. The rhyme works, as both *Contre Sainte-Beuve* and 'Contre l'Obscurité' imply, because emotional betrayal and artistic revelation break into the voice in similar ways, altering the syntax of the articulating mind into 'un désordre extrême', ringing out the private force of a deep feeling from the past, a disorder that Proust himself orders into an intelligible music.

When Racine in the first scene of *Andromaque* turns the alexandrines around word-play with these six words, 'courir', 'cours', 'courroux', 'cour', 'cœur', 'couronne', the word-play is truly earnest because they are the key-words for the plot and his characters' voiced imaginations. The pleasure in the word-play derives from how Racine's half-rhyming technique accords with the *raison d'être* of the rhymes. That *raison d'être* resides in the dramatic presentation of how the characters on stage agree on a commonly acknowledged series of key-words as well as how privately they understand these words differently. Proust's 'rimes intérieures' are dramatic in the same manner. Like the give-aways in Charlus's voice and face, the rhyme-features are among common resources of French speech and behaviour, whilst also being dramatic nervemarks of a private preoccupation.

The rhyme accent in the voice itself rhymes with that voice, motivated by it but introducing into it the new variation of 'ce qu'elle *omet*'. The rhymes can only be read and heard if the voice is allowed to run as a living voice, altering the material it utters with intentions and intonations that have lost their logical and reasonable origin to become the 'timbre' of another self. Prose rhymes, like Proust's musician, will tend to 'confondre les mots divers du livret dans un même rythme qui les contrarie et les entraîne' (*A la recherche du temps perdu*, ii. 351), creating a dramatic

---

[22] e.g. the Directeur of the Grand-Hôtel at Balbec 'émaillait ses propos commerciaux d'expressions choisies, mais à contresens' (ii. 24).
[23] Racine, *Andromaque*, I i.

'contresens' where the real individuality of the public actor, the public voice can be recognized.

Like Charlus's voice when he discusses Racine, Proust's prose rhymes are the murmur, rich as a chorus, of a self revealed in its passion:

> sa voix elle-même, pareille à certaines voix de contralto en qui on n'a pas assez cultivé le médium et dont le chant semble le duo alterné d'un jeune homme et d'une femme, se posait au moment où il exprimait ces pensées si délicates, sur des notes hautes, prenait une douceur imprévue et semblait contenir des chœurs de fiancées, de sœurs, qui répandaient leur tendresse. (ii. 122–3)

Charlus's voice has become a Racine play with a chorus of tender women behind the male and female leads. Its 'douceur' (a word Proust has associated with the narrator's grandmother, whom Charlus is charming here) rhymes richly with the feminine nature it reveals, with 'des chœurs de fiancées, de sœurs'; the drama is revealed by singing badly, singing contralto 'à contresens', creating a 'sens' that in Charlus's case is literally 'invers'. He is both Salomith and the chorus of 'jeunes filles de la tribu de Lévi' (Act III, scene viii in particular) from *Athalie*.[24] A dramatic internal voice rises above his cracked, broken intonations and goes against the grain of Charlus's expressed 'virilité'.[25] In the same way that a musical instrument gives a chorus-effect if slightly distorted, it is Charlus's inner distortion that, out of an uncultivated medium, gives rise, under the pressure of a passionate 'douceur' and 'désordre extrême', to a richly sweet and peopled voice. Charlus plays Racine and is discovered with a play of his own within him. The aptness of this joke stems from the fitting 'rhyme' Proust hears between the utterance and its matter, between the secret preoccupation and the changes wrought on the present substance of the voice. The rise from a badly mixed contralto duet to chorus moves with our sudden appreciation of the joke, of the rhymes, to a clear hearing of a voice ringing out its hidden nature with all contacts re-established.

[24] Later this play is used by the narrator as exemplary material for his analogy between the Jews and the secret homosexual community.

[25] 'J'essayai de peindre l'homosexuel épris de virilité parce que, sans le savoir, il est une Femme.' Letter to Gide 10/11 June 1914 on Charlus. (*Correspondance*, ed. Kolb, xiii. 246).

The sudden revelation of a complex secret nature within the known features of a voice and face, for Proust, could only be acutely felt by a mind attuned to noticing odd and disparate kinships in the minutiae of a sentence, a glance, a sequence of notes, that is, where the counter-senses to the public manifestation could be felt. And, the Charlus example shows us, the revelation strikes the truly attentive reader and watcher as a 'contresens' because what is revealed is foreign to the present-tense material, is constituted by other voices. It is instantly felt to be dramatic with Charlus because it would be a conscious mistake for him to reveal such foreign accumulated matter of an internal and historical past. Proust's play on words, his rhyme-play, become intimately dramatic at these points of revelation by themselves revealing the deep dramas within the subjects under consideration. This drama can be heard within the acoustics of the prose, the way the words pick up on themselves, remember themselves, and counter the thrust of their primary semantic point. And it is not a feature of the prose that is reserved for the narrator's analysis of the society that surrounds him. It is also a feature of Proust's own ironic presentation of his narrator's obsessions and hidden emotional life.

At a crucial point in that life, Proust has his narrator arduously disentangle something Albertine says, or rather stops herself saying about the Verdurins. The narrator has offered her money to buy clothes chic enough for a Verdurin evening, and Albertine replies: ' "Grand merci! dépenser un sou pour ces vieux-là, j'aime bien meux que vous me laissiez une fois libre pour que j'aille me faire casser . . ." ' and suddenly stops there, putting her hand to her mouth to break the phrase off in shame (iii. 840). He insists that she finish the phrase, but Albertine begs him not to force her to say what she was about to say, excusing herself for speaking 'sans rime ni raison' (iii. 841). The narrator, alone, racks his brain to fill out the dangerous fragment and his memory at last retrieves from the truncated 'mots de sa phrase' the street slang idiom, 'me faire casser le pot', a proof (for the narrator) of the lesbian street-world she inhabits in his absence.

As he neared completion of his reconstruction, the narrator had run the key term around his mind, rolling and revolving it to catch its habitual fellows within the context of Albertine's tone and gesture:

je m'étais hypnotisé sur le dernier mot: 'casser', elle avait voulu dire casser quoi? Casser du bois? Non. Du sucre? Non. Casser, casser, casser. Et tout à coup deux mots atroces, auxquels je n'avais nullement songé, tombèrent sur moi: 'le pot'. (iii. 842)

A spark of analogy leaps across the intervening sentences when we later hear the 'rimes intérieures' in the next passage, a rhyme forming with our own memory of the slang phrase:

malgré la souffrance que j'éprouvais à parler de notre séparation comme déjà entrée dans le passé—peut-être en partie à cause de cette souffrance même—je me mis à adresser à Albertine les conseils les plus précis pour certaines choses qu'elle aurait à faire après son départ de la maison. (iii. 844)

'Casser' connects eventually with words that bring alive the terrible truth of Albertine's sordid existence on the streets and it rhymes with words in the narrator's lies that bring out the true tones of the life of his feeling—'passé', 'adresser' with strong a and s repetitions. The atrocious words 'casser' and 'pot' ring out through stress-lines along p, s, and a: 'éprouvais', 'parler', 'séparation', 'passé', 'peut-être', 'partie', 'plus précis pour', 'après', 'départ'. The phrase is still beating within his mind with its heavy and shattering pressure.[26]

He had recuperated it from the depths of 'le sommeil fort vivant et créateur de l'inconscient (sommeil où achèvent de se graver les choses qui nous effleurèrent seulement, où les mains endormies se saississent de la clef qui ouvre, vainement cherchée jusque-là)' (iii. 842). And this creative, unconscious act of memory gives the lie to Albertine's lie, finds both a *reason* for her broken-off shame, and *rhymes* that stress the momentous weight of those 'deux mots atroces'. Proust's prose rhymes are giving a dramatic tone to the narrator's lying breaking-off of his relationship with Albertine. They give the note of stress along the stress-lines, while at the same time leaving readers free to judge the narrator's comic abandonment to his insanely jealous 'recherche'. Hearing those rhymes and the words they remember, a minute alignment is laid between reader and jealous character: both discover the truth of a hidden

[26] The phonemes aRsep constitute over 40% of the phonemes of the passage as opposed to the 30% in normal usage. Each phoneme is individually of significantly high percentage.

life and its memories through minute attention to the connections of verbal details and the attendant tone. The rhyme between our listening and his attention is oblique and indistinct but still present. It involves the manner in which some rhymes in prose are registered in reading, half-caught suggestions summoning detailed examination, strengthened and given body by the sudden appropriateness of the memory-contacts discovered within the context of the sentence and voice.

Their necessity is founded upon the technical means by which the reader is summoned to feel for those hidden memory-contacts in order to hear another experience and its accents. In this instance this entails hearing the pressures of the narrator's inner voice stressing the words he fears under the influence of his half-recalled horror at Albertine's suppressed phrase. This horrified accent is shadowed by one's suspicion of its insane and exaggerated music, the comic tyranny of a mind minutely interrogating the victim of whom he is himself a victim. Proust's prose rhymes are the facsimiles that fabricate the textual memories crazily made up by the narrator's jealousy, closely paralleling the way the sound-effects fabricate textual motifs summoned up by musical motifs. Across the distances set up between the narrator's voice of cold lies and the voice rolling 'casser' jealously around for its hidden kin, between the reader's and the narrator's nerves and pulses, between disparate words and sentences, sounds a contact re-established.

Wagnerian Leitmotif

Proust, in his study *La Mort des Cathèdrales*, had compared *Parsifal* with the way historical researchers make cathedrals sing again through the reconstitution of ancient rites and architectural symbols: 'cette résurrection des cérémonies catholiques, d'un tel intérêt historique, social, plastique, musical et de la beauté desquelles seul Wagner s'est approché, en l'imitant, dans Parsifal' (*CSB*, 142). For Proust, however, the true beauty lay in the celebration of those rites by priest and people within existing ancient churches—the persistence of those ceremonies, in other words, in living memory rather than the reconstructed, mimic memory of an aesthetic recollection. The living memory Proust records is the way Wagner is recalled, the manner in which his music lives within the mind of those who experience it, its aftershocks and rhythms, and how its motifs are adopted and translated by individuals to express the minutiae of their own lines of emotional force. Proust adopts and translates these motifs with his own facsimile brand of them: prose rhymes. This particular interest is partly fashioned by Wagner's own musical theory.

Writing *Siegfried*, Wagner discovered he needed a new language to correspond to the hero's 'geste joyeux'. He found that language in the alliterative verse of the old German myths:

Cette langue s'exprimait dans une forme qui retrouvait la véritable accent de la parole, épousait le rythme le plus naturel et le plus vivant, était capable sans effort d'une expression infiniment variée: *le vers allitéré*, l'instrument poétique dont le peuple se servait jadis du temps qu'il était encore poète et créateur de mythes. (143–4)

Behind these words, Wagner wrote a new form of thematic music with powerful links with the feelings expressed by the alliterative libretto:

c'était le discours lui-même, avec ce qu'il contient de sentiments, qu'il s'agissait de rendre [. . .] la mélodie devait naître tout naturellement du discours [. . .] l'expression la plus sensible d'un sentiment lui-même explicite dans le discours. (139–40)

The thematic material is itself organized into leitmotifs which are essentially a means of fabricating a musical memory and an organic *emotional* structure:

les motifs thématiques se lient et se ramifient [. . .] une tonalité propre à l'intérieur du sentiment général; aucune de ces tonalités ne devait être produite sans avoir un rapport essentiel avec les tonalités des autres scènes. (135–6)

Thomas Donnan has shown how Proust translated these motifs into *A la recherche du temps perdu* by resorting to alliteration and assonance. To create the necessary texture of 'contrapuntal interweavings of allusions and cross-references', Proust 'uses alliteration and assonance and sometimes rhythm to focus and intensify certain affectively charged phrases' (165). Proust was primarily interested in the resources that leitmotif theory gave him in his quest to represent complex remembering. As Donnan puts it, 'the use of leitmotifs is not only a means of signalization and an aid to organic structure, but a literary embodiment of the concept of 'la mémoire involontaire' (173). Donnan chiefly notices these motifs in the quasi-superstitious relationships between certain phonemes and certain names; so that the phoneme ã, for instance, has an 'organic relationship with the name "Guermantes" ' (160), and Donnan, following Milly, duly finds countless name-anagrams hidden in the sonorities of the prose. I have less time for these name games, which seem particularly futile versions of Wagner's *Grundthemen*, than with the essential idea of verbal motifs as signals of involuntary memory. The key-words are given emotional emphasis by surrounding phoneme repetition organized into stress-lines; this emphasis becomes an act of acoustic memory once the motif is re-established; the recall of that emphasis is involuntary precisely because, as counter-sense, it goes directly against the grain of the fully conscious articulations of the narrative voice.

An example to prove Proust's motif-work occurs when the narrator turns his mind to meditating upon Wagner himself. The narrator, free of his anxiety over Albertine for once, has time at last to listen closely and musically to the Vinteuil sonata. Playing it at the piano, he has just been struck by the uniqueness of the sonata's musical intelligence:

Au moment où je pensais cela, une mesure de la Sonate me frappa, mesure que je connaissais bien pourtant, mais parfois l'attention éclaire différemment des choses connues pourtant depuis longtemps et où nous remarquons ce que nous n'y avions jamais vu. En jouant cette mesure, et bien que Vinteuil fût là en train d'exprimer un rêve qui fût resté tout à fait étranger à Wagner, je ne pus m'empêcher de murmurer: 'Tristan!', avec le sourire qu'a l'ami d'une famille retrouvant quelque chose de l'aïeul dans une intonation, un geste du petit-fils qui ne l'a pas connu. (iii. 664)

The narrator's noticing of the musical allusion seems all there is to it, his smile a simple joy at capturing a kinship. It is a kinship, however, that accompanies the Vinteuil like a memory. Vinteuil is no longer alone. The alliterative play in the first sentence quoted might be merely amusing to notice ourselves: that is, the nasal stress-line that plays on the 'tan' of 'Tristan', as though the narrator literally *cannot* avoid murmuring it—'moment', 'pensais', 'pourtant', 'l'attention', 'différemment', 'pourtant', 'longtemps', 'en train', 'en jouant cette', 'étranger', 'retrouvant', 'dans une intonation'.[27] In other words, a witty joke that can afford to be over-looked. All the joke is saying, after all, is that Wagner's character-related motifs are recalled by other musicians in the same way that the narrator cannot help being transfixed by a loaded name like 'Tristan' in the very articulation of such 'sound'-resemblances. A very small-scale irony, one would think. Several considerations should warn us to listen again to those sound-repetitions.

First, that the sonata the narrator is playing has, with its 'combi-naison du motif voluptueux et du motif anxieux' (iii. 664), con-stantly shadowed his feelings for Albertine. For the moment, with the narrator relieved that Albertine is out of the house, the music seems simply to be recalling the Guermantes way and his purely aesthetic desires to become an artist. But a Wagner reference with-in the Vinteuil would tend to push musical interpretation away from purely formal analysis back towards dark, emotional read-ings. Baudelaire in his essay on Tannhäuser wrote on Wagner's music, we remember:

En feuilletant la Lettre sur la Musique, je sentais revivre dans mon esprit, comme par un phénomène d'écho mnémonique, différents passage de Diderot qui affirment que la vraie musique dramatique ne peut pas être autre chose que le cri ou le soupir de la passion noté et rythmé. ('Richard Wagner et Tannhauser à Paris', in *OC*, 515.)

Wagner's leitmotif theory, as Liszt put it (quoted in Baudelaire's essay), must necessarily contradict 'ceux aussi pour qui les croches et doubles croches sont lettres mortes et pures hiéroglyphiques.' (*OC*, 521) An allusion to Wagner in the Vinteuil sonata *cannot*, by definition, be simple; it *must* indicate some kind of involvement of the passions, some element of anxiety 'noté et rythmé'.

Secondly, that Wagner did not write *Tristan* but *Tristan und Isolde*. Prousts prose hints that stressing the name Tristan in isola-tion forms part of the narrator's sad pleasure; that is, the emphasis on the isolated name has something to do with his own isolation, and the absence of Albertine. His mind is unconsciously seeking self-accompaniments, musical and emotional. This is confirmed later on when the narrator implies that the theme Vinteuil's measure recalls from Wagner is the shepherd's flute-song 'avant le

[27] t = 5.4%; ã = 4.8%. Note also the i-string ('sourire'-'ami'-'famille'; 'petit-fils qui') at 3.0% which repeats the first vowel of the name.

grand mouvement d'orchestre qui précède le retour d'Yseult' (iii. 667). The opera's tragic lovers are unconsciously being adopted as shadow-figures for the narrator's internal emotional drama.

And thirdly, that immediately after recognizing the Wagner theme in the Vinteuil, the narrator describes Wagner's leitmotifs and reprises as *pathological* signs, not purely musical, compositional features:

ces thèmes insistants et fugaces qui visitent un acte, ne s'éloignent que pour revenir, et, parfois lointains, assoupis, presque détachés, sont à d'autres moments, tout en restant vagues, si pressants et si proches, si internes, si organiques, si viscéraux qu'on dirait la reprise moins d'un motif que d'une névralgie. (iii. 665)

The 's'-string in this passage (as though fabricated by the tensely shocked 'si' repetitions) mimes 'ces thèmes insistants', the sounds shadowing the great beating nervousness in the insistent adjectival rhythm.

Proust is deliberately aligning the narrator's consciousness of Wagner's neuralgic and passionate motifs with the presence of prose rhymes in the narrator's thought-patterns. The question remains open—what does the theme recalled from Wagner represent in its new Vinteuil context? This turns out to be the same question as asking what kind of neuralgia lies behind the 'tan' motif in the narrator's mind? The narrator seems to be avoiding the answer. We register this by hearing a curious awkwardness in the phrasing of the passage that stresses the 'tan' motif, an awkwardness emphasized by the alliterative play—its tone approaches tautology: 'une mesure [. . .] mesure que je connaissais bien pourtant [. . .] des choses connues pourtant depuis longtemps [. . .] jouant cette mesure [. . .] et bien que [. . .] retrouvant quelque chose [. . .] qui ne l'a pas connu.' The intonation of the two sentences betrays a certain neuralgic nervousness in the act of clearing its syntactical flow, in making its meaning clear. The return of the 'tan'-sound, in that it resembles the neuralgic return of the s sounds in the later passage, alerts us to the possibility that the sound-effects may be working to darker, more passionate purposes. These considerations make us wonder precisely why he finds solace in the 'Tristan' rhyme, and also why it may not be a solace at all. For this whole section on Vinteuil and Wagner ponders the relations between technical mastery and ordinary human passions, the narrator in the end coming away disappointed by Wagner's joyful detachment from 'la tristesse' (iii. 667), by the possibility that the rise of his music above the poet may simply be 'l'allégresse du fabricateur'.

The silent questions these doubts and suspicions raise seem to be confirmed by the curious ignorance the narrator shows when he emerges from his meditation on music:

Je ne sais pourquoi le cours de mes rêveries, qui avait suivi jusque-là des souvenirs de musique, se détourna sur ceux qui en ont été à notre époque les meilleurs exécutants et parmi lesquels, le surfaisant un peu, je faisais figurer Morel. (iii. 668)

It is a strange thing to wonder at, since it seems perfectly natural to move from 'souvenirs de musique' to the best interpreters of music at the time. The 'je ne sais pourquoi' betrays an odd discomfort and silent self-questioning in the narrator's tone. The unspoken embarrassment might have something to do with the fact that his thoughts on Morel dwell very little on his playing and shift with 'un brusque crochet' to consideration of his absurd lies and deceitfulness with Charlus, particularly how he manages to win time off from Charlus to pursue his lucrative street-trade. The analogy with Albertine is too close for comfort, 'vague, pressant, proche', to adapt a phrase.

The drama hidden in the rhymes, the leitmotif that though detached still runs pressingly through his prose, even during this period of calm, of blessed release from, and confidence in, Albertine, the time when he is most sure of a free descent 'en moi-même' (iii. 665), is the accent of his desire for her, the anxious intonation of his wait for her. She is the Yseult that troubles the free piping of the shepherd. For one remembers the last time in the novel that this motif, the shepherd's flute-song, had coincided with Albertine's absence, in *Sodome et Gomorrhe*:

J'étais torturé par l'incessante reprise du désir toujours plus anxieux, et jamais accompli, d'un bruit d'appel; arrivé au point culminant d'une ascension tourmentée dans les spirales de mon angoisse solitaire, du fond du Paris populeux et nocturne approché soudain de moi, à côté de ma bibliothèque, j'entendis tout à coup, mécanique et sublime, comme dans *Tristan* l'écharpe agitée ou le chalumeau du pâtre, le bruit de toupie du téléphone. Je m'élançai, c'était Albertine. (iii. 128–9)

The 'attention' that had suddenly recalled the Wagner motif within the Vinteuil itself recalls the spiralling anxiety of his 'attente' by the telephone.[28] The 'tan' stress-line that on the surface seems to celebrate the comfort of his solitariness, Tristan alone, in conjunction with the series of doubts and perplexities in the music section as a whole and in context, beats out the memory of 'l'incessante reprise du désir [. . .] d'un bruit d'appel', rises to the half-forgotten rhythms of his past 'ascension tourmentée'. The stress-line fabricates the leitmotif key-word 'attente' which gathers together all the anxiety and passion of its past occasions, transforming them into emphasis, intonation, and terrible intermittence. The passage in *Sodome et Gomorrhe* touches the same chord through 'incessant', 'ascension tourmentée' with the added and stronger 'i'-string (notably 'reprise du désir', 'bruit de toupie') that brings 'Tristan' and 'Albertine' into the same stress-line.[29] The nervousness of the later passage, its fits and starts, betrays a deep-seated anxiety that has to think of Albertine in the old ways, must remember and conserve the memory of anguish lived through.

In discovering a musical allusion in a piece of music too close to the heart of the intermittent rhythms of his passion for Albertine, the narrator lets slip into his prose the sharp nerve-racking ring of a buried anxiety which the *Tristan* motif had articulated.[30] The stress-line on the syllables of 'Tristan' has already worked itself into a context within his mind and life, sounding out a 'triste attente'. And, in a sense and sound closer than he can dare reveal to himself, his obstinate questioning of the true living value of

[28]   Proust remembers Romain Rolland in his use of the two moments of 'attente' in *Tristan*. Roland wrote, in 1899: 'Ainsi de certaines pages colossales de *Tristan*: par exemple, ces deux poèmes énivrés ou déchirés d'attente,—l'attente d'Isolde au second acte, dans la nuit chargée de volupté,—l'attente de Tristan au troisième, heurtée, frénétique, sanglante; l'attente du vaisseau qui apporte Isolde, et la mort;—ou le Prélude, ce désir éternel, qui se plaint, se rue et se brise, sans fin, comme la mer.' (*Musiciens d'aujourd'hui*, 81)

[29]   Also observable are p and b runs linking 'bruit d'appel' with 'Albertine'.

[30]   The musical crossed line the narrator is suffering from is well described by Anthony Newcombe in an essay on sound and feeling. One might say that the narrator is reacting to the music as though he were two kinds of music critic at once. Newcombe argues that there are those who hear music as 'metaphorical exemplification' based on the 'similarity of kinetic shape between the literal properties of music and our own physical symptoms when prey to agitation—rapid pulse, sudden gestures, and so on', and those who seek meaning in the individual musical image, the 'small-scale musical detail, interval, motive, theme or phrase [. . .] what happens to the material' ('Sound and Feeling', 625–6).

Wagner's music, deeper than the triumphantly artificial, has already answered itself, even in the manner of its articulation.

The pressing, intimate remembering of the sound (expected as well as real) of a telephone call that will re-establish the contact between Albertine and his jealous mind, even when he is at rest, detached from jealousy itself, secretly and internally justifies Wagner and Vinteuil, not only because their music understands the way feelings will return and persist over time ('ne s'éloignent que pour revenir'), but because that understanding creates a music that ministers to deep and complex articulations of feeling in those who attend to them, a music that can shadow, embody, and recall the chances of suffering. The sound-effects in Proust's prose are a tribute to such musical understanding, and they are the deepest way a prose imagination can be musical, with a music that resurrects past moods of the mind along stress-lines in the prose even when that music is 'tout à fait étranger' to the broad semantic run of the prose. Those stress-lines are true indicators of stress, concealed behind the screen of easy prose readibility.

Georges Matoré and Irène Mecz, in their fine work *Musique et structure romanesque dans A la recherche du temps perdu*, would assent to my understanding of the quality of Proust's musical motifs:

Les réminiscences involontaires qui font penser à la résurgence d'un thème musical se manifestent par une irruption du passé dans le présent. D'autres éléments de nature stylistique comme les parenthèses, les métaphores, les coordinations, les juxtapositions ou les multiples subordonnées que Proust introduit dans sa phrase, sont comparables à un accompagnement harmonique qui soutient et épaissit la ligne mélodique en lui superposant des résonances issues d'autres lieux, d'autres temps, d'autres 'moi'. (245)

This seems to me to be a perfect definition of the manner in which Proust's sound-motifs operate within his 'phrases', despite the fact that, for Matoré and Mecz, the leitmotif remains primarily a thing of sense, syntax, repeated material.

At the risk of over-stressing my point, I would like to quote this passage from *La Prisonnière* that comes just after the music interlude and the brief discussion of Morel's deceitfulness. Albertine has finally returned and the narrator slips oddly into a consideration of his jealousy and the bonds it creates, even though he says he feels clearly happy with her at the time: my point being Proust's determination to identify the 'tan'-rhyme with the narrator's need and 'attente' for her so soon after the 'Tristan'-passages:

autrefois une femme avait eu beau être dans la même voiture que moi, elle n'était pas *en réalité* à côté de moi, tant que ne l'y recréait pas à tout instant un besoin d'elle comme j'en avais un d'Albertine, tant que la caresse constante de mon regard ne lui rendait pas sans cesse ces teintes qui demandent à être perpétuellement refraîchies, tant que les sens, même apaisés mais qui se souviennent, ne mettaient pas sous ces couleurs la saveur et la consistance, tant qu'unie aux sens et à l'imagin-ation qui les exalte, la jalousie ne maintenait pas cette femme en équilibre auprès de nous par une attraction compensée aussi puissante que la loi de la gravitation. (iii. 672)

The 'tan'-motif is the key motif of the persistence of the narrator's jealous attraction: 'les sens, même apaisés mais qui se souvien-nent'. The words also remember (through the retrospective em-phases built up by the stress-lines become motif) other times when the body and mind had undergone real, active stress, particularly the anxiety of 'l'attente'. The narrator is movingly self-deceiving when he describes the shepherd's flute-song as motivated by the formal purposes of the whole of Wagner's work (iii. 667), moving-ly so because in dismissing to himself the clearest reason why the air moves him, he unwittingly and silently emphasizes that rea-son, a pure counter-sense.

Proust had described why that theme was so powerful in the first section of *En mémoire des églises assassinées*, that theme and also Isolde's scarf-signal at the beginning of the second act (also re-called in *Sodome et Gomorrhe*). He is describing the effect on him of hearing the horn of his chauffeur-driven car sound outside his parents' house: his parents are waiting for him. The strident mon-otonous sound of the horn is filled with a feeling of joyful expecta-tion within Proust's imagination: the parents hear the horn and

ne peuvent plus méconnaître le son devenu joyeux, presque humain, ne cesse plus de jeter son appel uniforme comme l'idée fixe de leur joie prochaine, pressant et répété comme leur anxiété grandissante. Et je son-geais que dans *Tristan et Isolde* (au deuxième acte d'abord quand Isolde agite son écharpe comme un signal, au troisième acte ensuite à l'arrivée de la nef) c'est, la première fois, à la redite stridente, indéfinie et de plus en plus rapide de deux notes dont la succession est quelquefois produite par le hasard dans le monde inorganisé des bruits; c'est, la deuxième fois, au chalumeau d'un pauvre pâtre, à l'intensité croissante, à l'insatiable monotonie de sa maigre chanson, que Wagner, par une apparente et géniale abdication de sa puissance créatrice, a confié l'expression de la plus prodigieuse attente de félicité qui ait jamais rempli l'âme humaine. (*CSB*, 68–9)

Here is the sad revelation. In altering the true and rich joy of his family reunion as the counterpart for Isolde's and Tristan's powerful 'attente de félicité', with car-horn for the flute and strings, into the narrator's 'attente' for Albertine by the muted telephone, something has been lost. Unable to join in with Wagner's joy, raising only a smile at a simple allusion, his prose becomes nervy not with 'la plus prodigieuse attente de félicité qui ait jamais rempli l'âme humaine' but with the kind of expectation that had characterized Tante Léonie's existence in Combray.

Again rhyme is the agent of the memory:

Je ne doute pas qu'alors [. . .] elle ne tirât de l'accumulation de ces jours monotones auxquels elle tenait tant, l'attente d'un cataclysme domestique, limité à la durée d'un moment, mais qui la forcerait d'accomplir une fois pour toutes un de ces changements dont elle reconnaissait qu'ils lui seraient salutaires et auxquels elle ne pouvait d'elle-même se décider. (i. 114–15)

The acoustic accumulation in 'elle tenait tant, l'attente' with the unspoken consonance with 'tante' is a strong enough alerting-device for the mind to register later uses of 'attente' with caution. In the music section, the narrator describes himself as 'baigné dans l'attente pleine de securité de son retour' (iii. 664), but the 'Sonate' recalls the darker side of his vigils before the 'sonnerie' of the telephone. His perplexity before Wagner's music discovers itself, through the counter-senses that the stress-line motifs sound out, as a deep fear that his happy security is not the joy Isolde and Tristan experience at the sight of the ships, but rather a short-term inhabiting of his aunt's habits of mind, a calm self-appeasement of his pain that is secretly, almost neuralgically, troubled by the gravitational forces, desires, and memories that his jealousy creates. The little 'tan' prose rhyme we hear in the currents of his prose articulates the accent of confused memory, doubt, and ambiguous expectation that sings out a dark opera of 'attente' within the sounds of his prose, within the silent stirrings of his memory. The smile he smiles when recognizing the intonation of 'l'aieul' in the 'petit-fils' cannot disguise how far Léonie in his voice falls short of the joy Proust felt on returning home.

My analysis of the Wagner section owes much to the work of Jean Milly, *La Phrase de Proust*, to which indeed I owe a more general debt. Milly noticed the 'tan' repetition in the first passage I analysed and much more besides. He reads the sound-repetitions in this section as a series of hidden anagrams. Thus one can hear 'Tristan' in the passage I quoted:

> Il est remarquable qu'à l'instant où surgit dans le texte le nom de Tristan, le phonèmes qui le constituent se trouvent repris et disséminés par petits groupes dans les mots voisines, comme si la phrase recélait déjà par fragments le mot-thème (ou hypogramme selon la terminologie de Saussure et de Starobinski) et que ce dernier fût en somme doublement présent. (67–8)

Milly discovers the rich field of key-word accentuation in this reading, runs and strings forming stress-lines ('repris et disséminés par petits groupes dans les mots voisines') that disseminate the phonemes of key-words, which by subsequent repetition become motif-terms ('mot-thème'). In the rest of his analyses, he discovers 'Wagner', 'Parsifal', and other 'mots-thèmes' hidden in the sound-repetitions. This sound-anagram technique, for Milly, 'serait le correspondant du leitmotiv dans la prose poétique' (72):

> comme lui elle procède par retour de séquences sonores [. . .] liées à un signifié identique. Comme lui, elle est moins un procédé de rappel explicite qu'un solicitation de l'inconscient. Elle aboutit d'une part à renforcer la présence d'un nom par répétition de ses éléments, d'abord dans un champ restreint, le *locus princeps*, puis dans un espace plus vaste, à la manière d'un halo d'intensité décroissante [. . .] d'autre part, en décomposant le signifiant et en dispersant ses éléments dans d'autres mots, à déployer le mot-thème en faisant jouer les capacités d'association de ses parties, d'où un notable enrichissement de sa signification. (72)

My only cavil against this fine description of the local effects of sound-repetition (that sit so closely with Delbouille's and Mourot's theories of key-word accentuation) is that Milly abandons the field at the essential point. That is, what point is there in stressing the 'mot-thème'?

Anxious to demonstrate Saussurian anagram-theory, he never answers this question, except to present the technique as merely symptomatic of certain acts of attention: 'L'écrivain, lorsqu'il fixe intensément son attention sur un mot, est amené à reproduire dans son écriture, volontairement ou non, les éléments phoniques de ce mot' (73). This begs the question. Milly is in effect answering a reader's query, why is our attention being drawn to this particular word? by simply saying, because the writer's is. More seriously, Milly's wholesale adoption of Saussure's anagram-theory seems to me to be singularly ill-advised. The use of this aspect of Saussure's work risks becoming dangerously normative, however, so deserves a short detour in my argument on Proust.

In 1971, Jean Starobinski published extracts from notebooks of Ferdinand de Saussure dealing with his strange and compelling anagram-theory. From 1906 to 1909, Saussure had obsessively ransacked Latin poems in search of anagrams concealed within the sound-effects. The sound-repetitions, according to Saussure, in the particular disposition of certain of their phonemes, obsessively repeat the phonemes of a name, usually of a god or goddess, to whom the poetry is, in an obscure sense, dedicated. I repeat the word 'obsessively' with malice aforethought: there seems to me to be a fruitful connection between Saussure's desire to find these hidden names and the whole issue of sound-repetition in texts.

Saussure's procedure throughout the ninety-nine 'cahiers' was rigorously single-minded. The name of the god or hero whose anagram is to be found in the text is called the 'locus princeps'. The words containing the relevant phonemes in the right order are called 'mannequins'. The 'locus' plus 'mannequins' form the 'hypogramme'. One example will suffice to illustrate Saussure's method. Basically, the 'mannequins' give a reduced form of the 'locus princeps', the initial and final phonemes, a kind of front-and-back version of a 'sigle'. So the Latin distich 'A̲D MEA TEMPLA̲ PORTATO̲' secretly gives us 'APOLLO'—the 'mannequin' is working through the phonemes underlined.

These phonemes have a double function, then, first, as ordinary participants in the poetic line, and secondly, as Starobinski points out, 'comme *souvenirs* du mot-thème, comme signes d'une règle respectée, d'un pacte tenu'. He goes on:

à travers les 99 cahiers de refléxion et d'enquête sur les anagrammes, (Saussure) pourchasse la similitude, l'écho épars où se laissent capturer, d'une façon presque toujours identique, les linéaments d'un corps pre- mier. Partout fonctionne la *même* loi anagrammatique, confirmée d'exemple en exemple (avec des résultats ici où là reconnus moins satis- faisants); et dans chaque exemple particulier, les phonèmes du mot- thème se redoublent, se diffractent, de façon à constituer une présence sur deux niveaux.[31]

At one point in his 'cahiers', Saussure investigates the possibility that the name 'Aphrodite' is to be found concealed and reverently repeated in the phonemes of Lucretius's invocation to Venus at the beginning of *De rerum natura*. As Starobinski puts it:

Dans l'admirable préambule du *De rerum natura*, Ferdinand de Saussure décèle la présence obsédante du nom d'Aphrodite. L'invocation à Vénus se construit sur le nom grec de la déesse: bien davantage, il continue à *retentir* alors même que l'invocation a pris fin. Tout se passe donc comme si le poète avait voulu, dans l'acte même de la composition, démontrer la fécondité, une puissance productive, dont le nom d'Aphrodite serait la source [. . .] A aucun moment n'apparaît l'hypothèse—si séduisante pour nous—d'une émanation des cinquante premiers vers du premier Chant à partir de la substance phonique d'Aphrodite—de son corps verbal: don maternel et amoureux d'une chair sonore, diffusion d'une présence fon- damentale à travers le chant. (Starobinski, *Les Mots sous les mots*, 80).

In this quotation, we are presented with the comic image of the editor, Starobinski, being thoroughly seduced by the hypothesis the scientist Saussure would not touch and letting his prose lilt to the sexy rhythms of its sonorous potential. But it is a hypothesis that charms because Saussure invites the accusation. Why this obsessive search? Why this silence about reasons and results?

These question become particularly pertinent in the light of the companion word Saussure finds in the Lucretius text, *postscenia*, or 'behind the scenes'. Again, Saussure gives no information as to why such a word should be there. Starobinski, as usual, gives us the unspoken answer, writing that the word, being found (in 'mannequin' form) throughout a passage where Lucretius de- nounces 'les mensonges de la passion' and the disgusting secrets

---

[31]   J Starobinski, *Les Mots sous les mots*: 63–4. Later references given after quota- tions.

of the woman loved, itself denounces 'une profondeur d'artifice, un lieu sans majesté où s'agence l'illusion' (Starobinski, *Les Mots sous les mots*, 100). The search for an elusive Venus in her ideal nature (pure name) and her unspoken sexuality (behind the scenes obscenity) is more than an apt image for Saussure's phonolinguistic studies: the search is the motive and definition of his research.

Saussure's research, by the way, ended in utter disillusionment— he had discovered a contemporary Italian poet who, according to him, used the same technique. But, it seems, the poet denied any conscious knowledge of the sound-repetition anagram-technique. Saussure gave it all up and went on, as we all know, to write *Cours de linguistique générale* where the signifier is stamped 'arbitrary'. And it is particularly arbitrary if one resorts to a *de facto* anagram-technique. This restricts uses of sound-repetitions to relatively pointless name-chants, like some childish version of cabalistic riddling. Any name might be construed from the normal frequencies of phonemes in initial and terminal positions. 'Ad mea templa portato' merely exploits the high frequency in Latin of the letter 'a' in these positions. Why not 'Minerva' ('mea templa')? Or 'Attica' ('Ad mea templa')? Or 'amato' ('Ad mea templa portato')? When Milly applies Saussure to Proust, he is careful to look only for pre-existing names in the text ('Tristan', 'Guermantes', etc.) which would seem sensible, but then mere stressing of names we are aware of seems rather a feeble discovery. If Proust is simply repeating the phonemes of 'Tristan' in the passage analysed above, then the sound-effects remain at the level of a weak and insignificant word-game, a poor man's Scrabble.

The Vinteuil sonata is not simply associated with the name 'Tristan'. For the narrator it is acutely involved with the repressed agonies of 'attente' and the emotional stresses his voice and memory undergo when suffering the long waiting that punctuates his life. It is something the narrator inherits from Swann, a lesson in the double translation Swann enacts each time he listens to the Vinteuil:

le violon était monté à des notes hautes où il restait comme pour une attente, une attente qui se prolongeait sans qu'il cessât de les tenir, dans l'exaltation où il était d'apercevoir déjà l'objet de son attente qui s'approchait, et avec un effort désespéré pour tâcher de durer jusqu'à son arrivée, de l'acceuillir avant d'expirer, de lui maintenir encore un moment de toutes ses dernières forces le chemin ouvert pour qu'il pût passer, comme on soutient une porte qui sans cela retomberait. Et avant que Swann eût le temps de comprendre, et de se dire: 'C'est la petite phrase de la sonate de Vinteuil, n'écoutons pas!' tous ses souvenirs du temps où Odette était éprise de lui, et qu'il avait réussi jusqu'à ce jour à maintenir invisibles dans les profondeurs de son être, trompés par ce brusque rayon du temps d'amour qu'ils crurent revenu, s'étaient réveillés et, à tire-d'aile, étaient remontés lui chanter éperdument, sans pitié pour son infortune présente, les refrains oubliés du bonheur. (i. 339)

The 'attente' motif originates in Swann's story,[32] a story so profoundly absorbed by the narrator that his own memory is occupied by, and preoccupied with, its narrative recurrences and intermittent structures. Swann's imagined memories are adopted by the narrator as his own. The rhyme of 'attente' with the Vinteuil motif is a motivating force summoning a complex system of memories into life as sound and feeling. The forgotten refrains of happiness that Swann recalls are, ironically, based on experiences that were *never* happy. The image of the door with the accompanying agonizing effort that obscurely embody the 'attente' motif recalls and inverts Swann's nightly returns to Odette's house, the knock on the window, signal to Odette to open the door and then play him the little Vinteuil phrase (i. 232), crossed with memories of the terrible search for her, and the long waiting (the 'grand souffle d'agitation' (i. 227)) that simultaneously creates both his love and jealousy for Odette's secret, absent life and its memories. The narrator's perplexity when listening to Wagner in Vinteuil is, in part, a perplexity at the sheer weight of tiny, painful recalls the 'attente' motif organizes and articulates. For the motif sings a song of many memories, his own mixed with Swann's and his aunt's, a song that recreates the desperate need, the desperate fabrications, and bewilderments provoked in the narrator's self by the mystery of absent lives, absent minds.

Allusion and 'Phrases Types'

The 'contresens' the rhymes stress along Proust's sentences, in discovering the pulses of a long-term interior life, do not function

---

[32] In this case, the motif is indicated by strong 't'-repetition ('monté'-'notes hautes'-'restait'-'attente').

as an inarticulate, hieroglyphic series of 'souvenirs de musique', but, with their 'délicate, minutieuse et douce précision' (iii. 290), press home to the heart of reader and narrator a detailed allusion to another painful context, a context that secretly moves the prose. In his essay on Baudelaire, Proust speaks of the way poetic allusion remembers other written contexts in a manner that makes this clear. He wonders there at the peculiar quality of a poet's prose, in particular Alfred de Musset's *Contes*:

Musset, quand il écrit ses Contes, ses essais de critique, ses discours d'Académie, c'est quelqu'un qui a laissé de côté son génie, qui a cessé de tirer de lui des formes qu'il prend dans un monde surnaturel et exclusivement personnel à lui et qui pourtant s'en ressouvient, nous en fait souvenir. Par moments, à un développement, nous pensons à des vers célèbres, invisibles, absents, mais dont la forme vague, indécise, semble transparaître derrière des propos que pourrait cependant tenir tout le monde et leur donne une sorte de grâce, de majesté, d'émouvante allusion. (*CSB*, 249–50)[33]

Proust's rhymes seem to me to be memory-signals in just such a relationship to the logical turn of the character's present-tense syntax. It is Musset's unconscious achievement dramatized within the voice-patterns of the narrating subject. Proust has his characters (including the narrator) unconsciously and movingly allude to exclusively personal patches of their past time with the dramatic pulses of the rhymes. Proust's own silent allusions to the 'vers célèbres' of past poets give body to this assertion.

One of the most interesting is in *Du côté de chez Swann* where Swann, at the Verdurins, is in secret agony over Forcheville's growing predominance and influence. The 'petite phrase' enters as if to reassure him:

sous l'agitation des trémolos de violon qui la protégeaient de leur tenue frémissante à deux octaves de là—et comme dans un pays de montagne, derrière l'immobilité apparente et vertigineuse d'une cascade, on aperçoit, deux cents pieds plus bas, la forme minuscule d'une promeneuse—la petite phrase venait d'apparaître, lointaine, gracieuse, protégée par le

[33] An example of Musset's poetic prose is this passage from the end of 'Histoire d'un merle blanc' who is in love with a rose and not his wife: 'son calice est fermé à l'heure qu'il est: elle y berce un vieux scarabée,—et demain matin, quand je regagnerai mon lit, épuisé de souffrance et de fatigue, c'est alors qu'elle s'épanouira, pour qu'une abeille lui mange le cœur' (*Contes*, 713).

long déferlement du rideau transparent, incessant et sonore. Et Swann, en son cœur, s'adressa à elle comme à une confidente de son amour, comme une amie d'Odette qui devrait bien lui dire de ne pas faire attention à ce Forcheville. (i. 260)

Like the Vinteuil phrase behind the cascade of the strings, the little line of poetry the passage alludes to lies half-hidden behind 'le long déferlement' of the sentence,[34] the great Romantic landscape the music paints for Swann obscuring in its wash the half-tangible presence of Baudelaire's great line:

Le violon frémit comme un cœur qu'on afflige

from 'Harmonie du Soir'. 'Violon', 'frémissante', and 'en son cœur' in the passage and the context itself (harmony at evening, Swann's jealousy), touch the Baudelaire line into the play of the two sentences, especially with our knowledge of Proust's own strong admiration for the breath-taking cruelty and compassion of the line. In the Baudelaire essay alluded to above, he quotes it with the two verbs stressed and adds, with a start of personal feeling, 'oh! ce frémissement d'un cœur à qui on fait mal' (CSB, 251).

With the poetic line alive in the words of the prose, resuscitated by our memory of it, the drama of Swann's feeling clears itself into definition. The strings correspond to Swann's jealous heart, tormented by Forcheville, deep in the heart of which the phrase (his dream of Odette shifted painfully here to the mere 'amie d'Odette') gracefully offers hope as if gathered 'du passé lumineux' (Baudelaire, Œuvres complètes, 69). The painful 'contresens' the Baudelaire line emphasizes, as Proust himself had done in the essay, is 'ce que le paragraphe omet', the connection between 'frémit'/'frémissante' and 'afflige'.

The internal rhyme-play in the passage quietly stresses it too. Baudelaire's internal f-string 'frémit-afflige' is echoed by the 'frémissante-phrase-déferlement-Forcheville' run in the Proust. The k-repetition in 'comme un cœur' is remembered in the repeated

---

[34] The cascade image is used elsewhere by Proust to describe the way a difficult truth is always half-concealed within the words one uses: 'Mes paroles ne seraient parvenues à Gilberte que deviées, comme si elles avaient eu à traverser le rideau mouvant d'une cataracte avant d'arriver à mon amie, méconnaissables, rendant un son ridicule, n'ayant plus aucune espèce de sens.' (i. 601). This is Proust at his most pessimistic about the communicability of lyrical sounds in prose, given the changes they must undergo in the alien context. Note the telling a, R and s repetitions so easily missed or made ridiculous by the rapidly skimming prose aural attention.

*comme*s, the comme-cascade trick and the 'sonore-cœur-comme-confidente-amour' stress-line. Just as the rhyme-parallel 'deux octaves de là . . . deux cents pieds plus bas' knits pitch, height, and what we hear together, the half-assonantal string, emphasized by the syntactical breaks, 'sonore . . . en son cœur . . . son amour', brings sound and heart together around their common cause. The harsh t and s runs down to 'minuscule', clustering (with our memory of the Baudelaire line) in stress-lines around 'frémissante', are gently and softly replaced by their muted counterparts in the rhyme-string 'promeneuse', 'la phrase', 'gracieuse' (which retrospectively makes 'l'immobilité apparente et vertigineuse' move with a more delicate life), and the t-repetitions (muted not phonetically but semantically) in 'petite', 'apparaître', 'lointaine', 'protégée'. Note also the return of Proust's paR motif (apparente-aperçoit-apparaître-transparent with accompanying runs on p and R).

The acoustic drama within the sentence is richly musical in the precise and minute ways Proust understood music to have when it deeply moved the mind: mimetic of motions of the mind deeper than those felt within the immediate time-signature, dramatized in the little accumulations of sound and emphasis to represent compositionally the memory of another time, other times that bring to bear their emotional rhythms and counter-senses upon the air and the page. The stress-lines in Proust's sentence remind us of the unspoken stress within Swann's mind, make us remember 'les harmonies oubliées' of 'Harmonie du soir', recall to our imagination how music itself, and the musicality of prose have, as the common core to their power, the recognition of their continued life in the listener, reader, character as modes for the sudden articulation of slowly accreted feeling.

My study of Proust's use of sound-effects has confirmed three things. First, that consideration of a variety of examples demonstrates that Proust consciously regulates the sound-system of his sentences to portray the reverberation of key terms within Swann's and the narrator's voices.

Secondly, that this reverberating effect is bound up with how memory acts upon the 'present-tense' voice. Thus, the key-words being emphasized by the prose rhyme technique simulate the internal 'accent' of the voice 'à contresens', suffering the flow of the currents of evaded remembered connotations.

And thirdly, that the local instances of memory-stress can, as in the 'attente'-'tan' rhymes for example, by themselves being repeated, build up into a motif that is, at root, the heart of a hidden argument about the relations between what is said and what is being remembered by the narrator. These three considerations bring into line the way a reader registers the prose rhymes in his or her memory and the memory-acts that the sound-effects imitate and articulate.

I would like to conclude this chapter by demonstrating how closely my suggestions as to how the key-word counter-senses are working at the level of the sounds of the prose accord with the narrator's own 'phrase-type' theories in *La Prisonnière*.

I have shown how the sound-effects in *A la recherche du temps perdu* act as lines of force that reveal concealed emotional emphasis on key memories. These memories, in my examples, have included the 'mémoire'-'cœur' link that revealed the jealous stress of the narrator's obsessive attention to detail, the 'passé' rhymes that circled round one of Albertine's suppressed phrases, the 'attente' rhymes that secretly informed his solitary enjoyment of music, the self-circling 'moi' rhymes that gave the selfish accent of his possessiveness with Albertine and his grandmother. The 'chant'-'accent' prose rhyme sequence at his grandmother's death is an untypical passage that unified the prose round a centre outside the narrator's preoccupations. And yet it also gives one a clue towards synthesizing the variety of memory-accents discussed in the chapter. For the 'chant'-'accent' motif unified a whole series of extreme revelations that the narrator undergoes concerning the nature of his grandmother's personality, before and after her death. Those revelations had made him see her and hear her voice at the two extremes of her nature, as pure tender voice and as absolutely foreign body. The 'accent' heard at her death-bed unified those shocking and moving revelations into one, just as the idea of a voice in print (on the one hand, impersonal, narrative, silent and on the other, personal, deeply felt, dramatic) is unified. This meeting occurs when the narrator manages to feel another's memory fully being revealed, rather than being isolated within the confines of his own intermittently selfish and artificial memory.

My analysis of the accents revealed by the sound-repetitions within the jealous voice demonstrates how, to a degree, the 'chant'-'accent' example is only a more spectacular revelation of a similar process. For both Swann and the narrator suffer, within their voices, the pain of being blocked between the habits of their own introspective memories and the mystery of the memory of their lovers. This pain breaks out into their voices along the prose rhymes, momentarily unifying their past selves with the possible other selves of Albertine and Odette whilst at the same time registering the internal shock this momentary unification causes. Similarly, the narrator's attempts to find a different, separate appeasement in music or the sleeping body of Albertine only serves to link those objects of desire to the recurrent and evaded memories of jealous stress and 'attente'.

The 'mémoire'-'cœur', 'passé'-'casser', 'attente'-'tan' prose rhymes, then, are operating in the same way as the 'phrase-types' the narrator discovers in Dostoevsky and Hardy, in essence because they, like the 'phrase-types', reveal a hidden past and articulate an accent of extreme emotion through repeated, remembered figures. The 'phrase-types' reveal 'une réalité cachée, révélée par une trace matérielle', the reality of 'le Passé' (iii. 877). The theory of 'phrase-types' originates in the narrator's attention to music, to 'la musique où les sons semblent prendre l'inflexion de l'être, reproduire cette pointe intérieur et extrême des sensations' (iii. 876). To make clear the rhyme between the music of inflection revealed by the typical phrase and the hidden jealous counter-senses concealed within his narrator's voice along the prose rhyme memory-accents, Proust alternates his narrator's discussion of his theory with the narrator's persistent obsessive jealous attention to Albertine's voice and its hidden memories. Immediately following his disquisition on Hardy's 'phrase-types', the narrator moves to an interrogation of Albertine's possibly lesbian relations with Gilberte (iii. 878). Proust here uses an alternating technique of Balzac's,[35] alternating Albertine's words with the narrator's own

---

[35] Balzac, Honoré de, *Le Curé de Tours* (Paris, 1976), 112–17. Madame de Listomère and l'abbé Troubert bandy diplomatic phrases about Birotteau's inheritance, whilst inserting, in parenthesis, the real meaning of what has been said. Balzac has this to say about this technique:

Quelques dessinateurs se sont amusés à représenter en caricature le contraste fréquente qui existe entre ce que l'on dit et ce que l'on pense. Ici, pour bien saisir l'intérêt du duel de paroles qui eut lieu entre le prêtre et la grande dame, il est nécessaire de dévoiler les pensées qui'ils cachèrent mutuellement sous des phrases en apparence insignifiantes. (112–13)

analysis of their secret sense in parentheses. This sudden move gives real, personal matter to the narrator's admiration for 'phrase-types' which reveal 'une réalité cachée', the reality of Albertine's past.

Proust makes this clearer later in this section:

Par instants, dans les yeux d'Albertine, dans la brusque inflammation de son teint, je sentais comme un éclair de chaleur passer furtivement dans des régions plus inaccessibles pour moi que le ciel et où évoluaient les souvenirs, à moi inconnus, d'Albertine. (iii. 887–8)

The hint that 'le Passé' sought for in the 'phrase-types' might be Albertine's hidden memories, is fully revealed in the narrator's description of her—'m'invitant sous une forme pressante, cruelle et sans issue, à la recherche du passé, elle était plutôt comme une grande déesse du Temps' (iii. 888). The link is confirmed and expressed by rhyme-play. In the passage above, the 'instant'- 'teint'-'sentais' stress-line allied to the repeated 'Albertine', is pressed home half-way through the paragraph where he says the 'beauté' he seeks in her, 'qui consistait en ce que mon amie se développait sur tant de plans et contenait tant de jours écoulés, cette beauté prenait pour moi quelque chose de déchirant' (iii. 888). The word 'passer' is repeated twice in the paragraph, before 'à la recherche du passé' occurs, once in the passage first quoted above, with a and s runs confirming it, and in this phrase 'je pouvais la caresser, passer longuement mes mains sur elle, mais [. . .] je sentais que je touchais seulement l'enveloppe close d'un être qui par l'intérieur accédait à l'infini' (iii. 888), where 'caresser' rhymes it into prominence again. The re-emergence of the 'tan' motif calls up all the anxiety of expectation it represents and here not only links it to the expectation of the revelation of Albertine's hidden memories but also rhymes it with 'Temps', the great motif of the book.

It thus, with the subsidiary rhyme-memory of the 'passer'- 'passé' motif, effects a back-translation of the real concealed meaning within the narrator's admiration for the typical phrase's access to 'le Passé', a translation he is half-aware of when discussing the ways the Vinteuil music had been 'une cause indirecte de

Proust inverts the technique: the 'pensées' in parentheses are the narrator's suppositions about what Albertine is really thinking. Prose rhymes are a more subtle form of this 'revealing' tactic.

jalousie pour moi' (iii. 875). These sound-effects, like the relations between 'passer' in this paragraph and 'le Passé', are as much symptoms of an anxiety to discover the true stories concealed in Albertine's memory as they are real revelations of the past present in the narrator's voice. The sounds of the prose rhymes pass over the body of the words and hint at complex textual 'souvenirs', momentarily take on 'l'inflexion de l'être', fleetingly reproduce 'cette pointe intérieure et extrême des sensations', but only at extraordinary moments will they, like the 'accent'-'chant' motif, give one memory and selves revealed, the voice, the body of the words, and 'le Passé' condensed into one.

The time sought after in the book is therefore partly but crucially the time concealed within the loved one's mind, the absent time of Albertine's unspoken memories provoking the intense fabricating processes of the jealous voice and its text, processes that slowly create a textual memory-system complete with its own complex structure of internal recalls, alerting-devices, and habit-forming repetitions. The arbitrariness, artifice, and chanciness of this system is conceded by Proust since he demonstrates that its chief agent is the sound of words. But Proust also shows how the historical music of words, broken up into painful counter-senses as it is, is nevertheless capable of constituting and constructing a mind in love, a mind in mourning, a mind hopelessly waiting. In all the uses of the memory-stress sound-effects technique, Proust records the meeting of such contradictions within the voice, from the tiny 'contresens' in Charlus's complex voice to the contradictions between dying body and pure tender voice within the narrator's loving and mourning perception of his grandmother, from the contradictions that reveal the jealous voice within Swann's habitual self-protecting memory to the Albertine-haunted contradictions within the narrator's love of pure music. Though they may contradict our own desires for a cleanly rational, silently skim-read prose, sound-repetitions in prose are tiny, minor traces we should learn to love to hear, for they may very well force us to acknowledge our own love for the fleeting, contradictory stories, passions, and fabrications of human memory and its texts.

3
Significant Lapses of Speech: rhymes and reasons in Joyce's prose

In *Finnegans Wake*, in the litany of inspired self-parody that is the 'Shem' section, Joyce describes his fictionalized self-image as an embodied 'lapsus lingua':

> a lapsis linquo with a ruvidubb shortartempa, bad cad dad fad sad mad nad vanhaty bear [. . .] if reams stood to reason and his lankalivline lasted he would wipe alley english spooker, multaphoniaksically spuking, off the face of the erse. (178. 01–07)

The toilet-humour of this delinquent exile shows just how far his tongue has fallen from his accusers' clean speech in the very act of articulating his angry multi-national linguistic manœuvre against the pure English tongue. That project relies on the rhymes in his book ('reams' as rhymes and paper) standing to reason. By this is meant an indivisible complex of sound and sense that reason will judge as making sound sense. This entailed a move out of English into other languages, other layers of historically significant sounds ('multaphoniaksically'), to reconstitute prelapsarian Babel before the babble set in. This mighty mission is ignored by his accusers however. All they remember is his dirty habits, his falls from grace. Rebuking the elders later in the book, Shem-Shaun as Yawn complains: 'I brought you from the loups of Lazary and you have remembered my lapsus langways'. (484. 25)

What they are remembering is his sexual misdemeanour, his incestuous coupling with his sister, a sideways version of messing about with your mother tongue. The Four disguised as sea-birds witness the act in Tristan's boat and hear 'like a lisp lapsing', either the end of a kiss or Tristan's withdrawal (396. 29). His control over the fragments of fallen language only remembers the fall, when the literal sexual acts of his tongue, the fatal kiss, gave all his kin away like Adam with the apple. The rhymes remember crimes: in Joyce's reworking of Swinburne's 'Ballad of Francis Villon' ('Villon our sad bad glad mad brother's name' (McHugh, *Annotations*, 178)), Swinburne's rhymes engender a similarly rich acoustic atmosphere in Shem's language, but Shem's rhymes accuse him: 'bad cad dad' identifies him with the betrayer of his father in Phoenix Park. The rhymes in his reams are the significant lapses of speech that betray Shem by remembering the sexual slip at the root of his mind.

Such significant lapses and their mode of recall seem to cross Freudian slips with Jungian race-memory. Indeed, as Clive Hart pointed out in *Structure and Motif in* Finnegans Wake (93), such cross-breeding seems to have been Joyce's intention as far back as the *Scribbledehobble* notebook where, in an entry significantly in the 'Scylla and Charybdis' section, Joyce noted, 'dream thoughts are wake thoughts of centuries ago: unconscious memory: great recurrence: race memorial: repressions: fixations: signs by'.[1] Frank Budgen in *James Joyce and the Making of Ulysses* told Clive Hart that Joyce 'prized memory above all human faculties' (53). In this chapter I shall sketch out the relations between Joyce's portrait of the workings of recollection and his use of sonic patterns, particularly his dense rhyme-play. Joyce's intentions as mapped out in the *Scribbledehobble* workbook entry will be criticized and redefined by considering the myth of his own prodigiously retentive memory, and his large-scale association of cultural and personal memory with a rhyming style. This style instanced a manner that Joyce remembered more and more as his reams stood the test of a lifetime's rationalization of the bonds between sound and sense.

The Myth of Joyce's Memory

The myth of Joyce's memory started early: friends recalled being startled by it, awed by its retentiveness. Though he might write of human lapses, his memory never failed him, the story went. As Budgen noted, 'most human memories begin to fail at midnight,

---

[1] *Scribbledehobble: The Ur-Workbook for Finnegans Wake*, ed. T. E. Connolly, 104. On the same page, interestingly enough, Joyce summarizes his reaction to Proust: 'Proust, analytic still life.'

and lapse into the vague and à peu près, but not that of Joyce' (181). C. P. Curran remembers Joyce's 'extraordinary memory [. . .] preserving for use immediately, or after a great space of years, what came his way' (*James Joyce Remembered*, 35–6). Joyce himself was proud of his retentiveness; he told Stanislaus in the early 1900s that 'like the Bourbons, "he never forgot" ';[2] this a devious reference also to his savage capacity to hold lifelong grudges. Stanislaus, however, immunized against the modish idolatry that surrounded his brother, was more surprised by his brother's control over his forgetfulness, as though understanding that a retentive memory relies on a practised capacity to forget:

He devoured books, while I was a slow reader. It sometimes surprised me, however, to find that my brother remembered little or nothing of most of the books he read so voraciously, and that at need he could make good use of the one or two things he did remember from his reading. He read quickly, and if the book or the author did not appeal to him he forgot them both. (*My Brother's Keeper*, 94)

Joyce's own idea of his own memory was skewed between astonishment at the monotonous regularity and vividness of his own recall and fear of losing such a necessary power. In the illnesses that were the consequence of overwork on *Ulysses* and his failing eye-sight, obliviousness was refused him. He wrote to Harriet Shaw Weaver in 1924, 'whenever I am obliged to lie with my eyes closed I see a cinematograph going on and on and it brings back to my memory things I had almost forgotten'.[3]

In the same letter, however, he fears a weakening in his retentive power so that he felt bound to practise his memory rigorously: 'I found that my memory was getting lame so in the clinic I started to learn by heart the Lady of the Lake by Sir Walter Scott, Bart. In three days I learnt 500 lines and can repeat them without mistake. Neither of my children can do this. It is not a sign of intelligence [. . .] but it is very useful'.[4] The more his eyes failed him the more Joyce had to rely on the infallibility of his memory in the complex

---

[2] Joyce, Stanislaus, *Dublin Diary*, 64 (entry for 31 July 1904).
[3] Letter to Harriet Shaw Weaver, 27 June 1924, *Letters*, i. 216.
[4] ˙ *Letters*, i. 216. Joyce remembers thinking this in the Wake. In Izzy's footnotes to the geometry lesson, she refers to 'that old Pantifox, Sir Somebody Something, Burtt' (*Finnegans Wake*, 293, fn. 2). The daughter of the book forgets what the father cannot.

work of proof-reading, note-assembling and expansion that the *Wake* demanded. In l928, for instance, he dictated a letter to Harriet Shaw Weaver saying his eyes were so bad that he could only read books for infants, and as a consequence had to memorize the whole of section three of Shaun (roughly a hundred pages of proof at that stage) 'to be able to find the places where I can insert from the twenty notebooks which I have filled up since I wrote this section' (*Letters*, i. 276—2.12.1928).

Identical with the practical usefulness of his memory was the hold it afforded him over the topography, lives, and history of pre-First World War Dublin, the enduring core of his material. Identical since his technical recall of 'the places where I can insert' was in a minute and intimate sense his control and organization of the memories of his characters. Eugène Jolas, one of the twelve friends/critics/amanuenses of *Exagmination*, the Joyce-controlled book of essays on *Work in Progress*, wrote in a 1938 edition of *transition*: 'nothing escapes his prodigious memory, whether the dialogues be in English, French, German, or Italian. It may be a slip of the tongue, a phantasmatic verbal deformation, or just a tic of speech, but it usually turns up later in its proper place'.[5] The verbal material Joyce chose to memorize is here specifically defined in terms of give-aways, particular distortions of many mother tongues, the telling lapsus linguae. The myth of Joyce's miraculous retentive memory is closely related to his and his entourage's desire to underwrite the authority in his readings and representations of slips of the tongue.

Joyce began to record Dublin slips of the tongue, verbal deformations and tics of speech from his earliest adventures into prose, the epiphanies. Stanislaus notes that the epiphanies began as 'ironical observations of slips, and little errors and gestures, mere straws in the wind—by which people betrayed the very things they were most careful to conceal' (*My brothers' Keeper*, 134). This preoccupation of Joyce's was never to leave him, and for him depended on an equally lordly sensitivity to those people's memories coupled with detailed knowledge of their environment and history. Many writers and critics have since commented on the effects of his lifetime's absorption in, and continuous recall of, Howth Castle and environs. Curran's comment: 'He knew the

---

[5] Jolas, 'Homage', 169–75. Quoted in Deming, *James Joyce*, ii. 658.

streets of Dublin by heart and his memory was a map of the town' (39); Wyndham Lewis's comparison of Joyce and Proust: 'Proust returned to the temps perdu: Joyce never left it. He discharged it as freshly as though the time he wrote about were still present, because it was his present' (*Time and Western Man*, 109); and Joyce's own remark: 'But every day and in every way I am walking along the streets of Dublin and along the strand. And 'hearing voices'. (*Letters*, i. 395—6.8.1937)

For Joyce, however, this display of his powers was not the vaudeville virtuosity of a memory-man. The display was to underpin the material thrown up by the observation of the telling straws in the wind. But it was also self-analytic in another sense. There are strong indications in his critical writings that he felt effortless recall, or rather inability to forget, was a political and racial inheritance of the Dublin scene. Reviewing William Rooney in 1982 as 'An Irish Poet', Joyce describes the narrative voice rising out of futile execrations of tyranny and 'with the gravity of one who remembers all the errors of his members and his sins of speech', goes into silence (*Critical Writings*, 87). In a review of Lady Gregory's work he exclaims, 'Out of the material and spiritual battle which has gone so hardly with her Ireland has emerged with many memories of beliefs, and with one belief—a belief in the incurable ignobility of the forces that overcame her' (*Critical Writings*, 105). The Irish citizen, Joyce writes in a 1907 discursive article,

does not forget the sack of Drogheda and Waterford, nor the bands of men and women hunted down in the furthermost islands by the Puritan, who said that they wanted to go 'into the ocean or into hell', nor the false oath that the English swore on the broken stone of Limerick. How could he forget? Can the back of a slave forget the rod? (*Critical Writings*, 119)

This national characteristic of the colonially oppressed merges with Joyce's youthful aesthetic preferences for the sanctuary of dream and for a pseudo-Blakean race-memory, both alluded to in his essay on James Clarence Mangan: 'One whose nature is so sensitive cannot forget his dreams in a secure and strenuous life'; 'In those vast courses of multiplex life that surround us, and in that vast memory which is greater and more generous than ours, probably no life, no moment of exaltation is lost' (*Critical Writings*, 181).

So two preoccupations lie within Joyce's interest in memory. First, as a form of Freudian observation of slips of the tongue that betray what people are most careful to conceal—this necessitated not only a myth about his own extraordinary powers of recall, but also a related myth about his miraculously detailed knowledge of Dublin in order to give authority to the secrets betrayed. Secondly, a Jungian concept of memory that understood the faculty in terms of racial recall, history, and world-spirit dream retention. The first covers the ground of personal memory; the second of broad cultural memory.

Personal and Race Memory

Brian Smith, in his book *Memory*, makes the broadest possible claims for memory: 'That we could not know the past without memory is true only because we could not *know anything* without memory, in the ordinary sense of the word "know" ' (22). Smith also interestingly blurs the distinction between memory and imagination: 'There is no reason why our imaginings, since they may be repeatedly entertained by us, should not become more familiar than actual experiences we have had only once' (42). 'Just as I can remember perceiving things so I can remember imagining things' (144). With this proviso in mind, Smith makes the following astonishing claim:

A set of coherent memories may be narrow and highly detailed, or it may be much wider and very sketchy; or it may be both at once—a nucleus, as it were, of detailed memories, fanning out into an extended context of less detailed memories, until it extends, however sketchily, over the whole of our past experience. (210)

Budgen's representation of Joyce's views on memory in *Ulysses* chimes in with Smith's. Discussing the peculiarity of self-portraiture in a novel, he notes that a writer's medium:

is not an active sense, but memory, and who knows when memory ceases to be memory and becomes imagination? No human memory has ever recorded the whole of the acts and thoughts of its possessor. Then why one thing more than another? Forgetting and remembering are creative agencies performing all kinds of tricks of selection, arrangement and adaptation. (63–4)

Budgen is explicitly saying that Joyce exploits the possible dubiety in memory's authority, memory *infida et labilis* , making a creative virtue out of the imagination invested in memory's organisation and mode of recall (122).

On the other hand, imagination itself is conditioned by large-scale cultural memories as Budgen goes on to suggest:

Imagination sees, remembers, foresees, divines. But that is not all. It is a heritage of human experience bequeathed from generation to generation and is therefore knowledge as such. If the poet had not this inheritance of race memory to draw upon he could never create a woman, so wide and deep is the gulf of desire and misunderstanding set between man and woman in the threescore years and ten of their experience. (292)

It is but a small step from this formulation to a reinterpretation of mystical race-memory:

From the dawn of life to the moment in which we live all experience is written in the structure and function of our bodies—all is preserved in the depths of our memories [. . .] In later years in Dublin Joyce lived in that philosophy which maintains that on the borders of our individual memory lies the memory of our race. (318)

That small step is through the middle term of how in a modern world racial memories are externally recorded: for Dubliners, 'all their yesterdays, that in an earlier age would have been quietly buried in the hope of a glorious resurrection as myth, lie embedded in files of newspapers and snapshot albums' (132).

If memory can expand by contextual and associative means 'however sketchily' to include the whole of our past experience; if past experience includes past imaginings; if it is also comprised of a vast cultural inheritance (not only etymologically, but historically and traditionally); if, further, the limits and detail of that inheritance are also allowed to lie in the public library; if all these descriptions of memory are admitted, then the thesis of *Finnegans Wake*, personal, local memories expanded by and cross-bred with bookish cultural memories, must also be admitted.[6] For a writer,

---

[6] The odder strands of both Smith's and Budgen's views are more difficult to incorporate into common-sense logic: Smith with his physiological description of how images are memorized, Budgen with the unconscious body-imprint of race-memory. If they mean no more than, respectively, 'automatically stored in the brain' and 'gestures and sex are as old as the species but have a historical development too which we remember', then they can pass.

acts of remembering will tend to expand backwards in the manner Budgen and Smith suggest because writing itself is an engagement with the sound and weight of words, their connotations and etymologies over time.

As T. S. Eliot put it when describing the auditory imagination:

What I call the 'auditory imagination' is the feeling for syllable and rhythm, penetrating far below the conscious levels of thought and feeling, invigorating every word, sinking to the most primitive and forgotten, returning to the origin and bringing something back, seeking the beginning and the end. It works through meanings, certainly, or not without meanings in the ordinary sense, and fuses the old and obliterated and the trite, the current and the new and surprising, the most ancient and the most civilised mentality. (118–19)

Race-memory, a national nostalgic temperament, dreaming recall are powerful and resourceful images for the working of the auditory imagination, especially so for a comic writer. And the image may work the other way, with the auditory imagination as Irish dream. Etymology shifts, for Joyce, to 'adamelegy' (*Finnegans Wake*, 77) in the 'earish' 'soundance' (130, 378) of the Dreamer's retrospect, a long lament for Adam's slip in the garden/Park, the primitive, forgotten 'lapsus linguae'. Like Hamlet, Joyce could never 'wipe away all trivial fond records,/All saws of books, all pressures past' (I. v. *Hamlet* 98–103) from the book and volume of his memory. Unlike Hamlet, he made of his retentiveness a great resource and created *quadrivial* fond records, to quote his wit.[7] His books hum with the rhymes, the syllables and rhythms of a powerful and continuously remembering auditory imagination.

Slips of the Tongue

Djuna Barnes, in the 1920s, asked Joyce about Irish garrulousness in relation to *Ulysses*:

'They are all there, the great talkers', he answered, 'them and the things they forgot. In *Ulysses* I have recorded, simultaneously, what a man says, sees, thinks, and what such seeing, thinking, saying does to what you

---

[7] From 'quadrivium', the higher division of the seven liberal arts in the Middle Ages.

Freudians call the subconscious—but as for psycho-analysis', he broke off, 'it's neither more nor less than blackmail.' ('I could never be lonely', 293)

Joyce's agile mind slips from forgetting to Freudian matters with an ease we would do wrong to ignore. His witty disclaimer of Freud's influence—psychoanalysts are blackmailers because they make their patients pay for knowledge about their intimate misdemeanours—masks Joyce's sustained interest in Freud's writings. Ellmann times his first exposure between 1910 and 1911 in Trieste where Italo Svevo would have brought him into contact with Dr Edoardo Weiss his nephew, the first to introduce psychoanalysis into Italy in 1910 (Ellmann, 340 n). He bought Freud's work on Leonardo that year, and though the list of his Trieste library shows that he acquired a 1917 edition of *Zur Psychopathologie des Alltagslebens* (Gillespie, *Inverted Volumes*, 94), Joyce's attention was focussed on slips of the tongue between 1911 and 1913.

One of his Trieste pupils, Paolo Cuzzi, remembers discussing Freud's *Five Lectures on Psychoanalysis* with him: 'he talked with Joyce' Ellmann records, 'about slips of the tongue and their significance. Joyce listened attentively, but remarked that Freud had been anticipated by Vico' (Ellmann, 340). Joyce is referring to Vico's imaginative use of etymology to prove the weight of a culture's history within individual utterances. Nevertheless, as Ellmann admits, Freud's influence was privately important for Joyce despite the public display of pre-cognizance. Joyce used to note down Nora's dreams in what Ellmann describes as a 'dream book' and furnish his own interpretations which 'showed the influence of Freud'.

Freud, in *The Psychopathology of Everyday Life*, provides numerous examples of slips of the tongue. For Freud, such slips cannot be analysed merely on the level of sound-resemblances, acoustic anticipations, or perseverations. The subtle disturbances of speech are influenced by material wholly outside the individual context motivated and distorted by repression using powers similar to the substitution work of childhood screen memories:[8]

[8] Freud provides an exhaustive comparison of the resemblance between the forgetting of names accompanied by paramnesia and the formation of screen memories, saying that both involve making mistakes in remembering, both involve a feeling that gives information of interference, and that both are marked by the interference of a tendentious factor, 'a purpose which favours one memory whilst

Among the slips of the tongue that I have collected myself I can find hardly one in which I should be obliged to trace the disturbance of speech simply and solely to what Wundt calls the 'contact effect of sounds'. I almost invariably discover a disturbing influence in addition which comes from something outside the intended utterance; and the disturbing element is either a single thought that has remained unconscious, which manifests itself in the slip of the tongue and which can often be brought to consciousness only by means of searching analysis, or it is a more general psychical motive force which is directed against the entire utterance. (*PEL*, 103)

Slips of the tongue are only one of the small betrayers. Amongst the other parapraxes Freud attends to are forgetting of names, slips of the pen, confusion in foreign languages, absent-mindedness, physical awkwardnesses and clumsiness and characteristic turns of phrase. All these chance actions betray a 'counter-will' (*PEL*, 206) internally opposed to one's own utterance which, though its manifestation tends through what Freud calls the 'defensive trend' (*PEL*, 199) to cancel out its own intentions, exposes an inner insincerity, becomes 'a mode of self-betrayal' (*PEL*, 131).

In particular, forgetting a place-name for instance, the mind's substitutes for the true place work through long cycles of acoustic similarities that dodge and echo a repressed element. Paramnesia, or false recollection, is an internal current (*PEL*, 57), an alien train of thought (*PEL*, 80) that diverts the attention away from 'an inner condition that attaches to the psychic material' (*PEL*, 44) but in so doing leaves a trace open to strict analysis, leaves 'echoes in a disturbance' (*PEL*, 51).

Joyce, it seems, was appalled by the humourlessness of such solemn scientificity and the arrogant assertions of expert right to know the subject's secret motives, which he thought merely masked prurient pleasure-seeking. In the *Wake* Yawn is subjected to vigorous cross-examination by the Four. They close in on the scene in the Park and homosexuality is in the air; they ask if there is a history of it in the family. Yawn answers with angry wit: '— Buggered if I know! It all depends on how much family silver you want for a nass-and-pair. Hah!' (522. 18–19). Here is Joyce's accusation of blackmail again. 'Nass-and-pair' is 'ass-and-pair', arse

striving to work against another', *Psycopathology*, 85–6. (Abbreviated to *PEL* throughout.)

and buttocks, the buggery charge. The 'Hah!' is at once triumph at the riposte and a laugh at his own joke. The Four do not get this at all. They, with *Psychopathology* up their sleeves, leap on the 'Hah!' as a perfect parapraxis. Freud's *Jokes and their Relation to the Unconscious* would also have told them that the formation of a joke entails a release of an inhibitory cathexis of psychical paths and is therefore a lead-in to the repressed element (199–203). 'What do you mean, sir, behind your hah!', they ask rather inexpertly. 'Nothing, sir. Only a bone moving into place. Blotogaff. Hahah!' Yawn replies. (*Finnegan's Wake*, 522. 22–3). Aware of their moves, he parodies the deterministic and materialist Freudian view of utterance with its physiologist extreme. 'Blotogaff' is one of Joyce's finer words: crossing 'photograph', 'blot', 'gaffe', and 'blow the gaff', a complex that organizes itself into something like this: the analyst feels he can see into the mind with X-ray scientific accuracy, using blotting-paper techniques to catch the patient out.[9]

Yawn's double laugh taunts the Four again with his next riposte, which is a mocking parody of their view of the subconscious self with its 'sordidly tales within tales': 'I didn't say it aloud, sir. I have something inside of me talking to myself.' (*Finnegan's Wake*, 522. 25–6) Yawn's wit is again lost on them:

But this is no laughing matter. Do you think we are tonedeafs in our noses to boot? Can you not distinguish the sense, prain, from the sound, bray? You have homosexual catheis of empathy between narcissism of the expert and steatopygic invertedness. Get yourself psychoanolised! (522. 30–5)

Yawn replies that he can psychoanalyse himself 'without your interferences or any other pigeonstealer' (522. 38–9).[10] Joyce here is not only having Yawn stand up for self-criticism against the self-pleasing, prying, and accusatory blackmail of the psychoanalyst; he hints that the Freudian view with its abstract distinctions and lack of wit over-distinguishes between sound and sense in its analysis. That is, in seeking ever for the hidden motive, the secret

---

[9] 'Blotogaff' is also responding to the Four's 'You don't hah to do thah, you know, snapograph,' which McHugh glosses with a quotation from *Souvenir of the* 25th Anniversary of the Gaiety Theatre, 1986: 'Thanks to X rays, the time will come no doubt when he will snapograph you wrong side out!' (*Annotations*, 522).

[10] 'Interferences' is of course a key-word in Freudian jargon, used also in relation to parapraxis (*PEL*, 85, for instance).

impulse in the brain ('the sense, prain'), they are tonedeaf to the weight of a judged accent ('the sound, bray' as Yawn's mocking parody). They accuse Yawn of repressing the implications of his 'nass-and-pair' sentence, believing him to have merely meant 'it depends how much you are asking for'. The 'hah!' after the sentence, therefore, is really a betrayal of his unconscious as it remembers the give-away in the utterance. By so doing they mishear Yawn's consciousness as it manipulates both sound and sense to parody their expectations. This indirectly works back against Freud's position on slips of the tongue. Freud, for Joyce, overestimates the unconscious motives external to the immediate context in which Wundt's 'contact effect of sounds' operates, not so much because Freud seeks sense rather than sound but because any utterance is not attended to until the full complexities of both the acoustic context and surface sense are *heard*.

Freud had argued against the position of the linguist Meringer who had asserted that slips of the tongue are products of the natural manner in which sounds in a sentence or utterance can be influenced by the intensity of certain of the vocables:

When we innervate the first sound or the first word in a sentence, the excitatory process already extends to the later sounds and the following words. (*PEL*, 96–7)

The 'excitatory process' concentrates around accented vowels and initial sounds, in Meringer's view. Freud rightly criticizes Meringer for his choice of the elements in a sentence with 'high valency': small 'insignificant' words can also affect the following sounds of a sentence; also key-sounds can be anticipated. But Freud uses such criticisms to distance his position too clearly from the arbitrary 'contact effect of sounds'. Proust's internal accentuations, the way they recall key-words against the 'sens' of the sentence seem to me to properly cross-breed Wundt's and Meringer's concentration on the actual acoustic context with the withheld but pressing anxieties that Freud, with much creative science, analysed. Joyce, with his expansive memory, his contempt for arbitrary restrictive distinctions, preferred to portray breadth of mind, Dedalus's keen intelligence, Bloom's temperance, Molly's unadulterated stream, the Dreamer's fabulous history of the world. Slips of the tongue, small-scale betrayals, chance actions were not signs of psychic repression for Joyce. They were mysteries of the

rich data of consciousness on its way, key-moments that concentrate occasional and painful cases of unwillingness to dwell upon
experiences—a dynamic act in which life presses upon and
changes attitudes to all that is remembered rather than the other
way around. One recalls Joyce's word-order to Djuna Barnes:
'what such seeking, thinking, saying does to what you Freudians
call the subconscious.'

Evacuated Auditory Imagination

Stephen Dedalus in *Ulysses* on the beach in Proteus, in fear of the
'vast memory' of his culture's long slavish history, contemplates
his people: 'Their blood is in me, their lusts my waves' (38). He
himself is half-consciously remembering his youthful fear of his
own sin, the first stirrings of lust in the *A Portrait of the Artist as a
Young Man*:

a presence subtle and murmurous as a flood filling him wholly with itself.
Its murmur besieged his ears like the murmur of some multitude in sleep;
its subtle streams penetrated his being. (*Portrait*, 91)

This wave of feeling flows throughout the *Portrait*, associated with
the rise of memory itself associated with sin and passion. Recalling
Ellen Clery's fingers touching him: 'suddenly the memory of their
touch traversed his brain and body like an invisible warm wave'
(*Portrait*, 77); the effect of the sermon on his guilt has him feel
waves of fire (125).[11]

These strange inchoate possessions, fits of contentless imaginings, are closely linked by Joyce with Stephen's creativity. The
villanelle comes on him like a wave of sound:

A soft liquid joy flowed through the words where the soft long vowels
hurtled noiselessly and fell away, lapping and flowing back and ever

---

[11] 'A wave of fire swept through his body: the first. Again a wave.' (*A Portrait of
the Artist as a Young Man* (abbreviated as *P*, throughout) 115). At school, Stephen's
darker moods are associated with sexual feeling and described as a 'stream of
moody emotions' (*P*, 71): 'the stream of gloomy tenderness within him had started
forth and returned upon itself in dark courses and eddies' (*P*, 71). These feelings
develop into a complex that unites sexual desire and poetic inspiration: 'Her
nakedness [. . .] enfolded him like water with a liquid life [. . .] the liquid letters of
speech, symbols of the element of mystery, flowed forth over his brain' (*P*, 201).

shaking the white bells of their waves in mute chime and mute peal and soft low swooning cry. (*P*, 204)

Merging Swinburne and sexual release, angelus with foam, the sentence gives subtle, murmurous flesh to pure rhythm and rhyme: rhythm becoming rise and fall of wave, rhyme the chime and peal of bells.[12] The acoustics take over the empty rhythms and pressures to connect that had characterized his sensual imaginings and guilt; waves of sensuous sound recalling the feelings of his senses. 'Vowels' flow and change along l and w stress-lines and carefully modulated long vowels and diphthongs into 'white bells'; 'words', through 'vowels', 'away' and 'white', turns into 'waves'; vowels resolve into over- perfect Masson patterns (ɔɪ – ɜː – ɒ – ɒ – ɜː – ɔɪ/eɪ – æ – æ – eɪ – eɪ – eɪ/uː – aɪ – uː – iː – uː – aɪ); strong fl and m stress-lines run flow and low, soft liquid objects together. This is an extraordinary display of almost narcotic possession, under the influence of strange unacknowledged passions. 'Pressures past' migrate into verbal textures in hazy synaesthetic flow.

It is a curious matter Joyce dwells upon here and in other contexts in the *Portrait*: how the subtle rising of past feelings and their merging into present ones with Stephen, entail an evacuation of sense and a creative flux:

he found himself glancing from one casual word to another on his right or left in stolid wonder that they had been so silently emptied of instantaneous sense until every mean shop legend bound his mind like the words of a spell and his soul shrivelled up, sighing with age as he walked on in a lane among heaps of dead language. His own consciousness of language was ebbing from his brain and trickling into the very words themselves which set to band and disband themselves in wayward rhythms:

The ivy whines upon the wall
And whines and twines upon the wall
The ivy whines upon the wall

[12] Bells have been associated with rhyme from Stephen's earliest experiences after being taught the castle bell song by Brigid: 'The bell! The bell! Farewell! O farewell!' (*P*, 22). The soft liquid joy of the later instances had also been occasioned by verse, a piece of Shelley—verse has always, with Stephen, had a direct access to his memory, forming it in many ways—'The verses crooned in the ear of his memory composed slowly before his remembering eyes the scene of the hall on the night of the opening of the National Theatre' (*P*, 204). The very first pages of the *P* are full of nursery rhymes, so much so that Dante's chance 'eyes' 'apologize' rhyme beats into the young Stephen's mind (*P*, 7–8).

The yellow ivy on the wall
Ivy, ivy up the wall

Did any one hear such drivel? (*P*, 162)

This passage follows the fierce erotic heroism Stephen felt on the beach after the revelation of the bird-like girl. There the tide had been out. She, in her wading in the ebbing water of the sea that Stephen dreads ('his flesh dreaded the cold infrahuman odour of the sea' (*P*, 152)), has concentrated all his flowing fears and guilt into affirmative power.

The passage above is the dark parody of that state of ecstasy—consciousness of language ebbing and trickling away like the sea, leaving the rhythms of creative energy. Instead of the girl, Stephen is haunted by the 'dark womanish eyes' of the priest-like Cranly (*P*, 162). Instead of 'swooning into some new world, fantastic, dim, uncertain as under sea' (*P*, 157), Stephen sinks into meaningless rhymes. 'Lord Almighty! Who ever heard of whining on a wall? Yellow ivy; that was all right. Yellow ivory also. And what about ivory ivy?', Stephen goes on (*P*, 162). The trouble is, 'wall' and 'ivory' have occurred before in his mental life. At school, he had remembered Eileen's long thin cool white hands: 'They were like ivory; only soft. That was the meaning of Tower of Ivory' (*P*, 39–40). In the next paragraph, the young Dedalus remembers graffiti in the closet-rooms—on the wall 'Balbus was building a wall'; the closet itself—'It was all thick slabs of slate and water trickled all day out of tiny pinholes and there was a queer smell of stale water there.' (*P*, 40). Cranly's priest-like face, his unsettling womanishness, the ambiguous resemblance to confessional of his 'listening face', have confused Stephen's feelings after the revelation of the girl on the beach. The rhymes that have paralleled and parodied his feelings of creative exaltation with their empty meaninglessness secretly recall his childhood religiose sexuality itself associated with fear of homosexual ambiguities at the Catholic school. His evacuated rhymes cross Cranly with the girl on the beach by hinting at Eileen and a Clongowes toilet.[13]

[13] The 'whines' part of the rhymes may recall the key-word that strikes Stephen very soon after the 'Balbus' and 'Ivory Tower Sequence: 'a faint winy smell off the rector's breath after the wine of the mass. The word was beautiful: wine'. (*P*, 43). Again this rhyme-reminiscence merges beauty with uncomfortable religious feeling—'the faint smell of the rector's breath had made him feel a sick feeling' (*P*, 43).

This style of discrete echo and reminiscence is a secondary motif behind the major drive to establish the grounds and means of an evacuated auditory imagination. Stephen's mind is inhabited by rhythm and rhyme 'emptied of instantaneous sense'. The fact that, on reflection, sense *can* be made of the purely verbal consciousness (that is, the vague recycling of religious and sexual preoccupations) would only confirm for Joyce the more important point. That point is that to be Jesuit-trained, an artist, and Irish is to suffer with an imagination that tends to bow before the flow of unaccommodated past pressures by deceiving itself into calling that flow its own present-tense passions transformed into a grand cultural act. The self-deception lies in the ceding of the self-regulatory power of personal memory to the 'vast' memory where every word has its dubious murmurous echo made resoundingly impersonal.[14]

It is an important aspect of *Ulysses* (hereafter abbreviated as *U*) that Stephen has turned against his *Portrait* self after the potentially crippling blow of his mother's death. He now recognizes the dangerous gravitational pull of his culture's whole desperate orientation towards empty-sounding words—'my lusts their waves'. The whole flow of the Irish mind towards rhythmical, rhyming rhetoric without hearted acts (analysed with such meticulous care in 'Ivy Day in the Committee Room') is grimly understood. 'Sounds are impostures', he tells Bloom in 'Eumaeus' (*U*, 509). In 'Ithaca', he declines Bloom's offer of a wash-basin because he is 'hydrophobe' and distrusts 'aquacities of thought and language' (*U*, 550). In 'Proteus', he wittily parodies his sensations of evacuation in the *Portrait* passage quoted above by reflecting on language as flow whilst pissing on the strand—literally evacuating:

Better get this job over quick. Listen: a fourworded wavespeech: seesoo, hrss, rsseeiss, ooos. Vehement breath of waters amid seasnakes, rearing horses, rocks. In cups of rocks it slops: flop, slop, slap: bounded in barrels.

[14] This point is supported by the hint that the 'ivy on the wall' in Stephen's senseless doggerel also crosses 'ivory tower' with 'Ivy Day', the Parnell anniversary. 'Ivy Day in the Committee Room' ends with an emptily rhetorical ballad which mutely awakens, mimes, and judges the empty patriotism of the committee. 'Ivy tower' and 'Ivy Day' together sketch out the path of Stephen's descent into confusion between Flaubertian impersonality (his personality replaced by a purely verbal consciousness) and an Irish nostalgic rhetoric (his poetry like the ballad first recalling then replacing a true historical attitude).

And, spent, its speech ceases. It flows purling, widely flowing, floating foampool, flower unfurling. (*U*, 101)

This passage parodies his revelation on the beach in *Portrait* where his soul enters the new world—'Glimmering and trembling, trembling and unfolding, a breaking light, an opening flower [...] unfolding and fading to palest rose' (*P*, 157). The eastern mysticism of Dublin at the turn of the century, Yeats's Rosicrucianism, Blavatsky's Buddhism, is brought mercilessly to book to serve the lower functions of the body. The unearthly acoustics of vague words emptied of sense, soft liquid vowels lapping and flowing to the murmurous rhythms of some multitude in sleep, are comically redefined in terms of the earthy banality of bodily waste-disposal, the continuity and monotony of the eternal rhythm of eating, drinking, and evacuation. It is now possible for Stephen to equate 'Flop, slop, slap' with 'purling', 'flowing', 'floating', 'unfurling'. Words that in the *Portrait* had become waves, here become a four-worded wave-speech that is also a four-letter word. Alliteration and assonance (with stress-lines along k<u>sr</u>, <u>slp</u>, <u>fl</u>, <u>sr</u> and accompanying heavy <u>s</u>-run), though literally wasted on the air as water on the beach, are not emptied of instantaneous sense but work here as a controlled release of self-mocking material that orders what lasts of the past into a comic, bodily frame.

Significant Lapses and Mocking Mirrors

By this change of heart Stephen moves spiritually closer to Bloom. Bloom at the end of 'Lotos-eaters', contemplates the heavenly weather:

Heatwave. Won't last. Always passing, the stream of life, which in the stream of life we trace is dearer thaaan them all.

Enjoy a bath now: clean trough of water, cool enamel, the gentle tepid stream. This is my body.

He foresaw his pale body reclined in it at full, naked, in a womb of warmth, oiled by scented melting soap, softly laved. He saw his trunk and limbs ririppled over and sustained, buoyed lightly upward, lemonyellow: his navel, bud of flesh: and saw the dark tangled curls of his bush floating, floating hair of the stream around the limp father of thousands, a languid floating flower. (*U*, II. 2. 175, 565–72)

Though Bloom achieves his mastering image by immersing himself in the stream become bath, whereas Stephen had achieved his by evacuation of his medium, both moments of self-contemplation create true flowers of rhetoric out of the flow of living and dead language. Bloom's mind merely wanders there, the stream of life becoming a bath in which he can serve himself a eucharist of his own anointed body through the agency of his domesticated associative imagination. Stephen's similar act of imagination—articulating the aquacities of his younger guilt-ridden flows of fancy—may seem at first far removed from Bloom's languor. The lotus that is created out of the mundanities of their bodies during their most private times of day is similar enough to establish a kinship, however: the repetition of 'floating flower', the little expansion of 'flow' into 'flower'.

Stephen's consciousness is mastering the power of words to rule and replace his passions and mask his fears. His is an act of hygienic control, a self-cleansing in the acrid tang of parody, a forced debunking of the watery in himself. Bloom's is involved in a similar act of self-cleansing. He is cleaning his mind of the persistent pain of his remembering. The song he sings, 'dearer thaaan them all', from Wallace's opera *Maritana*, is not about the stream of life at all, but about remembrance: 'Some th'ots none other can replace,/Remembrance will recall;/Which in the flight of years we trace,/Is dearer than them all.'[15] Bloom's attempts to replace his own remembrances of Molly with a song in a bath nevertheless recall them in the very act of cleansing forgetfulness. 'All' recalls its rhyme-word and summons up the rhyming act, 'Remembrance will recall'. Bloom is turning inwards and away to a pleasure in his body alone, a painful proof of his loneliness on this the day his wife joins her body with another. He is looking forward to a warm bath that is a womb, a withdrawal from the world, a small-scale retreat into the water removed from the stream of life, the flight of years, Henry Flower languid, floating. Whereas Stephen needs to train his voice down to earth to overcome the languishings of his and his people's history, Bloom attempts to slip into Omar Khayyám to have languid words lie light on his flesh, beyond recall.

But the song recalled by Bloom sings a silent lapsus, a lapse into evaded remembrance. Stephen, equally, cannot master the lure of

[15] Gifford and Siedman, 'Lotos-Eaters', Ulysses *Annotated*, 5. 563–4, 100.

evacuated sounds. The sea, as Buck Mulligan's mocking taunts in 'Telemachus' prove, is too mighty a mother. Mulligan's many voices in four consecutive speeches link the sea ('Our mighty mother!'), Stephen's guilt over his actions at his mother's death-bed ('You could have knelt down, damn it, Kinch, when your dying mother asked you'), and both Stephen's artificial poise and his own voice of insidious accusation ('—But a lovely mummer! he murmured to himself. Kinch, the loveliest mummer of them all!' (*U*, I. 1. 7)). Family guilt, maternal influence, silence, cunning and its mock are from the start intertwined in Mulligan's voicings of Stephen's unacknowledged pain and are sustained as an under-current to Stephen's hydrophobia, replacing the lust-directed guilt and exaltations of the *Portrait*.

Stephen is half-aware of this complex in Scylla and Charybdis when he talks about the ghost of Hamlet's father. The translation of mother to father is a desperate tactic of the Kinch:

He is a ghost, a shadow now, the wind by Elsinore's rocks or what you will, the sea's voice, a voice heard only in the heart of him who is the substance of his shadow, the son consubstantial with the father. (*U*, II. 6. 421, 478–81)

The voice is a voice of unremitting memory, a product of mem-ory's echoes, heard in the stress-line on sʌn ('o<u>n</u>ly'-'s<u>u</u>bstance'-'son'-'con<u>s</u>ubstantial'), the ʃæ–æʃ chiasmus, the <u>s</u> and <u>h</u> re-petitions: 'the speech (his lean unlovely English) is always turned elsewhere, backward [. . .] He goes back, weary of the creation he has piled up to hide him from himself, an old dog licking an old sore' (*U*, II. 6. 421). The paralysing effect of his nation's slavish, empty talk of the past joins hands with Stephen's personal anxieties to empty language of its hold on the body of the world, both finding expression here in the articulation of what it is to be a ghost of one's forbears. The significant lapse lies in the heavy-handed displacement of the sea's voice from mother to father.

For it is the ghost of his mother that plagues Stephen in 'Circe', sticking claws in his heart with fingers the shape of a green crab with malignant red eyes (*U*, 475). The subtle, murmurous acous-tics of a language ghosted of its sense finds sudden power in 'Circe' for Stephen as his true enemy rises out of his mind. He had tried to toughen the sinews of his prose musings with Aquinas, Newman, and seventeenth-century mystics and philosophers. But these are powerful ghosts with a powerful faith he had denied at his mother's bedside. Her crab-hand, his 'agenbite of inwit', is the hand of God ('Beware God's hand!'), the true father he cannot blaspheme well enough against. The control over acoustic context and his own *Portrait* past that Stephen's micturition had achieved has, nevertheless, not fully acknowledged the sources of his hydrophobia, his animus against aquacities of thought and language. For Stephen has refined the manner in which he had substituted his sexual energies with villanelle wave-rhythms in the *Portrait*: his consciousness has worked his own awareness of that rhyming substitution into a complex that side-steps the new more powerful guilt at his own betrayal of his mother and the way she had died to identify the sea with a custom-built mythology of race, a history of invasions. In both cases these rhyming evasions make play with the murmurous sounds of words. In the *Portrait* they only make sense by an unconscious recall of his past sense-perceptions; in *Ulysses* they make too much sense, sounding out long etymological histories, the dense compacted material of the rhetoric of past violent cultures.

For instance, when Stephen helps the 'weak watery' Cyril Sargent with his sums after his history lesson in 'Nestor':

Across the page the symbols moved in grave morrice, in the mummery of their letters, wearing quaint caps of squares and cubes. Give hands, traverse, bow to partner: so: imps of fancy of the Moors. Gone too from the world, Averroes and Moses Maimonides, dark men in mien and movement, flashing in their mocking mirrors the obscure soul of the world, a darkness shining in brightness which brightness could not comprehend. (*U*, I. 2. 55, 155–60)

The numbers are seen by Stephen in the fanciful light of their long dark history. His auditory imagination reads in the strange shapes of the sums hieroglyphics that summon up Moorish shades through an alliterative arabesque on <u>m</u>: 'moved', 'morrice', 'mummery', 'imps', 'Moors', 'Moses Maimonides', 'men in mien and movement', 'mocking mirrors', supported by an <u>n</u>-string and a mocking mirror rhyme in '<u>mocking</u>'-'<u>comp</u>rehend'.[16] Crossing imagery of medieval dance and theatre with heathen medieval thinkers succinctly portrays Stephen's mind in *Ulysses*: a mind that has

---

[16] There is also dense <u>ks/z</u> rhyming concentrated on 'darkness'.

trained itself to see, hear, and think of the world it experiences in terms of reminiscences, hints, and resurrections of the Dark Ages of the intellect.[17] But the shifts and dodges this refined and powerful auditory imagination unintentionally displays dance around a deeper, darker history in Stephen's mind, the history of that particular day in that particular year.

Cyril Sargent, the boy he is helping, is a weakling who painfully reminds Stephen of himself at that age and of *amor matris*, the only true thing in life according to the priest-like Cranly: Cyril is 'weak and watery' because fed by his mother's 'weak blood and wheys-our milk'. Stephen's own mother is being continuously recalled ('an odour of rosewood and wetted ashes'). Sargent, in short, typifies for Stephen the complex of feelings that manifests itself in his hydrophobia and distrust of aquacities in thought and language. Through all his distaste runs the unsteady stream of evasions and unacknowledged guilt surrounding his raw memory of his mother's death, the fear of her ghost. 'Mummery' recalls Mulligan's 'lovely mummer' taunt and with it the intuitive rhyme-play of that mocker as he connected 'mother' with 'mummery'. The 'mocking mirrors' recalls Mulligan again with his flashing shaving mirror. Stephen had called Mulligan an idle mocker (*U*, 39). The arabesque on 'm' in his meditation on the medieval exotic and hieroglyphic betrays the painful centre it avoids, recalls 'mother' though it attempts to stay mum.

Mulligan's mockery of his Hamlet thesis had directly challenged his motives for marshalling his attention around fathers and sons, by stressing the sweet mother, the sea, by reminding Stephen of his betrayal of his own mother, by linking both to Stephen's theatrical, mock-medieval artifice—all through the agency of rhyme-play on 'm'. Stephen's rhetorical triumph over his *Portrait* self whilst urinating on the strand, parody humanizing and giving low flesh to the false ecstasies of an evacuated auditory imagination, remains a hollow victory whilst he still cannot stage-manage his own Mulligan-mockery of this his deeper evasion, his

---

[17] This manner of seeing and remembering has been prepared for in the *P* where Joyce describes Stephen tasting 'in the language of memory ambered wines, dying fallings of sweet airs, the proud pavan' (*P*, 210), historical musical experience that dubiously masks sexual desire—'the tepid limbs over which his music had flowed desirously' (*P*, 211). The historical music of the language of memory ('the air is thick with their company' (*P*, 228)) in the *P* is closely shadowed by Stephen's particular sexual desires ('promise of close embraces' (*P*, 228)).

flight from his mother's watery shade. His stream of consciousness suffers from the possibility, still, of being publicly analysed as
a stream of the subconscious.

Stephen is wearily aware and afraid of this as he looks queasily
upon Sargent, the returned shade of his own mothered childhood.
He registers the secret distance between them through the distant
secrets that they share: 'Secrets, silent, stony sit in the dark palaces
of both our hearts: secrets weary of their tyranny: tyrants, willing
to be dethroned' (U, 57). Stanislaus remembered this shaky half-
admission of Stephen's in *My Brothers Keeper* when he wrote:

For [my brother] literature was not a comforting pastime that half lulls,
half encumbers the conscience. It offered other satisfactions, grim realizations that dethrone tyrannical secrets in the heart and awaken in it a
sense of liberation. (53)

In the newspaper office in Aeolus, Stephen ponders rhyme in the
abstract, for the moment returning to his *Portrait* evacuated imaginings, but here with an urge to make sense of it all:

RHYMES AND REASONS

Mouth, south. Is the mouth south someway? Or the south a mouth?
Must be some. South, pout, out, shout, drouth. Rhymes: two men dressed
the same, looking the same, two by two.

> . . . . . . *la tua pace*
> . . . . *che parlar ti piace*
> *Mentre che il vento, come fa, si tace.*

He saw them three by three, approaching girls, in green, in rose, in
russet, entwining, *per l'aer perso,* in mauve, in purple, *quella pacifica orifiam-
ma,* in gold of oriflamme, *di rimirar fè più ardenti.* But I old men, penitent,
leadenfooted, underdarkneath the night: mouth south: tomb womb.

—Speak up for yourself, Mr O'Madden Burke said. (U, 114)

This prose–poetic distinction between Italian and English rhyming power has already been unwittingly parodied ten headings
beforehand. Stephen had been rhyming a pastiche in his head,
'south' rhyming with 'mouth'. Professor MacHugh had spotted
Mr Deasy's article—'Foot and mouth? Are you turned . . . ? Bul-
lockbefriending bard' (U, 109). His rhyme-word is turned bestial
and diseased. In 'Rhymes and Reasons', seeking the reason for and

within rhymes, Stephen compares Dante's graceful triplets to the three graces, his English couplet to two old men. By so doing he is drifting into the territory of the Celtic Twilight. In his article on 'The Soul of Ireland', the young Joyce had complained that Lady Gregory and her Twilight compatriots were overly obsessed with old age.[18] Stephen's sorrow at his inability to match a European grace is confining him within the givens of the Dublin intelligent-sia. He has begun to fail here because, Joyce is implying, he is giving a ghostly physicality to empty sounds. Foot and mouth is a proper rebuke to the pale vampire.[19] So is Mr O'Madden Burke's 'Speak up for yourself'.

In the next chapter, 'Laestrygonians', Bloom also considers rhyme after his own creative effort (rhyming 'dull' with 'gull'):

That is how poets write, the similar sounds. But then Shakespeare has no rhymes: blank verse. The flow of the language it is. The thoughts. Solemn.

—*Hamlet, I am thy father's spirit*
Doomed for a certain time to walk the earth

—Two apples a penny! Two for a penny! (*U*, 125)

Bloom quotes the ghost of Hamlet's father in preparation for his own phantom fatherhood in 'Circe', prompted by a small-scale creative effort, thereby rhyming with Stephen's disquisition in 'Scylla and Charybdis'.[20] The fact that Bloom is thinking about rhyme so soon after Stephen seals the kinship, the wit lying in the ghostly imagination that Stephen's own rhymes had raised. The street-seller's cry (two apples for two rhyme words) recalls Stephen's momentary physicalization of his couplet into two old men, making mock of it in the 'foot and mouth' manner.[21]

But Bloom slips up in quoting Shakespeare. The line is really 'Doomed for a certain time to walk the *night*', not 'earth'. The slip ironically disproves Bloom's generalization about Shakespeare's blank verse. The similar sounds in 'spirit'-'time'-'night' are a kind of stress-line rhyming that establishes 'night' as a key-word in the

---

[18] *Critical Writings*, 'The Soul of Ireland' (1903): he criticizes Lady Gregory for portraying 'the old age of her country [. . .] a land almost fabulous in its sorrow and senility' (103).
[19] Stephen's rhyme—'On swift sail flaming/ From storm and South /He comes, pale vampire,/Mouth to my mouth' (*U*, 109).
[20] 'To a son he speaks, the son of his soul' (*U*, 155).
[21] Gulls, says Bloom here, 'spread foot and mouth disease' (*U*, 126).

play. The play opens at night, with repeated references to the 'minutes of this Night', 'this time of night'; Hamlet's imagination turns diseased under the pressure of the scenes of his uncle coupling with his mother every night ('Good night, but go not to mine Unkles bed,/Assume a Vertue, if you have it not, refraine to night'); Pyrrhus resembles the night, as does Hamlet; the play scene takes place at night, as does the 'very witching time'. Hamlet is doomed to think about the night and its hellish contagion. Why does Bloom misremember, substitute 'earth' for 'night'? The word has a charge for him, a music dark as Hamlet's night.

Remembering and Half-Conscious Evasions

Stephen's thoughts on rhyme refer us back to a short meditation by Bloom in his crazy jakes in 'Calypso' when he is thinking of Ponchielli's Dance of the Hours:

Evening hours, girls in grey gauze. Night hours then: black with daggers and eyemasks. Poetical idea: pink, then golden, then grey, then black. Still, true to life also. Day: then the night. (U, 57)

He is thinking of the dance because he had been remembering Molly's attitude the morning after the evening when she had met Boylan for the first time:

Morning after the bazaar dance when May's band played Ponchielli's dance of the hours. Explain that: morning, hours, noon, then evening coming on, then night hours. Washing her teeth. That was the first night. Her head dancing. (U, 57).

Bloom's poetical ideas issue from the particular stuff of his life. On the day when he fears the slow flow of time, approaching and receding from the dreaded half-past-four, Bloom thinks back to Molly's first encounter with the adulterer and shifts, exploiting the chance of the music played that night, to the poetry of time's motion.

His little paragraph about the dancing hours is tense with avoided pain. It follows this passage—Bloom remembers jotting Molly's questions and his own replies down on his cuff:

Her head dancing. Her fansticks clicking. Is that Boylan well off? He has money. Why? I noticed he had a good rich smell off his breath dancing.

No use humming then. Allude to it. Strange kind of music that last night. The mirror was in shadow. She rubbed her handglass briskly on her woollen vest against her full wagging bub. Peering into it. Lines in her eyes. It wouldn't pan out somehow. (*U*, 57)

The overtones from this strange recollection follow through into Bloom's consideration of the dancing hours. He is remembering planning to tell Molly the meaning of 'dance of the hours'. But Molly is too self-absorbed. Bloom's small disquisition on the poetical idea, then, is a lonely recap of what he would have said to Molly all that time ago. But the acoustic context hints that the turn to the hours is a sudden turn of the mind, an *emotional* paragraph-break. The more painful implications of the dance run through Bloom's head in the jakes: 'Dance' and her head 'dancing' the night before; her comment about Boylan's rich smell caught off his 'breath dancing'. The phrase 'Night hours' is painfully particularized in 'That was the first night' and his own ignored voice when saying 'Strange kind of music that last night'. The confused ending has a strange rhythm to it: 'Peering into it. Lines in her eyes. It wouldn't pan out somehow.' On the face of it, all these words mean is Molly's age caught in the mirror, followed by Bloom's shrug at his lack of success in getting Molly interested in the intelligent background to the music.

But the words are confused by Molly's question about Boylan, her remembering of his dancing breath, the present-tense understanding by Bloom of the after-effects of that particular dance, that particular night, his painful rereading of the little text on his cuff, the key-words of that dialogue, the strange music of its memory. 'Lines in her eyes' with 'mirror was in shadow' stress a hidden secrecy in her self-contemplation that the Bloom on the jakes now understands. There are hidden lines of internal monologue that make Molly entirely ignore Bloom's 'Strange kind of music that last night', hidden lines that, now known, discover dark musical overtones in 'night' and 'strange'. Bloom shifts quickly away from his helpless sense of loss and failure in 'It wouldn't pan out somehow' to cheer himself up by telling himself, at least, what Ponchielli meant. But the draw of his drift into memory (made painful by his present knowledge) is heard in the very means by which he had hoped to keep his mind off the particular implications of the dance of the hours. 'Evening hours, girls in grey gauze', a pretty piece of conventional poetic prose, repeats the rhythm of, and half-rhymes with, 'Lines in her eyes'. 'Lines in her eyes', laɪnz-n-aɪz; 'Evening hours, girls in grey gauze. Night hours', n-z-l-z-n-znaɪ-z. 'Lines' can also be heard in 'music that last night' (z-l-naɪ) and in general l, aɪ, n runs. Remembering this (and also the shadow of the mirror, the repeats of 'night'), the night hours are 'black with daggers and eyemasks', 'daggers' lightly reorganizing 'gauze'. Molly's secrets are 'musically' organizing the very rhythm and rhyme of Bloom's self-evasion. They are the centre around which semi-conscious stress-lines of remembrance flow. Her presence there gives an added stress to the last two sentences: 'Still, true to life also. Day: then the night.' What is true to Bloom's particular life in that day, the 'night' of Molly's silent deceit and secret betrayal, stabs Bloom in the back.

The next paragraph shows his sudden pain:

> He tore away half the prize story sharply and wiped himself with it. Then he girded up his trousers, braced and buttoned himself. He pulled back the jerky shaky door of the jakes and came forth from the gloom into the air. (U, 57)

Bloom's sudden activity, his girding, the rhyming of 'jerky shaky' with 'jakes' and 'gloom' with Bloom,[22] betray the man shaking off the implications within the dance of his words, avoiding the rhyme his seemingly careless thoughts about a poetical idea had summoned between night-time deceit, 'eyemasks' and Molly's consideration of adultery within the night of his memory ('Lines in her eyes'). These hidden lines of communication between sound and sense can be heard in the half-rhyme stress-line between 'jerky shaky' and 'jakes', soldering together the vulnerably emotional with the physically unsound. The jakes is a dangerous private retreat—it has a 'crazy door', is a place of yielded resistance and within there is the ominously named 'cuckstool' (U, 61). The tale he reads, the prize titbit, has certain dark overtones—Matcham winning the laughing witch (the very witching time). The pathos and ambiguity in the voice of his memory concentrates all these overtones into a sudden evasion that, however, stress-lines emphasize as a *continuation* of the dangerous line of thought.

---

[22] Masson patterns can be found in the sequence dʒkɪ−eɪkɪ−dʒeɪkɪ−keɪ and the vowel order ɔː−ɑː−ɔː−ɑː−ɜː−ɜː−eɪ−eɪ−ɔː

The light 'z'-alliteration in Bloom's poetic prose perpetuates the beat of anxiety and contained mystery in his memory of Molly's eyes.[23]

Stephen's thoughts on rhyme as imaginatively physicalized girls, then, recall Bloom's disquisition on the dance of the hours whilst also anticipating Bloom's consideration of the links between rhyme and the flight of his own language away from Molly. Stephen's distinction between Italian graces and old men sexualizes a desire for technical freedom whilst holding Stephen in the vice of his myth of Ireland's oppressive cultural memories. He is struggling against betraying symptoms. Joyce, however, uses Bloom to show how such static, self-betraying states of mind are not straightforwardly unconscious. Bloom is fully conscious of Molly's adultery. This is stressed throughout the novel. He hardly represses this working memory. In 'Circe', Bloom's fantasies acknowledge the tyrannical secret at the surface of his consciousness. Bloom represses nothing. He simply averts his mind.[24] Stephen attempts to master the memory of his mother's death by mastering a pseudo-physicalized rhetoric gleaned from distant cultures but this act masks his inability to comprehend the sheer particularity of that one death and his hand in it. His lazy disquisition on rhyme is not only rebuked by the context (cattle disease, O'Madden Burke) but by its recall of Bloom's struggle with the relations between poetical ideas and the particular lives in his memory.

That recall goes some way towards saving Stephen from resting subject to Freudian analysis and its preference for utterances as mere memory-tokens in a subconscious puzzle of other senses. Bloom lives in a continuum of memory, knowledge, and present

---

[23] There is, in his words, 'some goad of the flesh driving him into a new passion, a darker shadow of the first, darkening his own understanding of himself' (Stephen on Shakespeare, *U*, 161).

[24] As Karen Lawrence wrote on the extraordinary musicality of the 'Sirens' episode, 'the phonetic song played by the changing consonants', the way 'sounds migrate within a sentence': 'The play of the language is, in fact, a kind of linguistic diversion from the main event of the day [. . .] the reader is absorbed by the verbal surface of the prose just as Bloom momentarily escapes his loneliness, specifically his thoughts of his wife's adultery, by listening to music' (*Odyssey*, 99). 'Bloom's repression of the painful fact of Molly's adultery, evidenced in his gesture of scrutinizing his nails whenever her name is mentioned in an insinuating way, anticipates the narrative of "Ithaca", which focuses on material objects while we long to know the human emotions behind them' (13).

experience that, though escapist in its constant plunge into the actual, never splits into distinct categories. When contemplating a bath as consecrate womb, he is at the same time cleaning his mind of its memories. When considering rhyme and poetical ideas, he struggles and wrestles with his own life and his attempts to forget it. His example redefines Stephen's desperate repressions of sexuality and guilt as parallel failures of engagement resulting from a *half-conscious* fear of the dark matter of memory in the mind.

Stephen is prey to the consequences of his own false distinctions between the sounds of his own words and the senses they carry. The ghosts of his imagination remain to haunt him with the particular ghosts of his life. In a similar way, Bloom's direct knowledge and consciousness go through a desperate dance of evasion from the terrible fact of the day and its burden of anticipatory memories. 'Why all this fuss and bother about the mystery of the unconscious?' Joyce asked Budgen in Zurich, 'What about the mystery of the conscious?' (Ellmann, *James Joyce*, 436). The conscious, for Joyce, is the arena where remembering gives imagination the difficult matter it needs to work with and against the world and its stream of phenomena. The subconscious is interpreted, through the agency of Stephen's mind, as acts of thought that are *too* imaginative and lack the bolster of a detailed memory. They are thus creatures of unmediated desires. These desires are all too open to the cunning analysis of the Freudian precisely because the analyst can provide memory-contexts and memory-facts to inhabit the contentless imagining. Both Stephen and Bloom negotiate half-conscious manœuvres away from the dark centres of their minds, away from the rhymes that 'remember' in the words that they speak. But Joyce's writing of Bloom's internal talk rewrites Stephen's plausibly Freudian mind as half-conscious evasion and forgetting, not mere betrayal of unacknowledged symptoms.

The Secrets of Auditory Memory

In 'Telemachus', Stephen is divided between cultural and personal memory in his attitude to the flow of words themselves, and to the words he uses. Watching the sea, calmed down after Mulligan has left the top of the tower, he approaches near equanimity:

White breast of the dim sea. The twining stresses, two by two. A hand plucked the harpstrings, merging their twining chords. Wavewhite wedded words shimmering on the dim tide. (*U*, 8)

The rhythm of his own words—'white breast' . . . 'dim sea'— merge with the sounds into a twining of the acoustic elements of 'white' and 'dim' and of the double stress in the last sentence. Stephen is allowing his imagination to relax its hold on the world. The words, distantly Greek and lyrical, turn through cloudy bardic dream into purest Swinburne.[25] The language lies on the merest liquid surface of the world and twines together of its own accord, with some comic result. The heady run on w and d with alternating assonance on ɪ and aɪ make a gunshot wedding out of the meeting of sounds.

Joyce underlines the dilemma by having Stephen recall these heady sound-repetitions four short paragraphs later when Stephen remembers his dream of his mother's ghost:

In a dream, silently, she had come to him, her wasted body within its loose graveclothes giving off an odour of wax and rosewood, her breath, bent over him with mute secret words, a faint odour of wetted ashes (*U*, 9).

The 'wetted'-'words' doublet picks up 'wax' and 'wasted' at the start of the sentence, confirming the strong recall: 'wavewhite wedded words'—'mute secret words [. . .] wetted ashes'. 'Wavewhite' and 'wedded' resolve into 'wetted' (wt/d stress-line); the d-string in the earlier passage is heard again in the 'dream-had-wasted-body-odour-rosewood-words-odour' run, and both passages share stress-line play on st. This recall is a memory of a dream, coming after a series of true memories ('Memories beset his brooding brain'). As such they judge the dreamy chords struck by Stephen's pure imagination.

Joyce is dramatizing, down at the level of the acoustic surfaces of his prose, a conflict between a generalizing imagination and a memory and its particulars. What confuses the issue is that the

[25] The Swinburne sound I am thinking about can best be indicated by a few quotations: from 'Before Dawn'—'To laugh and love together/And weave with foam and feather/And wind and words the tether/Our memories play with yet'; 'this white wandering waste of sea' from 'In Memory of Walter Savage Landor'; from 'Hymn to Prosperine'—'Far out with the foam of the present that sweeps the surf of the past [. . .]/Waste water washes'. Swinburne, A. C., *Poems*, ed. E. Rhys (New York, n.d.), 101, 98, 57.

imagination is working with the surface of the world, whilst the memory is recalling the ghostly shades of past imagination. In both cases, the words are shown conspiring into analogous patterns of phonemic repetition. The 'accidental' nature of the rhyme-play in the prose is only in the confusion of Stephen's mind. Sound and sense merge into twining stresses as Joyce's conceptual rhyme between the possibility of 'wedded words' in the imagination and the 'wetted ashes' of a nightmarish memory merges them into twining chords. The middle term between the two is a song.

Stephen's thoughts about the sea were called into mind by Mulligan singing Fergus's song ('And no more turn aside and brood/Upon love's bitter mystery/For Fergus rules the brazen cars') to rebuke Stephen for his 'moody brooding' (*U*, 8). It also recalls his mother's death since it is the very song Stephen sang whilst his mother wept in the neighbour room—'Fergus' song: I sang it alone in the house, holding down the dark chords. Her door was open: she wanted to hear my music'(*U*, 8). The 'twining chords' of Stephen's pure imagination are given a dark and particular sense by Stephen's memory of those 'dark chords'. The bitter mystery is altered into a grim realization as the secret impulse towards solitary and internal imagining is revealed. What Stephen had thought was a peaceful shimmering of his auditory imagination on the face of all he sees, raised by the lyrical spur of Mulligan's song, is suddenly understood as an unconscious communion with the waves of the mighty mother, a resurgence from the secrets of his auditory memory.

Ulysses demonstrates the value of accidental rhyme as an artificial signal for the changing relations between the characters' flow of consciousness, the voices of the narrative and their medium, the sounds and senses of the words that 'weave in the wind'. The acoustic textures of the novel modulate across a scale from the evacuated rhythms and rhymes of senseless lyric (masking unacknowledged memories and desires) to the dense particularity of remembering touched into rhythm and rhyme by the pain of recall. In all cases, remembering inhabits the prose even when the articulating consciousness seems quite free of the past.

Rhyme is none the less at times used by Joyce to express a mind *emptied* of the material of memory, as in this quotation from *Stephen Hero* (abbreviated to *SH*):

The walk, the heat, the crush, the darkness of the chapel overcame Stephen, and, leaning against the lintel of the door, he half closed his eyes and allowed his thoughts to drift. Rhymes began to make themselves in his head. (*SH*, 105)

But in these cases too, the rhymes are reactions to context, be it the immediate physical and verbal surround, or the memory-contexts of the mind. In the passage above, Stephen begins his rhyming in a crowded chapel, refuge after some 'very solitary and purpose-less' wandering. The city wears an air of 'sacred torpor'. A lay-brother lies in a 'stupified doze' at the door. The chapel is run by Jesuits as 'a refined asylum, an interested, considerate confes-sional'. The choir is executing 'some florid tracery' (*SH*, 105). Joyce as early as *Stephen Hero* is aware of the dangers in vacant lyricism. Here it is diagnosed as a product of slavish Dublin piety, physical exhaustion, and a lazy reaction to a religiose musical stimulus. The rhymes are exemplified in the stress-lines along three groups of phonemes, hzd, ln, iːt, and a k-run.

Joyce's stream-of-consciousness model depends crucially upon a complex system of these rhyming reminders in the prose revealing hidden emphases in the characters' dispositional memory. The flow of language betrays counter-currents of remembered materi-al. Joyce in these sections demonstrates how the sounds of words can harbour evaded memories, and how (half)-consciousness of these memories can save the mind from the melodrama of the isolated individual imagination. In these considerations there is a broad agreement with Freud's theoretical understanding of the importance of verbal details and disturbances of speech as dis-guised repressed memories. Joyce's texts, however, in the very publicity of their representations of memory-acts, advocate the intelligibility of the mind's structures and the dominance of con-sciousness over its own unconscious memories. Joyce shows minds capable of living through and with psycho-sexual crises in the ordinary run of their everyday lives. The real pain in Bloom's story is not his incapacity to articulate his own memories, but in his *averting* manœuvres. Stephen, similarly, *can* face his deepest doubts (as in the confrontation with his mother in 'Circe'). Stephen's case is characterized by cultural urges to expand his real lack of material memory into a saving grace, a supratemporal icon; whereas Bloom tends to lose himself in the domestic, the petty details of the dailiness of his time. Joyce redefines Freud's preference for subconscious hidden memory-contexts as acts of *half-*conscious remembering, registered within the very textures of their speech.

Stephen's acute self-consciousness in the *Portrait* is the closest, ironically, that one gets towards a perfect psychoanalyst's daydream, because Stephen turns away from the world, the world's matter in his own memory, emptily watches himself, and inevitably scatters symptoms. Joyce uses the minutiae of his technique to manifest the adequacy of conscious utterance as the arena for both acknowledged and unacknowledged past pressures. Grim realizations of tyrannical secrets are discovered in the rhyme-play telling of the presence of other painful contexts. They are, importantly, *realized* there on the surface of the prose. Rhymes, miniature acts of memory, colour the surface of the conscious stream, telling stories of where the stream has flowed before, tiny signals of its countless origins in the complex past of memory, sound, and sense.

Beckett on Joyce and Proust

Beckett kindly donated his own copy of *A la recherche du temps perdu* to the Reading University Beckett archive, which contains markings, annotations, and a few notes towards his monograph on Proust. At the beginning of 'Nom de Pays: Le Pays' in *A l'Ombre des jeunes filles en fleurs*, Beckett underscored a long passage on memory-decay and wrote in the margin 'Utterly non-Joycian'.[26] Proust is demonstrating how the general laws of memory are ruled by the laws of habit, and that, as a consequence, memories will tend to fade away in a process of routine effacement. This is why what one recalls most clearly of someone in the past is precisely what one has forgotten, 'parce que c'était insignifiant, et que nous lui avions laissé toute sa force.' (II, 4) Here is the rest of the passage marked by Beckett:

[26] Proust, Marcel, *A la recherche du temps perdu* (15 vols.; Paris, Librairie Gallimard, Editions de la nouvelle revue française, 1925–29.) Reprint of 1919–1927 edns. Samuel Beckett's autographed presentation copies to Reading University Library, with his MS annotations. *A l'Ombre* ii. 60–1. I quote for convenience from the new Pléiade edn.

C'est pourquoi la meilleure part de notre mémoire est hors de nous, dans un souffle pluvieux, dans l'odeur de renfermé d'une chambre ou dans l'odeur d'une première flambée, partout où nous retrouvons de nous-même ce que notre intelligence, n'en ayant pas l'emploi, avait dédaigné, la dernière réserve du passé, la meilleure, celle qui, quand toutes nos larmes semblent taries, sait nous fait pleurer encore. Hors de nous? En nous pour mieux dire, mais dérobée à nos propres regards, dans un oubli plus ou moins prolongé. C'est grâce à cet oubli seul que nous pouvons de temps à autre retrouver l'être que nous fûmes, nous placer vis-à-vis des choses comme cet être l'était, souffrir à nouveau, parce que nous ne sommes plus nous, mais lui, et qu'il aimait ce qui nous est maintenant indifférent. Au grand jour de la mémoire habituelle, les images du passé pâlissent peu à peu, s'effacent, il ne reste plus rien d'elles, nous ne le retrouverons plus. Ou plutôt nous ne le retrouverions plus, si quelques mots (comme 'directeur au ministère des Postes') n'avaient été soigneusement enfermés dans l'oubli, de même qu'on dépose à la Bibliothèque nationale un exemplaire d'un livre qui sans cela risquerait de devenir introuvable. (ii. 4)

The words underlined are those specifically underscored by Beckett in his copy. By the first group he has written 'Utterly non-Joycian', by the second 'Non-Joycian'. The rest of the passage is marked by a single marginal line except for the last three sentences which are marked with a double line.

Beckett with his marginal notes is stressing how much Joyce is an exception to Proust's rule about the relativity of the utility of various perceptions for the habitual intelligence. Equally, as the second underscored passage implies, the conscious memory for Joyce preserved far more than Proust allowed. It therefore lacked the precious forgetfulness that Proust advocates as essential to the sudden retrieval of past sensation and past self. In the *Proust* monograph, Beckett analyses Proust's position as a function of a poor memory:

Proust had a bad memory—as he had an inefficient habit, because he had an inefficient habit. The man with a good memory does not remember anything because he does not forget anything. His memory is uniform, a creature of routine, at once a condition and function of his impeccable habit, an instrument of reference instead of an instrument of discovery [. . .] In extreme cases memory is so closely related to habit that its word takes flesh, and is not merely available in cases of urgency, but habitually enforced. (*Proust and Three Dialogues*, 29–30)

A good memory, Beckett mischievously implies, means that its possessor will be likely to be cursed with a world controlled by voluntary rather than Proust's involuntary memory.

Voluntary memory is the

uniform memory of intelligence; and it can be relied on to reproduce for our gratified inspection those impressions of the past that were consciously and intelligently formed. It has no interest in the mysterious element of inattention that colours our most commonplace experiences. (*Proust and Three Dialogues*, 32)

Whether Beckett noticed Proust's rhymes in the passage he underlined, is, as Johnson might say, lost in forgetfulness—'du passé pâlissent peu à peu, s'effacent'. Proust's stress on 'la dernière réserve du passé', on the grace that forgetfulness prepares for and enables, on the hierarchy of memories created by the 'habitude'-'oubli' split, would be for Joyce (as it was for Beckett in *Proust*) simply a sign of an inadequate memory. The resuscitation of past selves that involuntary memory entails for the rememberer in *A la recherche du temps perdu* is rather a general and continuous process in the *Wake* where each little act or word re-enacts and repeats ancient paradigms and original formulas. Beckett implies, when he writes 'Non-Joycian' beside the second underlined sentence, that the *Wake* is written in the daylight of 'mémoire habituelle' (even though it is a night-book), a daylight where the images of the past never pale and fade or quite disappear. They remain, rather, ever imminent in the most minor of one's everyday motions and syllables. For Joyce, the metabolic, paradigmatic nature of dreams proves this to be so.

An indication of the essential difference between the two writers would be their different notion of the auditory imagination. For the Joyce of the *Wake*, the auditory imagination both precedes and constitutes the rich and continuous recall, both personal and racial, that goes on within one's words. Auditory imagination is quasi-sexual at the same time as being constitutive of the imagination's return to the oldest of roots in primitive culture and childhood language-play. For Proust, however, the auditory imagination is very much more ephemeral. The sound-repetitions in the sentence underlined by Beckett, for instance: 'Au grand jour de la mémoire habituelle, les images du passé pâlissent peu à peu, s'effacent, il ne reste plus rien d'elles, nous ne le retrouverons plus.' Proust's wit here is to sustain the sound of the word 'passé' along stress-lines in the rest of the sentence just as the sense is denying its survival in habitual memory. It is this little sonic repetition that mimes the *possible* retrieval of the 'passé' by involuntary memory. The rhyming nature of the sentence is arbitrary, 'hidden' in the sense that a reader may very well pass over it without hearing it, and apt to be forgotten since prose-sounds will tend to enter a reader's 'oubli' almost immediately. The detail of the prose-sounds is 'like' the insignificant details ('un souffle pluvieux' etc.) given at the beginning of the passage marked by Beckett. The sound-repetitions, utterly non-Joycian, are a figure artificially representing the difference between regular and involuntary memory. This difference is rhymed by Proust with the difference between reading a sentence for its sense alone and hearing or attending to the aftershocks of a key-word ('passé') in that sentence's acoustics.

Later on in *A l'Ombre des jeunes filles en fleur*, Beckett marks half of a long paragraph about Saint-Loup with a marginal line (ii. 96 from sentence beginning 'En revanche' to end of paragraph, ii. 97, 'tant de prix') and underlines two sentences: 'Il n'était plus qu'un objet que ma rêverie cherchait à approfondir' and 'je me reprochais de prendre ainsi plaisir à considérer mon ami comme une œuvre d'art.' In the margin, Beckett has written 'Joycian'.[27] Proust's narrator is analysing the way Saint-Loup's perfect manners, physical grace, and generosity are an unconscious renaissance of his noble ancestors' hunter's physique, their disdain for their own wealth, their aristocratic condescension. This restitution of 'cet être antérieur, séculaire, cet aristocrate' within Saint-Loup's every gesture and act is all the more noticeable since Saint-Loup with his socialist and intellectual aspirations is trying very hard *not* to be feudal and noble.

This analysis of the hereditary traces of behaviour manifest in ordinary characteristic acts rhymes strongly with Joyce's *Wake*-practice and this is essentially why Beckett makes the comparison he does. But what clashes with Joyce's practice is the narrator's self-criticism with the art–idolatry charge and these are precisely the points that Beckett underlined. Saint-Loup, the narrator fears, is only interesting to him as an art-object, as a vehicle for the ghosts

[27] Beckett's *A l'Ombre*, ii. part 2, 188–9.

of his ancestors. He reproaches himself for considering his friend as a work of art, as mere material manifesting the powerful precedents in himself, as merely a particular example of a general idea in his family past that has sufficient authority to regulate his every movement, to harmonize his body and affections.

The Emersonian dissolution of personal identity into the province of the general governing idea,[28] betrayed by the behaviour one heeds least, Proust likens to an internal mind, an anterior self in ways that exactly accord with Joyce's project for the *Wake* as sketched out to Jaloux. The novel would be written, he told Jaloux:

> to suit the esthetic of the dream, where the forms prolong and multiply themselves, where the visions pass from the trivial to the apocalyptic, where the brain uses the roots of vocables to make others from them which will be capable of naming its phantasms, its allegories, its allusions. (Ellmann, *James Joyce*, 546)

For Beckett, with the narrator's self-criticism before him, Joyce's aesthetic mélange of psychological and mystic dream-material governed by habitual intelligence ('the brain') suffered from the very charge the narrator felt guilty about—considering human character (in the *Wake* the nuclear family of HCE, ALP, Shem, Shaun and Izzy) as material manifesting phantasms, allegories and allusions. The Four consider Yawn to be perfect material for psychoanalysis, a mere betrayer of symptoms and Joyce shows Yawn brilliantly parodying thus denying their superficial theory. And yet Yawn is still, from the level of the *Wake*, a servant of the general process of the book's own recall—he is felt and heard as archetypal, as Ymir and as guilty child. Just as Saint-Loup is a force-field for inherited behaviour patterns, so Yawn's own 'qualités propres' and 'valeur personelle' remain curiously detached from the mechanism of formal prolongation and multiplication which he articulates.

Joyce's technique in the *Wake* is nearer to a public version of this inner ancestor as manifested and preserved in libraries, tales, songs, riddles, jokes, jingles and slang. Larkin, reviewing the Opies' *The Lore and Language of Schoolchildren*, quotes a Wiltshire skipping rhyme that centres on the Kaiser and Napoleon:

[28] 'If the whole of history is in one man, it is all to be explained from individual experience [. . .] [Each man] should see that he can live all history in his own person.' (Emerson, Ralph W., 'History', in *Essays and Lectures*, ed. Joel Porte (Cambridge, 1983), 237–9).

To come upon the shadowy figure of Kaiser Wilhelm II, and the still more shadowy Napoleon Bonaparte, standing in a children's song like ghosts at midsummer noontide shows as well as anything could the way a particular rhyme will be transmitted unthinkingly from generation to generation until it loses all significance. (Larkin, 'The Savage Seventh', 114)

Joyce records these kinds of remnants of the past but mutated at the roots of vocables so that all significance is recalled. Beckett's marginal markings imply that Joyce with the *Wake* had discovered the most spectacular means of side-stepping the possible losses involved in being grounded in a superb voluntary memory by expanding that resource into an encyclopaedia of Nature's memory as manifested in language. Nature with its few laws becomes Everyman's family and their few stories. Trivial experiences of every day convert remembered words and signs into apocalyptic things by the mutation of everyday words back to their ghostly significance in the auditory memory.

This project however still flaunts Proust's warning. The problem centres upon whether the strange music of the *Wake*, with its eternally remembering textures, is not in itself a denial of the complex analyses in *Portrait* and *Ulysses* of the interplay between remembering and language-flow. The *Wake* is a perfect answer, formally speaking, to the queries raised by Bloom and Stephen, in that it steers between the Scylla of an evacuated lyricism that recalls the history of the world but evades the daily and autobiographical and the Charybdis of too great an immersal in the everydayness of ordinary language-use that evades the pain of recall. But, Proust might say, at what cost? Are the family in the *Wake* mere sounding-boards for the din of memory rhymes raised by Joyce's fiction? Have Ithaca's Listener and Narrator (*U*, 606) become mere abstract, overruling gods of the text?

Parody and Textual Memory

During the Four's interrogation of Yawn, Yawn is possessed of a ghost voice that tells them of the circumstances of the Fall. It describes a cold day with fog surrounding the hill of HCE and the lady of the valley ALP:

And the firmness of the formous of the famous of the fumous of the first fog in Maidanvale? Catchecatche and couchamed! From Miss Somer's nice dream back to Mad Winthrop's delugium stramens. One expects that kind of rimey feeling in the sire season? One certainly does. Desire, for hire, would tire a shire, phone, phunkel, or wire. And mares. (*Finnegans Wake*, 502. 26–33)

The hoar-frost over Ireland is a figure that recalls the fact that Yawn recumbent asleep on the land is a miniature reincarnation of Ymir the Rime-Giant, the original God out of whose flesh the earth was created in Norse mythology. (Hart, *Structure and Motif*, 139) Joyce has rime turn into and equal rhyme with the ludicrous play on 'sire'-rhymes. Those rhymes also stress the double-vision of the whole of the *Wake* which, throughout each of the few recycled tales, continually returns to distant origins, seeing at once intimations, hints, and guilty confessions of a primal scene and also the first beginnings of human and non-human development.

With 'sire' as sere, the rimey feeling is the dry, icy beginning of the year lost in the fogs of time—the beginning of natural creation in Norse myth. 'Sire' by means of the rhymes that prolong and multiply its sound in the context of its other sense (stallion father) alters rimey feeling to mean the poetics of sexual excitation. The 'phone, phunkel or wire' is the telephone line which is communicating the ghost voice through Yawn, also recalling Stephen's conceit about ringing Edenville through all the umbilical cords connecting the generations (*U*, 32). At the root of all the roots of Joyce's vocables, all the branching words of the Yggdrasil that is *Finnegans Wake*, is an inchoate rimey feeling, half-sexual, half coldly dormant, that underlies and gives indefinite context to the encounter of opposing principles—Miss Somer and Winthrop, at once an ill-matched couple from nineteenth-century melodrama (the lady a romantic dreamer, the gentleman an unhinged drunkard) and Summer and Winter. And the feeling is recalled by the ghostly voice of memory, both a race-memory of mythological origins and the personal memory of articulate subconsciousness.

At the same time, those rhymes are careless parodies of the Four's expectations, as they were when Yawn was interrogated about his sexuality. The serious enquiry about the weather at the crucial time of the Fall is turned into a piece of nonsense doggerel that takes 'rimey', hears its antique pomposity, turns it into 'rhymey' and spawns rhymes on 'the sire' in a glut of jester's ballad-innuendo. The ghost voice is nothing more than Yawn's mask of mockery. The rhymes are simply the product of a zest for comic reproduction of sounds that parodies the Four's desires to hear of the first act of sinful reproduction. The 'desire'-rhymes debunk the Four's 'one expects'.[29]

This double function of the rhyme-work in *Finnegans Wake*, on the one hand a serious technique that is the main agent for the reproduction of both a race- and a personal-memory (rhyming transformations are at the root of the creation of the compound vocables that name and thus recall the original phantasms) and on the other the touch of comic spirit and energy in the language (remembering the rhymes, riddles and songs of childish jesting), places an almost intolerable burden on each particular context. A riposte like Yawn's 'catchecatche and couchamed!', for instance, attempts too much. 'Cache-cache', French for hide-and-seek, is there, as is 'couché', lying down in heraldry. 'Couched' perhaps, to parody the Four's psychoanalyst's couch? Catching and couches and perhaps shame give a ghost of an eighteenth-century seduction scene. Should one allow the phrase 'catch as catch can' in? Is 'couch-aimed' included? Within the context, if there were such a thing as a certain context in the *Wake*, one might be able to say only those possibilities that are a proper answer to the Four's question should be admitted. So Yawn's reply means simply 'the fog was so thick it hid the ground'. But the rhyming reproduction of possibilities makes such decisions impossible. It in fact expands them beyond the wild guesses as to what one can draw out from or put into the words. The ktʃ stress-line connecting 'catche' and 'couch' leads everywhere and nowhere.

Yawn may also be responding comically to the Four's ponderous alliterative repetition of their adjective by spouting one of his own. The results are merely unsatisfactory since they seem the product more of one's own ingenuity than of what one has discovered to be there. Ingenuity, unfortunately, is quickly exhausted, and such

---

[29] McHugh, *Annotations*, 502. For this passage he provides the following notes which have aided me in my reading: 'Maida Vale' and Sanskrit 'maidan'—plain and name of great park in Calcutta; Latin 'fumus', smoke; French 'cache-cache', hide-and-seek; *A Midsummer's Night Dream*; Somer's shipwreck used in *The Tempest*, midwinter; delirium tremens; stramen—Latin for straw litter ; Deluge; sere: dry; funkel, German for spark; mehr: German 'more'; Rundfunk: wireless.

tiny challenges to one's wit as 'Catchecatche and couchamed!' with only the possibility of half-hearted self-congratulation at the end of them, swiftly become miniature powers of fruitless ambiguity. Rhyming music parodying sense becomes a mere parody of nonsense.

And perhaps it was parody itself that brought Joyce to believe that heavy rhyming was sufficiently explicable if the prose simply *remembers* enough. One can sense this with one of the parodies of 'Oxen in the Sun', the Newman parody :

There are sins or (let us call them as the world calls them) evil memories which are hidden away by man in the darkest places of the heart but they abide there and wait. He may suffer their memory to grow dim, let them be as though they had not been and all but persuade himself that they were not or at least were otherwise. Yet a chance word will call them forth suddenly and they will rise up to confront him in the most various circumstances, a vision or a dream, or while timbrel and harp soothe his senses or amid the cool silver tranquillity of the evening or at the feast, at midnight, when he is now filled with wine. Not to insult over him will the vision come as over one who lies under her wrath, not for vengeance to cut him off from the living but shrouded in the piteous vesture of the past, silent, remote, reproachful. (*U*, 344)[30]

These words recall evil memories hidden away in *Ulysses* itself. Stephen's mother had come to him 'silently' and 'reproachful' in the first passage that had invested the trite death-breath rhyme with such ghastly sense: 'Silently, in a dream she had come to him after her death [. . .] her breath, that had bent upon him, mute, reproachful, a faint odour of wetted ashes.' (*U*, 5)

The parody itself is remembered along with what it recalls in 'Circe' when Stephen suffers a vision of his mother to come to him 'when he is now filled with wine' (note how the Newman prose particularizes the 'they' of the memories into the 'her' of the vision). There the vision had been called forth by Stephen's chance word to the whores, 'Dance of death' (*U*, 472–3). And she wears

[30] The parodies of ' Oxen of the Sun' were indebted to Saintsbury's *A History of English Prose Rhythm* (London, 1912). The Newman passage Saintsbury uses is concerned with the resurgence of literary quotations in the mind long after reading (388–9). The mannerism which Joyce's parody remembers from Saintsbury's (they both concern memory) slyly indicates the consonance Joyce wants between his book's organization of its characters' recall and his own reorganization of his 'memory' of its literary styles.

the piteous vesture of the past: 'in leper grey with a wreath of faded orange blossoms and a torn bridal veil' (*U*, 3). The change that the dream of his mother remembered in 'Telemachus' has undergone (through Newman in 'Oxen of the Sun' to the vision in 'Circe') is that his mother has acquired a voice. She enters as a character in the hallucinatory drama of Bloom's and Stephen's memories. The voice, however, is as subtle as Emily Sinico's touching Mr Duffy's ears—'opens her toothless mouth uttering a silent word' (*U*, 3). Her voice *is* her breath, as this stage direction before one of her speeches indicates: '(comes nearer, breathing upon him softly her breath of wetted ashes)' (*U*, 3). Stephen's chance word has raised her ghost along with the breath that rhymes with it, that had rhymed with it so distressfully on the tower and in the classroom. The breath in 'Circe' is memory given voice, not as insult or vengeance (the manner of a stage-ghost), but as a public articulation of all that Stephen had averted his mind from when contemplating the sea.

Karen Lawrence makes this point well in her book on *Ulysses* : 'Somewhere in the middle of *Ulysses*, style goes "public", as language is flooded by memory of its prior use' (*Odyssey*, 8). 'Circe' for Lawrence, 'symbolically dramatizes those painful thoughts that we have learned of obliquely, by means of the characters' avoidance or narrative omission' (153) by way of technical transformations that manifest the general 'publicity' of internalized material during the latter half of the novel. '[S]imile gives way to literal representation, as human characters are transformed into animals' (148); 'analogy gives way to dramatized conceit' (149) demonstrating 'a libidinous release of tendencies in the language' (151). Joyce, in other words, has rhymed the rise of ghostly memories with the dramatic projections of figures of speech. The wedding of words in rhyme takes on ghostly flesh in the fully public waking nightmare of Bella Cohen's bordello. Joyce is demonstrating the extreme effects of remembering in language. As Beckett said in *Proust*, 'In extreme cases memory is so closely related to habit that its word takes flesh'. The habit here is the habit of Stephen's day, the habit of Joyce's own style as both establish the chances of rhyme and memory-association as habitually recalled necessities. What takes on flesh is the material thrown up by habitual animadversion from a painful centre of the mind, given flesh by the authorial, parodic, metalinguistic machinery of Joyce's systematized textual memory.

As Mr Duffy in 'A Painful Case' encountered physical memory because he had so habitually lived within an artificial medium of distancing recall,[31] so, in 'Circe', Joyce's artificial medium recollects the resisted memories of the day by making a drama out of the rhyming crises of all that the book remembers; Newman, Stephen, the sea, a death-breath rhyme and stage-managing it all, Mulligan with his little crucial run on 'm': 'She's beastly dead. The pity of it! Mulligan meets the afflicted mother. (*he upturns his eyes*) Mercurial Malachi! [. . .] The mockery of it! [. . .] Our great sweet mother!' (*U*, 473)

Similarly, Bloom's painful digression on the dance of the hours is given real flesh in 'Circe', not in the subtle manner in which his imagination had responded to the pressure to give Molly's body to the night hours, but with a cross between actual perception giving rise to memory (the whores dancing with Stephen giving a different pronunciation to 'hours') and fantasy-vision (the chance word 'dance' repeated by Zoe four times raising the evil memory) (*U*, 468–71). The masked night hours in Bloom's mind's eye are projected upon a prostitute's reel, opening up Bloom's unacknowledged feeling about Molly's act of adultery. Joyce's technique in the dance of the hours sequence in 'Circe' makes public both Bloom's and Stephen's painful memories; Bloom's feelings and memories on the jakes and Stephen's on the tower.

In its detail it actually merges them. As Zoe and Stephen dance they become Ponchielli's hours pointing Bloom's morning trial of memory just after he has imagined the full horror of the afternoon's adultery (*U*, 462). But Joyce's phrasing brings into play Stephen's meditation on numbers in the classroom with its submerged references to his mother's death preparing the revelation of the ghost. The noon hours 'catch the sun in mocking mirrors' (*U*, 470) recalling the dance of the numbers and the Eastern philosophers 'flashing in their mocking mirrors the obscure soul of the world'. The prose's rhyming recall makes of the real scene in the whore-house a mocking mirror of both men's memories,

---

[31] 'As the light failed and his memory began to wander he thought her hand touched his. The shock which had first attacked his stomach was now attacking his nerves.' (*Dubliners*, 129) (abbreviated to *D*)

particularizing the 'obscure soul of the world' into a double hallucination telling of the 'darkest places of the heart'.

Siren Sounds

What makes the public display of rhyming recall difficult to judge
in the later chapters of *Ulysses* is the extensive use of sound-
patterns in the prose. Whereas in the earlier chapters Joyce had
very subtly linked the acoustics to the active voices of his characters, midway though the novel, as Lawrence points out, the style
takes on an autonomous memory of its own that is a more public
demonstration of the internal life of individual memories in complex contact with the phenomena of the Dublin world. The play of
sound-resemblances that had signalled the intertwining of memory and imagination within the stream of the characters' consciousness becomes an interplay between the language's memory
of its prior use and that intertwining. In the later chapters of
Ulysses, style as public spectacle seems to convert what is private
and internalized into a generalized open system, with heavy
sound-repetitions threatening to mask rather than reveal the internal acts of recognition. The examples from 'Circe' discussed above
rise out of a general atmosphere of complex acoustic patterns and
so can be easily missed. They are thus potentially tendentious.

The difficulty can be faced most squarely by looking at the dense
musical patterns of 'Sirens' where the relations between the oblique internal pain of Bloom's mind and the acoustic atmosphere
seem arbitrary and purely organizational. It is a real question
about the craft of Joyce's fiction from 'Sirens' through to *Finnegans
Wake* whether the links between his characters' memory-contexts
and the prose's sound-system is broken, permitting the kind of
language that Stephen in 'Telemachus' and, before that, *Portrait*,
had been judged for indulging in. What Joyce may have risked in
the shift into style as public spectacle, parody, and creator of
ghost-visions was the self-communing of his textual memory
alone. Pound accused him of this once he started on the *Wake*. By
1934, Pound was writing about Joyce, 'He has sat within the grove
of his thought, he has mumbled things to himself, he has heard his
voice on the phonograph and thought of sound, sound, mumble,
murmur.' (Read, *Pound/Joyce*, 256). This is precisely the charge

Joyce's writing had brought against Stephen with Mulligan's murmuring mummer charge, and with the *Portrait*'s analysis of his evacuated auditory imagination. Did Joyce forget himself? Eliot tentatively criticized *Work in Progress* for similar reasons. He found in it 'an auditory imagination abnormally sharpened at the expense of the visual' and dated this change in Joyce's chosen technique back to the later part of *Ulysses* where he registered 'a turning from the visible world to draw rather on the resources of phantasmagoria.' (*Selected Prose*, 262) And it is in 'Sirens' that Joyce first reveals Bloom's physical world under the dissolving threat of audible rhythms and regulated sound-patterns.

'Sirens' has three 'voices': the strange musical and rhythmical voice of the narrator, the compound voices of the people at the Ormond Hotel, and Bloom's internal monologue. In the Prelude to the canon fugue these voices are mixed together as a rush of disjointed bits and pieces of language reduced to the level of sonic themes. It is harsh, sudden and incomprehensible like a parody of a modern musical score or of a modernist poem. What the prelude does is to articulate the musical narrator's control of the material that follows. This is a proof of the dominance of that voice's acoustic organization. It is the voice of Joyce's fugal form.

As the chapter progresses this voice interprets each intervening episode as a musical event in the curious syntax of its sentences. The two barmaids gossiping about the passing carriage of Earl and Lady Dudley are notated as pure rhyming grammatical units, their senses appropriated as musical notes in the flow of the voice's sentence-sound: 'Yes, bronze from anear, by gold from afar, heard steel from anear, hoofs ring from afar, and heard steelhoofs ringhoof ringsteel' (*U*, 212). Bloom's voice is interwoven with the voices in the bar even whilst he approaches and parts from the hotel, giving the fugal voice opportunity for some fancy contrapuntal weaving of melodies:

—O! shrieking, miss Kennedy cried. Will you ever forget his goggle eye? Miss Douce chimed in in deep bronze laughter, shouting:
　　—And your other eye!
　　Bloowhose dark eye read Aaron Figatner's name. [. . .] By Bassi's blessed virgins Bloom's dark eyes went by. Bluerobed, white under, come to me. God they believe she is: or goddess. Those today. I could not see. (*U*, 213)

The 'old fogey in Boyd's' the barmaids are joking about suddenly becomes Bloom, disfigured outcast wandering Jew, his very name altered by the fugal voice into a mysterious question, as well as cut into by the musical syntax. The counterpoint voice anticipates Bloom's words and rhymes his name with them, as well as with the coincidental parts of the world he is by chance attending to. The 'b'-alliteration in the things present to him but not articulate is given voice ('By Bassi's blessed virgins'), made to chime in with the 'Bloom' of narrative itself and then to coincide with Bloom's internal monologue ('Bluerobed') as he reacts. Bloom is being dissolved into fugue stretto and fugal rounds by the voice's canon counterpoint. The <u>blu:</u> stress-lines in the prose are taking his name in vain, taking its syllables up into their network of abstract acoustic tropes.

But curiously as the chapter develops these musical tricks, Bloom's inner voice takes over from the fugal musicality and sings a music of its own. It starts to happen whilst Simon Dedalus is singing M'appari:

— *. . . Sorrow from me seemed to depart.*

Through the hush of the air a voice sang to them, low, not rain, not leaves in murmur, like no voice of strings or reeds or whatdoyoucallthem dulcimers touching their still ears with words, still hearts of their each his remembered lives. Good, good to hear: sorrow from them each seemed to from both depart when first they heard. When first they saw, lost Richie Poldy, mercy of beauty, heard from a person wouldn't expect it in the least, her first merciful lovesoft oftloved word. (*U*, 225)

The fugal voice is merging into Bloom's, interrupting its musical flow with his consciousness (there clearly in 'whatdoyoucallthem dulcimers' and 'wouldn't expect it in the least'). It is an ambiguous moment. Si's voice is the sirens cry. Bloom may be being taken up into the generalizing dissolution of musical flow, the flow of immaterial nostalgia that Joyce identified with the Irish mind. The touch of the voice on 'their still ears' seems to activate personal memories ('each his remembered lives') but at the same time reduces the audience into a conglomerate being ('Richie Poldy' a compound of Bloom and Richie Goulding), and a musical babble, heard in the ɜː-repetitions, the <u>mst</u> Masson pattern and the ludicrous chiasmus of 'lovesoft oftloved'. The flow reduces them to simple human units in the same way that the fugal voice notates its human subjects into musical syntactical units—'they listened feeling that flow endearing flow over skin limbs human heart soul spine' (*U*, 225).

But Bloom's little interruptions are also resistances to the flow. The timbre of homely thinking with its specificity and easy conversational tone breaks the spell momentarily in this passage. The spell is not only one of nostalgic generalities. It is the flow of pure sexual desire. Bloom is surrounded with the language of flirtation, erotic connivance, and innuendo as well as by the ever-present fact that Boylan is precisely at this time visiting Molly. The flow around him of these cheating acts of union are the analogue to the sweet cheat in the music he hears and in the fugal voice one reads. The effect of these combined forces is momentarily to seduce him as his troubled mind loops and unloops an elastic band:

Bloom. Flood of warm jamjam lickitup secretness flowed to flow in music out, in desire, dark to lick flow invading. Tipping her tepping her tapping her topping her. Tup. Pores to dilate dilating. Tup. The joy the feel the warm the. Tup. To pour o'er sluices pouring gushes. Flood, gush, flow, joygush, tupthrob. Now! Language of love. (*U*, 226)

Bloom seems to have succumbed to the very processes that had evacuated Stephen's mind. The musical flow of language invades Bloom's stream of consciousness with a complex feeling that crosses his vision of Boylan's ejaculation and his own sensual desires. 'Words? Music? No: it's what's behind,' Bloom tells himself (*U*, 226). The ambiguity in that sentence is the arena of Bloom's struggle. Either 'what's behind' is the inchoate flow of feeling that floods the bar (sexual, nostalgic) or it is the specific memories which Bloom is harbouring that rise and fall within his consciousness.

Bloom follows the passage above with his own private act of distant seduction, called to his mind by the song he is listening to: 'Martha it is. Coincidence. Just going to write' (*U*, 226). His voice is immediately its old self again, untouched. The chapter's alternation of voices is being complicated by Bloom's own control over his flow of thought. As his voice continually resists the charm of the enveloping seductive musicality in the prose and in the air of the bar, as his privacy and his particular voice masters the generalizing flow, the chapter is itself altered by his presence there as a subject. Bloom is invisible to most of the people in the bar. He is absent in their eyes. 'Was he?' Dedalus asks once he has left (*U*, 237). Joyce, through most of the novel, portrays Bloom as a dark figure, ignored by all, flitting from place to place like a ghost. Stephen, in 'Scylla and Charbybdis', had defined a ghost as 'one who has faded into impalpability through death, through absence, through change of manners'. Melodramatically, he had asked of the ghost of Hamlet's father, 'Who is the ghost from limbo patrum, returning to the world that has forgotten him?' (*U*, 154). Bloom's isolation and loneliness (one of the most important verbal motifs in 'Sirens') has made a ghost of him. The music of generalized desire and regret threatens to finish him off because, as an out-sider, he can find no solace in being generalized into a community of vague feeling the way Simon Dedalus and his friends can with their common stock of comradely values.

'A Painful Case' had shown how, for the solitary man, a specific memory can appear as a ghost to teach him how much he is a single man by taunting him with musical acts of union. In 'Sirens', Joyce develops this idea to demonstrate how musical union can be resisted by specific memories to sustain Bloom's singleness of identity. He is a ghost for others but his stock of thoughts keeps him a man. Bloom listens to the music alert and conscious of its tricks: 'Wish they'd sing more. Keep my mind off' (*U*, 230). Here is that averting gesture caught in the interrupted sentence that liter-ally does keep his mind off. Karen Lawrence's point about 'Sirens' is just because 'momentarily' concedes Bloom's will to turn his mind away. As Bloom walks away from the acoustics and reson-ances of the echoing shell of the sirens, he distances himself from the community of pleasure-seekers and nostalgics like the ghost of their indifference and contempt, but also, privately, with the strength of a voice conscious and rounded:

Cowley, he stuns himself with it: kind of drunkenness. Better give way only half way the way of a man with a maid. Instance enthusiasts. All ears. Not lose a demisemiquaver. Eyes shut. Head nodding in time. Dotty. You daren't budge. Thinking strictly prohibited. Always talking shop. Fiddle-faddle about notes. (*U*, 236)

His thinking saves him. He succeeds in not being ghosted by the musical invasion of impersonal stress-lines in a hostile prose. His voice talks out of time or in time when it suits his inner self and its remembered life. Solitary though the achievement may be, Bloom manages to resist the generalizing musicality of the bar, and of Joyce's narrative voice. Its tracing of Bloom before and after his visit to the bar has not only failed to conquer him as part of the fiddlefaddle about notes; it has become a proof of Bloom's own influence over the music of the chapter. It is his fart that ends the chapter, interrupting the high patriotic music of Emmet's last words.

This is Joyce's comic salute to his creation whose bodied mind has resisted the ghosting generalities of his culture, of his own dangerous feelings. The music of his body incorporates the fortissimo and pianissimo expression marks of the music that had tried to seduce him into pure desire and regret ('Pprrpffrrppffff.' (U, 239)) and Bloom has done with it all. In Budgen's words, 'For Bloom the human body, its well-being and continued existence, is the greatest good'. This is so because its well-being is in itself a proof of the continuity of his affections, the identity of his particular hoard of random memories. Joyce, here, is resisting his own power secretly to involve his characters in musical structures of his own. It is also a form of resistance to the mechanical attractions of key-word emphasis: for the stress-lines in his prose may be taking up key terms too thoroughly and efficiently, transforming Bloom into a mere acoustic unit in a network of textual memories that have nothing to do with him. Joyce, with Bloom's 'Pprrpffrrppffff', warns himself not to take his auditory memory-system too far.

Sensual Private Memory

For Stephen it is memory alone that assures the identity of the self over time, as he proves when attempting to wriggle out of debt to A. E.—'Wait. Five months. Molecules all change. I am other I now. Other I got pound. [. . .] But I, entelechy, form of forms, am I by memory because under everchanging forms.' (U, 156) The self as a series of distinct selves ('I. I.') is recalled into one self continuously there at distinct moments ('I, I') against the body's alterations of itself. For Bloom his remembering self, in contact with the changing forms of the external world, is in league with his body, allowing a toleration of the random change and successiveness in his whole feeling of personal identity. This tolerance gives him the strength he shows in 'Sirens' to move in and out of the music's sphere of influence.

It also allows Bloom the gift of lyrical recall, moments that, with the power of the feeling and the physical sensuousness of the detail, bring rhythm and sound and his senses together into one force; a force moving round his memory and transforming it into a real presence. The memory of the day on Howth with Molly (that Molly herself recalls at the very end of *Ulysses* dismissing all suitors) converts all the tragic context of the book into its affirmative opposite. With this memory, Bloom makes his own past a palpable ghost to himself. It is a ghost that does not taunt but sings of real union with truly wedded words. A gulp of Burgundy summons it:

Seems to a secret touch telling me memory. Touched his sense moistened remembered. Hidden under wild ferns on Howth below us bay sleeping: sky. No sound. The sky. The bay purple by the Lion's head. Green by Drumleck. Yellowgreen towards Sutton. Fields of undersea, the lines faint brown in grass, buried cities. Pillowed on my coat she had her hair, earwigs in the heather scrub my hand under her nape, you'll toss me all. O wonder! Coolsoft with ointments her hand touched me, caressed: her eyes upon me did not turn away. Ravished over her I lay, full lips full open, kissed her mouth. Yum. Softly she gave me in my mouth the seedcake warm and chewed. Mawkish pulp her mouth had mumbled sweetsour of her spittle. Joy: I ate it: joy. Young life, her lips that gave me pouting. Soft warm sticky gumjelly lips. Flowers her eyes were, take me, willing eyes. Pebbles fell. She lay still. A goat. No-one. High on Ben Howth rhododendrons a nannygoat walking surefooted, dropping currants. Screened under ferns she laughed warmfolded. Wildly I lay on her, kissed her: eyes, her lips, her stretched neck beating, woman's breasts full in her blouse of nun's veiling, fat nipples upright. Hot I tongued her. She kissed me. I was kissed. All yielding she tossed my hair. Kissed, she kissed me.

Me. And me now. (*U*, 144)

Though Molly later pretends she was being calculating during this scene (she delights in the fact she was remembering her exotic Gibraltar life and manipulating him into a proposal), her own swoon into her own past with her repeated 'yes's reveals the moment as a creation of Bloom's own exotic and sensual love.

Bloom's memory is simply, lyrically monosyllabic, the sentences timed to the surrounding silence and the deep concentration on her body. The hidden Howth-mouth rhyme encapsulates the moment; the surrounds a screen of silent colours concentrating the close-up of the kiss. As the seedcake, emblem for Bloom of joy and young life, is exchanged, Joyce brings 'she' and 'me' together with 'seedcake' between both mouths—it is heard in the stress-lines along the massed m̲'s and iː's: 'Softly she gave me in my mouth the seedcake warm and chewed. Mawkish pulp her mouth had mumbled sweetsour of her spittle'. The rich connotations of 'seed', the fruitfulness of their sexual bond (this moment seals their marriage), filter into the surrounds with those iːs, the 's'-run (softly-seedcake-sweetsour-spittle) and the light d̲ and t̲ stress-lines repeating the sounds and the sense of the key-words 'touch' and 'touched'. The touch of memory is a real presence like the wine in his mouth repeating that miraculous kiss's exchange of fleshly life. The charge of the erotic prose at the end is intent with Bloom's wonder at the difference of his life and self 'now' but also of wonder at the life then being so richly remembered. The physicality of the prose, its simple sensuousness, make Bloom's memory almost synonymous with his senses as Joyce indicates in the equal value of 'moistened' and 'remembered'.

The delight in the simple things present to him in his memory expands his ample imagination into tasting the full senses and sounds of the simple words in the 'mouth' of his inner voice. The stress-line along s̲, m̲ and iː in the first two sentences merges sense and memory, making recall a touch on his tongue. And throughout the passage, little lines of repeated sounds are created, kissing their companions (for example, sleeping-sky-sound-sky, bay-by-by, lines-faint-brown-in, had-her-hair-heather), language itself at play with its own delight, its own chances. The precise, at times comically precise, details show a mind remembering everything and also delighting in the taste of the recall, the feel of its sounds: in the sentence beginning 'Pillowed', the earwigs, the relation of hand, nape, hair, the delightful word 'scrub', is minutely and distinctly seen as well as remembered. Yet the h̲-alliteration at the same time concentrates lightly and wonderingly on the sound of 'hair', 'hand', and 'her' lying so softly, easily and warmly together. The comic precision is the means towards that light and concentrated wonder.

The scene is a perfect image of the best of Bloom's mind: screened with veils, buried, pillowed, and hidden, the vision is like the exotic, sensuous nature Bloom hides from the world. Yet it took place in the open air, reflecting Bloom's open-heartedness. Within the hollows of his mind, as in the vision, Bloom's dreams are fleshly, sensuous and unwaveringly actual whilst simultaneously transforming all he sees and remembers into imaginative encounters. The whole of Howth becomes Molly's mouth, but it is a mouth surrounded and transformed by the colours, the strange and the comic words, the touch and the sensuousness of Bloom's soul tasting memory on the senses again with the sounds and senses of his auditory imagination kissing within his words. This is the true language of Bloom's love.

In 'Sirens' and the passage from 'Laestrygonians', Joyce demonstrates the double aspect of a musical prose. In the former, Bloom resists the flow of rhyming sounds around him. Rhyming stress-lines are a manifestation of the sweet cheat of a generalizing, weightless culture of desire and regret. It creates mechanical ghosts out of its audience and threatens absolute impalpability to the suffering, solitary Bloom. In the 'Laestrygonians' episode, the music of the prose is so intimate with the remembering self that the associations of and between the words are almost physical phenomena to Bloom's senses. The vision in his mind is as near to his body and mind as the things present to him. The prose rhymes here are the signal of real senses at play. 'Circe', and its phantasmagoria, crosses both aspects to create a waking nightmare of palpable and dangerous ghosts.

Rhyming Noise

Finnegans Wake, it seems to me, fails in that Joyce attempted to use the abnormally rich diction of 'Sirens' and 'Circe' without the counterweight of Bloom's hold on the sensual actuality of his perceptions and his memories. The ghost-voice of Yawn, with its auditory imagination in a continual state of absolute recall as a tap root to the most distant of origins, finds a rhymy feeling there that mutates all the vocables it uses. Joyce's attempt then to ground this extraordinary discovery in parodic tones (Yawn the mischievous jester mocking expectations) only manages to dismiss it whilst at the same time overloading the prose with indefinite musical associations.

He gets no further by parodying Bloom's tricks of speech either. Bloom's voice moves freely through harmony and struggle with his changing contexts. *Finnegans Wake* has no contexts in which the voices utter. The play-room, the pub, the ship, the river are unspecific mythological abstracts of physical place. Beckett's underlinings of Proust's criticisms of ways of seeing that reduce men to art-objects, slaves to the general ideas within their inheritance, must be a final critique of *Finnegans Wake*. It must be so because with the *Wake*, Joyce abandons his own complex analyses of the dangers and delusions of that very way of perceiving. To say that *Finnegans Wake*, by continually crossing mythological and cultural history with the parallel miniature experiences of the Earwicker family, manages all that *Ulysses* does but down at the level of individual syllable and rhythm, forgets that, at his best, Joyce with *Ulysses* shows Bloom resisting as well as harmonizing with the mythological structures of the prose's auditory textures. The family never have the life or the freedom to do so, being ghosts of the associations of Joyce's words.

The counter-movements in the *Wake* ironically narrow the possibility of each voice actively remembering down to the tight level of Freud's slips of the tongue. The give-aways in the *Finnegans Wake* voices continually manifest their seedy origins in history and infancy as mere symptoms. The Yawn-interrogation is Joyce's finest rearguard action against this possibility. Joyce blamed Freud for it but the fault was in the line Joyce himself had taken. One need only look at the earlier litany of incestuous but unconscious innuendo that characterizes Shaun's Lenten lecture to his sister(s) to realize the grievousness of that fault. A not untypical example: 'The pleasures of loves last but a fleeting but the pledges of life outlusts a lifetime. I'll have it in for you.' (*Finnegans Wake*, 444). 'Loves' taints 'lasts' to create 'outlusts' so that Shaun is easily condemned by Joyce as a lascivious and prurient preacher. The result is a cheap sexual innuendo in 'have it in', so cheap that it turns *Wake* into a schoolboy version of the professor's theory in the quiz chapter (bk 1, ch. 6), 'the inception and the descent and the endswell of Man is *temporarily* wrapped in obscenity' (*Finnegans Wake*, 150). The rhyme-play (heavy stress-lines along l̲s̲t̲ fabricating 'outlusts' as key-word) is reduced here to a simple mechanism of self-betrayal that clicks on unconsciously within the voice but is never truly part of it. Memories are transmuted into

'murmurrandoms' that, for far too much of *Finnegans Wake* , remind one only of the fluid, sexual atmosphere of the 'Sirens' bar
without Bloom's conscious presence.

Joyce wished to create a radical 'sound sense sympol' (*Finnegans
Wake*, 612) out of the 'crosscomplimentary crisscouples' (613) of
his characters that would reveal the 'secret working of natures'
(615) within language, the mind, and dream-fictions. He hoped to
do this without sacrificing wit for solemnity by playing his game
out with 'nonsery reams' (619) and the broad fantasy of pan-
tomime. The reason such a project fails so often in the *Wake* is that
Joyce is straining all he can from the myth of his own phenomenal
memory, recalling too much and losing the taste of real recollection. As the Dreamer slowly awakes he asks himself a question:
'What has gone? How it ends?' He answers himself:

> Begin to forget it. It will remember itself from every side, with all gestures,
> in each our word. Today's truth, tomo row's trend. (*Finnegans Wake*, 614)

The book's memory, the 'it', has such command over the material
that the Dreamer is finally irrelevant. Like Hegel's world-spirit
releasing itself from the unhappy consciousness, the book can do
without the minds, the histories, the memories of the creatures it
has exploited for its ends and trends. Each word will enable the
book to remember itself. The origins of Joyce's own act of creation
are revealed, with terrible anticlimax, as the centre of interest of
the Viconian circles. His rhymy feeling, as Pound and Eliot sus-
pected, is the final word back to and towards which the book is
written.

Joyce's own grimy self-parody as Shem writing the *Wake* on his
own flesh seems just another get-out clause, similar to the Yawn-
interrogation in that it attempts to forestall the real implications of
Joyce's method by parodying them beforehand. The real achieve-
ments of Joyce's rhyme-work, with the drama of minds ranging
from Stephen's evacuated lyricism and his side-stepping historical
rhetoric to his self-parodies, from Bloom's imaginative encounter
with the world to his painful aversion away from his own past,
from Bloom being ghosted by dissolving music to Bloom summoning up flesh spirits, all are forgotten as the *Wake* lapses into its
reams of rhyme and their oversimplified reasons. The '[t]hunner
in the eire' (565) (at once 'thunder in the air', 'the German in
Ireland', 'humming in the ear') that initiates and haunts the family

times and crimes of the book is the rhymy semi-conscious feeling of primitive sexuality in the blood, in the 'foreign' parts of one's own nature, in the deep, half-forgotten past of one's own culture. It is a 'thunner' that drowns out all the more intimate remembering sounds of Joyce's prose. *Finnegans Wake* suffers from too much rhyming noise.

Bloom, in the tranquillizing spectrality of 'Ithaca', was aware of the danger of too much noise in the morning when shaving:

matutinal noises, premonitions and perturbations, a clattered milkcan, a postman's double knock, a paper read, reread while lathering, relathering the same spot, a shock, a shoot, with thought of aught he sought though fraught with nought might cause a faster rate of shaving and a nick on which incision plaster with precision cut and humected and applied adhered: which was to be done. (*U*, 551)

The distraction of the noise of the world and in the mind is heard in the distracted rhymes, Masson patterns on ɔːt, mnm, and heavy stress-lines along p, ʃ, d. The distracting rhymes cause a slip of the hand. They are a disturbance of speech that disturbs the mind from the careful work of tending the surface of the body. Such care is forgotten in the *Wake*. The music of the prose, without Bloom's care and occasional disciplined need for it, becomes a painful series of perturbations, sign of a real lapse of speech.

Despite my reservations about the overworking of the memory rhyme contacts in *Finnegans Wake* , I believe I have shown that Joyce, with his work up to and including *Ulysses*, found many subtle uses for the key-word stressing technique of sound-repetitions in his research into the complexities of half-conscious memory in speech and thought. Though Beckett was right to contrast Joyce's and Proust's understanding of memory—Joyce's memory never lapsing so memory-sensations are habitual, Proust's memory always fading so a real memory is felt as a mystical shock—there is common ground.

The prose rhymes in both writers reveal the minute migrations of past key-words into the present-tense material. These key-words represent and half-consciously recall a string of resisted memories. These tiny memory-acts at times accumulate suddenly to express a real union of past and present selves, body and memory (the narrator at his grandmother's bedside, Bloom recalling Howth). Both writers are keenly aware of the dangers of a self-circling and self-communing poetic (Stephen's example in the *Portrait*, the narrator's porphyritic prose) and use heavy rhyme patterns to show their characters breaking away from the real struggle within actual memories into the fictive memories of artificial imagination. I will show with my Beckett chapter how these four aspects of the memory rhyme technique—migration of keywords, recall of resisted memories, union of selves, dangers of the selfish style—are also present in Beckett's work, though made extreme by the constant denial by his 'voices' of the faculty of memory itself.

4

Beckett's Prose Rhymes: remembering, companionability, self-accompaniment

Magessa O'Reilly, discussing the different versions of 'Texte pour rien XIII', noted that the echo system of the text had discernible purposes: 'Les mots répétés prennent immanquablement l'aspect de mots clés', she writes. She notices, too, revising choices that confirm a p-run when Beckett replaces the 'au fond des' of the *Disque vert* version with 'parmi':

se demander d'où elle sort, elle se le demande, et si ce n'est pas un petit espoir qui luit, méchamment, *au fond des* traîtres cendres, autres expression, petit espoir d'un petit être après tout[.]

O'Reilly suggests that this change contributes to 'la cadence large du début de l'extrait, avant l'accélération de la fin où la lettre *p* apparaît quatre fois plus rapidement, accélération qui souligne l'expressivité (*espoir*). Mais la préposition *parmi* est aussi un faible écho de la suite', that is, the phrase 'parmi les feuilles, parmi l'herbe, parmi le sable' (230-1). O'Reilly has in fact caught Beckett in the act of composing an acoustic motif centred on the keywords 'poussière' and 'traces',[1] in this instance with stress-lines emanating from the paR of 'parmi', which are so clearly brought to prominence by the alerting-device of two straight rhymes, 'traces'-'passe' and 'air'-'poussière':

quelque chose qui doit ouïr, et une main quelque part [. . .] [la voix] veut faire une main, enfin, quelque chose, quelque part, qui laisse des traces, de ce qui se passe, de ce qui se dit, c'est vraiment le minimum, non, c'est du roman, encore du roman, seule la voix est, bruissant et laissant des traces [. . .] l'air qui tremble un instant encore avant de se figer pour toujours,

---

[1] A motif he has 'borrowed', so to speak, from Flaubert's *Madame Bovary*.

une petite poussière qui tombe un petit moment. Air, poussière, il n'y a pas d'air ici, ni rien pour faire poussière[.]

The English translation performs the same feat with a 'voice'- 'trace' prose rhyme and the ʌst stress-line surrounding 'dust': 'the tiny flurry of dust quite settled' (*No's Knife*, 133).

The story is concerned with hearing down at the micro-level of 'every mute micro-millisyllable', with the strange sounds present in reading and composing 'du roman', sounds that threaten to counter no's knife and to confirm the little mimetic presence of the dust of memory and the trace of remembering among the words of a weak old voice. O'Reilly proves, at the micro-level of tiny acoustic revisions, Beckett's fidelity to the tandem rhyming motions of 'la langue logique et la langue lyrique' (233). Beckett's music, the 'coloration and accentuation of single words and phrases' as Michael Haerdter put it,[2] is a difficult music of memories struggling for tiny life within a formal system of echoes,[3] traces of a remembering voice. This chapter will attempt to follow up a few of Beckett's traces, raising the dust of his mute micromillisyllables, in order to catch the old voice in the act of construing its own fabricated remembering.

Semantic Amnesia and Fictional Remembering

The incident of the Galls father and son in *Watt* (abbreviated throught as *W*), piano-tuners who work briefly in Knott's house, is strangely transformed into an abstract impression with such power in Watt's mind that his own memories pale in comparison:

[the incident] developed a purely plastic content, and gradually lost, in the nice processes of its light, its sound, its impacts and its rhythm, all meaning, even the most literal [. . .] became a mere example of light

---

[2] Entry for Tues. 29 Aug., McMillan and Fehsenfeld, *Beckett in the Theatre*, 222.

[3] Rehearsing *Endgame* at the Schiller-Theatre in 1967, Beckett urged his actors to find, at certain key-moments of the play, a 'life-voice' 'What does it mean?' asks Haerdter: 'Bringing the words out, stressing them—a lyrical tone' (entry for Sat. 2 Sept., McMillan and Fehsenfeld, *Beckett in the Theatre*, 221). This tone, the colouration, is the tone of memory: ' "Colouration is only for their memories" ', said Beckett about Nag and Nell on 24 Aug. (ibid. 210), and is embedded within a complex of formal echoes: ' "The play is full of echoes; they all answer each other" ' (Wed. 23 Aug., ibid. 208).

commenting bodies, and stillness motion, and silence sound, and comment comment [. . .] The incident of the Galls [. . .] ceased so rapidly to have even the paltry significance of two men, come to tune a piano, and tuning it, and exchanging a few words, as men will do, and going, that this seemed rather to belong to some story heard long before, an instant in the life of another, ill-told, ill-heard, and more than half-forgotten. (W, 69–71)

This incident, 'of great formal brilliance and indeterminable purport' (W, 71), revisits Watt's mind in all its abstract phases, with a power and distinctness that torments him all the more because of the meaninglessness and absolute inconsequentiality of the non-event. To give the formal phantom a meaning becomes an obsession with Watt—'for to explain had always been to exorcize, for Watt' (W, 75). The incident plunges Watt into a state of endless thirst for 'semantic succour' (W, 79) within the formal qualities of language, a desperate urge for names to fit things, for his name to prove him a man, an urge Beckett exemplifies, and foils, with dense and ludicrous rhyme-play:

Looking at a pot, for example, or thinking of a pot, at one of Mr Knott's pots, of one of Mr. Knott's pots, it was vain that Watt said, Pot, pot. (W, 78)

The 'loss of species' (W, 82) Watt suffers as a result of this double failure, failure to be convinced of the word–thing, Watt–man relation (manic because instead of disbelieving words and names he disbelieves objects and bodies), has as its root, then, the substitution of his own memories by a trivial episodic memory which is itself transformed into 'an instant in the life of another'. This haunting of his mind by his own formal imagination exiles him into an obsessional world of rhyme patterns and private language games, lonely and 'longing for a voice [. . .] to speak of the little world of Mr Knott's establishment, with the old words, the old credentials' (W, 81). Watt is suffering from semantic amnesia.[4]

Beckett's early works are comedies that concern themselves with the pathological and formal manners by which a mind may

[4] Michel Beausang's work on amnesia, madness, and aphasia in Watt is crucial here, as are Jean-Michel Rabaté's studies of Murphy and Watt. Watt's language, according to Rabaté, 'est prise entre le délire et l'aphasie, inextricablement liés: mots manquants, réticences, répétitions, comme une rayure sur une disque, jamais assez de sens, toujours trop de mots.' (Rabaté, Beckett avant Beckett, 179). Cf. also Allbright, Representation, 180: 'Amnesia is the ideal condition of the inexpressive narrator', and Francis Doherty's essay on Watt, which deals with aphasia.

become locked permanently into a state of pure comedy as defined by Bergson: 'le comique exige donc enfin pour produire tout son effet, quelque chose comme une anesthésie momentanée du coeur. Il s'adresse à l'intelligence pure.' (*Le Rire*, 6) Bergson allies this state of mind with the quality of comic language, word-play in particular:

le jeu de mots nous fait [. . .] penser à un laisser-aller du langage, qui oublierait un instant sa destination véritable et prétendrait maintenant régler les choses sur lui, au lieu de se régler sur elles. Le jeu de mots trahit donc toujours une distraction momentanée du langage, et c'est d'ailleurs par là qu'il est amusant. (123–4)

Permanent anaesthesia of the heart (or rather permanent *amnesia* of the heart) and a *permanent* distraction of one's language from its natural purposes, however, divorces the subject from the society in which Bergson believed comedy should act as therapy, exiling him within the mind as surely as Dante's Belacqua is indolently, impudently paralysed in purgatory. A manic addiction to the forgetfulness necessary to preserve comic power over the particularities within the memory permanently dislocates the memory from the self.

Beckett, since these beginnings, has been concerned with the 'dribs and drabs' that remain of the heart, its old words and old credentials, after a general anaesthetic has been administered with language left amnesically distracted. In this section I shall examine the persistencies of memories in the various narrative voices and demonstrate how Beckett uses rhymes to locate stress-points in the formality of the voices' self-conceptions where those memories refuse to buckle beneath the weight of the reason-ridden imagination[5] and its forgetfulness. It may be language itself that fabricates these counteractive memories, or it may be the voice/mind itself. What is clear is that Beckett's prose rhymes, shot through with contradiction and ambiguity as they are, attest to this strange form of 'unheard' memory-work fitfully present within the syntax and convolutions of the prose on its way.

The Trilogy tracks the same withdrawal from personal episodic memory that had been diagnosed in *Watt*. Molloy, content to write a memoir, Moran to write a report, increasingly discover them-

---

[5] 'What kind of imagination is this so reason-ridden' (*Company*, 33).

selves caught within the 'mythological present' (*Molloy*, 27 (abbreviated to *M* hereafter)) and forgetful of the simplest details of their pasts. Distinctions between remembering and inventing become blurred—'Perhaps I'm inventing a little, perhaps embellishing [. . .] perhaps I'm remembering things' (*M*, 8–9). Malone is intent on play alone and his inventory, the memory he indulges in, is reduced to reminding himself briefly of his present state before embarking on his stories. His occasional forays into the past are stopped quickly in their tracks, as though memory were some lying form of self-indulgence on the part of a fictional self:

> What then could I be expected to remember, and with what? I remember a mood. My young days were more varied, such as they come back to me, in fits and starts. [. . .] All that belongs to the past. Now it is the present I must establish, before I am avenged. (*Malone Dies*, 10–11)

The Unnamable speaks beyond memory, equates pasts with illusions 'they' are trying to trick him into crediting as his own, along with all the other lies that would fictionalize him into real subject. The only memory he is prepared to acknowledge is the short-term memory of the words he is force-fed in the present tense, a tense he is also trying to deny. Any hint of an event as such is rejected as simply a built-in feature of the linguistic system he is forced to narrate/listen to: 'No matter how it happened. It, say it, not knowing what. Perhaps I simply assented to an old thing.' (*The Unnamable*, 7 (*abbreviated to TU*)) The old things of the past, locutions and syntax as mock memories, all are sentenced to death by the withering, suicidal narrative voice.

The Unnamable seems to be most clearly free of his own super-Cartesian, self-crippling doubt when he asserts that the enemy who foists civilization's lies on him is the very language he speaks. But at crucial times the voice betrays strange fear at the cold brutality of its own propositions, and it is the very words he speaks that register the shock:

> What I speak of, what I speak with, all comes from them [. . .] It's of me now I must speak, even if I have to do it with their language [. . .] My inability to absorb, my genius for forgetting, are more than they reckoned with. Dear incomprehension, it's thanks to you I'll be myself, in the end. Nothing will remain of all the lies they have glutted me with [. . .] On their own ground, with their own arms, I'll scatter them, and their miscreated puppets. Perhaps I'll find traces of myself by the same occasion. [. . .] I'll

fix their jargon for them, then any old thing, no matter what, whatever they want, with a will, till time is done, at least with a good grace. (*TU*, 297–8)

The Unnamable's militant bravado, rising in pitch and boast, suddenly forgets the means of his revenge and collapses into the mixed tones of guile and panicky resignation. The mixture of tones can be heard in the accumulation of rhymes—'what'-'whatever'-'want'-'with'-'will'-'with'-'will'-'till'—merging his and their will, collapsing his inherited language into a mess of odd stresses. The its and whats of ordinary English force him to acknowledge the quiddities within the syntax of his own desire for revenge. They force him to hear the desperate contradictions in his desires to blame his own language at the same time as fabricating an invisible presence 'behind' his own words. The phrase 'any old thing' assents weakly to the hold 'their' old words have over him, to the substance, even the acoustics, their words establish. Saying 'no matter what' finds matter in 'what' through the subsequent stress-line along <u>wt</u>. The miniature memories in his words panic him into a fleeting acknowledgement of his powerlessness to suppress his own traces. The grace of guileful resignation discovers the trace of a broken voice in its articulation, a voice hearing the distance between its past threats and the present compromise on stumbling into an unimaginable future. It is old Lear's voice crossed with Caliban's curses, beating around 'what', breaking on the future tense.

The Unnamable's main chance, his invincible forgetfulness, relies on the validity of his assertions that the memory he has is simply verbal: 'the same words recur and they are your memories' (<u>TU</u>, 113). But the assertion begs the question as to why those particular words recur. The ambiguity in 'they are your memories' has Worm turn against his so-called inventor and call him human—a lexical memory can accumulate a historical trace along the words the voice fails to suppress, and, by so doing, establish a humanized voice. The Unnamable's belief or hope that his narrative is a pure figment fabricated by the rhetoric of real presence is itself put in doubt. The self-killing processes begin to sound like desperate manœuvres to fend off a displaced episodic memory scattered among the words in one's head.

The Unnamable's struggles to fend off his own traces has its roots in *Murphy* with Mr Kelly, bedridden, 90, and lonely without Celia:

He found it hard to think, his body seemed spread over a vast area, parts would wander away and get lost if he did not keep a sharp look-out, he felt them fidgeting to be off. He was vigilant and agitated, his vigilance was agitated, he made snatches and darts in his mind at this part and that. He found it hard to think, impossible to expand the sad pun (for he had excellent French): Celia, s'il y a, Celia, s'il y a, throbbing steadily behind his eyes. To be punning her name consoled him a little a very little. What had he done to her, that she did not come to see him any more? (*Murphy*, 67–8)

The comic abandonment of the mind by the parts of the body is brought close to Mr Kelly's self-consoling rhyme-chant through the repeated phrase, 'he found it hard to think', stressing the relation between his preoccupation with his paralysis and Celia's abandonment of him. They are brought closer still by rhyme and stress-lines running through the phrases around the sad pun: 'hard', 'spread', 'parts', 'sharp', 'snatches', 'darts', 'at', 'part', 'that', 'hard', 'sad', 'had'. The darts of his mind, like Malone with his stick, beat out an agitated rhythm of self-commands, a teacher with his cane over unruly children—obsessed to such a degree with the bare act of recollecting his *disjecta membra* that the mind's action ('darts') shrinks to what it is about to lose ('parts'). The agitated pulse of the mind, its desperate recollection running through the acoustics of Beckett's prose, is a symptom of the narrow, throbbing headache of a rhyme that recollects Celia the only way he can. The text's cruel display of sympathetic wit puns her body with his through the rhymes in the old man's abandoned mind. In the Trilogy, this cruelty—capable of describing Mr Kelly's weeping like this: 'The human eye is not teartight, the craters between nose and cheekbones trapped the precious moisture, no other lachrymatory was necessary', a breath-taking anaesthetic—is ceded to the narrative voices, the body and loved ones wished away with a vengeance; yet the murmur of rhymes make Mr Kellys of them all.[6]

The Unnamable gives thanks for the passing away of his features:

Tout cela est tombé, toutes les choses qui dépassent, avec mes yeux mes cheveux, sans laisser de trace, tombé si bas si loin que je n'ai rien entendu, que ça tombe encore peut-être, mes cheveux lentement comme de la suie

[6] Mr Kelly—'extraordinarily like the Malone of *Malone Dies*', (Fletcher, *Novels of Samuel Beckett*, 46).

toujours, de la chute de mes oreilles rien entendu. Superflu, petite âme toujours, l'amour je l'ai inventé, la musique, l'odeur du groseiller sauvage, pour m'éviter. Des organes un dehors, c'est facile à imaginer, d'autres, un Dieu, c'est forcé, on les imagine, c'est facile, ça calme le principal, ça endort, un instant. Oui Dieu, je n'y ai pas cru, fauteur de calme, un instant. (*L'Innomable*, 31)

The near-perfect prose alexandrine couplet with the 'dépassent-trace' rhyme, reinforced by the 's' and 'z' run, backed up by the 'tout'-'tombé'-'trace' string and the 'yeux'-'cheveux' coupling, leave a trace of incompetent elegy, startlingly, on the surface of the prose. The rhymes measure out the amount of imaginative effort given to the literal fleshed-out implications of the bare denials the voice would wish to make, echo forth an imaginative space it cannot help describing. Indeed the phonemes of the word 'imaginer' pepper the last three sentences. 'Tombé', that one little word, necessitates a context, a height, a gravity. Saying 'tout cela' defines a previously existing and external state. Far from not leaving a trace, the facial features, 'all the things that stick out' (*TU*, 21), fashion a face in the very act of its denial.

The rhymes catch the sudden access into ease of the imagination as it settles itself into describing the memory of those 'things'. Like the tiny tenderness in imagining the hair falling like soot as he speaks, the rhymes sound out and mark the 'superflu' in the context around the statement of the 'rien entendu'. The superfluous feeling for the parts he denies writes the nostalgic score for the dart of the mind that imagines the present losing of them. The processes by which language fabricates presence may be diversionary gestures that keep the mind off the real job of dissolutionary logic. But it is a diversion that the rhyme-play reveals to be very passionately yearned-for.

Though the smart self-analysis brings 'inventer' and 'm'éviter' together, the sentence also has a melodramatic–sentimental counter-text, heard along the stress-lines connecting 'âme', 'amour', 'musique' with the 'm' of the reflexive. The elegiac relaxation into the imagining of what is denied, demonstrated by the rhymes, is there in the tiniest, oddest acoustic link, between 'oreilles' and 'groseiller'. What at first seems a cheap jibe at Proustian nature-sentimentalists for an instant turns into a real nostalgia. 'Oreilles' falls into 'groseiller', is heard again within it, and remembers, for a moment, the word 'oreiller'. The pillowed relaxation into half-hearing the fall, half-hearing the sweet resonances and music in words' memory, reminds us of Watt:

Not that for a moment Watt supposed that he penetrated the forces at play [. . .] But he had turned, little by little, a disturbance into words, he had made a little pillow of old words, for his head. (*W*, 115)

One of the novelist's most essential tasks, traditionally speaking, is the fabrication of memory. The characters in the novel must all have plausible pasts, must live, breathe and feel within sufficiently detailed and conceivable networks of memories which both they and reader have recall access to. This entails many hours of sensitive work creating personal memory stores, as well as significant semantic memory stores, for each and every character in the text. Proust's prose rhymes had administered to the nerves and pulses of his subjects' memories in contexts often surprisingly askew to the feelings being remembered. That sensitivity was a quality he admired in the novels of Balzac, particularly the occasion in *Illusions perdues* where 'Carlos Herrera demande le nom du château devant lequel passe sa calèche: C'est Rastignac, la demeure du jeune homme qu'il a aimé autrefois.' (ii, 1050). Herrera's 'Ah!' is all the indication we have from his voice—the memory drifts into the novel from outside it, from *Le Père Goriot*. Balzac's tact contrasts sharply with Vautrin's own evil exploitation of others (he passes himself off as Herrera, a Spanish priest). Having saved Lucien from suicide, he owns him ('Je vous ai pêché, je vous ai rendu la vie, et vous m'appartenez comme la créature est au créateur [. . .] comme le corps est à l'âme!' (*Illusions perdues*, 556)) and then drives him to suicide in *Splendeurs et misères des courtisanes*. Much of Balzac's skill, then, lies in his successful fabrication of long-term memory. His tact lies in the daring he displays in bringing his own creatorly procedures into mimetic contact with Vautrin's evil power over the lives of others.

Beckett in *Malone Dies* (abbreviated as *MD*) brings this tact out into the open, crossing Balzac with Vautrin to create Malone eager for the exploitative pleasure of having another's memory to play with, like Proust's narrator given unlimited power over an absolutely fictionalized sleeping Albertine. Malone's other is the stranger within him, the creature fabricated by the textual potential of language, a made-up memory system that resonates within the lazily fictionalizing discourse of the narrative voice. Malone remembers the love-affair he had imagined with that other:

celui qui m'attendait toujours, qui avait besoin de moi et dont moi j'avais besoin, qui me prenait dans ses bras et me disait de ne plus partir, qui me cédait la place et veillait sur moi, qui souffrait chaque fois que je le quittais, qu'j'ai beaucoup fait souffrir et peu contenté, que je n'ai jamais vu. Voilà que je commence à m'exalter. (*Malone meurt*, 34–5)

In the later English version, that last sentence is translated with genius by Beckett into 'There I am forgetting myself again.' (*MD*, 179). To forget oneself is to get carried away; but Malone is also forgetting his own self's part in the fabricating process. By exulting over the mind and body of his mock other, he momentarily forgets that it is his artificial creature, the voice rising to a mock acknowledgement of this fictional memory system as his very own.

In recognizing this, Malone suddenly hits upon the ideal relationship:

Ce n'est pas de moi qu'il s'agit, mais d'un autre, qui ne me vaut pas et que j'essaie d'envier, dont je suis enfin à même de raconter les plates aventures, je ne sais comment. Moi non plus je n'ai jamais su me raconter, pas plus que vivre ou raconter les autres. Comment l'aurais-je fait, n'ayant jamais essayé? Me montrer maintenant, à la veille de disparaître, en même temps que l'étranger, grâce à la même grâce, voilà qui ne serait pas dépourvu de piquant. Puis vivre, le temps de sentir, derrière mes yeux fermés, se fermer d'autres yeux. Quelle fin. (*Malone meurt*, 35)

This graceful dream of an end in the companionship of his creature is horribly parodied at the end of the book by Lemuel's raised axe. But here, despite the cauterizing tones of the self-critic ('pas dépourvu de piquant', 'Quelle fin'), a real tenderness slips through at the prospect of having his creature die, eyelids behind his, within his body as it dies. And despite his protestations ('pas de moi', 'moi non plus'), he does *not* forget himself in this selfless dream of self-possession. The sounds of 'moi' and 'me' run through the prose along stress-lines emanating from the dense alliterative string in '[m]e montrer maintenant'—'moi', 'mais', 'même', 'comment', 'moi', 'me', 'jamais', 'comment', 'jamais', 'me', 'montrer', 'maintenant', 'même', 'même', 'mes', 'fermés', 'fermer'— recalling as it does the etymological root of 'même', *egomet ipse*, 'moi-même en personne'.[7] The key-word fabricated by the stress-lines reveals a 'self exiled in upon his ego' (*Finnegans Wake*, 184), a myself as hypnotic sequence of phonemes forming themselves into the fiction of a self divorced from the self. He retells his 'other' exiled self in ceding his body to his other.

The elegant closure of the mirror-rhymes, 'derrière mes yeux fermés'-'se fermer d'autres yeux' with the 'mes'-'fermés' touch (matched in the two three-beat phrases in the English, with its soft 'z'-run and the my-eyes assonance: 'behind my closed eyes, other eyes close' (*MD*, 26)), is timed to the imagining feeling of his true self ('le temps pour sentir'). To be in the same time as another ('en même temps') is to realize in the mind that feeling of 'moi-même en personne' at the same time. This stranger, created in Malone's solipsistic melodramatic fiction ('qui souffrait'), is suddenly felt as *his* memory become another's. In imagining the perfect death for both of them, his dislocated memory comes home again and his prose is touched into telling of himself, fictional narcissism transposed onto another and revealing the pathetic accents of his loneliness. Balzac's ceding of life to Vautrin's memory has momentarily humanized Vautrin into Balzac, that moment, that 'maintenant' become 'le temps pour sentir'.

The language at such times is 'transformed, momentarily, perhaps because of the memories that motion revives', as Malone says of the cab-horse in its last years (*MD*, 70). In his extreme old age, Malone, though distracted from his language and his history, can suddenly be moved by the sensations of the distant past, as he is in one of his halts for breath during the telling of Sapo's story: 'Quand je m'arrête, comme tantôt, les bruits reprennent avec une force étrange, ceux dont c'est l'heure. De sorte qu'il me semble retrouver l'ouïe de ma jeunesse' (*Malone meurt*, 53). The sounds that the bedridden hear are rhymed with the sounds heard by the intent listening powers of childhood, a background roar, buzz, and song that through the coincidences of the chances of memory confuse past and present. Beckett's prose rhymes seem to reproduce such a sound-system, in little, within the time of the senten-

---

[7] 21 x $\underline{m}$ = 6.7%, as compared to 3.55% normal frequency. Allbright has described *Malone Dies* as ' a ghastly competition between I and self, vying over which of these twin phantoms will take preference' (*Representation*, 172). The competition often entails a 'tentative embrace of soiled images of oneself followed by strenuous repudiation of them' (ibid. 188).

ces. Being divorced from their memories, having turned their traces into fiction and denying them, Malone and the Unnamable at times rejoice in this feat and the fact that their memories are simply the small-scale pasts of the patch of sentence they have just written: 'the space of a moment the passing moment that's all my past', writes the voice in *How It Is* (80). The momentary transformation that occurs in the rhyme-cruces hints, however, at a feeling that is remembering, a voice that is feeling as though it were remembering.

Memory Traces and the Forgetful Textual Voice

The 'fizzles' (*For To End Yet Again*, abbreviated as *FTEYA*), 'Old Earth' and 'He is barehead', are both concerned with these kinds of rhyming memory formations and acts of *emotional* retentiveness. 'He is barehead' concerns a figure wandering along cave-like passages, struggling towards the light. The narrative voice describes the figure—its context and his manner of struggle onwards—in great detail and then considers his subject's memory:

He has already a number of memories, from the memory of the day he suddenly knew he was there, on this same path bearing him along, to that now of having halted to lean against the wall, he has a little past already, even a smatter of settled ways. But it is still all fragile. (*FTEYA*, 28–9)

There is a smatter of little rhymes in the passing of the sentence, the three half-rhymes 'still all fragile' remembering 'already', 'along', 'halted', 'wall', 'little', 'already', 'settled'; 'ways' recalling 'memories', 'day', 'was', 'same', and 'against' in the stress-lines along their phonemes; the acoustic past of the word 'past' in 'path' and 'against'; 'settled' reorganizing phonemes from 'little', 'already', 'smatter'; all the phonemes in 'smatter' find accompanying runs and strings. These internal little rhymes, though, on their own would not justify a memory-sentence rhyme. It is how the number of them, in little, support with their strands of similarity in sound and meaning a whole system of stress-line recalls that gather up the key terms and passages of the rest of the short story into the two summative phrases, 'a little past already, a smatter of settled ways' and 'But it is still all fragile'.

The two phrases recollect firstly the sounds described in the tunnel passages. There are two sounds, 'the sounds, intricate and faint, of the body on its way' (*FTEYA* 28) and the sound 'of fall', 'a solid mass that leaves its place and crashes down, lighter particles collapsing slowly' (28). The sounds of the summative phrase 'a smatter of settled ways' take up the sound of the 'body on its way'; 'all still fragile' recalls the sound 'of fall'; 'a little past' gathers up the memory of the acoustic runs in 'solid mass', 'its place', and 'lighter particles'. The sound of fall is described as having an echo 'as loud at first as the sound that woke it and repeated sometimes a score of times'. 'Fall' is echoed in the prose with strong rhyme and the word itself occurs nineteen times after this is said. 'All still fragile' stresses the fragility of its own acoustic recollection of that echo whilst also saying it 'still' is remembered (the sound 'all' is [here] still, fragile). The sound-effects, in subtly altering the stressing, change the meaning of the word 'still' from 'still merely' or 'still only' to 'still' as a mixed tone crossing persistence with the fragile immobility of sound and memory. Philip Davis, in *Memory and Writing*, writes about Wordsworth in ways it might be useful to remember with regard to Beckett: 'the poem's continuum is maintained by this internal reminiscence, this pick-up and retrieval of words, because it is as if the mind of the poet thereby rescues the meaning of the words of his own poetry from neglect; and because he does so seems in that to be learning from the language and from himself [. . .] memory, triggered within the words, becomes a form of discovery of truth to feeling' (76).

The sound of the body on its way becomes loudest in the prose when the clothes or the figure are described, the sound

of the clothes, singlet and trousers, espousing and resisting the movements of the body, coming unstuck from the damp flesh and sticking to it again, tattering and fluttered where in tatters already by sudden flurries as suddenly stilled (*FTEYA*, 28)

The phrase 'a smatter of settled ways' intricately arranges the faint recalls of the sounds of the clothes, 'tattering', 'fluttered', 'tatters', 'stilled'. The 'body'-'already' half-rhyme, emphasized by the rhythm, and by the 'sudden' and 'suddenly', is itself recalled by the passage quoted previously—'already a number of memories', 'he suddenly knew he was there', 'a little past already'. The intricate, faint sounds of the prose (stress-lines issuing forth from the summative phrase) are settled into a compact phrase, become a settled matter within the mind (stress-lines fabricating the summative phrase, transforming it into true motif).[8] The narrative voice, imagining the figure's memory accruing a fragile past out of the ways his body has been, gathers its own sounds up into a history. It takes up into its prose the delicately accrued sounds it has made on its way. The smatter of language gathers up the fragments of memory that the body has given the mind into its own dialect, settling the echoes of its dying falls into the ways of acoustic compassion and comprehension. The acoustic history of the text espousing and resisting the movements of the body to direct it to its own fragile summation, takes shape, the shape of the memory of the narrative voice. The voice rediscovers recall itself.

The 'fresh elements and motifs' (*FTEYA* 30) that enter the text, by recalling, within the textual 'short-term memories' of rhyme and repetition, the words that have preceded them, seem already to have been settled into a longer pattern. They approximate a long-term memory. This mimics the configurations discovered by the figure in the passage and his memory. He occasionally forgets his own small accumulated past and feels the same surprise at sounds and events 'as on that first day, which is his beginning, on days of great recall' (29). This freshness is changed by his memory:

memory returns and takes him back, if he will, far back to that first instant beyond which nothing, when he was already old, that is to say near to death, and knew, though unable to recall having lived, what age and death are, and other momentous matters. But it is all still fragile. (29)

His 'first steps' are 'merely the last or latest'. Within the amnesiac, contentless textual space he is condemned to, the narrated self discovers the contours of a long-term memory within the mere short-term passages of his discourse. Recalling that this long para-

---

[8] 'Il est tête nue' (*Pour Finir encore*, 15–25) has parallel sound-effects. The phrase 'il a déjà son petit passé' (21), remembering and made summative by the description of the 'corps qui avance' (20), particularly the hands, 'qui par moments passent et repassent sur toutes les parties du corps' (21), 'encore précaire' gathers a string of k-repetitions that stresses 'corps' (20–1). The major effect of the sound-effects is to rhyme his action ('passer') with the creation of memories ('passé')—the 'corps'-'encore' rapprochement has similar purposes. 'Souvenirs', 'souvent', and 'soudain' are similarly brought together (21–2), as are 'mémoire' and 'maintenant' (22). The 'smatter of settled ways' is simply 'presque des habitudes' (21) in the French. The French if anything is more efficient in showing the relations between present habitual action and memory-creation with its key-word rapprochements.

graph becomes the closed place of a short story distracted from living speech also reminds the voice how its sound-repetitions are instrumental in shaping a testimonial out of mere narrative time. Hearing the old voice listening to itself (sound-repetitions are proof of this), we hear the ghost of a real memory network within the smatter of short-term sound-effects, and the fabricated third person blurs into ghost first person.

'Old Earth' (*FTEYA*, 53–4), in the first person, is a brief tale of a self that has long outlived his loved ones, who dreams of death within the earth and yet remembers his pasts in complex visions in the sky he gazes upon. Only about three hundred words long, it splits naturally into three parts, though like 'He is barehead' it is one single paragraph. It splits naturally because of the suddenness of the changes in its subjects and the seeming separateness of the three subjects. The first section is preoccupied with an address to the old earth in which the voice forecasts a reunion of himself and the earth in the near future. The story then suddenly shifts to an odd little section about cockchafers and their natural habits. As suddenly again, the voice turns to his own habits at his windows, his sky-gazing and the memories that are screened there. These sudden shifts in purpose worry the mind into seeking a connection between the three sections.

A tiny key-word covers all three, the word 'gaze', yet it yields little of itself. It is rhymed in all three sections: in the first with 'lies' and 'eyes' and 'refuse'; in the second with 'rise, 'guzzle guzzle', and 'days'; in the third with 'skies', 'agonies' and 'skies' again. Hearing those rhymes emphasizes, across the three sections, all the plurals of the piece—the 'z'-string around 'gaze' accentuates the delicate 'z'-ending of English plurals with vowel or voiced consonant endings: 'shadows', 'moles', 'windows', 'agonies', 'loves', 'others', 'spasms', a small whirr of zeds trembles through the whole fizzle. One might like to leave it at that as a purely compositional grace linking three deliberately disjunctive passages. Except that one realizes there are also other strange links in the paragraph, as intricate as the rhyme-play.

In speaking to the earth, he addresses it as though it were a loved one, or more precisely in the tone of one speaking to a dead partner. He promises he will join the earth soon, he speaks of mutual refusal in present and past as though repeating a lovers' history, and of their future union as though it were a love song—

'it will be you, it will be me, it will be us'. The tone hints at a drama—a man suffers after the death of a woman who had loved him, whom he had never loved, whom he had refused. In guilt and love he visits her grave, desiring his own death, and promises her that he will soon be reunited with her. The old earth, then, is the plot of her grave. This drama is merely hinted lightly on the surfaces of the tone. This first section is telling us that an old voice may desire its own burial with the same passion and the same patterns of feeling as one who mourns and yearns for the company of a dead loved one.

In the last section, he imagines, like Malone with his creature, the perfect death, a death simultaneous with 'theirs, the last minute loved ones', a dream of happiness. This subtle link between the two sections, crossing a dreamt urge for death and the memory of loved ones dead, nevertheless skips over the cockchafer section and does not properly account for the strange rhythms and turns of the final words:

No but now, now, simply stay still, standing before a window, one hand on the wall, the other clutching your shirt, and see the sky, a long gaze, but no, gasps and spasms, a childhood sea, other skies, another body. (*FTEYA*, 54)

One of the keys to understanding contradictory material in any text is to go to the text and discover its own internal logic for its own contradictions. In 'Old Earth', we see a movement from the phrase 'Ah to love at your last and see them at theirs', to 'why ah, uncalled for' through to the 'No but now' that opens the final sentence. The voice, in other words, is swerving away from a too deeply felt and expressed yearning, with an aesthetic distaste that seems to believe that powerful feelings about love and death are necessarily bogus. In terms of Beckett's practice as a whole, this distaste might be defined as a sudden disgust for the melodramatic implications of the fictional memory system being fabricated. The movement away from the dream of dead loved ones to the attempt to concentrate on the 'present moment' of window and gaze is redefined here, then, as a movement away from mock-up mourning and its poetic prose. With this evidence, we can begin to account for the rest of the text's contradictions.

The cockchafer section swerves away from the earth so suddenly with the energy of such a turn. At the pitch of his mixed tone, 'you so refused', the imagination lurches away to the inconsequence of nature and its ravages. The cockchafers in rising from the earth through his oak-tree to the sky, might also be seen as mimicking the movement of his gaze, away from the compromisingly sentimental tones of mock mourning. The cockchafers also themselves recall an earlier moment in Beckett's compositional history, his translation of Apollinaire's 'Zone', where Apollinaire uses the chafer as an image for poetic prose (the 'cétoine' is the 'hanneton des roses'):

> Et tu observes au lieu d'écrire ton conte en prose
> La cétoine qui dort dans le cœur de la rose

Beckett translates:

> And you observe instead of writing your story in prose
> The chafer asleep in the heart of the rose (*Collected Poems*, 114–15)

The word 'prose' is itself rhymed with, made 'poetic', the chafers transforming the dull activity of prose-writing into poetic prose, prosaic poetry. The cockchafers' rise into the air announces the imminent flight of Beckett's prose up into the heart of poetic possibility. In other words, the shift in the subject's gaze, though superficially evading the pseudo-poetic sublime of the mourner at the graveside, is ineluctably sliding into the rhetoric it would wish to suppress.

The last turn, 'a long gaze, but no' is the sign of a similarly ambiguous change, settling the ways of the story and altering the whole memory of it. The voice has calmed itself down, disciplined itself to 'simply stay still [. . .] and see the sky'. What he wants to gaze at is the sky itself, without the confusion of memory and lament,[9] without it necessarily turning 'to faces, agonies, loves, the different loves', without the 'moments of life, mine too'. It is the word 'gaze' that foils the self-discipline, the word that with its accompanying rhymes and stress-lines on z and diphthongs recalls the whole story, recalls the intent, ambiguous gaze at the earth ('how I gaze on you [. . .] with my other's ravening eyes'), recalls the refusals, the 'guzzle guzzle' of his deep hunger for those he has been bereaved of, the standing at gaze before the window the first time, the plurals of the images, memories seen on the screen of the sky. To try and see 'the sky' singular with a gaze that

---

[9] 'Afar a bird', *FTEYA*, 40.

had always, in the time of the tale, perceived all things through the
plural vision of 'memory and lament', was a desperate move. His
first gaze at the sky had not managed it: 'For an instant I see the
sky, the different skies, then they turn to faces'. What the word
'gaze' touches into play at the last is the deepest feeling of all the
feelings the voice, at turns, tries to keep at bay: the terror at, the
lyrical beauty of, the plurality of selves remembered, imagined
and seen in the old narrator's mind, 'long gaze, but no, gasps and
spasms, a childhood sea, other skies, another body'.

The shock of that recollection makes him choke, as though
dying, makes him return deep into the past to see a context so
strange as to be other worldly. The words discovered at this
ending recall Tennyson's Tithonus in his extreme decrepitude
remembering falling in love with the Dawn:

> Ay me! ay me! with what another heart
> In days far-off, and with what other eyes
> I used to watch—if I be he that watch'd
> —The lucid outline forming round thee[.] ('Tithonus', 97)

Alain Girard, analysing the 'journal intime', remarks on how 'la
rémemoration aggrave l'impression de dissemblance intérieure'
(*Le Journal intime*, 516). With Tithonus and the narrator of 'Old
Earth', the dissemblance of their past selves within them is made
more painful by their desire to die and be forgotten 'earth in earth'.
Beckett's narrator is shocked permanently into the tone of memory and lament with its literally breath-taking visions and acute
dissemblances. Sound-resemblances accumulate and run counter
to his old wishes to be free of his charge of pasts. He discovers
there his memories, the long-term of the skies, the short-term of
'Old Earth' and its sounds, compacted and transformed into lyric,
recalling but departing from the body of the text and its gazes: 'a
childhood sea, other skies, another body'. The phrase is self-suffi-
cient in its echoes—child-hood-body; a-other-another; child-sea-
skies; sea-body—Masson patterns dʌðə/ʌðəd and aɪds/saɪd (with
accompanying z). The voice rises, towards rest, in strange eloquence, the internal echo of its imperfect sounds, heard in the
rhymes, creating 'trances of thought and mountings of the mind.'[10]
The voice rediscovers a lyrical childhood otherness within the

[10] Wordsworth, *The Prelude*, (1805), I, 18–21.

fictional memory system whose sentimentality he had been trying to repress.

Those concentrated memories in the strange last words of 'Old Earth' momentarily humanize the permanent state of comic amnesia that had characterized the predicament of Watt and the Trilogy-narrators. The manic transformation of an isolated episodic memory into 'an instant in the life of another' that had trapped Watt into distracted language and an anaesthetized heart, the withdrawal into a fictive denying of a personal past within the second childhood of decrepit forgetfulness in the Trilogy, rhyme richly with the mode of sudden transformation in 'Old Earth'. Both abstracting and imagining, the rhyming memory in the voice adopts the forces and means of the aged malady that had dislocated the mind into its close, narrow world in the first place. It takes up the energy of the effort to forget ('the sky, a long gaze') and rhymes it deep into remembered vision.

Rhyming Two Languages

In the last two sections, I have demonstrated how Beckett's prose rhymes act as faint, intricate reminders of persisting memory-traces within the forgetful textual voice, this after their value as purely compositional grace-notes in the prose: *after* that value because of the manner in which their accumulation over the time of the motion of the sentence 'revives the dead longings' (*MD*, 130) within the old words and their old credentials. Beckett's tact in bringing the stress-line traces in the memory of one's reading of the prose into relation with the long- and short-term memory of the narrator and narrated lies in how he presents the voice, at certain crucial moments, in the simultaneous act of espousing and resisting an acknowledgement of that rhyming relation itself. The act of espousing and resisting may take the form of the Unnamable's elegiac relaxation into the imagining of what he is denying, the faculty of memory itself, or, as with 'Old Earth', a sudden shocked recognition of a concentrated memory arising out of a desperate resisting of the tones of fictionalized memory and lament. I have also given some indication of the processes of dislocation that initiated the split between the memory and the self in the analysis of *Watt* and the Trilogy, and how the memory is ceded to the imagination of another, the stranger within, whilst at the same time demonstrating that the verbal recurrences and little acoustic pasts murmur of a deep-seated desire for a reunion. The rare movements of compassion in Beckett's prose, rarer and more fitful than Proust's rhyming accent of memory, compose themselves suddenly into brief sentences such as 'a smatter of settled ways' out of the fragile echoes of other rhyming contexts. Balzac's and Proust's sensitivity to the memories of their characters is dramatized by Beckett within the voices of his 'people' as they give utterance to their fictionalized selves and moods, lives 'invented remembered a little of each no knowing' (*How It Is*, 80).[11] That sensitivity to memory and lament survives the pressure of the unforgiving, anaesthetized prose in small pockets of resistance within the sentences that gather up and recollect out of the smatter of aged *obiter dicta*, the rhymes and rhythms of a humanized voice and its history.

I have attempted to show how a sensitivity to the sound-texture of Beckett's work is essential in order to respond to the crucial moments in the prose when a living memory rises out of the 'reason-ridden' voice of composition. Beckett's portrayal of memory is a complicated matter because of that voice's unchallengeable right and desire to disinvest itself of any true association with the 'memories' it narrates and to call them another's fiction. It is the comic step beyond Proust's awe at the multiplicity of past selves and Bloom's averting movements away from his memories. 'L'homme est,' Proust writes, 'cet être sans âge fixe, cet être qui a la faculté de redevenir en quelques secondes de beaucoup d'années plus jeune, et qui entouré des parois du temps où il a vécu, y flotte, mais comme dans un bassin dont le niveau changerait constamment et le mettrait à la portée tantôt d'une époque, tantôt d'une autre' (*A la recherche du temps perdu*, iii. 614). Beckett doubly marked this passage in his copy of *A la recherche du temps perdu*. He also marked these words from the next paragraph which describe the intelligent man's jealous attraction to 'la femme médiocre': 'Derrière chacune de ses paroles ils sentent un mensonge; derrière chaque maison où elle dit être allée, un autre maison, derrière chaque action, chaque être, une autre action, un autre être.'

[11] Related to what Beckett described as the 'mind to heart oneness' in Proust (Beckett Manuscripts, Trinity College Dublin: Dobbin notes).

(iii. 616). Beckett, in his fiction, crosses the implications of these two marked passages, internalizing the 'femme médiocre' by having her articulate the very voice of memory itself. Within 'cet être sans âge fixe', 'un autre être' narrates its fabrications. What Beckett's rhyme-effects achieve, however, is a momentary bridging of the cruel and artificial gap between voice and remembered experience by articulating (through the memory-network and associations put into play by the sound-resemblances) an imaginary recall of living memory itself, back into the closed mind.

In this next section I should like to show how far Beckett goes to demonstrate this imaginary recall of memory. The recall of memory finds its strongest presence in the prose in the form of imagined encounters between fictional selves. The fictional 'others', like Mahood in *The Unnamable*, the mother's voice in *Footfalls*, are, I believe, to be read as potential memory-images, concentrated essences of the many selves discarded in a long life of solitude amongst words. Much of the rhyme-work in this section transforms these encounters into moments of unity and identity where the 'femme médiocre' of the denied memory-traces is momentarily embraced and loved, so to speak, as the voice's own.

Fully aware of how much I risk the charge of sentimentality with such readings, I would argue strongly that this is precisely what the rhyming connections themselves do within the voice itself, namely, risk the charge of sentimentality. The most difficult problem about such a reading of the prose is the harsh, bleak voice's consciousness of its own artificial desires for such meetings and its subsequent wheedling parody of them.[12] Examples of such parodies include the open, bare-faced pathos of the voice in *From an abandoned work*:

Now I am old and weak, in pain and weakness murmur why and pause, and the old thoughts well up in me and over into my voice, the old thoughts born with me and grown with me and kept under, there's another[.] (*No's Knife*, 143)

The cynical sneer at Augustinian and pseudo-romantic nostalgia in *Mercier and Camier*:

You cultivate your memory till it's passable, a treasure-bin, stroll in your crypt, unlit, return to the scenes, call back the old sounds (paramount), till

---

[12] Paul Lawley identifies Hamm as a 'parody presence' in his attempts to 'finish off' a self imperfectly created ('Symbolic Structure', 45–68).

you have the lot off pat and you at a loss, head, nose, ears and the rest what remains to snuff up, they all smell equally sweet, what old jingles to play back! Pretty beyond! (108)

And the coldly compositional tone of the note-book in *Company* where the voice deliberates on the best attributes for his 'hearer' to make him more 'companionable':

An attempt at reflexion at least. At recall. [. . .] A trace of emotion. Signs of distress. A sense of failure. Without loss of character. Delicate ground. (28).

Many critical approaches to Beckett's work are already imagined within the work and lamed there by their context, not least mine. One *is* on delicate ground seeking amongst the minutiae of the voice's tones for traces of emotion, signs of distress within attempts at recall. Criticism might be wishfully creating its own companionable creature to comfort it within the harsh contexts of Beckett's prose. For instance, it is fashionable to quote the Unnamable's last words, 'I can't go on, I'll go on' (*TU*, 132) as a moving affirmation of human endurance without stopping to consider whether one would really wish the immeasurably cruel, chilling nihilist of a voice to go on, or at least to wonder whether it might be truly pitiful that it must. When engaging with Beckett's prose, it is necessary to judge to what extent one believes or disbelieves the voice. The possible delicate ground of distinction would be within the reader's own human confidence in, for instance, hearing the ambiguity in 'Delicate ground'—a mere compositional difficulty, or an area dangerous because it has to do with delicacy itself. The parodies of the wish to find a meeting-ground may, in themselves, be crossed by ambiguous tones that surrender traces of emotion, signs of distress.

In this section I shall present Beckett's prose rhymes as acoustic images of memory-encounters, particularly in the light of his remarkable feats of self-translation, encounters that translate the terms in which they are expressed into 'un langage nouveau', as Mayoux says of *Molloy* (269), that gives utterance to a genuine 'sense of failure' in the killing style of the reason-ridden voice. The 'langue étrangère' of Proust's counter-senses is translated into a language created by the encounter between two languages, a language that fails at a deeper level than the texts' failure to make clear, to comprehend a context, to sustain a belief, the deeper failure to stop the life in the feeling imagination. I shall contrast the English and French versions of the texts to establish my ground for human confidence in the moments where one disbelieves the remorselessness of the form, where a purer imagination finds a form of life. The encounter between different aspects of the self, different selves to be precise, is externalized and given flesh by Beckett and is consequently strangely dehumanized. What the externalization does is to present the split selves as merely other, not memory-images at all. Watt's transformation of the piano-tuners into someone else's ill-told tale is achieved with the faculty of memory itself. The pseudo-couples are past selves fictionalized into unfeeling strangers, like French and English facing each other across the untranslatable. The rhyme-work, however, establishes a true meeting of those selves within the arena of felt memory recollected, in the same way as it demonstrates the common ground possible between Beckett's two languages. When the two meet, a true memory is resuscitated (and/or fabricated) and the imagination is shown breathing again.

At the beginning of the French *Molloy* (abbreviated to *FM*), Molloy recalls two men coming towards each other outside the town:

C'étaient deux hommes, impossible de s'y tromper, un petit et un grand. Ils étaient sortis de la ville, d'abord l'un, puis l'autre, et le premier, las ou se rappelant une obligation, était revenu sur ses pas. L'air était frais, car ils avaient leur manteau. Ils se ressemblaient, mais pas plus que les autres. Un grand espace les séparait d'abord. Ils n'auraient pas pu se voir, même en levant la tête et en se cherchant des yeux, à cause de ce grand espace, et puis à cause de vallonnement du terrain, qui faisait que la route était en vagues, peu profondes mais suffisament, suffisament. Mais le moment vint où ensemble ils dévalèrent vers le même creux et c'est dans ce creux qu'ils se rencontrèrent à la fin. (*FM*, 9–10)

Molloy remembers what amounts to a staged act of memory. 'Le premier', prompted by memory, retraces his steps. The sound-effects make clear, however, that 'revenu sur ses pas' is identical with the motive 'las ou se rappelant', the 'rappelant'- 'pas' sound-resemblance sufficiently reinforced by the surrounding phonemes to alert our attention—('le premier, las ou se rappelant une obligation, étaient revenu sur ses pas'). The sound of 'pas' echoes through the succeeding sentences in the repeated 'grand espace' with 'séparait', in 'pas plus', 'pas pu' and 'puis à', with minor echoes in the 'vallonnement'-'vague' link and the phrase 'peu profondes mais suffisament, suffisament'. The first, by remembering, retraces his steps and meets himself walking along the road just where he had been moments before. It is the prose rhymes that tell us that this is so by identifying 'pas' with the act of weary memory and by then repeating the sound of his retracing mind on its way towards the meeting with the self of the immediate past.[13]

Other features in the passage confirm this. For instance, Molloy's odd assertiveness that it was 'deux hommes', as though there could have been some doubt; the way calling one of the men 'autre' subtly changes the sense of the denial of likeness ('pas plus que les autres')—other past selves are suggested; the odd way Beckett manipulates common features of French, the reflexive, the 're-' verbs, a phrase like 'ils avaient leur manteau', hinting at an identity. The repetitions in the passage are curious too ('grand espace', 'suffisament', 'creux')—and even more so in the light of the fact that Molloy is remembering an act of memory. The two men are repetitions of each other brought together by the sound of their footfalls ('pas') which are little externalized acts of recall in action.

Here is the English version:

It was two men, unmistakably, one small and one tall. They had left the town, first one, then the other, and then the first, weary or remembering a duty, had retraced his steps. The air was sharp, for they wore greatcoats. They looked alike, but no more than others do. At first a wide space lay between them. They couldn't have seen each other, even had they raised their heads and looked about, because of this wide space, and then because of the undulating land, which caused the road to be in waves, not high, but high enough, high enough. But the moment came when together they went down into the same trough and in this trough finally met. (M, 9)

'Rhymes: two men dressed the same, looking the same, two by two', Stephen had thought. One of Watt's backward sentences remembers Stephen's thoughts about rhyme: 'Dis yb dis, nem,

[13] The unpublished draft "8" is a specific denial of the *Molloy* meeting: the 'ways' are one-way, there is no 'retracing the way up back down', there is 'no sign that none before' (Lake, *No Symbols*, 173).

owt' (*Watt*, 166), or 'two men, sid by sid'. Watt and Knott are literally rhymes of each other, and Molloy's pseudo-couple rhyme too—'small' and 'tall'. It is memory that, by repeating its original, creates a rhyme, the present self living side by side with its twin dead self. As in the French, 'remembering' and 'retraced' are aligned ('weary or remembering a duty, had retraced his steps', an alignment reinforced by the r-run). The 'pas' rhymes are left un-translated, but 'retraced' is echoed in the 'wide space' repetition with a supporting eɪ-run (all the 'they's, 'lay', 'raised', 'waves'). The rhyming identity between the two men ('one small and one tall') leads to a rhyming meeting-place—'high enough, high enough [. . .] the same trough and in this trough'.

The possibility that the scene is an allegory of memory, remem-bering mind retracing its steps to meet its trace, is underlined by the French 'pas'-string, and in the English with the full rhymes. In the English the two men are made one by the implications of the rhymes—they are rhymes of each other. In the French the two men are made one by the identity of their 'pas' with the act of recall itself. The two different routes meet in the final analysis, just as the two men meet finally in the same trough. The rhyming approach between the two versions sets out a memory-encounter that speaks of translation itself, the resemblances and differences be-tween the two languages and their encounter in *Molloy*, Beckett's second major venture into French.[14] Northrop Frye first described the two halves of *Molloy* as a representation of an encounter be-tween Irish English and French.[15] Over the undulating prose of the novel, Beckett's Irish–English imagination meets its French counterpart, his 'secondmouth language' (*Finnegans Wake*, 37); 'traduced into jinglish janglage for the nusances of dolphins born' (*Finnegans Wake*, 275) the way is vice versa, a rhyme of itself.

The act of self-translation, then, could be seen as the linguistic manifestation of the particular malaise of the voice and its mem-ory. The self over time is split into a series of distinct successive

[14] Molloy was written in French between Sept. 1947 and Jan. 1948. In 1947, Beckett had translated *Murphy*, written *Mercier et Camier* (the first major venture into French), 13 French poems, and also the early play *Eleuthéria* and *Quatre Nouvelles* in French. *Molloy* was translated into English in 1955 by Beckett in collaboration with Patrick Bowles.
[15] 'The Nightmare Life in Death', 442–9; corroborated by Hugh Kenner: 'Molloy and Moran are more or less the author's Irish and French selves respectively' (quoted Alvarez, *Beckett*, 53).

selves. Beckett's two languages make each other foreign. The persistent memory of the other language in the mind dislocates the lexical accents of the voice, making the native unfamiliar and the foreign close to home:

Mahood's stories are not any old thing, though no less foreign, to what, to that unfamiliar native land of mine, as unfamiliar as that other where men come and go, and feel at home [. . .] Not any old thing but as near as no matter. (*TU*, 31)

On one level, Beckett is talking about the strange relationship between his French stories and his Irish memory. The Unnamable, in keeping them distinct, wishes them both devoid of any relation to each other or to the real world, the 'dead tongue of the living' (*TU*, 54). Rhyming-effects, present in both versions, bring them close together, implying rough identity between Mahood and voice, memory and self, and a certain kinship between French and English.

And they appear at the very point the Unnamable is asserting their differences:

Here, in my domain, what is Mahood doing in my domain, and how does he get here? There I am launched again on the same old hopeless business, there we are face to face, Mahood and I, if we are twain, as I say we are. (*TU*, 31)

The rhymes are there in the French: 'Ici, dans mon pays, que fait Mahood ici [. . .] Mahood et moi, si nous sommes deux, comme je le dis' (*L'Innomable*, 47). The rhymes bring both the Unnamable and Mahood together, just as the languages are by translation, together against the voice's arbitrary distinguishing of itself from Mahood. This rough unity is brought into a rhyming relation with the languages he speaks, the 'pays' of the original, the 'domain' of the translation. 'The self-accompaniment of a tongue that is not mine' (*TU*, 22) murmurs his deeper confession even when the voice believes itself to be coming clean. The 'tongue' is the voice of the 'autre être', the past self made stranger by the voice's extreme old age and by comic, manic dislocation.

It is also the foreign language Beckett prefers to write in and then translate out of. In 1977, Beckett told Charles Juliet that 'il écrit maintenant en anglais, car cette langue est devenue pour lui la langue étrangère' (Juliet, 49). The persistence of the 'pas' and rhyme-sounds in the two versions of the passage from *Molloy* creates a background accompaniment to the fleeting, inconsequential meeting of the two men which parallels the 'superflu' of the Mahood–moi rhyme in the later work. It merges the sounds the two men make beyond the limited encounter in the trough. Two languages, two selves pace out a secret acoustic kinship unawares.

The 'pas' rhymes of the French *Molloy* are of particular importance to Beckett. He told Juliet, friend of Bram van Velde, of 'l'importance du pas de l'homme, de nos pas sur cette terre':

Toujours ce va-et-vient... (Et de la main, il décrit ce mouvement du prisonnier dans sa geôle, du fauve dans sa cage.) C'est quelque chose que Bram connaît bien, ce bruit des pas ... (47–8)

But their importance lies not only in the fact that they create the impression of men and women as prisoners, circus animals in endless come-and-go, but also in the fact they remind each man and woman of the species to which they belong. They recall to the isolated mind its elemental bodied humanity, the rhythm of the species. All Beckett's pseudo-couples reject this fundamental kinship in discarding all vestige of human mercy and companionship, and in so doing, reject each other's part in their lives. 'Pas' rhymes, 'ce bruit des pas de l'homme' to condense Beckett's phrasing, recall each one back into themselves, gather both divided selves into human history and into fleeting communion.

Encounters of Memory, Voice, Body

In *Footfalls*, May treads a narrow strip on the stage as though on a phantom treadmill, or like a sentry, guarding her pain, whilst the voice of her dead mother sounds in the auditorium—they alternate speeches, interspersed with some dialogue. From the theatrical cliché 'treading the boards', Beckett creates a chilling and moving dramatic image of an old age endlessly repeating her grief at the loss of a mother, stepping out the close, narrow limits of her maddened solitude. Beckett stresses in the stage-directions that May's steps must have 'a clearly audible rhythmic tread', and the 'woman's voice', in her fourth sentence beats out the steps May makes, her voice 'synchronous with the steps' (*Ends and Odds*, 33).

The distinction is blurred between May and the other voice. Beckett strictly avoids saying 'her mother's voice': though May and 'V' talk to each other as mother and daughter, in both of their long speeches they show themselves capable of mimicking such a dialogue in monologue. Both May and mother may very well be each other's fictions.

The play's language is gently lyrical with the rhythms of dying falls resolving into simple rhymes. It begins in a rhyming stride: 'M: Were you asleep?/V: Deep asleep. (Pause) I heard you in my deep sleep. (Pause) There is no sleep so deep I would not hear you there' (33). The extraordinary nature of the majority of the rhymes, however, is their consonance with the title of the play, *Footfalls*: 'It all' which ends both sections, repeated eleven times in a five-page play; 'nightfall', 'wall', and the half-rhymes 'till', 'still', 'tell' and 'little' are repeated so often as to make the sound the dominant one of the play, rhyming not only with the title but also on the word in the text: 'I mean, Mother, that I must hear my feet, however faint they fall' (35).

All these points give a secondary sense to V.'s speech:

V. Will you never have done? [*Pause.*] Will you never have done . . . revolving it all?

M. [*Halting.*] It?

V. It all. [*Pause.*] In your poor mind. [*Pause.*] It all. [*Pause.*] It all.

[M resumes pacing . . .] (*Ends and Odds*, 34)]

'It's all in the mind' sounds out through the phrasing, transforming stage into May's mind, having her rhyming tread and voice seem to echo off the walls of her skull. Fictionalizing habits begin to sound like the self-soothing rituals of mad memory.

As Beckett's stage-directions indicate, many of the footfall-rhymes occur during a halt in May's pacing, or cause her to halt. The voice assumes the rhymes in the halts of the imagination. The auditor begins to feel and hear the strangest supposition: that the dominant sound in both heard voices is rhyming with the word that *names* May's physical action, the sound of her pacing. Stress-lines issue forth from the word that defines her pacing, translating bodily movement into the rhythms fabricated by phoneme repetition and full rhyme. May's footfalls beat out a rhythm that both voices seem to follow ('synchronous with the steps') and also impose, through the mind's translation of the body's action ('footfall, footfall . . .', etc.), a rhyming pattern. The same air that had shuddered to the audible tread of May's pacing beats with the returning stress-lines and stress-patterns of the sounds of that tread translated into voiced breath. The echo of the rhymes in the voice resounds in its pauses, whilst the voice itself rhymes clearest in the halts of the body: the voiced breath is at once echoing, remembering, and conserving the body's rhythm. The footfalls have become pantings in the breath that in rhyming the heard noise and its rhythm into the ghostly externalities of the voice's acoustics, gathers the stage and what is seen and heard into voice. The inner rhythm of May's history takes up the body into staged mind,[16] just as the body and its halts seem, inversely, to generate the voices and their pauses.

This two-way, simultaneous rhyming transformation of voice-breath and the sound of the body on its way is deepened by the gathering weight of the story the voices have to tell. The two voices re-enact the beginning of May's habit when very young and, it is hinted, soon after her mother's death. The pacing starts first within a church at nightfall, then within the room where she was born, this retreat strangely confusing her own life with her mother's taken away. This doubling is emphasized further in the subsequent strange and dislocated story May tells of Mrs Winter and her daughter, an argument at table where the mother swears she heard Amy respond 'Amen' in the church when the daughter was not there. The tale is a close, internal inversion of the present state of May's mind, the grey ghostly semblance in the church (that could be either mother or daughter), the imagined voice on the stage twisted into the mother's mishearing of Amy's response. May's habit seems to be reproducing her own actions soon before and after her mother's death—she had tended her dying mother for years, and then her grave (the church). She seems to be adopting the rhythms of her mother's illness from rhymes upon the pacings of her own past service and mourning at her mother's bed- and grave-side.[17] Though we are looking at a stage inhabited and generated by the fictional procedures of May and/or mother, the stage is transformed by the intensity of story and rhyme into the physical, external arena for May's grief, waste and possessed,

---

[16] I am grateful to Eric Griffiths for the felicitous phrase, 'staged mind'.

[17] 'It is the revolving, the incessant reliving of a traumatic experience which clearly is the foundation of the insistent pattern of seven steps, turnabout, seven steps, turnabout, seven steps', Martin Esslin (McCarthy, *Critical Essays*, 197).

shuffling pain. The rhymes that bring 'It all' and her footfalls together as echoes of each other spell out in the air of the auditorium the conceptual rhyme between the rhythm of tormented remembering and the habits of the body, a rhyme as much a cause as a symptom of the stage of mind we see. What had seemed the mere performative of narrative, dramatic power is heard anew as the true painful fabrications of displaced memory and its rituals.

How the title-rhymes deepen and are deepened by the substance of the voices' story is strengthened by the confirmation of Beckett's French version *Pas*, where the dominant sound is also created by rhymes on the title, an extraordinary translating achievement. The 'It all' section from *Footfalls* runs in the French:

V.—N'auras-tu jamais fini de ressasser tout ça?

M. s'immobilise de face G.

M.—Ca?

V.—Tout ça. [Un temps.] Dans ta pauvre tête. [Un temps.] Tout ça. [Un temps.] Tout ça.

[Un temps. M. repart. (*Pas*, 10)]

The rest of the text is similarly preoccupied with the 'pas' assonance: 'déjà' and 'jadis' are repeated, the preposition 'à' after 'jouer' and 'se mit' is emphasized by pause-breaks. There are three extended sections of involved and gravely comic repetitions in the dialogues, one of 'pas là', the other two almost ludicrously alternating 'ça' and 'commença' and 'suffit pas' and 'pas'.[18] 'Pas' is heard discretely within phrases such as 'Cette impassibilité apparente!' and 'pauvre bras'. Supporting this sustained play is the past historic tense in May's story about Amy and many of the negatives.

What the French confirms is the necessity of reading and seeing *Pas* as bringing simultaneously before the mind's eye and the physical eye the suddenness of contacts recognized. The rhymes bring voice and body together. The dislocated, revolving pain of being possessed by a voice, at once May's own become her mother's and her mother's heard, comes into contact with May's body. The body's halts and revolutions and ghostly look may be a

---

[18] It has been objected to me that 'pas', a 'back' *a*, cannot rhyme with 'déjà', 'ça', and the others which are 'front' 'a's. But since poets have been rhyming the two a's together since Baudelaire—('Bénédiction' rhymes 'pas' with 'crachats' for instance, Verlaine rhymes 'naviguat' with 'délicat' in 'Non il fut gallican', Apollinaire 'pas' with 'bras' in 'Au Platane', Supervieille 'pas' with 'soient' in 'Whisper in agony')—I have trusted that the French hear it as a rhyme.

haunting of the mind, or created by its words; none the less they are physically *there* on stage. The rhymes bring all four into complicated contact. May's memory inhabits and is inhabited by the mechanics of the stage-directions. The 'pas' and 'footfall' rhymes identify the voice of the past with the movements of the present. They bring them together. The body is at once a manifestation of the accent and rhythm of the voice of memory, and the creator of it. The mother's presence is recalled out of the dark by May's whole being, action, and voice. This is brought into rhyming contact with the other need, to hear the feet fall however faintly; in other words to hear herself alive.[19]

These meetings of memory, voice, and body change the stage into a space of deep rhyme. The space May paces out, the footfalls that sound in the air and in the words fashion a habitation, a manner of habitual life out of the internal shudders, torments and revolutions of the imagination's struggle with itself. That habitation, though it brings no comfort, brings May's mind into intimate rhyming touch with her past and her flesh. A remembered life is discovered, made out of madness, itself fashioned out of pure theatre.

The 'footfall' and 'pas'-rhymes then, echo in the audience's auditory memory, rhyming with the audible tread of the actress's pacing. Beckett brings this voice–sound link into rhyming relation with May's own consciousness of the mysterious but necessary identity between the voice of memory and her body and life in the present. The 'pas'-rhymes in Beckett's work, from *Mercier and Camier* onwards, force into rough unity the feelings of isolation and detachment of a prisoner (where the single fictionalizing mind is ghosted of all real relation with the past) and essential human continuity (the mind in remembering step with its body and the body of all past human selves). By so doing they succeed in crossing the aspects of the self in precisely the manner which Krapp most earnestly desires. As Rosette Lamont put it, the two voices in *La Dernière bande* trace a 'double mouvement' in the air: 'course vers un but intellectuel, encore éloigné, de celui qui *fut* par rapport à celui qui écoute, retour de celui qui *est* vers celui qui *semble être*, sa présence rendue vivante, presque tangible par la

---

[19] May *soothes* herself with these multiple recognitions and rhythmical procedures. Beckett told David Warrilow to treat *Ohio Impromptu* 'like a bedtime story and let it be soothing.' (Kalb, *Beckett*, 223).

bande.' What the elder Krapp seeks is 'un point de rencontre dans l'entrecroisement des deux mouvements, course vers l'avenir, recour au passé, ou aux passés. Il se retrouvera dans l'adieu à l'amour, épisode auquel l'intelligence n'a pas de part' ('Krapp, un anti-Proust', 347–8). Krapp finds a release, a real 'point de rencontre' in a powerful nostalgia for what his intelligence had detached his fictional self from, just as May's selves discover their 'entrecroisement' when the 'pas'-rhymes identify her urge to hear herself alive not as mere theatricalized performative but as the dislocated, narrative voice of memory. The habits of failure rediscover the roots of feeling that had been abandoned in the initial decision to create an abstract drama. Acts of memory in the terrible predicament of Krapp and May attempt to counter the ravages of loss by replaying and retreading the moment of abandonment.

These last sections have sought to establish Beckett's rhymes as signals or creators of memory-encounters in the prose and drama that marry traces of emotion with the purely abstract and fictionalized words and contexts that seem to belie them. The move from a linguistic encounter, between two languages as between rhyme-fellows, to a meeting of selves, minds, and the life of other bodies is actuated by a pause in the imagination that concedes and allows for the persistence of a double consciousness and its two-way echoes. In *All Strange Away*, the narrator, by virtue of his tiny concessions to Emmo's and Emma's emotional life, allows into his text the sighing breath of an intimacy and its rhyming life:

no sound, well say a sound too faint for mortal ear (22)

Memories of past felicity no save one with faint ripple of sorrow of a lying side by side (37)

no sound and so exhaled only for the moment with faint sound, Fancy dead, to which now add for old mind's sake sorrow vented in simple sighing sound black vowel a (43)

no other sounds than these and never were that is than sop to mind faint sighing sound for tremor of sorrow at faint memory of a lying side by side and fancy murmured dead. (43–4)

The narrator's voice, in these tiny concessions, shifts into rhyming mode. He allows an affecting memory to ripple through his detached prose (the detached tones of a narrative technician, arranging his fictional characters), a memory registered in the ranked s̲ sounds. The faint ripple of the stress-line along a̲i̲ and s̲ culminates on 'side by side', the prose rhyme recall of 'simple sighing sound' and 'sorrow' preparing for and initiating a sorrow-ful, sighing accent on the very words 'side by side', discovering the emotional connotations of the summative key phrase.

The 'faint memory', the one memory of past felicity the voice lets slip by, inhabits his voice with all the emotional history implicit in Emma's and Emmo's pose and retrospectively alters his technical-narrative voice into one that desires to imagine love and its memories. The stress-line build-up, the manner in which it emo-tionally accentuates 'side by side', releasing connotations of re-membered affections, mimes the narrator's failure to differentiate himself from the real urgencies of momentary sops to mind, faint memories fitfully imagined. The shift from the acoustic to the semantic rhyme may be a mere matter of imagination, but Beckett, by dramatizing the voices imagining the imagination of it, like Malone dreaming of dreaming, like May hearing her mother hear her and her footfalls together, shows how crucial such mere matter is in rediscovering the gentle suddenness of felt memory when all has been abandoned.

The voice may, only for the moment, for old mind's sake, pause then touch and meet its own humanity and externalized memory. But the emotional power of the rhyme-accents bear witness to the importance of these memory-encounters and the way they alter the detached perspectives of the whole text within which they occur. The rhymes cross 'the simple feeling and its voice' with the self-accompaniment of the foreign tongue of the stranger, the other, the body on its way to create bonds of feeling that last long enough to sound like memory felt and recognized.

Rhymes Lyrical, Rhymes Authorial

Marjorie Perloff, in an article on Beckett's late rhymes, discusses *Ill Seen Ill Said* (abbreviated to *ISIS*), remarking on its binary rhythms, its associative 'thought-breath', or 'free prose' as she dubs it, and analysing the basic unit of the late Beckettian text, 'the short phrase of irregular length and primitive syntax'. She has this to say about the opening paragraph:

Six dimeter lines, five of them rhyming, followed by three trimeters made up primarily of anapests, the whole bound together by the alliteration, of voiced and voiceless spirants [. . .] The paragraph—or is it a strophe?—is punctuated twice by the refrain word 'On' which rhymes with 'sun'. ('Between Verse and Prose', 415–33)

This is all she says. Her only theory as to the purposes of such close rhyming is an ill-developed suggestion that it emphasizes plurality of voice in the text, though she does not say how this is done. Her book on indeterminacy sets out to prove that such voice-conflicts, to paraphrase her rather roughly, cancel each other out. Other Beckett critics seem even less sure of the purposes of the sound-repetitions in the texts. Moorjani, having noticed complex sound-patterns in Beckett's late work, resorts to vague Kristeva references to 'pre-symbolic pleasure of sound-play'(*Abysmal Games*, 67), as though Beckett were romping in a sonic sandpit. Pilling notices the alliteration and assonance in *Ill Seen Ill Said* but cannot say why they are there, except to underline the curious fact that Beckett strove to have parallel sound-effects in both French and English.[20] Perloff, in another article, attempts to account for the rhyming in *Ill Seen Ill Said* by arguing for some network of Nineties vocabulary and metre. How she could possibly hear 'elegant variations on Wildean or Paterian discourse'[21] in the work is beyond conjecture, though this particular howler does prove how desperate Beckettians have become to have some kind of 'learned' response to Beckett's complex sound-repetitions. I would like to take up the problem of the lyrical patterning in that first paragraph in the light of the remarks I have made on the perplexities rhyme suggest in the later prose, for I believe Beckett *does* have complex reasons for the presence of the heavy rhyming-patterns in his late prose.

One of the most difficult decisions to make when encountering rich rhyming-patterns in a text is to make up one's mind about whether they are designed to act as signs of deep lyrical feeling or as signs of authorial power over fictional material. What makes Beckett's work doubly difficult is the fact that he has internalized

---

[20] 'In general Beckett has striven to preserve the phonetic values of the original whenever there are instances of "rhyme", e.g. "Yet brunette"(25) and "Fillette brunette" (*MVMD*, 31).' (Pilling, 'A Criticism of Indigence', 143 n.).
[21] 'Une Voix pas la mienne', 40.

such readerly perplexities deep within the narrative voice itself. Not only does Beckett do this, but he hopelessly mixes both possibilities up within the voice, making it increasingly unclear *to the narrative voice itself*, whether any occasion is sentimentally lyrical or coldly authorial.

As an example of this Beckettian procedure, we might ask ourselves as readers what would happen if *Ill Seen Ill Said* were to begin in the past tense and lose its initial rhyme? Instead of 'From where she lies she sees Venus rise', 'From where she lay she saw Venus rise.' What would be the difference? In shifting the tense into the past, this revision would casually damage one of the central, particular perplexities of the whole novel: 'all this in the present as had she the misfortune to be still of this world.' (*ISIS*, 7) The narrative voice would prefer her at times not to be 'of this world', to see her to death and destroy this world—which world 'this' is is at the nagging heart of that tense-perplexity. If she is properly 'past' then she might be the mere matter of memory, of finished literary text. In the present tense she might be pure figment or actually there: 'If only she could be pure figment. Unalloyed. This old so dying woman. [. . .] How simple all then' (20). To make up one's mind about the tenses as they happen is to make up the voice's mind for him, to mock up the black brain as real. Our perplexity turns out to be the narrative voice's too.

The present tenses in the first paragraph seem delicately judged —they are passive, habitual, immobile, and, in series, approach the quality of a past tense. The narrator seems to be working out a past-tense narrative as he speaks. 'On' as a motor-command is half-stilled by its positional, temporal verbal use: 'On. She sits on erect and rigid' (7).[22] His character's movements are stilled down to suit his contextual power over her. Yet it is equally conceivable that what he is seeing *is* in the real present tense, that 'on' is a movement out of his control. The reader has to make his or her mind up about whether the narrator is in control over his fictional material (we may be 'listening' to a writer sketching out a story),

---

[22] The English language is itself sometimes confused as to the distinction. As the *OED* points out, discussing the history of the preposition: 'the primary division into senses implying position and those implying motion or direction is difficult to carry out in the figurative uses, in some of which the point of view has gradually changed since they first arose, so that what was originally felt to express a direction of the mind towards something is now felt as a static attitude or mental state.' This is not a change that would have surprised Beckett.

or whether he is simply a passive spectator before a vision (he may be lover watching loved one under the influence of Venus). But it is a question that perplexes the narrative voice itself. He cannot make up his mind either. What disturbs him, perhaps, is how much power she may have. She may be reacting against the imposition of narrative time itself, to her own position within the tenses the voice describes 'her' as inhabiting.

The rhyme would be lost too along with the tense. Is all one loses when the rhyme goes a shape, a pattern in the voice? One might say that the rhyme 'lies-rise' reinforces a four-beat rhythm in the sentence (x/x/xx/x/). This rhythm, one discovers, is the main rhythm of the story, that and a ghost heptameter, 4:3 (for example, 'Heading on foot for a particular point often she freezes on the way.' (7)). One might also say it is an important rhythm to hear with rhyme because it beats out suggestions of ballad, lullaby, lyric love—lyric because, one could say, Venus dominates that rhythm, because that star summoned love-lyric into being.

But the false timing in saying 'the rhymes reinforce the rhythm' stumbles over another of the narrator/reader's particular perplexities in *Ill Seen Ill Said*: how can one say the rhythm comes first, as though it were mysteriously inherent there on the page hovering before/behind/above the words that actually constitute it.[23] Similarly one cannot say that the words 'strike up a rhythm', or 'fall into a rhyming pattern' because there is no time for them to fall or strike anything before they are printed/said.[24] One's own

[23] I must distinguish this statement from Valéry's analysis of his working-methods when composing 'Le Cimetière marin' and 'La Pythie' in his essay 'Poésie et Pensée Abstraite', in *Oeuvres*, ed. Jean Hytier, (2 vols.; Paris, 1960), i. 1338–9: 'Mon poème Le Cimetière Marin a commencé en moi par un certain rythme, qui est celui du vers français de 10 syllabes, coupé en 4 et 6. Je n'avais encore aucune idée qui dût remplir cette forme. Peu à peu des mots flottants s'y fixèrent, déterminant de proche en proche le sujet, et le travail (un très long travail) s'imposa. Un autre poème, 'La Pythie', s'offrit d'abord par un vers de 8 syllabes dont la sonorité se composa d'elle-même.' My statement restricts itself to what one can say about the text as written and does not address the common artistic experience of hearing a foundational rhythm. In fact, Beckett with *Footfalls* gets close to a demonstration of the links between wordless rhythm and subsequent words (Valéry, incidentally, describes an experience in which his walking creates a rich, rhythmical atmosphere in his mind in the essay referred to above). In the case of Beckett's play, however, such links are *there* on the page. The rhythm must be articulated and *represented* before one can begin to analyse its 'pre-existence' in a text.
[24] This, of course, rhymes with the difficulty I discussed in my introduction concerning the illusion of a cause–effect chronology in descriptions of the way stress-lines and key-words are related.

imagination about the rhyme and the rhythm must accord with the 'present tenseness' of their occurrence in the sentence. This perplexity is the voice's too—problems with the eye and the mind and the treacherous word are an essential moment in the overall rhythm of the paragraphs, from the mere particularity of seeing and hearing 'her' and her situation to panicky generalizations as to his own purposes and the validity of his techniques of apprehending—how can he get close to her, in the right time and in time, to finish her off right.

To imagine oneself so close to the words that the rhyme and rhythm begin to mean something other than the words they run through might also threaten the sequence of fragile fixities the particular tenses of each paragraph say and see. For instance, reader/narrator might dream a loveliness into the first five sentences. 'From where she lies she sees Venus rise' alternates i: and aɪ in a delicate see-saw, the 'ize'-sound softens and soothes the s's in 'sees' and 'Venus'. With 'skies' in the third sentence, these soft, sweet vocables are taken up against the sun (that is in 'rails'), whilst 'all life' is remembered in an aɪ and l stress-line through 'lies' and 'rise'. The sun rhyming with the motor-command 'On' is set against the r, l, and z that haze 'she' and Venus' together in the sentence they both inhabit. The drama of the sentence, dreams the reader/narrator, is enacted in words that shift from entranced seeing to sweet-voiced saying. The title, *Ill Seen Ill Said*, is belied in this dream of Venusian sights and sounds.

But one can never make the distinction between saying and seeing in sentences, for one has not the time to do so before the words are read and said, and there is no space inside the words to make room for such a distinction. One can make stands and judgements 'after' the event about the simple ballad-tenderness of the r, l, ɪ, aɪ stress-lines under the influence of our feelings for the word Venus, the rich, simple pleasure touched into life by the rhythm and lightness of it in context.[25] But there the timing is recalled, savoured again, taken up into our habitual responses— our past feelings are actuated by the present-tense utterance. The tenderness, the loving delicacy in soft sounds are *after* the words, so to speak, are the words' imaginary future. We assume a drama

[25] Nicholas Zurbrugg has said that this initial 'lies-rise' rhyme shows language fading 'in and out of focus, somewhat as the narrator's memories hover to and fro, in and out of view' ('*Ill Seen Ill Said* and the Sense of an Ending', 153).

there: we assume that her gaze is watching out for Venus as though desiring love and death against the influence of the 'source of all life'. The word 'revenge' supports this, but this could simply be a matter of time, a colourful way of saying morning and evening star. The evidence that one might have for an acoustic drama is a double act of memory (for all the associations Venus has) and imagination (softness and sweetness in vowels as softness and sweetness as values).[26] The narrator cannot work out if he is generating what he sees and says, or whether he is seeing something out there which he is forced to narrate. If he were able to work out whether the rhymes and rhythms in his voice were sentimentally mimetic in the Venusian dream manner outlined above, his perplexity would be solved, for he would be able to acknowledge the influence of Venus on his prose patterns.

The question as to how much we read into the acoustic effects rhymes I think quite clearly with the difficulties the eye has in seeing the old so dying woman. The movement and life in the words or rather how much we allow ourselves to say about their movements, are co-substantial with the desires, the emotions that the voice seems to discover within itself and to find itself betraying. The severe ambiguity between bereavement and predatoriness in the eye's actions and the voice's tones is matched by the perplexities one has in giving the rhyme-effects in the text either a sensuous, lyrical life or a rhetorical and cruel playfulness.

This ambiguity is involved in the more complex perplexity which the narrator/reader has to struggle with. For any text has its internal memory system, its intratextual networking of recalls, repetitions, memory motifs. The perplexity about the text's status as either pure fiction or real powerfully re-imagined memory store becomes impossibly complex when we (as reader/narrators) have to work within the text's own system of internal recalls. This perplexity could be instanced by the three uses of the word 'grace' in the story. The three instances demonstrate three kinds of acoustic grace in such prose and

---

[26] I have been to Reading University to obtain material on *ISIS* from the Samuel Beckett Manuscripts Collection. I examined MSS 2200–2207 which include all the drafts and typescript MSS of both the French original and the English translation. In the first draft of his English translation, Beckett wrote 'sky' rather than 'skies' (MS 2200, p. 1). This was altered in the next revision, a deliberate rhyming move, rather like his creature in 'Old Earth'. Other examples of 'rhyming' revisions include altering 'Panic passed on' to 'Panic past pass on' in the first draft (MS 2200; cf. *ISIS*, 58).

the perplexities of their contradiction. These perplexities rhyme richly with how much grace we (and the narrator) can allow ourselves to find in such a word, and in such a world.

First, the lyrically specific, tenderly detailed description of her eating:

At last in a twin movement full of grace she slowly raises the bowl toward her lips while at the same time with equal slowness bowing her head to join it. Having set out at the same instant they meet halfway and there come to rest. (*ISIS*, 35).

The twin movement is a rhyming move, with 'bowl' and 'bowing' approximating themselves through 'slowly' and 'slowness'; stress-lines along s̲, l̲ and t̲; the way 'raises' gently picks up 'grace' has an awkward gracefulness that fits—the tone is a delicate Ave.

The second use is when the eye, after hearing the curtains fall, dreams of a future collapse of it all: 'Then far from the still agonizing eye a gleam of hope. By the grace of these modest beginnings. With in second sight the shack in ruins' (*ISIS*, 55). The word here is part of a system of very immodest '-ace' rhymes that accelerate into the voice at the end of the story. In the same paragraph, it rhymes with 'face' and 'trace'. Six paragraphs later, the rhyming is too much, becomes ludicrously foregrounded:

no more trace. On earth's face. [. . .] Till no more trace. On earth's face. Instead of always the same place. Slaving away forever in the same place. At this and that trace. [. . .] say farewell. If only to the face. Of her tenacious trace. (*ISIS*, 58–9)

Rhyming of this regularity and formality, simple, end-stopped, short-rhythmed, reveals the voice safe in the privacy of the fierce intoxicating tones of its dreamed-of triumph. Rhyme here has a violent purpose, the word 'grace' appropriated by brute force for personal needs and desires, the language of the text by this stage having accelerated into the voice's solipsistic register. There is a real menace in 'grace' in such hands.

The last use is the last two sentences:

Not another crumb of carrion left. Lick chops and basta. No. One moment more. One last. Grace to breathe that void. Know happiness. (*ISIS*, 59).

The grace here is reduced to a parody of postprandial thanksgiving, solitary, glutted and relieved after wholesale slaughter. The difference between the first and last instances shows this: 'grace' is not gently given to another's action, heard within her 'raises'. It is there to feed a need, the eye's desire (how 'grace' is consumed by its acoustic surrounds, 'basta', 'last, 'happiness').

The difficulty we have in understanding the acoustic effects is compounded, however, once the reader/narrator has to bring these instances together, when he has to integrate them into the text's memory system. Saying 'Grace to breathe that void' *recalls* 'Twin movement full of grace'. This allusion troubles our hearing of the rhymes and of the word 'grace' itself. The question is whether the grace in the first instance should be allowed to colour how we hear it in the final paragraph and thus alter the driving accent of the whole host of '-ace' rhymes that seem so triumphantly to prove the voice luxuriating in its own words, free of her, and in command over the treacherous word that suits his treachery. In both cases, the movement described and the emotion guessed at are concerned with eating, devouring, consumption. He watching her eat is how he eats: his eye is the devourer. The yearning one hears in the first instance, how strongly he might feel bereaved of her, might be allowed to carry over and rewrite the yearning of the last instance, the yearning to have time to savour the end of it all. In other words, it might rewrite that yearning as a secret desire to relish, for one moment more, her slow grace. The eye as bereaved or as predatory discovers its own twin movements within the rhyming recall the perplexing rhymes stress.

'Grace', at the three moments of its use in the story, finds its definition in three types of time. Her slowness is what makes the twin movement graceful. The grace of these modest beginnings is in the future possibility of total annihilation. Grace to breathe that void is 'grace' as leave, as breathing-time after that annihilation. Severally, a present time that is as slow as a past remembered, a future that presses on the inner eye as a present-tense grace ('With in second sight the shack in ruins' is both within seconds, present, and second sight, imagined), and lastly a future felt as past. Crossing the wide conceptual differences between last and first, crossing those three times, is the little half-assonance, 'last'-'grace': 'At last in a twin movement full of grace' (*ISIS*, 48), 'One moment more. One last. Grace to breathe that void.' In the first typescript, Beckett had altered 'Finally in a twin movement full of grace' to 'At last . . .' partly, I believe, to confirm this half-assonance (MS

2200, para. 31). It brings the sigh of wonder and the sigh of relief together. Once again, such an acoustic detail, in challenging
reader/narrator to bring the instances together, in constituting
and generating the text's acoustic and key-word memory system,
brings the doubled perplexity of our interpretation of the text
(as Venusian, or as authorial exercise of power) to a head.
With both 'last' and 'grace' carrying over and being fully remembered, her spell would be there at the last. Her trace would thus
alter the whole accent of the text's last words. She would trace her
memory over his wish to have one last moment more on earth's
face.[27] Her grace however lilts too softly in the word itself. Our
confidence, human and humane may breathe a little freer in the
habits of reading soft sounds into and out of Venus. But the doubt
too carries over. 'Grace' can as easily be forgotten as recalled.

The problem with the sound-effects in *Ill Seen Ill Said* may then
simply be that they instance to us the perplexities Beckett feels that
the voice learns to have about the intrusion of rationality into a
purely visual field. To argue that there is no such thing as a purely
visual thing begs the question that the narrator precisely desires,
in his panicky paragraphs, no-such-thing. His panic that his intent
gaze does not sweep her off her patch of planet into the night of
light or darkness is not ours, though. One is not ferociously hun-
gry for the end of the tale and a neat line on how the voice's reason
and manner knit up. But one is unaccountably moved. The strange
time the story and the world it describes run to is close to but
askew from our reading speed. Similarly the voice's rhymes touch
the prose into a gracefulness at times in line with our wish to be
moved by the sight of the old so dying woman, at others only
recollecting the times we were. The more this occurs, the more we
as readers feel ourselves becoming more and more detached from
the narrator's own purposes, from his own control over his own
perplexities.

The most curiously detached paragraph, describing the watch-
face, is perhaps the key paragraph instancing this detachment and
its consequences:

[27] Zurbrugg talks about a more general ambiguity in Beckett's characters: the
'poignant discrepancy between these protagonists' wish to attain immunity to their
'need' for others, and their compulsive instinct to return, over and over again, to
their loved ones' ('*Ill Seen Ill Said* and the Sense of an Ending', 154).

Sixty black dots. No figure. One hand only. Finest of fine black darts. It advances by fits and starts. No tick. Leaps from dot to dot with so lightning a leap that but for its new position it had not stirred. Whole nights may pass as may but a fraction of a second or any intermediate lapse of time soever before it flings itself from one degree to the next. None at any moment overleaping in all fairness be it said. Let it when discovered be pointing east. Having thus covered after its fashion assuming the instrument plumb the first quarter of its latest hour. Unless it be its latest minute. Then doubt certain—then despair certain nights of its ever attaining the last. Ever regaining north. (*ISIS*, 45–6)

What is one to make of this stop-watch? He is looking at his watch to see how time flows in this place. How long it takes to stop her. Also how long his paragraphs are taking, their curious detachment from each other. There are sixty-one paragraphs in *Ill Seen Ill Said*, the last a desperate coda, a surplus minute or hour, after the final farewell midnight at 'north'.[28] The paragraphs encircle their subject within their time, the guardians like the twelve hours around Aphrodite, the formless place the watch-face of the earth.

Read this way, past paragraphs gain retrospective force: 'At this rate it will be black night before she reaches home. Home! But time slows all this while. Suits its speed to hers' (*ISIS*, 24). The joke in 'time slows all this while', that 'this while' is somehow not time, is

[28] From the earliest drafts Beckett had planned to have more than 60 paragraphs. In the French it remained at around 63 or 64 until very late when Beckett began to think of cutting down on the scribe's overflow. The novel from its inception had been conceived in terms of numbered paragraphs, as only a glance at the French notebook (MS 2203) shows, where the paragraphs are planned separately on different pages and under their number. The paragraphs are plotted in terms of their key phrases, with numerous references to other paragraphs when repetitions are planned. These cross-references also record every contradiction the narrator will utter, usually where her movements and habits contradict previous judgements he has made on them. For instance, he denies the fact that she has a pillow (*ISIS*, 39) when in a previous paragraph he had thought her album could be hidden 'under her pillow' (*ISIS*, 14). In the notebook, the page under the heading '38' (for para. 38) has the note 'Pas d'oreiller—contredit 9 (album sous l'oreiller)'. The contradictions her sight causes him, and the importance Beckett placed on them, support my argument that the rhyme-memories counter his will to be clean of her by way of hidden contradictions. Such contradictions are altered by the rhyme-memories from being simple signs that she is beyond his control to standing for emotional breaks in his voice. In his production notebook for *Happy Days*, Beckett took great care to detail the 'défaillances' Winnie suffers, the moments where her voice breaks (*Happy Days: The Production Notebook of Samuel Beckett*, 85–123). The prose rhymes, as with Proust, work at times like stage-directions with dramatic purposes in revealing the memories hidden in the relations between the words.

another time within which time slows, almost makes 'slows' transitive, 'this while' a physical thing, the space she inhabits. It is the paragraph's timing of the narration of her as well as the time we learn to expect is the case in this close world. The dwelling, one remembers, is 'under constant watch' (*ISIS*, 12). But this watch moves to suit her vigils and timed rituals, her changes, appearances, and disappearances. The eye's vision of the dial should be a dream of an object that has no woman to see, he the imaginary stranger craving to betray all sign of life. No woman with her rags of sky and earth ('Nothing else'). But the sentences are still timed to her time—'Then doubt certain—then doubt certain nights'; his certainty, that of absolute doubt, is altered by her, even here within this cold paragraph, altered by the memory of her place under the eye's constant watch into a hopelessness particularized by her time-scale ('certain nights').

It is these considerations that make the rhyme-play complex and tactful—one must *remember* to hear the true pitches of their traces, recall the accumulation of paragraphs and their times and moods. But one must remember not with the technical expertise of a quasi-authorial command over the text's intratextuality, but with the recall of an emotional rememberer.

Sixty black dots. No figure. One hand only. Finest of fine black darts. It advances by fits and starts. No tick. Leaps from dot to dot with so lightning a leap that but for its new position it had not stirred.

Apart from the dial seen, the eye is also describing the prose of the drivelling scribe—we see no figure, only the hand of the author. He is describing the rhythm of his sentences as they leap from punctuation mark to punctuation mark, paragraph to paragraph: it is a dream of a pure prose clean of its subject ('Finest of fine black darts. It advances by fits and starts'). In one sense, he is merely timing himself, free of her, momentarily free from the terms of his own perplexity over her and the text's status, free to say to himself that all that is real here is myself and narrative time.

But here in this paragraph the real feeling is there, the true troubling rhythm is there, infinitesimally trembling to the memory of another's rhythm and rhyme. In watching his one hand ('Finest of fine black darts. It advances by fits and starts'), he recalls her hands:

Tightening and loosening their clasp. Rhythm of a labouring heart. Till when almost despaired of gently part. Suddenly gently. (*ISIS*, 32)

The fits and starts of his prose are timed to her heart, are locking in an unwished-for rhyming imitation of its slow systole and diastole (*ISIS*, 31). The prose through the rhymes and through its rhythm is ticking, though it would wish to have no heart, ticking to how he secretly imagines her to feel.

The prose is also, in describing the dial face, despairingly facing the real difference between the eye of the beholder and the strange beauty it cannot divine. For she does not leap from place to place. She sees north when she wishes. Her comings and goings are sudden, one suspects, because the eye cannot stand her sight, is subject to his own peculiar fits and starts of panic and despair. The gradualness of her going is imperceptible, her changes shadowy. Her labouring heart is dying, his labouring (creating) is on centennial leave from where tears freeze, Caina, ninth circle of the betrayers. She may be frozen from time to time by the memory of some ancient horror. One sometimes feels it must be the eye she is sensing (Dante speaks of the chilling paralysis he experiences when some of the damned look at him)[29] or remembering (the ambiguity in 'shocked still'—suddenly shocked into immobility, shocked even after all this time).[30] But she is free of him. He is beating out the radical difference between their two rhythms, and they are the two rhythms of the prose, the two manners of attending to it.

[29] 'Then saw I countless visages, alas!/Purpled with cold, that made me shudder and still/The shudder comes when frozen pools I pass', *Inferno*, xxxii, 70–3, Binyon's translation, *Dante Alighieri 1265–1321: The Portable Dante* (New York, 1969), 173. Beckett, in the first MS of the French original, quotes from this ninth circle canto under para. 25 (now para. 23, in English beginning 'The eye will return to the scene of its betrayals. On centennial leave from where tears freeze' (*ISIS*, 27)). This quotation is explained in the notebook (MS 2203) under '25' where Beckett has written 'Préciser deux allusions à la D. C.' The quotation appears like this:

A XXXII 47
9me cercle de l'enfer: traitres
'gli occhi lor, ch'eran pria pur dentro molli,
gocciar super li labbri, e il gelo strinse
le lacrime tra essi, e risserrolli.'
                    (Ms 2205, para. 25)
The quotation actually begins on line 46.

[30] Her hair is described as staring: 'Stares as if shock'd still by some ancient horror' (*ISIS*, 28). His eye is literally riveting: 'The eye rivets the bare window' (*ISIS*, 19), but can itself be moved: 'Riveted to some detail of the desert the eye fills with tears' (*ISIS*, 17), though here there is some doubt as to whether he is describing her eye rather than his own.

By recalling the 'heart'-'part' rhyme and by responding to the rhythm of the sentence 'rhythm of a labouring heart', within the texture of a paragraph dealing on the face of it with a clear view of a dial, one hears the true complexity at the surface of the prose.[31] The one hand of the author, handicapped by its love for those two hands, betrays itself into a deep acknowledgement of a heartfulness in his voice. So intent on betrayal is he that he betrays himself at the heart of his prose. Wishing to still life to 'nature morte', the prose trembles, still, with life. The prose darts and starts into sudden life through the recall of her labouring heart, into a sudden shocked gentleness. The eye's vigilant pose, stone-faced and predatory, discovers its own laws of motion and time in being moved by her even when contemplating abstract time. The rhymes sound comic and cold at first sight, but the reader's memory, in giving them life, in receiving the life in the prose from them, discovers the heart of the story 'with in second sight'—that heart being nothing so simple as the discovery of the real question of *Ill Seen Ill Said*—how much he loves her. The question is timed outside narrative time, secret rhymes and stress-lines signal and constitute the patterns of emotional remembering the prose responds to, heart-beat accents come from that other time. What they bear witness to, against the grain of the narratorial cold-blooded textuality, is that, finally, she is not helpless to move in the dial the paragraphs draw around her. Rather he cannot help being moved by her.

The real gentleness of the rhymes lies in how they show his time and his timing rising and lapsing to hers, how they, for good and all, rhyme his cold abstract narrative time with the labouring heart of the fictional subject as free, loved memory-image. The reader/narrator's perplexity about the Venusian or authorial status of text and rhyme is resolved not by choosing between the two. For the sound-effects remain, for the most part, deliberately undecided and ambiguous. The perplexity is resolved by the sudden collapse of the terms of the perplexity itself. By positing authorial intervention and power as the only valid question within the fiction, the narrator/reader loses himself (and hopes to

---

[31] The recall is not only sealed by the rhyme but by the prose rhymes that surround the two passages. In the later passage, strong use of s̲t̲ branches out from the key phrase 'fits and starts', recalling the 'tightening' 'loosening' 'part' 'suddenly' of the earlier para.

drown his subject) in a false epistemological polemic. The dial paragraph's 'heart-part' rhyme signals a different loving order, translating the text's intratextual, 'graceful' memory system of undecideable contradictions onto another plane, into another time, the time of true, heart-felt remembering.

Narrative Voice and the Shadow of Memory

This timed turn against the increasingly vicious rhyming tongue of the imaginary stranger in *Ill Seen Ill Said*, the heart-rhyme deep in his reason-ridden abstraction of his imagined hunger for clean and ordered time, finds a rhyming companion in *Company*. In *Company* the rhyming is at times so dense as to approach tongue-twisting babble:

Can the crawling creator crawling in the same create dark as his creature create while crawling? (52).

In fact this particular example is a complication of a real tongue-twister, adopted by Joyce for HCE in *Finnegans Wake*, 'Creator he has created for his creatured one a creation' (*Finnegans Wake*, 29), raising interesting questions about Beckett's reading of Joycean late prose rhymes as overly reason-ridden. And then again:

For with what right affirm of a faint sound that it is a less faint made fainter by farness and not a true faint near at hand? Or of a faint fading to fainter that it recedes and not in situ decreases. (*Company*, 33).

Both quotations discretely question the status of the rhyming tongue they are articulated in. In the first, the voice analyses its own heavy prose-rhyming as a feature of narcissistic creativity, a symptom of the self-entangled ways the creator fabricates its own mock other, its own creaturely memory system and artificial afflatus. With the second, he analyses his obsessive concerns with the sounds of his prose as a symptom of his own coldly and comically pseudo-scientific meticulousness about empty epistemological questions (like the Venusian–authorial bugbear of *Ill Seen Ill Said*). In both cases, the excessively rhyming tongue is an ethical marker indicating emptily self-reflexive, reason-ridden authorial obsession with the (for the narrator) remarkable nature of his own fictionalizing.

Alternating with these self-involved exercises in narrative procedure, we find simple memory visions, heightened and lyricized by
a gentler rhyming rhetoric:

By the time you open your eyes your feet have disappeared and the skirts
of your greatcoat come to rest on the surface of the snow. The dark scene
seems lit from below. You see yourself at that last outset leaning against
the door with closed eyes waiting for the word from you to go. To be gone.
Then the snowlit scene. (*Company*, 35)

The sentence-end rhymes (snow-below-go) seem gently to order
thoughts into a cadence that calms the voice around the sound of
the word 'snow' that has pacified and charmed the imagined
landscape. Masson patterns appear with the siːn-siːm-siː-siːn-siːn
sequence and the lt stress-line, making 'snowlit scene' the summative phrase that dominates the paragraph.

Yet the paragraph immediately preceding this has wondered
how to improve the voice to make it 'more companionable' and
muses:

Same flat tone as initially imagined and same repetitiousness. No improv-
ing those. But less mobility. Less variety of faintness. As if seeking
optimum position. From which to discharge with greater effect. (34)

Those 'snow'-rhymes, in such a formal pattern, their calming
pacification of the voice, are they not precisely the kind of im-
provements the reason-ridden narrative voice ordered? The
rhymes themselves become indices of the perplexity the narrator
suffers as to whose voice it is that returns to him with such vivid,
particular sights and rhythms. The memory paragraphs, as in *Ill
Seen Ill Said*'s vision of the old so dying woman, are condemned to
remain within the narrator's own controlled system of obstinate
self-questioning. That is, they remain fruitlessly ambiguous, being
either imaginary visions, or written-up 'memory' purple passages,
mere material feeding the question 'am I truly creating them out of
divine inspiration, or am I imagining a beautiful memory bank for
myself?' Either way, they serve the controlling reason's narcissistic obsession with his own fictionalizing procedures.

The question turns, as in *Ill Seen Ill Said*, on who really controls
narrative time, for rhymes, memory, and rhetorical control depend so much on a stable system of repetitive structures. And, as
in *Ill Seen Ill Said*, it is within the paragraph that coolly considers

narrative time in the novel that a different order of rhyme-play arises from the emptily procedural prose. The paragraph imagines 'you' waking and contemplating his watch, becoming obsessed by the minute relations between the second hand and its shadow on the dial:

From 30 to 60 shadow follows hand at a distance increasing from zero at 30 to maximum at 45 and thence decreasing to new zero at 60. Slant light now to dial by moving either to either side and hand hides shadow at two quite different points as for example 50 and 20. Indeed at any two quite different points whatever depending on degree of slant. But however great or small the slant and more or less remote from initial 60 and 30 the new points of zero shadow the space between the two remains one of 30 seconds. (58).

The fact that this passage occurs within a memory paragraph nudges us into thinking about parody. The parody is devious, studding itself with rhyme-play ('either to either side and hand hides', 'zero shadow', stress-lines on zəʊ d and aɪd) which, interspersed with the over-complex numbers and their repetitions, perfectly captures and judges the nature of the twisted rhymes in the reason-ridden voice.

At the end of the paragraph, the voice describes 'you' turning away from the contemplation of 'second hand and its shadow' in exhaustion, and, for the first time in the novel, we can be certain that the narrator is really being watched by other eyes. We have entered into a prose that is free of narratorial concerns, a prose that is watching the dreamer of empty fictional memory systems and seeing him anew:

But unable to continue you bow your head back to where it was and with closed eyes return to the woes of your kind. Dawn finds you still in this position. The low sun shines on you through the eastern window and flings all along the floor your shadow and that of the lamp left lit above you. And those of other objects also. (59).

The rhymes in this closing section of the paragraph ('bow', 'closed', 'woes', 'low', 'window', 'shadow', 'also') shadow the voice with the intimacy of the 'snow'-rhymes, three Masson patterns in the phrase 'with closed eyes return to the woes of your kind' alone (kn, wəʊz, daɪ). They pick up and transform the 'shadow'-'zero', 'side'-'hides' rhymes in the parody before—the shadow no longer rhyming with nothing ('zero') but with the woes of others through the window.

The rhyming tongue is a shadow of his reason-ridden perplexity, obsessed rationality, and stop-watch empty time. The dawn, like Venus, brings the two voices together, recalls the two shadows into rhyming contact. The recognition of this alters the rational voice's words into a moving description of his own yearning for the true company of his own memory. The watching of the approach, unity, and departure of the shadow from the hand is a dream of a constant seconding of his voice by the shadow of his memory-based imagination. The woes of his kind are suddenly illumined by this gentle, sudden raising and rising of the two voices together in the shadow-rhymes, the kind of its own lit up by the kind dawn of memory. The charity of this remembering voice's imagination in parodying the watchful voice of reason in order to bring them into a contact as close and as sure as a shadow and its body may be a slender comfort, a comfort denied as soon as imagined in the next paragraph ('Quick leave him.' (60)). But it reinvests the reasonable voice's own parodies of easy seeking after company with a deeper intention and lonelier life. Narrative voices, however clinically involved they may be in their own powers to fabricate memory and vision, can never lose their shadow, the shadow of the true companionability of the subtle chains of memories and rhymes, that couple voices to their pasts within the tenacious trace of their twin movements.

Conclusion

I hope this book will prove useful to others when they encounter complex sound-patterns in prose. My terms, runs, strings, stress-lines, key-words, motifs, are not ruinously technical in the manner the perplexed narrator/reader of *Ill Seen Ill Said* might prefer. I believe they are flexible enough to be taken up even by those who would contest the mimetic grounds of my argument. What I have proved is simple: that sound-effects in prose are often organized around key terms. Those key terms may be read as fabricating the local stress-lines along their repeated (or disseminated) phonemes in the surrounding syntax, or they may be read as themselves being fabricated by the stress lines. As a textual event, it is irrelevant whether it is one or the other. But as an emotional event, by which I mean an event where the possibilities of memory, imagination and conceptual rhymes enter into play, the fabrication of stress-lines and key-words becomes a miniature act of readerly and narratorial memory, with the stress-lines potentially read as emotional memory-markers. The sound-repetitions involved in this process are neither essentialist signs of ideal feeling, nor are they purely musical features signifying authorial structural control (though writers' irony may use them to parody these expectations). They are short-term, ephemeral features in the prose that may be used to mime memory's brief and fleeting inhabiting of the present-tense narrative voice. The process by which stress-lines indicate key summative phrases and promote them into motifs shadows the way memory, as fabricating fictional process, organizes its material into key sequences and charged language events.

Dieter Wellershoff, writing about L'Innommable, distinguishes between 'Le Moi' and 'la voix', describing the disjunction in terms of a life-and-death struggle. The voice

semble parler à la fois au-dedans et au-dehors, elle a son siège dans la tête et vient de loin comme un murmure indistinct, parfois comme un bruit qui ne signifie rien. Ce parler intérieur et extérieur est l'obscurité dans laquelle le Moi reste caché à lui-même. (138)

I suggested in my Beckett chapter that this disjunction could very well be analysed as a consequence of childhood amnesia in reverse, rhyming with the dislocation of the self from its own memory. The memory, in such an extreme case, seems external to the self and yet, because of its nature, deep within it as well. Memory speaks of many anterior selves as though they were others and will tend to arrange previous experience into indistinct narratives, at times into stories. It is registered by the present-tense self (that wishes to deny, abandon, or forget it) in ways subtle, murmurous, and obscure. The sound-system of a novel in its relation to the sense accords with such a description. The sound-effects seem external to the sense-context and yet cannot be separated from it. They are heard as an indistinct murmur 'parfois comme un bruit qui ne signifie rien'.

Stephen, in *Portrait*, hears the language of history around him as a vague music:

He heard a confused music within him as of memories and names which he was almost conscious of but could not capture even for an instant; then the music seemed to recede, to recede: and from each receding trail of nebulous music there fell always one longdrawn calling note, piercing like a star the dusk of silence. (*P*, 152)

The 'confused music' of sound-repetitions in prose acts just in this manner. They create a music 'as of memories and names' in the way they cluster around the remembered material in key-words. They, as the reading-attention recedes, concentrate through stress-lines on those key-words and make them sing ('there fell always one longdrawn calling note') and, crucially, they alter the emphasis of the voice that is 'almost conscious' of them but cannot 'capture' them. The calling note alters the stress of the voice often in contradiction to the surface modulations of the sense, like the 'contresens'-patterns in Proust's writing. And with Proust, the resurfacing of past material arranged around a key phrase brings two selves into contact as though in argument. The effect is like the manner in which Bergotte's voice alters itself when arguing with an interlocutor with oppposing views:

Une idée forte communique un peu de sa force au contradicteur. Partici-pant à la valeur universelle des esprits, elle s'insère, se greffe en l'esprit de celui qu'elle réfute, au milieu d'idées adjacentes, à l'aide desquelles, re-prenant quelque avantage, il la complète, la rectifie; si bien que la sentence finale est en quelque sorte l'œuvre des deux personnes qui discutaient. (I, 562)

Mallarmé's prose rhymes effect a kind of 'amplification' of the key-words in the narrator's obsessive search for lost memory indi-cators, occasioned by the desiring imagination, and creating its own remembering. 'Rimes dissimulés' bring the fleeting memory of words into strange contact with fugitive memory of the fictional dead. Beckett's dislocated murmuring voice, Joyce's half-con-scious confused music, Proust's contresens'-rectifications, Mal-larmé's bereaved transformations all express themselves in the sound-repetitions in their prose and represent the subtle concen-trations, collusions, and after-effects of key-word memory.

This book has revealed some dominating strains in the memory-rhyme technique, despite the different attitudes towards the faculty of memory in general. First, there is the demonstration of the way currents of resisted memory-material will flow through the present-tense voice. Mallarmé's narrator in 'Le Démon de l'analogie', for instance, finds his voice possessed by the rhyming accents of the dead Pénultième. With Proust, I show how the narrator's voice breaks and reveals its past anxieties, stranded as he is between his own habitual memory and the mystery of Alber-tine's. Stephen's overly historical imagination is shot through with pressing guilty memory after his mother's death. Beckett's voices are revisited by the tones of real memory, stressing their confusion between their own imagination and another's memory.

Past phrases migrate (in the form of key-word stress-lines) into the voice and their 'accent' functions as a counter-sense to the drive of the syntax. Israfel's divine emphases, the rhythms of English, and prose poetic conceits, inhabit Mallarmé's narrator's memory and voice along 'nul' and 'souvenir' prose rhymes. In Proust, the phrases in Aimé's letter, the word 'casser' let slip by Albertine, the 'tan'-repetitions in the narrator's mind whilst listen-ing to music, run on and alter the voice revealing the narrator's deeper distress and the persistence of his pain. Despite Bloom's strong averting gestures, Joyce reveals the persistence of loaded phrases such as 'Lines in her eyes' in Bloom's subsequent thoughts, again there as an emotional rhythm, a heart-beat of avoided feeling. The narrative voice in *Ill Seen Ill Said* beats to the rhythm of his subject's labouring heart even when luxuriating in the cold efficiency of abstract narrative time and its false perplexities.

The second abiding strain in the uses of the memory-rhyme technique is the expression and judgement of a comic, selfish style of speech that manufactures artificial memory to cushion the voice's desire for free control. These are expressed through over-rich rhyme patterns and over-stylized, rhetorical recall. Humbert Humbert's super-parodic discourse and Derrida's empty supplementary rhyme-play haunt the comic self-parodies that Mallarmé saw as integral to post-Baudelairian prose poetry. There is a nagging possibility that the Pénultième is a mere trick of prose nostalgia for poetic resources. Proust had demonstrated this self-circling manner in his narrator's luxurious preciousness when freeing himself from the constraints of the real memory of, and attention to, his grand mother's plight, also when sinking into an artificial tyranny over Albertine's sleeping body. Both acts entailed a shift from subtle to overt sound-effects, and both demonstrated this shift as a consequence of a substitution of the limits and difficulties of living with another's independent memory by the manufactured memory of easy, self-cherishing delusion. Joyce had judged such self-defining pseudo-memories with his analysis of Stephen's self-deluding apocalyptic dramas. With 'Sirens', Joyce allowed this rhetorical memory to go public and it is my contention that *Finnegans Wake* can itself be judged as pandering to Joyce's own capacity to indulge in Stephen's evasions. Beckett's prose, particularly *Ill Seen Ill Said* and *Company*, analyzes this self-centred, tyrannical manufacturing of memory in terms of the reason-ridden imagination's violent desires for rhetorical control. In both Joyce and Beckett, this style is expressed and judged by over-rich rhyme-patterns that seek to remember or forget everything to death.

The third dominating use of the memory rhyme link is in the demonstration of sudden crossing of selves that alter the 'pastness' of the narrative tense into the feeling of memory quasi-actualized. Mallarmé's narrator changes places, momentarily, with the mourning creature summoned by his elegiac philological and literary imagination, and discovers real mourning for the absent loved one. Proust's prose reaches this height when describing the grandmother's death where 'accent' becomes pure 'chant'. The minor painful resuscitations of past feeling that the 'rimes inté-rieures' had hinted at develop into a full-scale unity of body, heart and memory at the miracle of the sight of pure voice and pure body simultaneously in concert. Joyce finds a similar miracle in the tangibility of Bloom's memory when recalling the kiss on Howth hill. Beckett's *Ill Seen Ill Said* narrator finds his style tuned into the dying woman's heartbeat. The sound-effects mime the reunification of past selves with the present self, changing memory into presence, uniting body, heart, and past experience, with the prose rhymes actually heard, like May's footfalls on the stage.

These three uses of the memory rhyme technique to express migration of past key-words, self-centred comic tyranny, and uni-fication of body and memory, persist in the four writers' prose despite the wide difference in their portrayal of memory. Beckett had distinguished between Proust's stress on forgetfulness and sudden retrieval of difficult material and Joyce's belief in the half-conscious retention of all of one's past in the mind.[1] Beckett's own practice concentrated on the extremes of violent forgetful-ness[2] (*The Unnamable*) and being absolutely stuck in the past (*Foot-falls*). In so doing he forged lines of contact with Mallarmé's investigation into the relations between prose writing, remembe-ring, and bereavement.

Yet despite these differences, all four writers reveal a certain community of understanding in the use of the key-word stress technique. This community of understanding points up an essen-tial definition of the craft of fiction. The definition recognizes the real parallels between memory-acts within the living voice and the way a narrative is created. These parallels work at three levels.

[1] Proust would have certainly looked askance at Joyce's belief that a very good memory was a virtue for a writer interested in memory. 'Une mémoire sans défaillance', he wrote, 'n'est pas un très puissant excitateur à étudier les phé-nomènes de mémoire' (III, 52). This passage is marked in Beckett's copy of *A la recherche du temps perdu*.
[2] Beckett's interest in extreme forgetfulness is clearly influenced by this daring statement of Proust's: 'Si je puis avoir en moi et autour de moi tant de souvenirs dont je ne me souviens pas, cet oubli (du moins oubli de fait puisque je n'ai pas la faculté de rien voir) peut porter sur une vie que j'ai vécue dans le corps d'un autre homme, même sur une autre planète' (III, 374).

First, that memory organizes the past into sequences of key-moments, arranging them into stories in its habitual form and into centres of resisted power in its involuntary form.[3] A prose-writer similarly creates a narrative sequence out of imaginative key-moments with, hidden in this material, certain centres of concealed power.

On a second level, a prose-writer's task is essentially a creation of his character's memory, his narrative tense keeping each 'present-tense' experience on hold, so to speak, within the developing past of the book as a whole. Each experience immediately enters the book's textual memory[4] as well as defining the characters' memories.

Thirdly, the manner in which memories enter the mind, unbidden as well as recalled, is perfectly mimed by the half-conscious retention of stress-lines surrounding, fabricating and being fabricated by key-terms—both processes bring times together (repetition of sound, repetition of self), the past times altering the stress, rectifying the sense, contradicting the feeling and comparing the weight, of the present time of the voice. The alignment between key-words and key-moments is emphasized by this miming of memory and rhyme.

It is at this third level, I believe, that writers prove the strange consonance between their craft and the act of human memory. The murmur of memories in the voice on its way revealed in the 'remembering' connotations of unacknowledged key-words and their sounds concentrate the attractions and perils of a writer's belief in that consonance so essential for fiction's links with the

---

[3] As Proust puts it: 'A n'importe quel moment que nous la considérions, notre âme totale n'a qu'une valeur presque fictive, malgré le nombreux bilan de ses richesses, car tantôt les unes tantôt les autres sont indisponibles, qu'il s'agisse d'ailleurs de richesses effectives aussi bien que celles de l'imagination, et pour moi par exemple, tout autant que de l'ancien nom de Guermantes, de celles, combien plus graves, du souvenir vrai de ma grand'mère' (iii, 153). The almost fictive nature of memories is the key to the complex exchange between real memories in the world and the art of fictional imagination. As Bersani stated, more bluntly, *A la recherche du temps perdu* 'shows how the disappointments the narrator suffers as a result of his extraordinarily rich imagination lead him to give up novelizing in life in order to reminisce about the way he used to novelize in art' (Bersani, Leo, *Marcel Proust: The Fictions of Life and Art* (London 1965), 17). The middle term, for Proust, is the liaison between strong feeling and memory-changes: 'Car aux troubles de la mémoire sont liées les intermittences du coeur' (iii, 153).

[4] This term, 'textual memory', is usefully defined by John Rickard's book *Exercising Mnemotechnic* (See Joyce Bibliography).

world of human speech. The accompaniment of prose rhyme memory alongside the drift of the words in time not only shows the voice half-remembering, creating artificial memory, and suddenly being possessed by the past—it demonstrates the essential companionability of fictional narrative with the complexity of human memory in voice. Prose rhymes, though artificial, are the proof of the real way art touches life—through memory. The mind in the world is full of the accents of both its personal past and its culture's past and the inflections of its voice play a confused music of memories and names; the narrative voice is full of the prose rhymes of the other voices of memory—'the air is thick with their company' (P, 228). With the prose rhyme memory technique, a writer keeps company with the ordinary courses of human speech, its accents, and subtly acknowledged memories. The key-word accentuation of sound-repetitions, in miming the currents of memory in the human voice, does not prove that fiction reflects life; rather it demonstrates that fiction, at its best and in its details, attempts to remember it.

Appendix 1
Sound-Frequency Percentages
'It is not to be Thought of'

The sonnet has 377 phonemes. The phonemes occuring are listed below in the form of percentage of the sonnet's phonemes taken as a whole. The first number is the frequency percentage of the phoneme occurring in accented words; the second both accented and non-accented. The number in bold is the frequency of phonemes in colloquial Received Pronunciation in percentage (D. B. Fry 'The Frequency of Occurrence of Speech Sounds in Southern English', *Archives Néerlandaises de Phonétique Expérimentale*, 20 (1947), 103–6.) As a rough guide as to actual occurrences in the poem: 1% = 4 times; 1.6% = 6; 2% = 8; 7% = 25. The occurrence of the schwa (ə), has not been tabulated, but is roughly normal at around 11 %.

ɪ	= 1.6 / 7 **8.33**	p	= 2.65 / 2.65 **1.78**
e	= 1.3 / 1.3 **2.97**	t	= 4.5 / 7 **6.42**
æ	= 1 / 1 **1.45**	k	= 1.6 / 1.6 **3.09**
ʌ	= 1.6 / 1.6 **1.75**	f	= 2.65 / 3.18 **1.79**
ɒ	= 1.85 / 1.85 **1.37**	θ	= 1 / 1.3 **0.37**
ʊ	= 0.8 / 1.3 **0.86**	s	= 4.2 / 6.1 **4.81**
iː	= 1.85 / 2.65 **1.65**	ʃ	= 0.8 / 1 **0.96**
ɑː	= 0.5 / 0.5 **0.79**	h	= 1 / 1.6 **1.46**
uː	= 0.3 / 0.5 **1.13**	m	= 2.4 / 2.9 **3.22**
ɔː	= 0.8 / 1 **1.24**	n	= 3.2 / 4.8 **7.58**
ɜː	= 1 / 1 **0.52**	ŋ	= 1 / 1 **1.15**
eɪ	= 1.3 / 1.3 **1.71**	tʃ	= 0.5 / 1 **0.41**
aɪ	= 0.8 / 0.8 **1.83**	b	= 1.6 / 2.4 **1.97**
aʊ	= 1.3 / 1.85 **0.61**	d	= 4.5 / 4.8 **5.14**
ɪə	= 0 / 0.5 **0.21**	g	= 0.5 / 1 **1.05**
əʊ	= 1.3 / 1.85 **1.51**	v	= 1 / 3.2 **2.00**
		ð	= 0.5 / 3.8 **3.56**
		z	= 2.9 / 3.5 **2.46**
		l	= 4.5 / 4.5 **3.66**

$$r \quad = 4 \, / \, 4 \, \textbf{3.51}$$
$$w \quad = 1.3 \, / \, 2.65 \, \textbf{2.81}$$

Summative phonemes (both accented and non-accented)

iː ɜː p f θ z l

Appendix 2: French Sound-Frequency Percentages

Phoneme frequencies are taken from Marc Hug *La Distribution des phonèmes en français*, (Geneva, 1979), 26–7. Hug tabulates five studies of French phoneme frequency. I have taken the mean of those five studies. The first number after each phoneme indicates the percentage of each consonant amongst the consonants as a whole, of each vowel amongst the vowels as a whole (100 in consonants, 100 in vowels). The second number shows the percentage of each phoneme of the phonemes taken as a whole (100 in both vowels and consonants taken together).

CONSONANTS			VOWELS		
b	2.43	1.37	a	14.56	6.36
p	6.41	3.58	ɑ	1.58	0.68
d	7.97	4.48	ɛ	12.12	5.26
t	8.82	4.96	e	11.82	5.17
g	0.98	0.56			
k	6.63	3.73	i	11.59	5.1
v	4.61	2.58	y	4.51	1.93
f	2.47	1.39	u	5.83	2.57
z	3.01	1.71	o	3.36	1.48
s	9.91	5.61			
ʒ	2.62	1.47	ɔ	4.46	1.96
ʃ	1.13	0.65			
ʀ	14.21	7.96	ø	1.63	0.73
l	11.2	6.28	œ	1.42	0.59
m	6.33	3.56			
n	5.07	2.85	ə	11.13	4.91
ɲ	0.22	0.13			
j	3.04	1.71	ã	7.55	3.31
ɥ	0.89	0.51	ɛ̃	2.63	1.15
w	2.05	1.15	ɔ̃	4.55	2.01
			œ̃	1.26	0.55

Bibliography:

INTRODUCTION

BACHELARD, GASTON, *On Poetic Imagination and Reverie*, translated C. Gaudin (New York, 1971).

BALLARD, P. B., *Thought and Language* (London, 1934).

BARBIER, JOSEPH, *Le Vocabulaire, la syntaxe et le style des poèmes réguliers de Charles Péguy* (Paris, 1957).

BARBIZET, J., *Pathologie de la mémoire* (Paris, 1970).

BARTHES, ROLAND, *Essais Critiques* (Paris, 1964).

BARTLETT, J., *Remembering: A Study in Experimental and Social Psychology* (Cambridge, 1965).

BATAILLE, GEORGES, *Œuvres complètes* (5 vols.; Paris, 1973).

BERGSON, HENRI, *Le Rire: Essai sur la signification du comique* (Paris, 1908).

BOWER, R. A. (ed.), *On Translation* (Oxford, 1966).

BRADBURY, M. and MCFARLANE, J. (eds.), *Modernism* (London, 1981).

BRIDOUX, A., *Le Souvenir* (Paris, 1953).

BROWN, HUNTINGDON, *Prose Styles* (Minneapolis, 1966).

CERMAK, LAIRD S., *Human Memory* (New York, 1972).

CHASTAING, MAXIME, 'Si les r étaient des l' (Part 1) *Vie et langage*, 159 (1966), 468–72; (Part 2) *Vie et langage*, 174 (1966), 502–7.

CHATMAN, SEYMOUR and LEVIN, SAMUEL, *Essays on the Language of Literature* (Boston, 1967).

CLANCHY, M., *From Memory to Written Record: England 1066–1307* (Bath, 1979).

COFER, C. N. (ed.), *The Structure of Human Memory* (San Francisco, 1976).

CRESSOT, MARCEL, *Le Style et ses techniques* (Paris, 1976).

CROLL, MORRIS, *Style, Rhetoric and Rhythm* (Princeton, 1966).

DARBELNET, JEAN, *Le Français en contact avec l'anglais en amérique du nord* (Quebec, 1976).

DARBELNET, JEAN and VINAY, JEAN-PAUL, *Stylistique comparée du français et de l'anglais* (Paris, 1958).

DAVID, DONALD, *Articulate Energy* (London, 1966).

DAVIS, PHILIP, *Memory and Writing: From Wordsworth to Lawrence* (Liverpool, 1983).

DELAY, JEAN, Les Dissolutions de la mémoire (Paris, 1950).

—— *Les Maladies de la mémoire* (Paris, 1970).

DELBOUILLE, PAUL, *Poésie et sonorités* (Paris, 1961).

DELISLE, JEAN, *L'Analyse du discours comme méthode de traduction* (Ottawa, 1980).

DICKENS, CHARLES, *David Copperfield* (London, 1985).

DOLEZEL, LUBOMIR and BAILEY, RICHARD W. (eds.), *Statistics and Style* (New York, 1969).

DU BOS, CHARLES, *Choix de textes*, ed. E. Gibson (Paris, 1959).

DUGAS, L., *La Mémoire et l'oubli* (Paris, 1919).

ELIOT, T. S., 'The Music of Poetry', in *Selected Prose of T. S. Eliot*, ed. Frank Kermode (London, 1984), 107–14.

EYSENCK, MICHAEL, *Human Memory* (Oxford, 1977).

FISCHER, KURT and CORRIGAN, ROBERTA, 'A Skill Approach to Language Development', in *Language Behaviour in Infancy and Early Childhood*, ed. Rachel Stark (Oxford, 1981), pp. 245–74.

FITZGERALD, ROBERT, *Enlarging the Change: The Princeton Seminars in Literary Criticism 1949–1951* (Boston, 1985).

FOCCI, MARIO, *La Langue indiscrète: essai sur le transfert comme traduction* (Paris, 1984).

FOWLER, R., *Essays on Style and Language* (London, 1966).

FRIDAY, NANCY, *Jalousie* translated T. Carlier (Paris, 1985).

FUSSEL, PAUL, *Poetic Meter and Poetic Form* (New York, 1965).

GIRARD, ALAIN, *Le Journal intime* (Paris, 1963).

GRAMMONT, MAURICE, *Le Vers français* (Paris, 1937).

—— *Petit Traité de versification française* (Paris, 1966).

DE LA GRASSERIE, RAOUL, *De l'accent comparé dans les diverses langues* (Paris, 1909).

GUSDORF, G., *Mémoire et personne* (2 vols.; Paris, 1951).

HALBWACHS, M., *Les Cadres sociaux de la mémoire* (Paris, 1925).

HALLIDAY, M. A. K., 'One Child's Protolanguage', in *Before Speech: The Beginning of Interpersonal Communication*, ed. Margaret Bullowa (Cambridge, 1980), pp. 171–90.

HARDY, THOMAS, *The Return of the Native*, ed. James Gindin (London, 1969).

HATZFELD, HELMUT, *Initiation à l'explication de textes français* (Munich, 1957).

HAZLITT, WILLIAM, 'Coriolanus', *Characters of Shakespeare's Plays*, (London, 1954).

—— 'Character of Mr Wordsworth's New Poem, The Excursion', in *The Complete Works of William Hazlitt*, ed. P. P. Howe (21 vols.; London, 1933), xix. *Literary and Political Criticism*.

—— 'On the Periodical Essayists', in *Lectures on the Comic Writers* (London, 1913) (1819).

HEANEY, SEAMUS, *Preoccupations: Selected Prose 1968–1978* (London, 1980).

HERDAN, G., *Language as Choice and Chance* (Groningen, Holland, 1956).

HILLIS MILLER, J., *Fiction and Repetition: Seven English Words* (Oxford, 1982).

HOLLANDER, JOHN, *Vision and Resonance* (New York, 1975).

HOSKINS, JOHN, *Directions for Speech and Style* (Princeton, 1935).

HOUGHTON, E. (ed.), *The Wellesley Index to Victorian Periodicals 1824–1900*, iii (5 vols.; Toronto, 1979).

HOUSTON, J. P., *The Traditions of French Prose Style* (London, 1981).

HOWELLS, W. D., *Criticism and Fiction* (New York, 1959).

HRUSHOVSKI, BENJAMIN, 'The Meaning of Sound Patterns in Poetry', *Poetics Today*, 2:1a (Autumn 1980), 29–56.

HUGUET, EDMOND, *L'Evolution du sens des mots* (Paris, 1934).

HYMES, DELL, H., 'Phonological Aspects of Style: Some English Sonnets', in *Essays on the Language of Literature*, ed. Seymour Chatman and Samuel Levin (Boston, 1967), pp. 33–53.

JAKOBSON, ROMAN and WAUGH, LINDA, *La Charpente phonique du langage*, translated Alain Kihm (Paris, 1980) (*The Sound Shape of Language*, 1979).

JAMES, HENRY, *The House of Fiction: Essays on the Novel*, ed. Leon Edel (London, 1957).

JANET, PAUL, *L'Evolution de la mémoire et de la notion du temps* (Paris, 1928).

JESPERSEN, OTTO, 'Symbolic value of the vowel I', in *Linguistica* (Copenhagen, 1933), pp. 283–303.

JOFFUS, ELIZABETH, *La Mémoire* (Quebec, 1983).

KER, W. P., *Form and Style in Poetry* (London, 1966).

KRISTEVA, JULIA, *La Révolution du langage poétique* (Paris, 1974).

—— *Polylogue* (Paris, 1977).

LADMIRAL, J-R., *Traduire: Théorèmes pour la traduction* (Paris, 1979).

LANZ, H., *The Physical Basis of Rime* (Stanford, Calif., 1931).

LATFORD, J. C., *A Linguistic Theory of Translation* (Oxford, 1974).

LECLERCE, LOUIS, *Rousseau et l'art du roman* (Paris, 1969).

LECOCQ, PIERRE and TIBERGHIEN, GUY, *Mémoire et décision* (Lille, 1981).

LEFEBVRE, HENRI, *Le Langage et la société* (Paris, 1966).

LINCH, J. J., 'The Tonality of Lyric Poetry: An Experiment in Method', *Word*, 9 (1953), 211–24.

LUCAS, F. L., *Style* (London, 1955).

LURIA, A. R., *Une Prodigieuse mémoire* (Neuchâtel, 1970).

—— *The Neuropsychology of Memory* (London, 1976).

MCCLUSKEY, KATHLEEN, *Reverberations: Sound and Structure in the Novels of Virginia Woolf* (Ann Arbor, 1986).

MASSON, DAVID, 'Patterns of Vowel and Consonant in a Rilkean Sonnet', *Modern Language Review* (1951), 419–30.

—— 'Vowel and Consonant Patterns in Poetry', *Journal of Aesthetics and Art*, 12 (1953), 213–17.

—— 'Free Phonetic Patterns in Shakespeare's Sonnets', *Neophilologus*, 28 (1954), 277–89.

—— 'Wilfred Owen's Free Phonetic Patterns: Their Style and Function', *Journal of Aesthetics and Art Criticism*, 13 (1955), 360–9.

—— 'Sound Repetition Terms', *Poetics Poetyka*, International Conference of Works-in-Progress Devoted to Problems of Poetics (Warsaw, 1961), 189–99.

—— 'Sound and Sense: Mechanisms in a Middle Rilkean Sonnet', *Modern Language Review*, 59 (1964), 237–43.

—— 'Thematic Analysis of Sounds in Poetry', *Essays on the Language of Literature*, ed. Seymour Chatman and Samuel Levin (Boston, 1967), pp. 54–68.

MAURIAC, FRANÇOIS, *Mémoires intérieures* (Paris, 1959).

MELTON, A. W. and MARTIN, E. (eds.), *Coding Processes in Human Memory* (New York, 1972).

MICHAUD, GUY, *Message poétique du symbolisme* (Paris, 1947).

MICHAUX, LÉON, *La Mémoire* (Paris, 1974).

MILES, JOSEPHINE, *Style and Proportion: The Language of Prose and Poetry* (Boston, 1967).

—— *Wordsworth and the Vocabulary of Emotion* (New York, 1965).

MOUROT, JEAN, *Le Génie d'un style: Chateaubriand—Rythme et sonorité dans les Mémoires d'outre-tombe* (Paris, 1960).

NABOKOV, VLADIMIR, *Lolita* (London, 1980) (1955).

NEISSER, ULRIC, *Memory Observed: Remembering in Natural Contexts* (San Francisco, 1982).

NELSON, CARY, *The Incarnate Word: Literature as Verbal Space* (Urbana, Ill., 1973).

NESS, FREDERICK, *The Use of Rhyme in Shakespeare's Plays* (Newhaven, 1941).

OLLER, D. KIMBROUGH, 'Infant Vocalizations: Exploration and Reflexivity', in *Language Behaviour in Infancy and Early Childhood*, ed. Rachel Stark (Oxford, 1981), 85–97.

PEGUY, CHARLES, 'Le Commentaire d'"Eve": Entretien de Péguy avec Joseph Lotte', 4 Jan. 1914, *Cahiers de l'amitié Charles Péguy* (Paris, 1948), nos. 3–4.

PORTER, KATHERINE ANNE, *The Collected Essays and Occasional Writings of Katherine Anne Porter* (New York, 1970).

DE QUINCEY, THOMAS, *Selected Essays on Rhetoric*, ed. F. Burwick (London, 1967).

RAY, WILLIAM, *Literary Meaning: From Phenomenology to Deconstruction* (Bath, 1984).

REIMAN, DONALD, *Shelley's 'Triumph of Life': A Critical Study* (Urbana, Ill., 1965).

REY, ANDRÉ, *Les Troubles de la mémoire et leur examen psychométrique* (Brussels, 1966).

RICHARD, J-P., *Littérature et sensation* (Paris, 1954).

RIFFATERRE, MICHEL, 'Stylistic Approach to Literary History', in *Langue française* no. 3 (Sept. 1969), 46–60.

ROACH, PETER, *English Phonetics and Phonology* (Cambridge, 1988).

ROGERS, NEVILLE, *Shelley at Work: A Closer View* (Oxford, 1956).

SAINTSBURY, GEORGE, *A History of English Prose Rhythm* (London, 1912).

SAYCE, R. A., *Style in French Prose* (Oxford, 1953).

SEBEOK, THOMAS (ed.), *Style in Language* (New York, 1980).

SHELLEY, MARY, 'Rome in the first and nineteenth century', *New Monthly Magazine and Literary Journal*, vol 10, (Mar. 1824), 217–22.

—— 'Byron and Shelley on the Character of Hamlet', *New Monthly Magazine and Literary Journal*, 29:2 (1830), 327–36.

SHELLEY, PERCY BHYSSHE, 'A Defence of Poetry', in *The Complete Works of Percy Bysshe Shelley*, V, ed. R. Ingpen and Walter Peck, (10 vols.; New York, 1965).

—— *Peacock's Memoirs of Shelley*, ed. H. F. B. Brett-Smith, (London, 1909).

SMITH, BRIAN, *Memory* (London, 1966).

SPEAR, NORMAN, E., *L'Evolution des souvenirs* translated B. Deweer (Paris, 1980).

SPIRE, ANDRÉ, *Plaisir poétique et plaisir musculaire* (Paris, 1949).

STARK, RACHEL, 'Early Development of the Forms of Language', in *Language Behaviour in Infancy and Early Childhood*, ed. Rachel Stark (Oxford, 1981), pp. 77–82.

STEINER, T. R., *English Translation Theory 1650–1800* (Amsterdam, 1975).

STEVENS, WALLACE, *The Necessary Angel* (New York, 1982).

SUTHERLAND, JAMES (ed.), *The Oxford Book of Talk* (Oxford, 1953).

SWIFT, JONATHAN, *Swift*, ed. John Hayward (London, 1990).

TAMBA-MECZ, IRÉNE, *Le Sens figuré* (Paris, 1981).

TENNYSON, ALFRED LORD, *Tennyson: A Selected Edition*, ed. Christopher Ricks (London, 1989).

THIBAULT, E., *La Sensation du 'Déjà Vu'* (Bordeaux, 1899).

THOMSON, WILLIAM, *The Rhythm of Speech* (Glasgow, 1923).

VAGAR, GEORGES, *A la Recherche de la mémoire* (Paris, 1976).

VALERY, PAUL, *Cahiers I*, ed. Judith Robinson (Paris, 1973).

VESTER, FREDERIC, *Penser apprendre oublier* (Paris, 1984).

WEBBER, JOAN, *Contrary Music: The Prose Style of John Donne* (Madison, 1963).

WEBSTER, OWEN, *Read Well and Remember* (London, 1965).

WEISSMAN, FRIDA, S., *Du Monologue intérieur à la sous-conversation* (Paris, 1978).

WELLEK, RENÉ and WARREN, AUSTIN, *Theory of Literature* (London, 1966).

WELSH, ANDREW, *Roots of Lyric* (Princeton, 1978).

WETHERILL, P. M., *The Literary Text: An Examination of Critical Methods* (Oxford, 1974).

WIMSATT, W. K. JR., 'One Relation of Rhyme to Reason', *Modern Language Quarterly* 5 (Mar., 1944) no. 1, 323–38.

WORDSWORTH, WILLIAM, *The Convention of Cintra*, in *The Prose Works of William Wordsworth*, ed. W. J. B. Owen and Jane Worthington Smyser, (3 vols.; Oxford, 1974), 224–343.

—— 'Preface to Lyrical Ballads (1800)'; in *The Prose Works of William Wordsworth*, i, ed. W. J. B. Owen and Jane Worthington (3 vols.; Oxford 1974).

—— Poems, in *Two Volumes and Other Poems 1800–1807*, ed. J. Curtis (New York, 1983).

—— Appendix, 'Preface to Poems (1815)', in *William Wordsworth: The Poems*, ii, ed. John Hayden (3 vols.; London, 1977).

—— 'Essay on Epitaphs', in *Wordsworth's Literary Criticism*, ed. W. Owen (London, 1974), 120–69.

MALLARMÉ

AUSTIN, LLOYD, *L'Univers poétique de Baudelaire: Symbolisme et symbolique* (Paris, 1956).

BAUDELAIRE, CHARLES, *Œuvres complètes*, ed. Claude Roy and Michel Jamet (Paris, 1980).

BENJAMIN, WALTER, *Charles Baudelaire—A Lyric Poet in an Era of High Capitalism*, translated H. Zohn (London, 1973).

BERNARD, SUZANNE, *Le Poème en prose de Baudelaire jusqu'à nos jours* (Paris, 1959).

BERTRAND, ALOYSIUS, *Gaspard de la nuit* (Paris, 1953).

BROMBERT, VICTOR, 'Lyrisme et dépersonalisation—Charles Baudelaire', *Romantisme*, 6 (1973), 29–37.

BUTOR, MICHEL, *L'Emploi du temps* (Paris, 1957).

CASSAGNE, ALBERT, *Versification et métrique de Charles Baudelaire* (Geneva, 1972).

CAWS, MARY ANN and RIFFATERRE, HERMIONE (eds.), *The Prose Poem in France: Theory and Practice* (New York, 1983).

CHESTERS, GRAHAM, *Some Functions of Sound-Repetition in 'Les Fleurs du mal'* (London, 1975).

DERRIDA, JACQUES, *La Dissémination* (Paris, 1972).

—— *La Vérité en peinture* (Paris, 1978).

FAIRLIE, ALISON, *Imagination and Language* (London, 1983).

FINCH, ALISON, BOWIE, MALCOLM, and FAIRLIE, ALISON (eds.), *Baudelaire, Mallarmé, Valéry: New Essays in Honour of Lloyd Austin* (Cambridge, 1982).

FRANKLIN, URSULA, *The Rhetoric of Valéry's Prose Aubades* (Toronto, 1979).

GARDES-TAMINE J. and MOLINO J., *Introduction à l'analyse de la poésie* i. *Vers et figures* (Paris, 1982).

GIBSON, ROBERT, *Modern French Poets on Poetry* (Cambridge, 1979).

GIDE, ANDRÉ, *Le Traité du Narcisse (Théorie du symbole)* (Ottawa, 1978).

GUIRAUD, PIERRE, *Langage et Versification d'après l'oeuvre de Paul Valéry* (Paris, 1953)

HIDDLESTON, J. A., *Baudelaire and Le Spleen de Paris* (Oxford, 1981).

HOPKINS, GERARD MANLEY, *Selected Letters*, ed. Catherine Phillips (Oxford, 1990).

HUNTER, IAN, *Memory* (London, 1972).

JOHNSON, BARBARA, *Défigurations du langage poétique* (Paris, 1979).

JOUVE, N. W., *Baudelaire: A Fire to Conquer Darkness* (London, 1980)

JOUVE, PIERRE JEAN, *Proses* (Paris, 1960).

LLOYD, ROSEMARY, *Baudelaire's Literary Criticism* (Cambridge, 1981).

LOUGH, JOHN, *Writer and Public in France* (Oxford, 1978).

MALLARMÉ, STÉPHANE, *Œuvres complètes* (Paris, 1945).

MICHON, JACQUES, *Mallarmé et Les Mots anglais* (Paris, 1978).

MORIER, HENRI, *Le Rythme du vers libres* (Geneva, 1973).

NABOKOV, VLADIMIR, *Lolita* (London, 1980) (1955)

OLOVSSON, HALVAR, *Etudes sur les rimes des trois poètes romantiques: Alfred de Musset, Théophile Gautier, Charles Baudelaire* (Lund, 1924).

PARENT, MONIQUE, *Saint-John Perse et quelques devanciers: Études sur le poème en prose* (Paris, 1960).

PATTERSON, WILLIAM, *The Rhythm of Prose* (New York, 1916)

PAXTON, NORMAN, *The Development of Mallarmé's Prose Style* (Geneva, 1968).

PICKERING, ROBERT (ed.), *Paul Valéry poète en prose: La Prose lyrique abstraite des Cahiers* (Paris, 1983).

POPKIN, D. and POPKIN, M. (eds.), *Modern French Literature* (New York, 1977).

RABATÉ, JEAN-MICHEL, *La Penultième est morte* (Seyssel, 1993).

RICHARD, JEAN-PIERRE, *L'Univers imaginaire de Mallarmé* (Paris, 1961).
RONSARD, PIERRE DE, *Les Amours* (1552–1584), ed. Marc Bensimon (Paris, 1981).
SAINTE-BEUVE, CHARLES AUGUSTIN, *Vie, poésies et pensées de Joseph Delorme* (Paris, 1956) (1829).
SCHERER, JACQUES, *Grammaire de Mallarmé* (Paris, 1977).
SIMON, JOHN, *The Prose Poem as a Genre in Nineteenth-Century European Literature* (New York, 1987).
TODOROV, TZVETAN, *Poétique de la Prose* (Paris, 1971).
ULLMANN, STEPHEN, *Style in the French Novel* (Oxford, 1964).
WRIGHT, BARBARA and SCOTT, DAVID, *'La Fanfarlo' and 'Le Spleen de Paris'* (London, 1984).

PROUST

PRIMARY TEXTS

A la recherche du temps perdu, ed. Jean-Yves Tadié (4 vols.; Paris, 1987–9).
Contre Sainte-Beuve précédé de Pastiches et mélanges et suivi de Essais et articles, ed. Pierre Clarac (Paris, 1971).
Jean Santeuil précédé de Les Plaisirs et les jours, ed. Pierre Clarac (Paris, 1971).
John Ruskin: Sésame et les lys, *traduction et Notes de Marcel Proust précédé de Sur la Lecture de Marcel Proust* (Paris, 1987).
Correspondance, ed. Philip Kolb (13 vols.; Paris, 1985).
Albertine disparue: Edition originale de la dernière version revue par l'auteur, ed. Nathalie Mauriac and Etienne Wolff (Paris, 1987).
Poèmes, ed. Claude Francis and Fernande Gontor, *Cahiers Marcel Proust*, 10 (Paris, 1982).
Two microfilms of Proust's manuscripts consulted, held at the Bibliothèque Nationale, Paris: 1. MS NRF 16737 M. 619 Le Côté de Guermantes; 2. MS NAF 16721 M. 603 Cahier XIV.

SECONDARY TEXTS

(All texts published in Paris unless otherwise stated.)
ALBARET, CÉLESTE, *Monsieur Proust*, souvenirs recueillis par Georges Belmont (1973).

BACKHAUS, INGE, *Strukturen des Romans: Studien zur Leit- und Wiederholungsmotivik in Prousts 'A la recherche du temps perdu'* (Berlin, 1976).

BALDRIDGE, WILLIAM, 'The Time-Crisis in Mallarmé and Proust', *French Review*, 59:4 (Mar., 1986), 564–70.

BARRES, MAURICE, *Mes Cahiers 1896–1923 (1963)*.

BAUDELAIRE, CHARLES, *Œuvres complètes* (1968).

BAUDRY, JEAN-LOUIS, *Proust, Freud et l'autre* (1984).

BEAUCHAMP, LOUIS, DE, *Le Petit Groupe et le grand monde de Marcel Proust* (1990).

BEDRIOMO, ÉMILE, *Proust, Wagner et la coincidence des arts* (Tübingen, 1984).

BERSANI, LEO, *Marcel Proust: The Fictions of Life and Art* (London, 1965).

BILLY, ROBERT, DE, *Marcel Proust: Lettres et conversations* (1930).

BLANCHE, JAQUES-ÉMILE, and MAURIAC FRANÇOIS, *Correspondance 1916–1942* (1976).

BOSQUET, ALAIN, *Saint-John Perse* (1971).

BOURGET, PAUL, *Portraits d'écrivains* (1905).

BOWIE, MALCOLM, *Proust, Jealousy, Knowledge* (Leeds, 1978).

BOYER, VÉRONIQUE, *L'Image du corps dans A la recherche du temps perdu* (1984).

BRADY, PATRICK, *Marcel Proust* (Boston, 1977).

BRUN, BERNARD, 'Sur le Proust de Beckett', in *Beckett avant Beckett : Essais sur le jeune Beckett (1930–1945)*, ed. Jean-Michel Rabaté (1984), pp. 79–91.

CABANIS, JOSÉ, 'Bergotte ou Proust et l'écrivain', *Proust* (Collection Génies et Réalités) (1965), 185–97.

CATTAUI, GEORGES, 'L'Amitié de Proust', *Les Cahiers Marcel Proust* (1953) viii. 119–49.

CHANTAL, RENÉ DE, *Marcel Proust: Critique littéraire* (Montreal, 1967).

CHARDIN, PHILIPPE, 'Sortie du dédale et temps retrouvé: le dénouements de A la recherche du temps perdu de Proust et de A Portrait of the Artist as a Young Man de Joyce', in *Cahiers Marcel Proust*, no.9 (Études Proustiennes III) (1979) pp. 95–120.

—— *L'Amour dans la haine, ou, la jalousie dans la littérature moderne: Dostoievski, James, Svevo, Proust, Musil.* (Geneva, 1990).

COCHET, MARIE-ANN, *L'Âme Proustienne* (Brussels, 1929).

COHN, ROBERT G., 'Proust and Mallarmé', *French Studies* 24: 3 (July, 1970), 262–75.

COMPAGNON, ANTOINE, *Proust entre deux siècles* (1989).

CONTINI, ANNEMARIE, *La Biblioteca di Proust* (Bologna, 1988).

CURTIUS, ERNST ROBERT, *Marcel Proust*, translated Armand Pierhal (1928).

CZONICZER, E., *Quelques antécédents de* A la recherche du temps perdu (1957).

DAUDET, LÉON, *Souvenirs littéraires* (1968).

DE MAN, PAUL, *Allegories of Reading* (1989).

DESCARTES, RENÉ, *The Philosophical Works of Descartes*, translated E. S. Haldane and G. R. T. Ross, (2 vols.; Cambridge, 1973).

DESCOMBES, VINCENT, *Proust: Philosophie du roman* (1987).

DONNAN, THOMAS M., 'Proust "reprit à la musique son bien": A Study in Analogies between Wagnerian and Proustian Composition', *Stanford French Review*, 13: 2–3, (Fall-Winter 1989), 159–74.

DU BOS, CHARLES, *Journal 1921–1923* (1946).

DUGAST-PORTES, FRANCINE, 'Le Goût selon Odette' in *Marcel Proust: Geshmack und Neigung* ed. Volker Kapp (Tübingen, 1989), pp. 43–60.

ELLISON, DAVID, *The Reading of Proust* (Oxford, 1984).

ERICKSON, JOHN and PAGES, IRÈNE, *Proust et le texte producteur* (Guelph, 1980).

ERMAN, MICHEL, *L'Œil de Proust: Écriture et voyeurisme dans* A la recherche du temps perdu (1988).

FERNANDEZ, RAMON, *Proust ou la généalogie du roman moderne* (1979).

FRANCE, PETER, *Racine's Rhetoric* (Oxford, 1965).

GENETTE, GÉRARD, *Narrative Discourse* (Oxford, 1980).

—— *Palimpsestes* (1982).

GIORGIO, GIORGETTO, *Stendhal, Flaubert, Proust* (Milan, 1969).

GIRADOUX, JEAN, *Littérature* (1941).

GIRARD, RENÉ, *Mensonge romantique et vérité romanesque* (1961).

GOURMONT, RÉMY DE, *Promenades Philosophiques II* (1920).

GRIFFITHS, ERIC, *The Printed Voice of Victorian Poetry* (Oxford, 1989).

HENRY, ANNE, *Marcel Proust: théories pour une esthéthique* (1981).

—— *Proust romancier: le tombeau égyptien* (1983).

—— *Proust* (1986).

HILDEBRANDT, HANS-HAGEN, *Becketts Proust-Bildee: Erinnerung und Identitat* (Stuttgart, 1980).

HOUSTON, J. P., *The Shape and Style of Proust's Novel* (Detroit, 1982).

HUMPHRIES, JEFFERSON, *The Otherness Within* (Baton Rouge, L., 1983).

IFRI, P. A., *Proust et son Narrataire* (Geneva, 1983).

JAECK, LOIS MARIE, *Marcel Proust and the Text as Macrometaphor* (Toronto, 1990).

JAMMES, FRANCIS, *Le Roman du Lièvre* (1922).

JEFFERSON, LOUISE M., 'Proust et Racine', *Yale French Studies*, 34 (June, 1965) 99–105.

JOHNSON, LEE MCKAY, *The Metaphor of Painting: Essays on Baudelaire, Ruskin, Proust and Pater* (Ann Arbor, 1980).

LATTRE, ALAIN DE, *La Doctrine de la réalité chez Proust* (2 vols.; 1981).

LEHMANN, A. G., *The Symbolist Aesthetic in France 1885–1895* (Oxford, 1968)

MCGINNIS, REGINALD, 'L'Inconnaissable Gomorrhe: A propos d'*Albertine disparue* ', *Romantic Review*, 81:1, (Jan. 1990), 92–104.

MAETERLINCK, MAURICE, *Les Sentiers dans la montagne* (1919).

MALLARMÉ, STÉPHANE, *Divagations* (Geneva, 1954).

MANSFIELD, LESTER, *Le Comique de Marcel Proust: Proust et Baudelaire* (1953).

MATORE, GEORGES ET MECZ, IRÈNE, *Musique et structure romanesque dans* A la recherche du temps perdu (Strasbourg, 1972).

MAURIAC, CLAUDE, *Proust* (1953).

MAYER, DENISE, *Marcel Proust et la Musique d'après sa correspondance* (1978).

MEIN, MARGARET, *A Foretaste of Proust: A Study of Proust and his Precursors* (Farnborough, 1974).

—— *Proust et la chose envolée* (1986).

MIGUET-OLLAGNIER, MARIE, *La Mythologie de Marcel Proust* (1982).

MILLY, JEAN, *La Phrase de Proust* (1975).

—— *Proust dans le texte et l'avant-texte* (1985).

—— 'Proust: le jaloux dans tous ses états', *Magazine littéraire*, no. 267–268 (July–Aug. 1989), 34–9.

MORAND, PAUL, *Papiers d'identité* (1931).

MOREAS, JEAN, *Esquisses et souvenirs* (1908).

MOUTON, JEAN, *Le Style de Marcel Proust* (1968).

MUSSET, ALFRED DE, *Contes* (1867).

—— 'Histoire d'un merle blanc', *Œuvres complètes en prose*, ed. Maurice Altem and Paul Courant (1960).

NATTIEZ, JEAN-JACQUES, *Proust musicien* (1984).

NEWCOMBE, ANTHONY, 'Sound and Feeling', *Critical Inquiry* (June 1984), 640–9.

NYKROG, PER, *La Recherche du don perdu: points de repère dans le roman de Marcel Proust* (Cambridge, Mass., 1987).

PICON, GAETAN, *Lecture de Proust* (1963).

RACZYMOW, HENRI, *Le Cygne de Proust* (1989).

RAIMOND, MICHEL, *Proust romancier* (1984).

REILLE, J. FRANCIS, *Proust: le temps du désir: une lecture textuelle* (1979).

REMÂCLE, MADELEINE, *L'Elément poétique dans* A la recherche du temps perdu (Brussels, 1954).

RICHARD, JEAN-PIERRE, *Proust et le monde sensible* (1974).

RIVERS, J. E., *Proust and the Art of Love* (New York, 1980).

ROGERS, B. G., *Proust's Narrative Techniques* (Geneva, 1965).

ROLLAND, ROMAIN, *Musiciens d'aujourd'hui* (1908). The article on Tristan first appeared in *La Revue d'Art Dramatique* in November 1899.

ROSASCO, JOAN TERESA, *Voies de l'Imagination proustienne* (1980).

SCHER, LAWRENCE R., *Flaubert and Sons: Readings of Flaubert, Zola and Proust* (New York, 1986).

SEGAL, NAOMI, *The Banal Object* (London, 1981).

STAROBINSKI, JEAN, *Les Mots sous les mots* (1971).

TADIE, JEAN-YVES, *Proust et le roman* (1971)

—— *Proust* (1983).

TAYLOR, ELIZABETH, *Proust and his Contexts* (New York, 1981).

VALÉRY, PAUL, *Cahiers*, i, ed. Judith Robinson (1973), 'Mémoire' section (pp. 1211–62) [note 1911].

VAN DE GHINSTE, J., *Rapports humains et communication dans* A la recherche du temps perdu (1975).

WAGNER, RICHARD, *Une Communication à mes amis suivi de Lettre sur la musique*, translated Jean Launay (1976).

WINTON, ALISON, *Proust's Additions: The Making of* A la recherche du temps perdu (2 vols., Cambridge, 1977).

JOYCE

PRIMARY TEXTS

Epiphanies, ed. O. A. Silverman (Buffalo, NY, 1956).

Chamber Music, ed. William York Tindall (New York, 1954).

Collected Poems (New York, 1936).

Stephen Hero (London, 1961).

Dubliners (corrected edition), ed. R. Scholes (London, 1975).

Exiles: A Play in Three Acts (London, 1951).

Giacomo Joyce (New York, 1968).

A Portrait of the Artist as a Young Man (London, 1987).

Ulysses: The corrected text (student edition), ed. Hans Walter Gabler (London, 1986).

Finnegans Wake (London, 1975).

Poems and Shorter Writings: Including Epiphanies, Giacomo Joyce *and 'A Portrait of the Artist'*, ed. Richard Ellmann and A. Walton Litz (London, 1991).

The Mime of Mick, Nick and the Maggies, illus. Lucia Joyce (London, 1934).

The Critical Writings of James Joyce, ed. E. Mason and R. Ellmann (London, 1959).

Letters of James Joyce, i, ed. Stuart Gilbert (London, 1957).

Letters of James Joyce, ii, ed. Richard Ellmann (London, 1966).
The main drafts and notebooks consulted were:
Dubliners: A Facsimile of Drafts and Manuscripts, ed. H. W. Gabler (London, 1978)
Joyce's Ulysses Notesheets in the British Museum, ed. Phillip F. Herring (Charlottesville, 1972).
Joyce's Notes and Early Drafts for Ulysses: Selections from the Buffalo Collection, ed. Phillip F. Herring (Charlottesville, Va., 1975).
James Joyce: Ulysses 'Wandering Rocks' and 'Sirens': A Facsimile of page proofs for episodes 10 and 11, ed. Michael Groden (London, 1978).
Scribbledehobble: The Ur-Workbook for Finnegans Wake, ed. T. E. Connolly (Kingsport, Tenn., 1961).
A First-Draft Version of Finnegans Wake, ed. David Hayman (Austin, Tex., 1963).

SECONDARY TEXTS

(All books published in London unless otherwise stated.)
ATHERTON, JAMES, *The Books at the Wake: A Study of Literary Allusions in James Joyce's* Finnegans Wake (New York, 1979).
ATTRIDGE, DEREK, *'Finnegans Wake*: The Dream of Interpretation', *James Joyce Quarterly*, 27: 1 (Fall, 1989), 11–30.
AUBERT, J. and SENN, FRITZ, *James Joyce* (Cahiers de l'Herne) (Paris, 1985).
AVERY, BRUCE, 'Distant Music: Sound and the Dialogics of Satire in "The Dead" ', *James Joyce Quarterly*, 28: 2 (Winter, 1991), 473–85.
BARNES, DJUNA, *'I could never be lonely without a husband'*, ed. Alyce Barry (1985).
BAUERLE, RUTH, *The James Joyce Songbook* (1982).
BEACH, SYLVIA, *Ulysses in Paris* (New York, 1956).
BECKETT, SAMUEL, and others, *Our Exagmination round his Factification for Incamination of Work in Progress* (Paris 1929).
BEGNAL, MICHAEL H., *Dreamscheme: Narrative and Voice in* Finnegans Wake (Syracuse, NY, 1988).
BENSTOCK, BERNARD, *Joyce-Again's Wake* (Washington, 1965).
—— (ed.), *James Joyce: The Augmented Ninth*, International James Joyce Symposium 9th (Frankfurt, June 1984), (Syracuse, NY, 1988).
—— and STALEY, T. F., *Approaches to Joyce's Portrait* (Pittsburgh, 1976).
BLOOM, HAROLD (ed.), *James Joyce's* Ulysses (New York, 1987).
—— (ed.) *James Joyce's* Dubliners (New York, 1988).
—— *James Joyce's* Portrait (New York, 1988).
BOWEN, ZACK, *Musical Allusions in the Works of James Joyce* (Albany, NY, 1974).

—— and CARENS J. F. (eds.), *A Companion to Joyce Studies* (Westport, Conn., 1984).

BRANDABUR, EDWARD, *A Scrupulous Meanness: A Study of Joyce's Early Work* (1971).

BRIVIC, SHELDON, *Joyce between Freud and Jung* (New York, 1980).

BUDGEN, FRANK, *James Joyce and the Making of Ulysses* (1937).

BURGESS, ANTHONY, *Joysprick* (1973).

BUTTIGIEG, JOSEPH A., *A Portrait of the Artist in Different Perspective* (Athens, Oh., 1987).

BYRNE, J. F., *Silent Years* (New York, 1953).

CARD, JAMES VAN DYCK, *An Anatomy of 'Penelope'* (1984).

CIXOUS, HÉLÈNE, *L'Exil de James Joyce ou l'art du remplacement* (Paris, 1968).

COLUM, PADRIAC and COLUM, MARY, *Our Friend James Joyce* (New York, 1958).

CROSS, RICHARD, *Flaubert and Joyce: The Rite of Fiction* (Princeton, 1971).

CURRAN, C. P., *James Joyce Remembered* (1968).

DALTON, JACK and HART, CLIVE (eds.), *Twelve and a Tilly* (1966).

DEMING, R. H. (ed.), *James Joyce: The Critical Heritage* (2 vols.; 1975).

DERRIDA, JACQUES, *Ulysse gramaphone* (Paris, 1987).

ELIOT, T. S., *Selected Prose*, ed. Frank Kermode (1984).

ELLMANN, RICHARD, *James Joyce* (Oxford, 1983).

EPSTEIN, E. L. (ed.), *A Starchamber Quiry* (1982).

ERZGRÄBER, WILLI, 'Auditive und visuelle Appelle in James Joyces *Finnegans Wake*', *Anglia*, 106, i–ii (1988), 111–23.

FERRER, DANIEL, *Genèse de Babel: Joyce et la création* (Paris, 1985).

FRENCH, MARILYN, *The Book as World: James Joyce's Ulysses* (1982).

FREUD, SIGMUND, *Jokes and their Relation to the Unconscious*, translated James Strachey (1966).

—— *The Psychopathology of Everyday Life* translated Alan Tyson (Aylesbury, 1976).

FRIEDMAN, M. J., *Stream of Consciousness* (1955).

GIFFORD, DON and SEIDMAN, ROBERT J., Ulysses *Annotated : Notes for James Joyce's* Ulysses (2nd edn.; Berkeley and Los Angeles, 1989).

GILLESPIE, MICHAEL P., *Inverted Volumes Improperly Arranged: James Joyce and his Trieste Library* (Epping, 1983).

GLASHEEN, ADALINE, *Third Census of* Finnegans Wake (1977) (1956).

GOLDMAN, ARNOLD, *The Joyce Paradox: Form and Freedom in his Fiction* (1966).

GORMAN, HERBERT, *James Joyce: His First Forty Years* (New York, 1924).

GOTTFRIED, ROY, *The Art of Joyce's Syntax in Ulysses* (1980).

GRODEN, MICHAEL, *Ulysses in Progress* (Princeton, 1977).

GWENS, SEON, *James Joyce: Two Decades of Criticism* (New York, 1963).

HALPER, NATHAN, *Studies in Joyce* (Ann Arbor, 1983).

HANSON, CLARE, *Short Stories and Short Fictions 1880–1980* (1985).

HART, CLIVE, *Structure and Motif in* Finnegans Wake (1962).

—— *A Concordance to* Finnegans Wake (New York, 1974).

—— and HAYMAN, DAVID (eds.), *James Joyce's Ulysses: Critical Essays* (1974).

HARTY III, JOHN, *James Joyce's* Finnegans Wake: *A Casebook* (New York, 1991).

HAYMON, DAVID and ANDERSON, Elliott (eds.), *In the Wake of 'The Wake'* (1978).

HODGART, MATTHEW and WORTHINGTON, MABEL, *Song in the Works of James Joyce* (New York, 1959).

HOLLANDER, JOHN, *The Figure of Echo: A Mode of Allusion in Milton and After* (Berkeley, 1981).

HOUSTON, JOHN PORTER, *Joyce and Prose : An Exploration of the Language 'Ulysses'* (Lewisburg, Pa., 1989).

HUMPHREY, ROBERT, *Stream of Consciousness in the Modern Novel* (1954).

JANUSKO, ROBERT, *The Sources and Structures of James Joyce's 'Oxen'* (Ann Arbor, 1983).

JOLAS, EUGENE, 'Homage to the Mythmaker', *transition*, 27 (May, 1938), 169–75.

JOYCE, STANISLAUS, *Recollections of James Joyce by his brother Stanislaus Joyce* translated E. Mason (New York, 1941).

—— *My Brother's Keeper* ed. Richard Ellmann (1958).

—— *The Dublin Diary of Stanislaus Joyce*, ed. G. H. Healey (1962).

JUNG, C. G., *Modern Man in Search of a Soul* (New York, 1933).

KELLOG, GENE, *The Vital Tradition* (Chicago, 1970).

KELLY, DERMOT, *Narrative Strategies in Joyce's 'Ulysses'* (Ann Arbor, 1988).

KENNER, HUGH, *Dublin's Joyce* (1955).

—— *Flaubert, Joyce and Beckett* (Boston, 1964).

KERSHNER, R. B., *Joyce, Bakhtin and Popular Literature* (Chapel Hill, NC, 1989).

KNAPP, BETTINA L., 'Joyce's "A Painful Case": The Train and an Epiphanic Experience', *Études Irlandaises*, 13 (Dec. 1988), 45–60.

—— *Music, Archetype, and the Writer : A Jungian View* (Philadelphia, 1988).

LARKIN, PHILIP, 'The Savage Seventh', in *Required Writing: Miscellaneous Pieces 1955–1982* (London, 1983).

LAWRENCE, KAREN, *The Odyssey of Style in Ulysses* (Princeton, 1981).

LEMONT, GEERT (ed.), Finnegans Wake: *Fifty Years, European Joyce Studies* 2 (Amsterdam, 1990).

LEVIN, HARRY, *James Joyce* (New York, 1960).

LEWIS, WYNDHAM, *Time and Western Man* (1927).
—— *Men Without Art* (New York, 1964).
MCHUGH, ROLAND, *Annotations to* Finnegans Wake (1980).
MADTES, RICHARD, *The 'Ithaca' Chapter of Joyce's* Ulysses (Ann Arbor, 1983).
MAHAFFEY, VICKI, *Reauthorizing Joyce* (Cambridge, 1988).
MARTIN, AUGUSTINE (ed.), *James Joyce: The Artist and the Labyrinth* (1990).
NABOKOV, VLADIMIR, *The Annotated Lolita*, ed. A. Appel (New York, 1970).
NESBITT, LOIS ELLEN, *Critical Insomnia: Reading and Rereading Joyce, Proust and Beckett* (Ann Arbor, 1988); Princeton University diss. DA1 48 (May 1988): 2867.A.
OWEN, RODNEY WILSON, *James Joyce and the Beginnings of* Ulysses (Ann Arbor, 1983).
PARIS, JEAN, *Joyce par lui-même* (Paris, 1957).
PARR, MARY, *James Joyce: The Poetry of Conscience* (Milwaukee, 1961).
PARRINDER, PATRICK, *James Joyce* (Cambridge, 1984).
READ, FORREST (ed.), *Pound/Joyce* (London, n.d.).
REYNOLDS, MARY, *Joyce and Dante* (Princeton, 1981).
RICKARD, JOHN, *Exercising Mnemotechnic: The Odyssey of Memory in James Joyce's 'Ulysses'* (Ann Arbor, 1989).
RIQUELINE, J. P., *Teller and Tale in Joyce's Fiction* (Baltimore, 1983).
ROSE, DARIUS and O'HANLON, JOHN, *Understanding* Finnegans Wake (New York, 1982).
ROSS, MARTIN, *Music and James Joyce* (New York, 1973).
SAN JUAN, EPIFANIO, *James Joyce and the Craft of Fiction: An Interpretation of Dubliners* (Cranbury, NJ, 1972).
SCOTT, BONNIE K. (ed.), *New Alliances in Joyce Studies* (Newark, 1988).
SENN, FRITZ (ed.), *New Light on Joyce: From the Dublin Symposium* (Bloomington, Ind., 1972).
—— *Joyce's Dislocutions* (Baltimore, 1984).
SMITH, BRIAN, *Memory*, (1966).
STALEY, T. F., *Fifty Years*: Ulysses (Ontario, 1974).
STEINBERG, ERWIN, *The Stream of Consciousness and beyond in* Ulysses (Pittsburgh, 1958).
SVEVO, ITALO, *James Joyce—A Lecture Delivered in Milan in 1927 by his Friend Italo Svevo*, translated Stanislaus Joyce (New York, 1950).
THOMAS, BROOK, *James Joyce's* Ulysses: *A Book of Many Happy Returns* (Baton Rouge, La., 1982).
TRISTRAM, HILDEGARD, 'Why James Joyce Also Lost His "Brain of Forgetting": Patterns of Memory and Media in Irish Writing', *Anglistentag 1988 Göttingen*, ed. H. J. Müllenbrock and R. Noll-Wiemann (Tübingen, 1989), pp. 220–33.

UNTERECKER, J. and MCGORY, K., *Yeats, Joyce and Beckett* (1976).
WEIR, LORRAINE, *Writing Joyce* (Bloomington, Ind., 1989).
ZACCHI, ROMANA, 'Quoting Words and Worlds: Discourse Strategies in *Ulysses*', *James Joyce Quarterly*, 27: 1 (Fall, 1989), 101–9.

BECKETT

PRIMARY TEXTS IN ENGLISH.

All texts published in London unless otherwise stated.
Whoroscope (Paris, 1930).
Echo's Bones and Other Precipitates (Paris, 1935).
Murphy (1975).
Molloy (1966).
Malone Dies (1968).
The Unnamable (1975).
Waiting for Godot (1956); critical edition, ed. Colin Duckworth (1966).
Watt (1972).
No's Knife (1967).
All That Fall (Faber, 1957).
Endgame (1958).
Act Without Words I (1958).
From an Abandoned Work (1958).
Krapp's Last Tape (1959).
Happy Days (1962).
How It Is (1964).
Proust and Three Dialogues (1965).
Cascando and Other Short Dramatic Pieces (New York, 1969).
More Pricks than Kicks (1970).
First Love and Other Shorts (New York, 1974).
Mercier and Camier (1974).
For to End Yet Again, and Other Fizzles (1976).
Four Novellas (1977).
Collected Poems in English and French (1977).
Ends and Odds (1977).
Six Residua (1978).
All Strange Away (1979).
Company (New York, 1980).
Ill Seen Ill Said (1982).
Worstward Ho (1983).

Disjecta: Miscellaneous Writings and a Dramatic Fragment, ed. Ruby Cohn (1983).
Collected Shorter Prose 1945–1980 (1984).
Collected Shorter Plays (1984).
Stirrings Still (1989).
As the Story was Told: Uncollected and Late Prose (1990).
Happy Days: The Production Notebook of Samuel Beckett ed. James Knowlson (1987).

PRIMARY TEXTS IN FRENCH.

(All texts published in Paris by Editions de Minuit.)
Murphy (1947).
Watt (1969).
Premier amour (1970).
Mercier et Camier (1970).
Molloy (1982).
Malone meurt (1971).
En attendant Godot (1952).
L'Innomable (1971).
Nouvelles et textes pour rien (1958).
Fin de partie (1957).
Tous ceux qui tombent (1957).
La Dernière bande (1960).
Comment c'est (1961).
Oh les beaux jours suivi de *Pas moi* (1975).
Comédie et actes divers (1970).
Têtes-mortes (1966).
Le Dépeupleur (1970).
Théâtre I (1971).
Pour finir encore et autres foirades (1976).
Pas suivi de *Quatre esquisses* (1978).
Poèmes suivi de *Mirlitonnades* (1978).
Compagnie (1980).
Mal vu mal dit (1981).
Catastrophe et autres dramaticules (1986).

Beginning to End: A Selection from the Works of Samuel Beckett, adapted by Samuel Beckett and Jack MacGowran (New York, 1988).
Translation of Anna Livia Plurabelle ('Anna Lyvia Pluratself') in conjunction with Alfred Péron, in *James Joyce*, ed. Jacques Aubert and Fritz Senn (Paris, 1985), pp. 417–24.
Beckett's copy of RTP: held at Reading University Library: Paris, Librairie Gallimard, Editions de la nouvelle revue française, 1925–9, 15 vols.

Reprint of 1919–27 edns. Autographed presentation copies with his manuscript annotations.

'PSS', *New Departures*, 14 (1982), 64.

'what is the word', *Sunday Correspondent*, 31 December 1989, 32.

At Reading, the main manuscripts consulted were:

Mal vu mal dit notebook MS 2200, notebook MS 2203, 4 loose sheets MS 2204. Original manuscript (1979) MS 2205. Typescript and MS corrections Ms 2206, 2 corrected typescripts Ms 2207.

Ill Seen Ill Said: 2 corrected typescripts Ms 2202. 'The Dial' corrected typescripts Ms 2201.

Also consulted:

Rockaby: MSS 2196, 2197.

Footfalls: MSS 2461, 1552–7.

Company: MSS 1765, 1822.

Beckett Manuscripts, Trinity College, Dublin.

Notes taken by Rachel Dobbin, later Mrs Rachel Burrows, from Beckett's lectures on André Gide, Racine and Proust. Microfilm, October 1976.

SECONDARY TEXTS.

(All texts published in London unless otherwise stated).

ACHESON, JAMES and ARTHUR, KATERYNA, *Beckett's Later Fiction and Drama* (1987).

ADMUSSEN, RICHARD, L., *The Samuel Beckett Manuscripts: A Study* (Boston, 1978).

ALLBRIGHT, DANIEL, *Representation and the Imagination: Beckett, Kafka, Nabokov and Schoenberg* (Chicago, 1981).

ALVAREZ, A., *Beckett* (1974).

ANDONIAN, CATHLEEN, *Samuel Beckett: A Reference Guide* (Boston, 1989).

ASMUS, WALTER, 'Rehearsal Notes for the German Première of Beckett's *That Time* and *Footfalls* at the Schiller-Theater Werkstatt, Berlin (directed by Beckett)', translated Helen Watanabe, *Journal of Beckett Studies*, 2 (Summer, 1977).

AVILA, WANDA, 'The Poem within the Play in Beckett's *Embers*', *Language and Style*, 17 (Summer, 1984), 193–205.

BAIR, DEIRDRE, *Samuel Beckett: A Biography* (1978).

BALZAC, HONORÉ DE, *Illusions perdues* (Paris, 1983).

BANGERT, SHARON, *The Samuel Beckett Collection at Washington University Libraries: A Guide* (St. Louis, Mo, 1986).

BARNARD, G., *Samuel Beckett: A New Approach* (1970).

BEAUSANG, MICHEL, 'Watt: logique, démence, aphasie', in *Beckett avant Beckett: Essais sur le jeune Beckett (1930–1945)*, ed. Jean-Michel Rabaté (Paris, 1984), pp. 153–72.

BEJA, MORRIS, GONTARSKI, S. E. and ASTIER, PIERRE, *Samuel Beckett: Humanistic Perspectives*, based on 7–8 May 1981 symposium, College of Humanities, Ohio State University (Columbus, Oh. 1983).

BEN-ZVI, LINDA, 'Fritz Mauthner for Company', *Journal of Beckett Studies*, 9 (Autumn, 1984), 65–88.

—— *Samuel Beckett* (Boston, 1986).

—— 'Phonetic Structure in Beckett: From Mag to Gnaw', in *Beckett Translating/Translating Beckett*, ed. Alan W. Freidman, Charles Rossman and Dina Sherzer, (London, 1987), pp. 155–64.

BERGSON, HENRI, *Le Rire: Essai sur la signification du comique* (Paris, 1908).

BISHOP, TOM and FEDERMAN, RAYMOND (eds.), *Samuel Beckett* (Cahier de l'Herne) (Paris, 1976).

BOVE, EMMANUEL, *Mes Amis* (Paris, 1977) (1921).

—— *Armand* (Paris, 1977) (1925).

BRATER, ENOCH, 'Still/Beckett: The Essential and the Incidental', *Journal of Modern Literature*, 6:1 (Feb., 1977), 3–16.

—— 'Light, Sound, Movement and Action in Beckett's *Rockaby*', *Modern Drama*, 25:3 (Sept., 1982), 342–9.

—— *Beckett at 80/Beckett in Context* (Oxford, 1986).

—— *Why Beckett* (1989).

BRUN, BERNARD, 'Sur le *Proust* de Beckett', in *Beckett avant Beckett: Essais sur le Jeune Beckett (1930–1945)*, ed. Jean-Michel Rabaté (Paris, 1984), pp. 79–91.

BURKMAN, KATHERINE, *Myth and Ritual in the Plays of Samuel Beckett* (London, 1987).

CHAMBERLAIN, LOVI, ' "The Same Old Stories": Beckett's Poetics of Translation', *in Beckett Translating / Translating Beckett*, ed. Alan. W. Freidman, Charles Rossman and Dina Sherzer, (London, 1987), pp. 16–24.

COE, R. N., *Beckett* (1964).

COHN, RUBY, *The Comic Gamut* (New Brunswick NJ, 1962).

—— *Back to Beckett* (Princeton, 1973).

—— *Just Play: Beckett's Theater* (Princeton, 1980).

—— (ed.) *Samuel Beckett: Waiting for Godot: A Casebook* (Basingstoke, 1987).

—— (ed.) *Samuel Beckett: A Collection of Criticism* (New York, 1962).

CONNOR, STEVEN, *Samuel Beckett: Repetition, Theory and Text* (Oxford, 1988).

COOK, VIRGINIA, *Beckett On File* (1985).

CROUSSY, GUY, *Beckett* (Paris, 1971).

DAVIS, PHILIP, *Memory and Writing* (Liverpool, 1983).

DAVIS, ROBIN, J., *Samuel Beckett: A Checklist and Index of his Published Words 1967–1976* (Stirling, 1979).

DEARLOVE, J. E., *Accomodating the Chaos* (Durham, 1982).

DOHERTY, FRANCIS, 'Watt in an Irish Frame', *Irish University Review*, 21:1 (Autumn/Winter, 1991), 187–203.

ELIOPULOS, JAMES, *Samuel Beckett's Dramatic Language* (The Hague, 1975).

ESSLIN, MARTIN, (ed.), *Samuel Beckett: A Collection of Critical Essays* (Princeton, 1965).

—— *Mediations: Essays on Brecht, Beckett, and the Media* (1980).

—— 'A Theatre of Stasis—Beckett's Late Plays', in *Critical Essays on Samuel Beckett*, ed. Patrick McCarthy (Boston, 1986), pp. 192–8.

FINNEY, BRIAN, *Since 'How It Is'. A Study of Beckett's Later Fiction* (1972).

FITCH, BRIAN, T., *Dimensions, structures et textualité dans la trilogie romanesque de Beckett* (Paris, 1977).

—— 'The Relationship between *Compagnie* and *Company*: One work, Two Texts, Two Fictive Universes', in *Beckett Translating/Translating Beckett*, ed. Alan W. Freidman, Charles Rossman and Dina Sherzer (London, 1987), pp. 25–35.

—— *Beckett and Babel: An Investigation into the Status of the Bilingual Work* (Toronto, 1988).

FLETCHER, JOHN, *The Novels of Samuel Beckett* (1970).

—— and SPURLING, JOHN, *Beckett: A Study of his Plays* (1972).

FRANKEL, MARGHERITA, S., 'Beckett et Proust: Le Triomphe de la parole', in *Samuel Beckett*, ed. Tom Bishop and Raymond Federman, (Cahier de l'Herne) (Paris, 1976), pp. 316–40.

FRIEDMAN, ALAN, W., ROSSMAN, CHARLES and SHERZER, DINA (eds.), *Beckett Translating/Translating Beckett* (Philadelphia, 1987).

FRIEDMAN, MELVIN, *Samuel Beckett Now* (1970).

FRYE, NORTHROP, 'The Nightmare Life in Death', *Hudson Review* 13 (Autumn, 1960), 442–9.

GASS, WILLIAM, H., *Fiction and the Figures of Life* (Boston, 1971) (1958).

GIDAL, PETER, *Understanding Beckett* (1986).

GIRARD, ALAIN, *Le Journal intime* (Paris, 1963).

GONTARSKI, S. E., *The Intent of Undoing in Samuel Beckett's Dramatic Texts* (Bloomington, Ind., 1985) .

—— *On Beckett: Essays and Criticism* (New York, 1986).

GRAVER, LAWRENCE and FEDERMAN, RAYMOND, (eds.), *Samuel Beckett: The Critical Heritage* (1979).

HARTMAN, GEOFFREY, 'Evening Star and Evening Land', in *Post-Structuralist Readings of English Poetry*, ed. Richard Machin, and Christopher Norris, (Cambridge, 1987), 264–93.

HARVEY, LAWRENCE, *Samuel Beckett, Poet and Critic* (Princeton, 1970).

HESLA, DAVID, H., *The Shape of Chaos: An Interpretation of the Art of Samuel Beckett* (St Paul, Minn., 1971).

HUBERT, MARIE-CLAUDE, *Langage et corps fantasme: Ionesco, Beckett, Adamov* (Paris, 1987).

JACOBSEN, JOSEPHINE and MUELLER, WILLIAM, R., *The Testament of Samuel Beckett* (1966).

JOUBERT, J., *Pensées* (Paris, 1928).

JULIET, CHARLES, *Rencontre avec Samuel Beckett* (Montpellier, 1986).

KALB, JONATHAN, *Beckett in Performance* (Cambridge, 1989).

KENNEDY, ANDREW, K., *Samuel Beckett* (Cambridge, 1989).

KENNER, HUGH, *Samuel Beckett: A Critical Study* (Berkeley and Los Angeles, 1968).

KNOWLSON, JAMES, *Light and Darkness in the Theatre of Samuel Beckett* (1972).

—— (ed.), *Samuel Beckett: Krapp's Last Tape: A Theatre Workbook* (1980).

—— (ed.), *Happy Days: The Production Notebook of Samuel Beckett* (1985).

—— and PILLING, JOHN, *Frescoes of the Skull* (1979).

LAKE, CARLTON, *No Symbols Where None Intended: A Catalogue of Books, Manuscripts and Other Material Relating to Samuel Beckett in the Collections of the Humanities Research Center* (Austin, Tex., 1984).

LAMONT, ROSETTE, A., 'Krapp, un anti-Proust', in *Samuel Beckett*, ed. Tom Bishop and Raymond Federman, (Cahier de l'Herne) (Paris, 1976), pp. 341–60.

LAWLEY, PAUL, 'Symbolic Structure and Creative Obligation in Endgame', *Journal of Beckett Studies* 5, (Autumn, 1979), 45–68.

LEVY, ERIC, P., *Beckett and the Voice of Species* (Dublin, 1980).

LYONS, CHARLES, R., *Samuel Beckett* (1983).

MCCARTHY, PATRICK, (ed.), *Critical Essays on Samuel Beckett* (Boston, 1986).

MCGORY, KATHLEEN and UNTERECKER, JOHN, (eds.), *Yeats, Joyce and Beckett: New Light on Three Modern Writers* (1976).

MCMILLAN, DOUGALD and FEHSENFELD, MARTHA, *Beckett in the Theatre: The Author as Practical Playwright*, i. *From Waiting for Godot to Krapp's Last Tape* (1988).

MCQUEENEY, TERENCE, *Samuel Beckett as a Critic of Joyce and Proust* (Ph.D thesis, Berkeley and Los Angeles, 1977).

MCWHINNIE, DONALD, *The Art of Radio* (1959).

MAYOUX, JEAN-JACQUES, 'Molloy: Un événement littéraire, une œuvre', short essay appended to *Molloy* (Paris, 1982).

MEGGED, MATTI, *Dialogue in the Void: Beckett and Giacometti* (New York, 1985).

MERCIER, VIVIEN, *Beckett/Beckett* (New York, 1978).

MITCHELL, BREON, 'A Beckett Bibliography: New Works 1976–1982', *Modern Fiction Studies*, 29 (Spring, 1983), 142–3.

MOLLER, HANS-MARTIN, *Adorno, Proust, Beckett* (Frankfurt, 1981).

MOORJANI, ANGELA, B., *Abysmal Games in the Novels of Samuel Beckett* (Chapel Hill, NC, 1982).

MOROT-SIR, EDOUARD, HARPER, HOWARD and MCMILLAN, DOUGALD, (eds.), *Samuel Beckett: The Art of Rhetoric* (Chapel Hill, NC, 1976).

MORRISON, KRISTIN, *Canters and Chronicles: The Use of Narrative in the Plays of Samuel Beckett* (Chicago, 1983).

NEISSER, ULRIC, *Memory Observed: Remembering in Natural Contexts* (San Francisco, 1982).

O'DONOVAN, PATRICK, 'Beckett's Monologues: The Context and Conditions of Representation', in *Modern Language Review*, 81: Pt. 2 (Apr., 1986), 318–26.

O'REILLY, MAGESSA, '*Texte pour rien XIII* de Samuel Beckett: édition critique et variantes', *Revue d'Histoire littéraire de la France*, mars/avril 1990, 90e année, 2, 227–37.

PAINE, SYLVIA, *Beckett, Nabokov, Nin: Motives and Modernism* (1981).

PERLOFF, MARJORIE, 'Between Verse and Prose: Beckett and the New Poetry' *Critical Inquiry* 9:2 (Dec.1982), pp. 415–33.

—— *The Poetics of Indeterminacy* (Princeton, 1983).

—— 'Une Voix pas la mienne: French/English Beckett and the French/English Reader', in *Beckett Translating/Translating Beckett*, ed. Alan W. Freidman, Charles Rossman and Dina Sherzer (London, 1987), pp. 36–48.

PILLING, JOHN, *Samuel Beckett* (1976).

—— 'Beckett's "Proust" *Journal of Beckett Studies*, 1 (Winter, 1976), 8–29.

—— 'The Significance of Beckett's *Still* ', *Essays in Criticism*, 28, (Apr. 1978), 155–7.

—— 'A Criticism of Indigence: *Ill Seen Ill Said*', in *Critical Essays on Samuel Beckett*, ed. Patrick McCarthy, (Boston, 1986), pp. 136–44.

PYLE, HILARY, *Jack B. Yeats: A Biography* (1970).

RABATE, JEAN-MICHEL, (ed.), *Beckett avant Beckett: Essais sur le jeune Beckett (1930–1945)* (Paris, 1984).

—— 'Quelques figures de la première (et dernière) anthropomorphie de Beckett', *Beckett avant Beckett*, 135–51.

—— 'Watt à l'ombre de Plume: l'écriture du désœuvrement', in *Beckett avant Beckett*, 173–85.

RABINOVITZ, RUBIN, *The Development of Samuel Beckett's Fiction* (Champaign, Ill, 1984).

—— 'The Self Contained: Beckett's Fiction in the 1960s', in *Beckett's Later Fiction and Drama*, by James Acheson and Kateryna Arthur (1987), pp. 50–64.

READ, DAVID, 'Beckett's Search for Unseeable and Unmakeable: *Company* and *Ill Seen Il Said* ', *Modern Fiction Studies*, 29 (Spring, 1983), 111–25.

READING UNIVERSITY, *Samuel Becket: An Exhibition*, Reading University Library, May–July 1971 (1971).

REAVEY, GEORGE, 'Poems by George Reavey', chosen by Samuel Beckett, March 1977, *Journal of Beckett Studies*, 2 (Summer, 1977), 2–3.

ROBINSON, MICHAEL, *The Long Sonata for the Dead* (1969).

RODGER, IAN, *Radio Drama* (1982).

SAINT-MARTIN, FERNAND, *Samuel Beckett et l'Univers de la fiction* (Montreal, 1976).

SHERINGHAM, MICHAEL, *Beckett, Molloy* (1985).

SILVERMAN, SUSAN, *Time and the Problem of Self-Definition and Uncertainty: Proust, Beckett and Stravinsky* (Stanford, Calif. 1988).

SIMON, ALFRED, *Beckett* (Paris, 1983).

SMITH, JOSEPH, H. (ed.), *The World of Samuel Beckett* (Baltimore, 1990).

ST-JOHN BUTLER, LANCE and DAVIS, ROBIN, J., *Rethinking Beckett* (Basingstoke, 1990).

STEWART, GARRETT, *Death Sentences: Styles of Dying in British Fiction* (Cambridge, Mass., 1984).

TAGLIAFERRI, ALDO, *Beckett et la surdétermination littéraire* translated N. Fama (Paris, 1967).

TENNYSON, ALFRED LORD, *Poetical Works* (1904).

TOPSFIELD, VALERIE, *The Humour of Samuel Beckett* (Basingstoke, 1988).

WATSON, DAVID, *Paradox and Desire in Samuel Beckett's Fiction* (1991).

WEBB, EUGENE, *Samuel Beckett: A Study of his Novels* (1970).

WELLERSHOF, DIETER, 'Toujours moins, presque rien', in *Samuel Beckett*, ed. Tom Bishop and Raymond Federman (Paris, 1976), 123–47.

ZILLIACUS, CLAS, *Beckett and Broadcasting* (Abo, 1976).

ZURBRUGG, NICHOLAS, *Beckett and Proust* (Totawa, NJ, 1988).

—— 'Ill Seen Ill Said and the Sense of an Ending', in *Beckett's Later Fiction and Drama*, by James Acheson and Kateryna Arthur (1987), pp. 145–59.

Index